War Stories

War Stories

THE CAUSES AND CONSEQUENCES OF PUBLIC VIEWS OF WAR

Matthew A. Baum & Tim J. Groeling

PRINCETON UNIVERSITY PRESS
PRINCETON AND OXFORD

Published by Princeton University Press, 41 William Street, Princeton, New Jersey 08540
In the United Kingdom: Princeton University Press, 6 Oxford Street, Woodstock,
Oxfordshire OX20 1TW

Library of Congress Cataloging-in-Publication Data
Baum, Matthew, 1965–
War stories : the causes and consequences of public views of war / Matthew A. Baum, Tim
J. Groeling.
    p. cm.
Includes bibliographical references and index.
ISBN 978–0–691–13858–9 (hardback : alk. paper) — ISBN 978–0–691–13859–6
(pbk. : alk. paper)   1. War—Press coverage—United States.   2. Foreign news—United
States.   3. United States—Foreign relations—Public opinion.   4. Iraq War, 2003—
Journalists.   5. Public opinion—United States.   6. Press and politics—United
States.   I. Groeling, Tim J.   II. Title.
PN4888.W37B38 2010
070.4′333—dc22   2009015445

British Library Cataloging-in-Publication Data is available

This book has been composed in Sabon

Printed on acid-free paper. ∞

press.princeton.edu

Printed in the United States of America

10 9 8 7 6 5 4 3 2 1

To Mom, Dad, Kristen, and Jee, the people most responsible
for who I am
And to Téa, for showing me that there are an infinite number
of stars in the sky
With all my love and gratitude.

    —M.B.

To Dad, who taught me to think like a scientist
To Mom, who taught me to see the wonder in the world
To Vicki, who let me know it all makes sense
And to Laura and Carrie, who have made it all worth while.

    —T.G.

Contents

Figures

Tables

Preface

In January 2001, Matt was writing a paper about the "rally-'round-the-flag" phenomenon and came across an intriguing paradox: presidents seem to enjoy larger rallies in public support during crises when their political enemies (the opposing party) control the legislature. As it turned out, Tim's recently completed dissertation provided a theoretical argument that predicted exactly that outcome, and a citation was born. Later that year, we first broached the possibility of expanding our brief discussions to collaborate on a paper at some future date.

After we met Lori Cox Han and Diane Heith at the 2002 Western Political Science Association Conference, they approached us independently about contributing to an edited volume they were putting together on the president in the public domain. As newly minted assistant professors, we were both keenly aware of the ticking tenure clock and worried whether devoting time to an edited volume would "pay off" at tenure time. Cox Han and Heith eased our concern by suggesting that if we did not have enough time to write separate chapters, we could collaborate on one in order to divide the work. This proved to be the nudge we needed to turn our sketchy conversations into a tangible research program.

Although we had been friends in the same graduate program, shared an adviser (Sam Kernell) and research interests, and been hired into the same department at UCLA, in the decade we had known each other we had never worked together on a research project. In late 2002, we decided to meld our respective work on public opinion during foreign policy rally events, partisan communication, and the news, for what we thought would be a one-shot book chapter. Fortunately, combining Matt's research on public opinion and foreign policy with Tim's work on partisan communication produced what we later concluded was a conceptual framework that exceeded the sum of its theoretical parts. Building on this integrated framework, we soon had plotted out the structure of a much more ambitious study. Even as Matt relocated twice (to UCSD and Harvard) over the next few years, the book continued to develop during numerous trips to the Van Nuys Metrolink station, more than 10,000 separate e-mail messages, and countless minutes' worth of cell phone overage charges. While the geographic distance of our collaboration has presented some obstacles, it has allowed a near-seamless workflow in which the combination of time zones and odd sleeping patterns allowed each of us to hand off work before retiring for the night, only to be greeted with an updated draft upon awaking. As was said of the British Empire in its heyday, the sun never set on our work on this book over the past seven years.

Those seven years, which coincided almost exactly with the presidential term of George W. Bush, proved to be among the most fascinating years in recent American history for scholars of the media, public opinion, and foreign policy. Following on the heels of the 9/11 attacks in 2001 and the resulting invasion of Afghanistan, we began working in earnest on this book at a time when President Bush enjoyed near-record approval ratings, Republicans had recently achieved unified control of government for the first time in half a century, and war with Iraq was appearing more likely with each passing day. When war finally arrived, it became a central touchstone of this book, providing clear and consequential examples of many of the key concepts we had developed and serving as the empirical foundation for two new chapters. No one would welcome the catastrophe and devastation unleashed by war. However, the historic polarization engendered by the conflict in Iraq helped dash the polite fiction that Washington politics "stops at the water's edge." In doing so, it underlined the critical role of partisan communication and persuasion in any such future conflicts.

Acknowledgments

We could not have completed this work without the financial assistance of the UCLA Academic Senate, the Harvard Kennedy School of Government, Harvard's Joan Shorenstein Center on the Press, Politics, and Public Policy, and the University of California's Institute on Global Cooperation and Conflict (IGCC). For valuable comments on earlier drafts, we thank participants in the following meetings and workshops: the IGCC Junior International Relations Faculty Colloquium, the University of Wisconsin, Madison, Department of Communication Colloquium, the Harvard Kennedy School's Faculty Workshop, Harvard's Department of Government's Political Psychology and Behavior Workshop, Stanford's Department of Political Science's International Relations Workshop, and Georgetown University's Public Policy Institute Seminar Series and American Politics Speaker Series, as well as numerous panelists, discussants, chairs, and thoughtful audience members at the annual conferences of the American Political Science Association, International Studies Association, Peace Science Society (International), and International Communication Association, at which we presented segments of this work. We also wish to thank several anonymous reviewers and our editor, Chuck Myers, for helpful comments on our Princeton proposal and manuscript drafts.

In completing our work, we were ably assisted by literally dozens of colleagues and institutions. First and foremost, we gratefully acknowledge the research assistance of Catie Bailard, Kim Yi Dionne, Jamie Georgia, Phil Gussin, Delynn Kaufman, Phil Potter, Rachel Potter, and Alan Potter. Our graduate research assistants also helped serve as field marshals for a vast army of UCLA and UCSD undergraduates we enlisted to help with our content analysis. For their assistance with content analysis, we commend Alexander Akerman, Raul Alvarez, Jennifer Arnold, Jeff Barry, Suzanne Bell, Alexandra Brandt, Ross Bul, Stephanie Chambers, Frank Chang, Tim Chettiath, Connie Choe, Francis Choi, Blaire Cirlin, Jenny Cocco, Nicole Corpuz, Elizabeth Cummings, Sarah Davis, Jennifer Dekel, Melinda Dudley, Betty Fang, Brette Fishman, Nicole Fiss, Roxana Fouladian, Kristin Gatfield, Rita Ghuloum, Christina Gibson, Angela Gill, Daniel Gordon, Sasha Gorelick, Anjana Gupta, Kazue Harima, Megan Hayati, Julia Heiser, Jennifer Herriot, Candice Hyon, Marchela Iahdjian, Ruoyang Jin, Avraham Kalaf, Sangeeta Kalsi, Robin Kelly, Robert Kelly, Angela Kim, Jihyun Kim, Alain Kinaly, Daniella Knelman, Priya Koundinya, Lauren Kubota, Matt Lacoff-Roberts, Jennifer Lee, Leona Lee, Marissa Levi, Yanyi Mao, Blake Marchewka, Gerri Marshall, Frank

Martinez, Joe Mason, Jennifer Murakami, Jennifer Muise, Jenna Murphy, Shaudee Navid, Kim Newin, Maria Nickerson, Maya Oren, Justin Pak, Leeja Patel, Lauren Patterson, Andrea Peterson, Kate Pillon, Anthony Pura, Lee Razo, Brittney Reuter, Tate Rider, Bryan Riggs, David Rigsby, Brooke Riley, Justin Ryan, Dean Sage, Sundeep Sahni, Nirmaljit Samra, Michael Sefanov, Matthew Seibert, Taleen Serebrakian, Sara Shamolian, Mariel Shaw, Paula Simon, Eric Simpson, Erin Skaalen, Ashley Skipwith, Skye Smith, Jessica Spivey, Katherine Steele, Mark Stefanos, Benjamin Steinlechner, Casey Tillett, Julia Tozlian, Jonathan Tran, Jenny Triplett, Elisabeth Turner, Ummkulthum Vakharia, Caroline Van Der Harten, Phuong Vu, Andrew Wang, Spencer Westcott, Shira Wheeler, William Whitehorn, Barri Worth, Sossy Yazaryan, Jordan Yurica, and Jennie Zhu. We are also grateful for the meticulous and insightful research assistance of Kellan Connor, Andrea Evans, Kuros Ghaffari, Chance Goldberg, Kirstin Jeffries, Clint LaVigne, Meredith McNaughton, Daniel Prager, Clare Robinson, Alyson Tufts, and Kate Wagner.

In addition, we benefited tremendously from the helpful suggestions and support of our colleagues in the UCLA and UCSD Communication Studies and Political Science Departments, and at the Harvard Kennedy School and Harvard College's Department of Government. We are particularly grateful to the following individuals for valuable comments and critiques: Jeeyang Rhee Baum, Adam Berinsky, Jeffrey Cohen, Pepper Culpepper, David Ellwood, Jim Fearon, Claudine Gay, Vicki Groeling, Kim Gross, Dan Hallin, James T. Hamilton, Sunshine Hillygus, Will Howell, Gary Jacobson, Sam Kernell, Doug Kriner, David Lake, Ashley Leeds, Jeff Lewis, Tom Patterson, Ken Schultz, Lynn Vavreck, Stephen Walt, Michael Xenos, John Zaller, and Richard Zechauser.

Portions of several chapters of this book were previously published in the *Journal of Politics* ("Crossing the Water's Edge: Elite Rhetoric, Media Coverage, and the Rally-Round-the-Flag Phenomenon," 70, no 4: 1065–85), *Political Communication* ("New Media and the Polarization of American Political Discourse," 25, no 4: 345–65), *Political Behavior* ("Shot by the Messenger: Partisan Cues and Public Opinion Regarding National Security and War," 31, no 2: 157–186), *International Organization* ("Reality Asserts Itself: Public Opinion on Iraq and the Elasticity of Reality," forthcoming), and *Conflict Management and Peace Science* ("Journalists' Incentives and Coverage of Elite Foreign Policy Evaluations," 26). This material is reprinted herein with the permission of Cambridge University Press, Taylor and Francis Press, and Springer Verlag.

Finally, we thank our wives, Vicki and Jeeyang, and daughters, Téa, Carrie, and Laura, for patiently tolerating our marathon phone consultations, odd work schedules, frequent travel, and tortured analogies over the seven years we worked on this project. Without the support of our families, none of our endeavors would be possible.

War Stories

CHAPTER ONE

News, Opinion, and Foreign Policy

ON AUGUST 21, 2005, Senators Chuck Hagel (R-NE) and George Allen (R-VA) appeared together on the ABC Sunday morning political round-table program *This Week* to discuss American involvement in Iraq. The senators were of comparable stature; both were considered credible aspirants for the 2008 Republican presidential nomination, both were forceful and articulate for their respective positions, and both spoke for similar lengths of time. Yet they differed in one key respect: Hagel criticized U.S. policy in Iraq, while Allen defended it. Commenting on the Bush administration's just released proposal to "possibly" keep over 100,000 troops in Iraq "for at least four more years," Hagel scoffed: "I think that it's just complete folly. ...The fact is I don't know where he's going to get these troops . . . there won't be any National Guard left. . . . No Army Reserve left. . . . There's no way America is going to have 100,000 troops in Iraq, nor should it, in four years. It would bog us down, it would further destabilize the Middle East . . . we need to be out." Allen responded by defending the proposal: "This was a worst case scenario. And I think that . . . if they can constitute a free and just society with this constitution that they're working on right now, I think that that will be something, a real measurement, a real benchmark that Chuck [Hagel] talks about."

We have recounted this anecdote on numerous occasions to audiences of students, scholars, and journalists. In each instance, we asked the audience to guess which senator's comments were broadcast on the network news that evening. Without exception, most of our audience members—and frequently all of them—anticipated that post-interview media coverage would heavily emphasize Hagel and largely ignore Allen. In this respect, our audiences were prescient: in the two weeks following the interview, journalists broadcast over 30 times more television stories about Hagel's criticism of the war than about Allen's defense of it.[1] What accounts for the vast difference in media attention devoted to these prominent Republicans' comments? Clearly, many people—indeed, nearly everyone to whom we have ever posed the question—intuitively assume that the news media prefer to cover criticism of the president's Iraq War policy

---

[1]Specifically, a search of Lexis-Nexis online transcripts produced 277 hits for stories that mentioned only Hagel, compared to just nine that mentioned only Allen. An additional 61 stories mentioned both.

over support for it, at least when the critique is offered by a senator from the president's own party. However, as intuitive as this assumption may be, the prevailing views of the causes and consequences of public support for foreign policy, both in Washington and in the academy, have failed to consider this common assumption and its implications. In this respect, the coverage of Hagel and Allen illustrates an important limitation to our understanding of the dynamics of public support for American foreign policy. That is, the information on which the public depends in determining whether or not to support a foreign policy initiative may be systematically distorted for reasons having more to do with the professional incentives of journalists than with the merits of the policy. This limitation has important consequences both for understanding whether and when the public is likely to support the president in times of foreign conflicts and for assessing the likely implications of public opinion for the political viability and sustainability of military actions under different circumstances.

The goals of this book are first, to identify the conditions under which the American public will or will not support their president when he or she leads the nation to war; second, to determine precisely when those conditions will tend to prevail (and for how long); and third, to assess their implications for the future of American foreign policy.

To accomplish these goals, we focus on the primary source of public information about politics and foreign policy, the mass media. The mass media are the key intermediaries between citizens and their leaders, particularly with respect to policies and events being implemented far from American shores. Citizens learn virtually everything they know about foreign policy from the mass media, whether through direct personal exposure or indirectly, via conversations with friends or family members who gained *their* information from the media. This makes understanding how the media select stories concerning foreign policy (the *supply* of information) central to any effort to account for public attitudes toward those policies (the *demand* for policy).

This focus in turn leads us to three central questions that guide this book. First, to what extent do the media's representations of foreign policy rhetoric and events account for variations in public support for presidential foreign policy initiatives, and do these effects vary over the course of such initiatives? Second, does media coverage of foreign policy rhetoric and events faithfully reflect their intensity, substance, or variance? Finally, do the incentives and interactions of citizens and media differ substantially in the so-called new media, and if so, how? To address these questions and their implications for the conduct of U.S. foreign policy, we develop a "strategic-bias" theory of elite–press–public interaction. Our theory, which we present in detail in the next chapter, explains the foreign policy communication process as the outcome of a three-way strategic interaction between and among the press, the public, and the political elite, each of which has distinct preferences, interests, and capabilities.

MEDIA COVERAGE OF ELITE RHETORIC, AND PUBLIC ATTITUDES ABOUT FOREIGN POLICY

For reasons we describe below, in foreign policy matters, citizens are highly responsive to what they see and hear from political elites—more so than in most aspects of domestic policy. Hence, the degree of public support for a presidential foreign policy initiative depends on the mix of elite rhetoric about the president's policy to which citizens are exposed. (This statement is consistent with the prevailing view in the literature [e.g., Brody and Shapiro 1989; Brody 1991], and hence is relatively uncontroversial.) When citizens observe elites expressing bipartisan support for a policy, they typically respond favorably (Larson 1996, 2000). This tendency accounts for much of the so-called rally-'round-the-flag phenomenon, in which citizens reward the president with an upward spike, if often short-lasting, in his approval ratings when the president engages the national honor abroad, typically by using military force (Mueller 1973; Russet 1990; Brody 1991; Baum 2002).

In contrast, when citizens observe elites engaging in partisan bickering about the merits of a policy, they tend to choose sides, largely though not perfectly along partisan lines. In this respect, citizens employ the opinions of trusted elites as an information shortcut or heuristic cue, allowing them to reach a judgment that most of the time reflects their perceived self-interest, without expending a lot of time and energy to become perfectly informed (Popkin 1994; Lau and Redlawsk 1997; Lupia and McCubbins 1998). We refer to this pattern as the Opinion Indexing hypothesis, reflecting the tendency of the public to index their opinions to the tenor of elite debate to which they are exposed. This hypothesis is most closely associated with the work of Richard Brody (1991).[2]

Our theory highlights the central role of credibility in mediating the persuasiveness of information to consumers (Lupia and McCubbins 1998; Druckman 2001, "Using Credible Advice"). The credibility of media *messages*, their *sources*, and the *messengers* communicating those messages, as well as the *context* within which the messages are delivered, all mediate the influence of news on consumers. The reason is that citizens depend on credibility assessments in determining which information shortcuts to rely on in rendering political judgments.

---

[2]For additional arguments and evidence substantiating the Opinion Indexing hypothesis, see Brody and Shapiro (1989), Oneal, Lian, and Joyner (1996), Baker and Oneal (2001), Hetherington and Nelson (2003), and Eichenberg, Stoll, and Lebo (2006).

*The Accuracy of Media Representations of
Foreign Policy Rhetoric and Events*

Our second key question addresses the accuracy of media coverage of foreign policy rhetoric and events. An additional scholarly prevailing view, closely related to the Opinion Indexing hypothesis, holds that owing to journalists' dependence on official government sources, media coverage is itself indexed to elite rhetoric in Washington (e.g., Hallin 1986; Bennett 1990; Page and Entman 1994; Zaller and Chiu 2000). We refer to this argument as the Media Indexing hypothesis. The implication is that the media are, at least most of the time, largely passive and nonstrategic, like a conveyor belt faithfully transmitting what elites, especially the most powerful elites (Zaller and Chiu 2000; Bennett, Lawrence, and Livingston 2006), are saying.[3] However, contrary to this sometimes implicit and at other times explicit prevailing wisdom, we argue that news coverage typically does not faithfully reflect the mix of elite rhetoric in Washington. Consequently, to the extent the Opinion Indexing hypothesis is valid, citizens frequently base their decisions regarding whether or not to support a president's foreign policy initiatives on an inaccurate representation of what elites are actually saying about the policies.[4] Prior research into the Media Indexing hypothesis tended to focus on the *reporting* function of journalists. In particular, this view holds that journalists tend to overrepresent authoritative political elites, or those in the strongest positions to influence policy outcomes. A fair amount of evi-

[3]Bennett, Lawrence, and Livingston (2007) update the traditional Media Indexing hypothesis, arguing that certain "notable conditions" may lead to some degree of press independence from official government sources, including a willingness to challenge those sources, and hence a reduced predominance of indexing. As they observe, "It goes without saying that press dependence on government is not absolute" (60). Examples of such notable conditions the authors cite include the aftermath of Hurricane Katrina and the second Iraq War (Operation Iraqi Freedom and its aftermath). However, while Bennett and colleagues suggest several sets of circumstances likely to give rise to such notable conditions (for instance, major breakthroughs by investigative journalists), it is difficult to precisely define and measure them, and even more difficult to determine ex ante which events are likely to give rise to them. After all, they are presumably "notable" in part because of their exceptional infrequency. (Otherwise, of course, indexing itself would be the notable departure.) Consequently, the core of the Media Indexing hypothesis, namely, that *most* of the time the press is *mostly* dependent on and responsive to official government sources, and especially so in foreign policy, remains intact.

[4]Even early formulations of the Media Indexing hypothesis (e.g., Bennett 1990) do allow for the possibility that in the presence of significant elite discord, journalists might be relatively more inclined to look beyond official government sources. This would appear at least partially inconsistent with the implicit passive media assumption. However, to the extent that it is the presence or absence of elite consensus that drives such behavior, and given that such proactive reporting by journalists is limited to cases of elite discord, news coverage of controversial policy debates is likely to be observationally equivalent, whether or not they include nonofficial government sources. After all, such nonofficial sources are most likely of

dence supports this assertion (see, e.g., Zaller and Chiu 2000; Cook 1994). Yet this emphasis tends to overlook the fact that journalists are not solely *reporters*; they are also *interpreters*. Their interpretations regarding the newsworthiness of different pieces of information in turn color the representation of politics to which citizens are ultimately exposed. To the extent this representation is distorted, so too most likely will be the conclusions citizens draw from it by indexing their opinions to media coverage of elite debate. The implications of such inconsistency between elite rhetoric and media representations of that rhetoric are potentially quite troubling for democratic representation.

Senator Arthur Vandenberg famously opined that when it comes to foreign policy, "politics stops at the water's edge." Our research reveals little evidence supporting this view. Rather, we find strong evidence that partisan politics has long crossed the water's edge, even during the cold war, and has extended even to the "high politics" of foreign policy. Moreover, as the Hagel-Allen anecdote illustrates, the qualities that journalists prefer in news stories result in a strong tendency to overrepresent negative, critical coverage of the president, particularly when it originates within his own party. We argue that this overrepresentation stems not from any partisan preferences of the news media but rather from pervasive institutional and professional incentives that shape journalists' standards of newsworthiness.

From these first two elements of our argument, we conclude that journalists' preferences shape the representation of elite discourse available to citizens in times of foreign crises. Indeed, they suggest that the media may systematically distort public perceptions of policy debates in Washington by presenting to the public an unrepresentative sample of elite rhetoric. This in turn seems likely to influence the public's propensity to support presidents' foreign policies. Indeed, for presidents to build support for their foreign policy initiatives via the mass media, they must overcome a significant institutional bias toward overrepresenting criticism of their policies.

Nevertheless, as we explain below in our discussion of the "elasticity of reality," policymakers' information advantage vis-à-vis the public in the realm of foreign affairs nearly always affords them at least some leeway in framing foreign policy events to their own advantage. This leeway arises to some extent independent of the true nature of such events. Yet the extent of this elite discretion varies over time and with circumstances, typically contracting as the public and the media gather more information.

---

interest to journalists only to the extent they are critical of the government. Given that such sources are sought out only when elites themselves are critical of the government's policy, the public would presumably become aware of the policy controversy, with or without a broader search by journalists.

Effects of the New Media

The third question guiding our research concerns the new media, by which we mean cable news channels and the Internet.[5] Do the new media affect the relationships predicted in our investigations into the first two research questions, and if so, how? The answer, we argue, is that they increasingly allow citizens to self-select into ideologically friendly environments while discounting information they may encounter in environments perceived as ideologically hostile.

From a strictly economic standpoint, the availability of more news choices is a positive development. After all, individuals are, to a greater extent than in prior decades, able to consume news products suited to their specific tastes. Liberals can consume "liberal" news while conservatives can consume "conservative" news, thereby presumably making everyone happier. From the standpoint of democratic theory, however, this trend may have unfortunate consequences. Most notably, if individuals attend to news sources that present only one side of a story, they may be less willing to believe sources or information at odds with their prior views, and ultimately their willingness to moderate their positions or fashion compromises may diminish.

For much of the past century, the mass media, especially television, have served as an important common civic space, providing citizens with a shared understanding of their culture and of the major issues and events of the day. In the age of new media, this common space is eroding. The end result may be a hardening and polarization of partisan attitudes in general, and with respect to foreign policy in particular. Conversely, partisan media might impart even greater credibility to messages viewed as running counter to their institutional biases. If a prior generation believed "only Nixon can go to China," some in the next may believe "only Fox can legitimize Obama 'going to' Iran."[6]

THEORIES OF PUBLIC OPINION AND FOREIGN POLICY

The causes and consequences of public support for the overseas application of military force are subjects of longstanding scholarly debate (e.g., Lippmann 1934; Almond 1950; Rosenau 1961; Baum 2003; Holsti 2004;

[5]Some scholars (e.g., Davis and Owen 1998) include political talk radio within the category of new media. However, politically oriented talk radio, which dates back to the 1920s in the United States, is not, strictly speaking, a new phenomenon. More important, we have no theoretical reason to anticipate that the hypothesized relationships will differ materially for talk radio. Hence, we focus on cable TV and the Internet.

[6]For a theoretical argument along these lines, see Schultz (2005).

Eichenberg 2005; Howell and Pevehouse 2007). Research in this area has focused on the characteristics of the conflicts themselves (hereafter "event-based" explanations), the domestic political circumstances surrounding them ("domestic political" explanations), or the internal characteristics of individual citizens ("individual-level" explanations).

Event-based explanations focus primarily on *longer-term* public support, or more precisely everything beyond the immediate effect of the initiation of a crisis event. Such explanations hold that a president's ability to sustain public support for a U.S. military engagement depends primarily on its degree of success (Kull and Ramsay 2001; Feaver and Gelpi 2004; Eichenberg 2005; Gelpi, Feaver, and Reifler 2005–2006), or alternatively on the *number* (Milstein and Mitchell 1968; Milstein 1969, 1973, 1974; Mueller 1973, 1994; Gartner and Segura 2000), *rate* (Slantchev 2004), *trend* (Gartner 2008), and *framing* (Boettcher and Cobb 2006) with respect to U.S. casualties. While such explanations could potentially account for longer-term trends in public responses to a U.S. military engagement (but see Cobb 2008), in many instances they seem less well-suited to account for the presence or absence of a public opinion rally at the *outset* of a military conflict, before the public observes either the ultimate costs or the outcome (for critiques of these literatures, see Berinsky 2007; Berinsky and Druckman 2007).

Jentleson (1992), however, advances an event-based theory that can potentially account for both initial and longer-term public support for U.S. conflicts. He argues that the American public is more likely to support military actions perceived as defensive (aimed at imposing "foreign policy restraint" on an adversary) than it is to support those perceived as offensive (aimed at imposing "internal political change") in nature (see also Oneal, Lian, and Joyner 1996; Jentleson and Britton 1998; Eichenberg 2005). Yet research into both the rally-'round-the-flag phenomenon (e.g., Brody 1991; Baum 2002) and, more generally, the framing of foreign policy (e.g., Entman 2004; Patrick and Thrall 2007) calls this argument into question. Such scholarship has shown that public perceptions concerning the offensive or defensive nature of U.S. military engagements are often endogenous to the domestic political circumstances surrounding them, including the efforts of elites to frame events to their own advantage (Entman 2004; Baum and Potter 2008).

Presidents routinely seek to frame their military actions in terms of national self-defense (e.g., Baum 2003; Perla 2005). At the same time, most Americans know relatively little about foreign affairs (Almond 1950; Lippmann 1955; Erskine 1963; Converse 1964; Edwards 1983; Sobel 1993; Holsti 2004; Canes-Wrone 2006; Page and Bouton 2006; Berinsky 2007). Consequently, in determining whether to support or oppose a conflict, typical Americans are ill-equipped to independently assess the president's "true" motivations, especially in the short term. Instead, as noted above, they rely on information shortcuts, or heuristic cues (Sniderman, Brody, and Tetlock 1991; Popkin 1994), most notably the opinions of trusted political elites, and primarily as reflected in the mass media (Iyengar and Kinder 1987; Krosnick and Kinder 1990; Zaller 1992; Rahn 1993; Larson 1996, 2000). Trust in turn frequently hinges on one particularly accessible heuristic: party identification (Rahn 1993; Popkin 1994; Nelson and Garst 2005).[7] Individuals' interpretations of heuristic cues depend in significant measure on their preexisting belief systems (Hurwitz and Peffley 1987; Herrmann et al. 1997), for which party identification is typically an important (Rahn 1993; Popkin 1994; Lupia and McCubbins 1998; Groeling 2001; Nelson and Garst 2005) if incomplete (Herrmann, Tetlock, and Visser 1999; Holsti 2004) element. The party affiliations of information sources (e.g., elites) and receivers (e.g., citizens) in interaction thus serve as a cognitive filter, mediating the selection and implications of the information shortcuts typical individuals rely on in making political judgments.[8]

In contrast to scholarship focused on longer-term public support for U.S. overseas conflicts, research on the public's *immediate* reactions to such events—the so-called rally-'round-the-flag phenomenon—focuses far more on domestic politics in general, and on the influence of public statements by political elites in particular. In fact, the most widely accepted domestic political explanation for the rally phenomenon, which we earlier termed the Opinion Indexing hypothesis, argues that the extent of elite, and particularly congressional (Hallin 1986; Bennett 1990; Zaller and Chiu 2000), criticism of the president determines the magnitude of a post-use-of-force rally (Brody 1991; see also Brody and Shapiro 1989; Oneal, Lian, and Joyner 1996).[9] Brody's theory implicitly assumes that the Media Indexing hypothesis is

[7]Individuals also employ other heuristics in evaluating foreign policy, such as accessible "images" of potential adversaries (e.g., enemy vs. friend) and core values, such as isolationism versus internationalism (Herrmann et al. 1997; Holsti 2004). Still, elite communication plays an important role in priming such images and values, and thereby in framing events for individuals. While some research (Herrmann, Tetlock, and Visser 1999; Campbell et al. 1960) has found that party identification is not a good predictor of public support for military conflict, in chapter 9 we discuss the findings of Holsti and Rosenau (1990, 1996), who report, based on research supporting the so-called Militant Internationalism (MI)/Cooperative Internationalism (CI) Index (Maggiotto and Wittkopf 1981), that a majority of liberals are accommodationists (opposing MI and supporting CI), while conservatives are about equally divided between hard-liners (supporting MI and opposing CI) and internationalists (supporting both MI and CI). In addition, party *does* mediate elites' capacity to successfully frame events for different individuals (Druckman 2004).

[8]For an investigation into the effects of partisan cues on post-9/11 public opinion on U.S. foreign policy, see Hindman (2004).

[9]For a systematic investigation of the nature and extent of congressional influence on public opinion regarding foreign policy and war, see Howell and Pevehouse (2007). For

valid. That is, it assumes that media coverage accurately reflects elite debate. As noted earlier, this implies that the media are largely nonstrategic.[10]

In contrast, we argue that the true nature and extent of elite debate may matter less than *media coverage* of any such debate and the partisan makeup of the debaters, and that this is the case well beyond the short-term or "rally period" of a foreign policy crisis or conflict. These differences do not stem from partisan bias in the news or from journalists being cowed by political elites but rather from commonly held professional incentives and norms that lead journalists to strongly prefer certain stories over others. For example, highlighting discord within the president's party, particularly when such internecine clashes occur in unified government, is an especially attractive story element, as Republican Senator Hagel found when he characterized the Iraq War as similar to Vietnam. Conversely, there is relatively little reward for covering boosterism of the president by his own party, as George Allen discovered after his appearance on that same program. Across the aisle, for reasons we discuss at length, journalists cover statements from the opposition party with somewhat less regard to whether they are supporting or criticizing the president or whether they take place during unified or divided government (Groeling 2001).

Like event-based theories, the Opinion Indexing hypothesis also discounts differences in the characteristics of individual consumers. In contrast, consistent with substantial prior research, we argue that not all elite statements are equally persuasive to the public. For example, opposition party endorsements of, or presidential party attacks on, the president should be extremely credible to viewers because they are atypical and represent costly (that is, potentially self-damaging) signals (Dutton 1973; Eagly, Wood, and Chaiken 1978; Lupia and McCubbins 1998; Groeling 2001). Similarly, typical individuals will likely view statements by their fellow partisan elites as more credible than statements by opposition elites (Rahn 1993; Popkin 1994; Lupia and McCubbins 1998; Groeling 2001; Nelson and Garst 2005).

In the new media (e.g., cable news, Internet blogs), in turn, consumers frequently attribute partisan preferences—that is, ideological orientations—to media outlets (Baum and Gussin 2008). As a consequence, partisan and costly credibility increasingly apply not only to messengers but also to the context, or media outlet, within which those messages are embedded.

---

more in-depth reviews of the vast literatures on the interrelationships of the mass media, public opinion, and foreign policy, see Powlick and Katz (1998), Entman (2004), and Baum and Potter (2008).

[10]Others go a step further, arguing that elite debate actually bounds the range of arguments considered sufficiently "acceptable" to receive any news coverage (Bennett 1990), or that support and consensus among elites will short-circuit broader debate by constraining journalists' willingness to challenge an administration (Hallin 1986).

Finally, we seek to bridge the divide between the aforementioned theories emphasizing rational public responses to empirical indicators of a war's success or failure, such as U.S. casualties (e.g., Mueller 1973, 1994; Gartner and Segura 2000; Feaver and Gelpi 2004; Eichenberg 2005), and those emphasizing the centrality of elite rhetoric in mediating public support (e.g., Brody 1991; Zaller 1992, 1994; Perla 2005; Berinsky 2007). In the latter case, while prior research (e.g., Zaller 1994; Berinsky 2007) has shown that elite cues influence public opinion regarding war beyond rally periods, such studies do not directly measure or compare the evolving relative effects of rhetoric and reality over the course of an extended conflict. Nor do they consider the intervening effects of the mass media in shaping the representation of elite rhetoric to which the public is exposed.

To bridge this theoretical divide, we develop an alternative conceptual framework, termed the "elasticity of reality" (Baum and Potter 2008). We argue that the information advantage of policymakers vis-à-vis the public in the realm of foreign affairs nearly always affords them at least some leeway in framing foreign policy events to their own advantage, to some extent independent of the true nature of such events. After all, the public rarely observes foreign policy directly. Rather, it observes and responds to a framed representation of such events, in both the short and the longer term.[11] However, the extent of elite discretion in framing events—that is, the elasticity of reality—varies over time, typically shrinking as the public and the media gather more information about an event and have the opportunity to retrospectively assess the reliability of prior elite rhetoric.[12] (An exception may arise if a substantial and sustained

[11]This is not to say that the media are the only route through which such information can flow. For instance, while relatively few Americans personally venture into war zones, many have familial or social ties to combatants who can serve as exceptionally credible sources of information about the true state of a conflict. Those same personal networks are also likely to highlight the costs of the conflict by increasing the knowledge and salience of casualties among linked service members. Moreover, Americans gain at least some independent information about the costs and benefits of a conflict through their daily lives. Increases or decreases in taxes, gas prices, deficits, or even terrorist attacks are examples of data Americans can easily track as by-products of their daily lives (Popkin 1994) and that they might, over time, employ in weighing the wisdom and success of a foreign policy venture.

[12]Brody (1994) offers a complementary argument regarding the 1990–91 Persian Gulf crisis and war. Consistent with our argument, Brody (1994: 210) observes "[T]he public can also respond to directly experienced indications of presidential policy performance. However, he concludes that "[I]t is not clear what switches public attention from mediated to unmediated indications of policy success or failure." In this book, we directly model the effects of and evolving relationship between elite rhetoric and reality, and do so over a much longer period of time than Brody's study of the eight-month-long (August 1990–March 1991) Persian Gulf crisis and war.

change emerges in the status of a conflict. If so, the elasticity gap may reopen to some extent.) Consequently, while both rhetoric and reality influence public attitudes, we argue that absent a substantial and sustained change in events, the former will tend to matter more in the early stages of a conflict, whereas given a sufficiently extended conflict, the latter is likely to catch up and eventually surpass the former over time. We thus show how both rhetoric and reality matter, albeit to varying degrees under differing circumstances and at different points in time. We also show that, far from a passive conveyor belt, the media play an active role in shaping the nature and extent of citizens' exposure to rhetoric and reality.

Our theoretical framework draws on widely recognized characteristics of human information processing, elite incentives, and journalistic preferences. Hence, taken individually, our assumptions are not novel. However, combining these relatively common assumptions concerning the distinct choices of the makers, transmitters, and receivers of news yields a variety of nonobvious and consequential predictions. Further, our argument applies not only to foreign policy but also, in varying degrees, to many high-profile domestic political issues, such as energy policy and domestic responses to global climate change. We focus on foreign policy crises, however, as a particularly interesting and we believe useful application of our framework, because prior theories of public opinion and foreign policy have generally ignored the strategic incentives of media actors and their potential effects on the nature of the information on which distinct subgroups of the public base their opinions.

We also view foreign crises (particularly those involving military mobilizations and conflicts) as especially hard cases in which to find an independent effect from media or elite rhetoric, because they involve life-and-death risks and large-scale movements of people and equipment. Such crises thus tend to be unusually visible and salient to the public, relative to the material costs and benefits of most domestic policy initiatives, such as tax or welfare reform, which tend to be observable only gradually and primarily over the long term, if at all (Arnold 1992). Finally, because, as noted, typical Americans tend to know relatively little about foreign affairs, and less about foreign policy than about domestic policy (Edwards 1983; Sobel 1993; Canes-Wrone 2006), they are particularly dependent on elite cues in determining whether to support or oppose a presidential foreign policy initiative such as a military conflict. This makes citizens' credibility assessments especially important in the realm of foreign policy.

In short, we argue that only by studying the information and incentives of, as well as the interactions between, elites, the public, and the press can we account for variations in public responses to presidential foreign policy initiatives over time.

IMPLICATIONS FOR U.S. FOREIGN POLICY

Our theory suggests that presidents who lose public support for their foreign policy initiatives will face tremendous difficulty sustaining them. Former President Bill Clinton's 1997 National Security Strategy document described this difficulty as follows: "One . . . consideration regards the central role the American people rightfully play in how the United States wields its power abroad: the United States cannot long sustain a commitment without the support of the public" (National Security Council [NSC] 1997). Similarly, President George W. Bush's "National Strategy for Victory in Iraq" listed "continued support of the American people" as one of six "conditions for victory" in the Iraq conflict (NSC 2005). As we will show, most of the time (with the possible exception of large-scale military invasions), public support is difficult to sustain. Moreover, doing so appears to be growing more difficult over time. We further argue that, seemingly paradoxically, unified control of government can make sustaining public support more rather than less difficult.[13] President George W. Bush confronted this paradox directly when, after twice successfully campaigning to ensure that the Iraq War would be fought under unified Republican control of government, he arguably achieved his most reliable Republican legislative support once his colleagues were in the minority again after 2006.

As we shall see, new media are partly responsible for these patterns. A consequence of the self-selection they engender is that presidents increasingly find themselves preaching to the choir. In other words, the audiences for presidential appeals tend to be limited to a president's ex ante supporters. For instance, one study (Kernell and Jacobson 2006) reports that the president's fellow partisans increasingly dominate the television audiences for presidential State of the Union addresses. This will make it more difficult for future presidents to reach beyond their base in order to achieve or maintain bipartisan support for foreign policy initiatives.

In this book we demonstrate that even after controlling for a wide range of indicators of empirical reality, communication still plays a crucial and independent role in influencing public support for the president during foreign crises. We show further that, rather than simply parroting the opinions of Washington elites, public opinion in these crises varies systematically with the institutional context in which political communication takes place, the media context within which the message is communicated, and the characteristics of the speakers and receivers—that is, depending on who the president is at the time of a crisis, who is

---

[13]See Groeling (2001) for a parallel discussion of how unified government can undermine the presidential party's ability to favorably define their brand name with the public.

speaking about it, what medium or channel is carrying the speech, and who is listening.

PLAN OF THE BOOK

In chapter 2, we begin by explicating our strategic-bias theory of elite–press–public interaction. From our theory we derive a series of hypotheses, which we test in the remainder of the book. The theory consists of three factors, reflecting the aforementioned corresponding research questions guiding the book. These factors are (1) the effects of media coverage on public opinion regarding foreign policy (in both the short and the longer term), (2) the nature of media coverage of foreign policy, including the accuracy or inaccuracy of its representation of elite rhetoric, and (3) the effects of new media on factors 1 and 2.

In chapter 3, we focus on the first two factors: patterns of elite discourse in the news and the implications of those patterns for public opinion. As a validity check on several of our theoretical assumptions, we first present the results of a survey of a national sample of citizens and journalists regarding their news preferences. We then formally test several of our hypotheses against a new data set consisting of all evaluations of the president or his administration by members of Congress (MCs) that appeared on the evening newscasts of ABC, CBS, or NBC between 1979 and 2003, during 61-day windows surrounding the start dates of major U.S. deployments or employments of military force. In addition to providing a detailed picture of partisan evaluations in the news across nearly a quarter century, these data allow us to examine the impact of coverage of these evaluations on partisans and independents, during both normal times and crisis periods. For this analysis, we merge partially disaggregated data on public approval of the president with the aforementioned content analytic data set.

It is important to note that the data in chapter 3 encompass only congressional evaluations that journalists selected for broadcast, making it difficult to determine whether they selected those statements based on standards of newsworthiness (as we argue) or were simply presenting an accurate representation of elite debate (as the Media Indexing hypothesis implies).

Although surveys can enhance our confidence that journalists apply common standards of newsworthiness in their story selections, rigorously testing this assumption potentially runs afoul of the so-called unobserved population problem (Groeling and Kernell 1998; Groeling 2008). That is, without some means of observing the stories *not* chosen by journalists, we cannot rule out the possibility that the representation of elite rhetoric in the news may accurately reflect what elites are actually saying in the real world. In chapter 4 we address precisely this issue, thereby continuing our investigation into the second factor in our theory. To separate the media's independent effect from that of the actual tenor of elite discourse itself as presented on the evening news, we investigate a class of stories for which we *can* observe a full population of potential elite evaluations of the president: interviews with MCs on the three major broadcast networks' Sunday morning political interview shows. We therefore analyze the content of all congressional appearances on *Meet the Press* (NBC), *This Week* (ABC), and *Face the Nation* (CBS) during the same 61-day windows surrounding foreign conflicts between 1979 and 2003. Such interviews afford elites a chance to present their views to a politically attentive audience in a relatively unfiltered, "open mic" format. More important, these interviews represent low-hanging fruit for all three broadcast networks' evening news programs, providing readily accessible content from which evening news producers can easily select excerpts for broadcast. To test our hypotheses, we investigate which comments are selected for inclusion on the evening news and compare the characteristics of such comments with those of comments that were not selected during periods immediately following major U.S. uses (deployments or employments) of military force and during normal time periods.

In chapter 5, we take up the third factor in our analysis, the impact of new media on story selection patterns and public opinion, by conducting a series of experiments intended to determine the effects of media outlet brand reputations on consumers' credibility assessments regarding elite rhetoric, and the effects of those assessments on the influence of that rhetoric. To do so, we exposed participants to a series of carefully edited video and text-based news reports on issues related to national security. The eight treatment conditions entailed members of the president's party or the opposition party either praising or criticizing the president's policies (two evaluation types × two evaluation source treatments). We also modified the treatments so they would appear to have originated on either Fox or CNN (two network treatments). These experiments also allow us to retest our opinion hypotheses from chapter 3 under more tightly controlled conditions.

Next, in chapters 6 and 7, we undertake a systematic case study of elite rhetoric, media coverage, public opinion, and the "situation on the ground" in the U.S. war in Iraq. Chapter 6 addresses all three factors in our theory by comparing the content of new and traditional news media coverage of foreign policy in general, and Iraq in particular (in this instance, contrasting such coverage on cable to that on network television news). We introduce the Iraq case through brief vignettes, or mini-case studies, of six events in the conflict that a panel of foreign policy experts we polled rated as especially consequential. We then investigate 30 months of daily content analysis of the nightly national newscasts of ABC, CBS, and NBC, as well as of *Fox News Special Report with Brit Hume,* in order to compare story selection patterns and the resulting effects on consumer attitudes across the new and old media, thereby addressing all three factors in our theory. With respect to public opinion, these data make it possible to investigate longer-term public opinion dynamics, which in turn allows us to determine whether and to what extent the hypothesized communication effects described in chapter 4 persist over the longer term. In other words, these data allow us to directly pit the event-based theories that dominate much of the literature on public opinion and foreign policy (e.g., casualty aversion, principal policy objectives, perceptions of success) against our strategic-bias theory. In contrast to these event-based arguments, our theory, derived primarily from the literatures on framing and the rally phenomenon, emphasizes the elite contest to *frame* reality via news media populated by journalists with distinct preferences and goals.

As noted, event-based theories typically focus on longer-term or sustained public opinion. In contrast, the rally literature underpinning our theory largely focuses on the immediate or short-term effect of dramatic events on public attitudes. Comparing the efficacy of these two theoretical perspectives over a 2.5-year period thus represents a particularly difficult test for our theory, as we conduct it largely on the turf of the long-term-focused, event-based theories.

In chapter 7 we continue our case study of news coverage, media consumption patterns, and public opinion regarding the Iraq War between 2003 and 2007. We employ a variety of public opinion surveys, as well as the aforementioned content analysis of network newscasts and the Fox News Channel. For this analysis, which again addresses all three factors in our theory, we extend the media content analysis series through November 2007.[14] This allows us to explore the implications of the elasticity of reality for news coverage of and public opinion regarding the Iraq conflict over an extended period, including the so-called "surge"—the U.S. counterinsurgency campaign initiated in March 2007 that increased the U.S. troop presence in Iraq by over 30,000.

In chapter 8 we turn to the Internet, thereby focusing squarely on the third factor in our theory. Here we present the results of a content analysis of a variety of politically oriented Internet sites. Specifically, we compare daily wire service "political news" summaries to see which stories liberal, conservative, and nonpartisan web sites selected for their respec-

---

[14]It should be noted that our extended data set has large gaps in its coding (at the time of this writing, several intervening months remain uncoded by Media Tenor), limiting our ability to apply these data to our time-series analysis in chapter 6.

tive "top news" summaries. We also investigate differences in partisan polarization over the Iraq conflict between individuals who rely primarily on traditional news sources and those who rely primarily on the Internet for their news. Through these investigations, we explore the processes by which the changing media environment is shaping political discourse, particularly with regard to foreign policy.

Finally, in chapter 9 we consider the ramifications of the answers to our three central research questions for U.S. foreign policy. We draw conclusions from our empirical investigations and consider the present and future implications of our study for politics in general, and for presidential leadership in foreign policy in particular.

CHAPTER 2

Politics across the Water's Edge

SPEAKING IN ST. LOUIS on July 5, 2008, then-Democratic presidential candidate Barack Obama outlined his plans for withdrawing U.S. troops from Iraq: "The tactics of how we ensure our troops are safe as we pull out, how we execute the withdrawal, those are things that are all based on facts and conditions. I am not somebody—unlike George Bush—who is willing to ignore facts on the basis of my preconceived notions" (Loven 2008). In his statement, Obama accused President Bush, in effect, of ignoring reality in his Iraq policies, and implied that his own promised timetable for withdrawal might be adapted to reflect the actual situation there.

Obama's statement drew heavy coverage throughout the news media and exposed the presumptive Democratic presidential nominee to sharp criticism from both the Left and the Right for his apparent "flip-flop" regarding withdrawal (Hurst 2008), especially among online commentators (Harper 2008). Upon calling another press conference to refine his stance mere hours after making his initial statement, Obama confessed that he was "a little puzzled by the frenzy that I set off with what I thought was a pretty innocuous statement" (Reuters 2008).[1] The campaign of Republican candidate John McCain in turn attacked Obama both for his initial speech and for his subsequent puzzlement about the furor. "What's really puzzling is that Barack Obama still doesn't understand that his words matter," said McCain spokesman Tucker Bounds (Reuters 2008).

This incident brings into focus several vital components of public opinion and foreign policy in the modern American context. First, it illustrates that the statements of politicians, which studies of politics often dismiss as "cheap talk," can be consequential. Second, it highlights the importance of events on the ground in a conflict even as it demonstrates the degree to which politicians can politicize and manipulate public perceptions of such "reality." Third, Obama's puzzlement regarding why this particular statement provoked such massive media comment draws attention to the news choices of journalists, who generally stand between

---

[1]Interestingly, Obama's statement about troop withdrawal timelines (complete with a near-instantaneous follow-up press conference to clarify his remarks) was a repeat of a similar series of events earlier in the week (Cooper and Zeleny 2008), which probably magnified its impact.

politicians and the public they hope to persuade, and new media actors, who helped stoke the fires of the controversy online. Finally, Obama's accusation that Bush would "ignore facts" because of "preconceived notions" about Iraq calls into question the degree to which prior opinions, political rhetoric, and reality can alter public opinion over the course of a conflict.

Building on the three key factors we identified in chapter 1, we develop a theory to explain the relationships between public opinion, media coverage of elite rhetoric, and the reality of a conflict. In particular, we seek to explain *how* various partisan messages emanating from different sources and media outlets influence public opinion, particularly with respect to foreign policy crises and wars. In addition, we seek to explain how these effects on news content and public opinion might systematically change with time and the flow of events. Finally, we seek to determine exactly *which* elite messages are likely to make it into the news under different circumstances, and how new media actors might alter those patterns.

Our strategic-bias theory considers journalists' incentives to cover various types of partisan evaluations of the president, the effects of these evaluations on different groups of individuals, and how varying the sources of such messages (both the speakers and the outlets covering the rhetoric), as well as the circumstances surrounding their delivery, affects their impact on public opinion. We also examine the relative influence of elite rhetoric and objective indicators of reality, in both the short and the longer term of foreign policy events, in shaping journalists' assessments concerning the newsworthiness of stories regarding such events, as well as public attitudes toward them. In both cases, we consider the implications for public opinion of differing journalists' preferences and consumers' credibility assessments in traditional and new news media. From this discussion, we derive a series of hypotheses concerning both the types of stories journalists are likely to prefer to cover and which messages are likely to be persuasive to consumers. Subsequent chapters test these hypotheses, as well as various subhypotheses that emerge along the way.

A STRATEGIC-BIAS THEORY OF POLITICIAN–PRESS–PUBLIC INTERACTIONS

We assume that the evaluative statements of partisans break down into four basic categories: (1) attacks on the other party (cross-party attacks), (2) support for one's own party (intraparty praise), (3) support for the other party (cross-party praise), and (4) attacks on one's own party (intraparty attacks). Below we delineate additional assumptions concerning the preferences and incentives of politicians, journalists, and citizens.

What Politicians Want from the Media

We begin by examining the incentives of politicians. Politicians expend considerable effort in shaping their messages and images in the news media. The most universally accepted assumption in U.S. electoral politics is that politicians seek, first and foremost, reelection (Mayhew 1974). We generalize Mayhew's famous observation by assuming that politicians seek reelection both for themselves and for their fellow partisans. After all, winning an election holds dramatically different implications, with respect to both resources available for subsequent election campaigns and a party member's ability to influence public policy, if one is a member of the majority party in Congress, and particularly when that party also controls the executive branch (Cox and McCubbins 1993; Cox and Magar 1999).[2] Winning election or control of government in turn requires making one's self and one's fellow partisans look good, while casting members of the opposition party in a negative light. The implication for politicians' preferences regarding media coverage is straightforward: typical politicians prefer stories that praise themselves and fellow partisans, or criticize their opponents and the opposition party.

In the context of interbranch relations, this further implies that, any journalistic preferences for *covering* particular statements notwithstanding, members of the presidential party (PP) in Congress are likely to *express* rhetorical support for the president, while members of the opposition party, or nonpresidential party (NPP), should be more likely to oppose him. While periodically there are incentives for individual members to depart from these strategies, particularly if they are running for president or wish to gain press coverage by taking "maverick" stances, the perceived novelty of such instances highlights the prevailing baseline from which they depart.

Senator John McCain's (R-AZ) campaigns for the 2000 and 2008 Republican presidential nominations provide perhaps the most famous recent example of this tendency. In both elections, McCain ran campaigns that initially challenged the Republican Party leadership, instead relying heavily on what he jokingly referred to as "my base"—the national news media (Tumulty 2007).[3] While this close relationship was undoubtedly

---

[2] However, see Groeling (2001) for a discussion of how unified government can paradoxically reduce a party's ability to cohesively communicate a valuable party brand name.

[3] In fact, before McCain secured the 2008 nomination, Republican partisan media (particularly talk radio hosts such as Rush Limbaugh and Hugh Hewitt) vociferously opposed his nomination (Bigg 2008).

attributable in part to McCain's comparatively open access to members of the press, reporters viewed his "defiant character" in the Senate, in which he broke with his own party over campaign finance reform and other key issues, as "delightfully subversive" (Weisberg 1999). Even before McCain's candidacy, Republicans had complained that journalists granted conservatives who took liberal positions fawning press coverage that emphasized the person's growth and the "strange new respect" they were receiving in Washington (the term is attributed to Bethell 1992).

If journalists *do* consistently report discord among the president's fellow partisans more frequently than affirmation, as we demonstrate in chapter 3, there can be only two explanations. Either such coverage must reflect journalists' preferences, or elites from the president's own party must be routinely criticizing the president more often than they praise him during times of foreign crises—thereby supporting the passive media assumption of the Media and Opinion Indexing hypotheses discussed in chapter 1. We consider the latter possibility highly improbable, especially given that in the most public of all representations, votes for or against presidential legislative initiatives, recent presidents have typically received overwhelming support from members of their own party and similarly strong opposition from the opposing party.[4] (Nonetheless, we explicitly test this assumption in chapter 4 by examining which partisan statements from Sunday morning interview shows are selected for broadcast on the evening news.)

What Journalists Want from Politicians

Despite politicians' best efforts to control their public communication, journalists and news organizations have historically maintained ultimate control over the content of their news programs because of their function as gatekeepers of political news content. In deciding what political material is or is not news, certain characteristics of stories or sources make them more (or less) desirable for journalists. In particular, professional journalists generally prefer stories that are novel, conflictual, balanced, and involve authoritative political actors (Graber 1997; Groeling 2001; Project for Excellence in Journalism [PEJ] 2002).[5] Below, we consider exactly how each of these characteristics applies to news about politics.

[4]*Congressional Quarterly* reports that since the Eisenhower administration, an average of about two-thirds of presidents' fellow partisans support them on votes where they stake a position. Presidents since Reagan have greatly exceeded that average. Conversely, opposition party support for presidents is generally low, with no president managing to break even on such votes (*Congressional Quarterly Almanac* 1953–2006).

[5]In chapter 8 we evaluate how online communication, particularly through weblogs, has diffused the traditional power of the press to select news to a far broader set of gatekeepers. In addition, later in this chapter we examine how explicitly partisan media might vary in their story preferences. This is not meant to be a comprehensive listing of all factors that

The most obvious characteristic of newsworthiness is that it places a premium on stories that are actually new. Informing readers or viewers of unexpected, inconsistent, or novel information is the core value provided by news organizations. In fact, without novelty, it makes very little sense to speak of news organizations at all. This preference leads reporters to strongly resist attempts by politicians to deliver scripted, consistent messages to the public. As Andrew Rosenthal (2007), *New York Times* editorial page editor, put it, "We like to be surprised, and to surprise our readers." CBS's chief White House correspondent noted when covering the 2004 Republican National Convention that journalists want "to find the inconsistency here, to find the people who aren't quite agreeing with the script that's going on any given convention night, to get behind the story" (Kurtz 2004). Journalists participating in Bush press conferences have tellingly described their interactions with the president as a "contest between Bush's desire to repeat his previously articulated views ('sticking a tape in the VCR,' as one frequent Bush questioner puts it), and the reporters' quest to elicit something that will contribute to democracy, not to mention getting them on television or the front page" (Allen 2005).[6] Along these lines, Robin Sproul, Washington Bureau Chief for ABC News, commented in an interview with one of the authors that she prefers stories "that are counterintuitive or present a point of view that we haven't focused on as much."[7] In brief, *journalists prefer stories that contain new or unexpected information to stories presenting old or expected information.*

A second characteristic of "good" news is, ironically, a preference for bad news. Numerous scholars (e.g., Sabato 1991; Patterson 1996; Cappella and Jamieson 1997) have observed that while negativity and conflict have long been staples of American journalism, the news media have increasingly embraced "attack journalism" and cynicism since the 1960s. Indeed, there seems to be a consensus within the scholarly literature that negativity is pervasive and dominant in modern news coverage.

While not all politicians go so far as former Vice President Spiro Agnew in characterizing the media as "nattering nabobs of negativism," recent politicians appear to share the view that the press favors negativity and

---

might contribute to journalists' determinations of newsworthiness vis-à-vis a particular story. Indeed, some scholars have argued that standards of newsworthiness are evolving. (For instance, Downie and Kaiser [2002] argue that novelty is less central to such determinations than in the past.) Rather, our theory highlights several of the most widely cited and broadly observed factors influencing such perceptions.

[6]In the same article, Dana Bash of CNN observed, "Bush, like most skilled politicians, will tend to answer the way he wants, no matter what the question. The hardest thing is to ask the question in a way he can't do that."

[7]Interview with author (M.B.), October 10, 2007, Cambridge, Mass. (The full transcript is available online at http://www.sscnet.ucla.edu/comm/groeling/warstories/sproul.html.)

conflict in its story choices. Early in his first year in office, President Bill Clinton had already concluded that, for the media, "success and lack of discord are not as noteworthy as failure."[8] As one prominent journalist bluntly observed, "Well, journalists are always looking for conflict. That's what we do" (Saunders, in Kurtz 2004). Therefore, we argue that *journalists prefer stories in which political figures attack each other to stories in which political figures praise each other*.

Considerable ink, in turn, has been spilled debating whether the media might be more likely to attack liberal or conservative points of view in their coverage (e.g., Efron 1971; Alterman 2003; Coulter 2003; Goldberg 2003; Franken 2004). As Rosenthal (2007) explained, the role of journalists is "to provide a dispassionate accounting of events, free of political or ideological coloration." Gaye Tuchman (1972) famously argued that, in part to counter such bias accusations, journalists have a strong incentive to use procedures or strategic "rituals" of objectivity in doing their jobs. The main ritual Tuchman and others discuss is presenting *both sides of the story*. News organizations, particularly broadcasters, have long practiced this balancing. For most of the twentieth century, FCC regulations held broadcast stations and networks to an exceptionally high standard of fairness (the so-called fairness doctrine).[9]

Journalists have also internalized these standards through professional ethics and norms, which require them to make every effort "to assure that the news content is accurate, free from bias and in context, and that all sides are presented fairly" (American Society of Newspaper Editors [ASNE] 2002).[10] Indeed, Robin Sproul commented that, in her judgment, "there would be a professional price to pay" for a professional journalist who consistently privileged one political perspective over others, adding, with respect to covering the Iraq conflict, "My expectation for ABC is that we would put a balanced story on the air."[11] We thus assume *journalists prefer stories that include both parties' views to stories that present only the views of members of a single party*.

Finally, journalists place a premium on including the most authoritative and high-ranking sources in their stories. As Graber (1997, 116) ar-

[8]From a May 7, 1993, Clinton press conference.

[9]See Hazlett and Sosa (1997), though, for an analysis arguing that the fairness doctrine actually served to chill political speech rather than merely balance it.

[10]These norms are further reinforced by the policies of news organizations themselves. For example, Reuters's Independence & Trust Principles argue the company is "dedicated to preserving its independence, integrity, and *freedom from bias* in the gathering and dissemination of news and information" (emphasis added. See http://about.reuters.com/aboutus/overview/independence.asp). Similarly, AP identifies their mission as "providing distinctive news services of the highest quality, reliability and *objectivity* with reports that are accurate, *balanced* and informed" (emphasis added. See http://www.ap.org/pages/about/about.html).

[11]Interview with author (M.B.), October 10, 2007, Cambridge, Mass.

gues, the "gatekeeping process winnows the group of newsworthy people to a very small cadre of familiar and unfamiliar figures . . . predominantly political figures." Sigal (1986, 20) adds that "by convention, reporters choose authoritative sources over other potential sources," and that "the higher up an official's position in government, the more authoritative a source he or she [is] presumed to be, and the better his or her prospects for making the news." Lippmann (1920) agrees, arguing, "The established leaders of any organization have great natural advantages. They are believed to have better sources of information. . . . It is, therefore, easier for them to secure attention and speak in a convincing tone." Finally, Rosenthal (2007) concurs, noting, "When an editorial page comments on the government, it makes a lot more sense to comment on the party in power than the party in opposition. . . . The focus of all newsgathering tends to be on the party in power." In other words, *journalists prefer to include sources with greater authority in their stories over less authoritative sources.*

For our purposes, the key implication of the authority assumption is that its significance varies systematically from unified to divided government. For instance, during unified government, the NPP will be disadvantaged in attracting news coverage because it lacks control over either the legislative or executive branch. Conversely, during divided government the NPP will be exceptionally newsworthy, all else equal, by virtue of controlling the legislative branch and its consequent relatively greater capacity to influence policy outcomes. Sproul thus observed that "somebody with stature in politics, somebody who can have an impact on policy or could be leading others," is particularly newsworthy, "because they can impact the direction the country is going . . . they have a voice that other people don't have. I do think they drive the coverage in some ways." This, she added, meant that statements by leaders from the majority party are typically more newsworthy because of their greater "potential impact."[12]

Because we are primarily concerned with coverage and opinion related to foreign policy, we focus our attention here on party messages about the executive branch, especially the president. The top section (part A) of table 2.1 applies the aforementioned assumed story preferences to four types of partisan evaluations of the president, allowing us to determine which types of stories are most likely to gain airtime.[13] Table 2.1 shows that evaluations of the president by the opposition party (that is, the NPP) tend to be at least somewhat newsworthy, regardless of which party controls Congress, although they are somewhat more so

[12]Interview with author (M.B.), October 10, 2007, Cambridge, Mass.

[13]Because these evaluations are all directed at the president or administration, the stories already presumably contain some exposition of the president's or administration's position or actions.

in divided government, when NPP rhetoric has greater authority by virtue of a legislative majority. Such comments are always either novel, if they support the president, or conflictual, if they criticize him. Airing NPP comments also adds balance to stories about the president and his policies.

In contrast, praise of the president by his own party (or PP praise) has little novelty, balance, or conflict, and thus is of little interest to journalists. As Sproul observed, "[PP praise is] like the plane took off and flew safely. . . . [I]t's not really news unless that were a big change."[14] During divided government, PP praise of the president is even less interesting to journalists than in unified government because the PP does not control Congress. This makes all PP rhetoric less authoritative than in unified government. Thus, as table 2.1 shows, PP praise is especially uninteresting, particularly in divided government, where it lacks appeal for journalists on all four dimensions.

Conversely, PP criticism of the president is particularly attractive to journalists, especially during unified government, because it is highly novel, conflictual, and in unified government authoritative (again, because the PP controls both branches). In her interview, Sproul rated PP criticism the most appealing type of story, commenting that during the Republican Bush administration, "[The] number one [most appealing story] would be [a] Republican breaking from the President."[15] Sproul further explained that part of the reason she ranked Republican criticism of President Bush as the most appealing type of story was "because it's the president's policy. With Clinton I would have led with the Democrat breaking away. . . . In this case, it's which party is in the White House."[16] Along these lines, in a question-and-answer session with *New York Times* readers, Rosenthal (2007) observed, "An Op-Ed by a Republican criticizing the Democrats, or vice versa, is easy to come by and not that interesting. But a Democrat who takes issue with his or her party, or a Republican who does that, is more valuable." A hypothesis follows. (Here and in each subsequent hypothesis specifying certain conditions or states of the world, we assume that other such conditions are held constant or remain unchanged—in other words, ceteris paribus).

HYPOTHESIS 1: OVERSAMPLED PRESIDENTIAL PARTY CRITICISM
Because PP criticism is far more newsworthy than PP praise, the news media will present more negative than positive evaluations of the president by his own party in the news.

[14]Interview with author (M.B.), October 10, 2007, Cambridge, Mass.
[15]For the second-most newsworthy story, she chose "[a] liberal Democrat who's supporting the president" (interview with author [M.B.], October 10, 2007, Cambridge, Mass.).
[16]Interview with author (M.B.), October 10 2007, Cambridge, Mass.

TABLE 2.1
Newsworthiness, Novelty, and Credibility of Rhetoric Regarding President from
Presidential Party (PP) and Nonpresidential Party (NPP) Elites

	PP Praise	PP Criticism	NPP Praise	NPP Criticism
A. Newsworthiness of Partisan Evaluations of the President				
Novelty	Low	High	High	Low
Conflict	Low	High	Low	High
Balance	Low	Low	High	High
Authority (unified government)	High	High	Low	Low
Authority (divided government)	Low	Low	High	High
B. Change in Novelty during Salient Rally Periods				
Novelty during salient rallies	Lower	Higher	Lower	Higher
C. Partisan and Costly Credibility, by Party of Speaker and Viewer				
Costly Credibility				
All partisans and independents	Low	High	High	Low
Partisan Credibility				
Presidential partisans	High	High	Low	Low
Independents	Low	Low	Low	Low
Nonpresidential partisans	Low	Low	High	High

Salient Crises as Special Cases for Journalists

If the top section of table 2.1 delineates the newsworthiness of "politics as usual," this raises the question of how newsworthiness might systematically differ during a major foreign crisis. For much of the post-Second World War era, the Republican and Democratic parties are commonly viewed as having achieved near consensus in foreign policy, especially with respect to the cold war. Implicit in the very notion of rallying 'round the flag is that major international crises will induce each party to close ranks and increase its support for the president.

From a standpoint of newsworthiness, however, the impact is somewhat more complex. If journalists *expect* partisans from both parties to rally behind the president when American troops are in harm's way, criticism of the president by *either party* should become even more newsworthy than during noncrisis periods. After all, criticizing the president during a particularly high-profile foreign crisis is especially risky. Research (e.g., Zaller 1994; Zaller and Chiu 2000) has shown that risk-averse members of Congress (MCs) typically prefer to avoid such criticism until the political ramifications of the crisis outcome are relatively clear. Part B of table 2.1 illustrates this point. While the table tells us little about each party's *intent* to support the president in crisis periods, it does suggest that if members of either party choose to criticize the president, they should find journalists even more eager to air their comments than during other times. This suggests a second hypothesis:

HYPOTHESIS 2: SALIENT CRISIS NOVELTY
    For MCs from both parties, the ratio of presidential criticism to presidential praise selected to appear on the news will be greater during high-salience crisis periods than during other periods.

Partisan Media

The rise of new media, and particularly the Internet, has challenged and begun to redefine the business of news. As media have fragmented and some news outlets have begun to cater to partisan audience niches (Hamilton 2003), the underlying preferences and routines of news organizations have shifted markedly. As we demonstrate in chapters 5 and 8, these changes have widened the gap between the true nature and extent of elite rhetoric and public perceptions of such rhetoric. Whereas traditional journalistic norms and preferences have for the most part persevered, their applicability clearly varies across media outlets, particularly for the norm of offering balanced coverage. Indeed, sophisticated and motivated consumers are increasingly able to seek out news sources, from cable news to partisan web sites to political talk radio, that reflect their own ideological preferences.

One clear manner in which the Internet appears to differ from other mass media is the degree of niche targeting by political web sites. To be sure, some Internet outlets seek mass audiences. But these sites tend to represent the online versions of traditional mainstream news media, such as the *New York Times* or CBS News. Many other Internet outlets, including but not limited to weblogs, or "blogs," are overtly niche-oriented, aimed at attracting a smaller but more loyal segment of the overall audience. While political partisanship is by no means the only dimension on which niche marketing strategies might be based, in the realm of political information, partisanship is one of the key lines of demarcation allowing web sites to attract a relatively loyal audience.[17] It is therefore not sur-

[17]Of course, many bloggers care little about the commercial implications of their writing, instead embodying a modern version of political pamphleteers. As one blogger put it, "Lumping 'bloggers' together as if they were some sort of monolithic force, with predictable behaviors is deceptive" (Scott Ott [http://scrappleface.com], e-mail correspondence with author [M.B.], December 21, 2007). Our research does not address the *causes* of ideological polarization in online media, instead focusing on the *implications* of such segmentation, given that it exists.

prising that many of the most widely visited political blogs, and certainly those with the most loyal audiences, tend to be overtly partisan, ranging from sites like MoveOn.org and DailyKos.com on the left to FreeRepublic.com and Instapundit.com on the right. Based on these observations, we derive the following hypothesis:

HYPOTHESIS 3: MEDIA PARTISANSHIP
    Left-leaning news outlets will be more likely to feature stories that are harmful to Republicans or helpful to Democrats, relative to the opposing types of stories. Conversely, right-leaning news outlets will be more likely to feature stories that are harmful to Democrats or helpful to Republicans, relative to the opposing types of stories. Nonpartisan news outlets should be equally likely to feature stories that are harmful to Democrats and Republicans.[18]

Message Impact on Public Opinion

In determining each message type's effect on viewers, it is important to note not just the content of the message itself but also the credibility of the message and its speaker. Parties do not inject messages into a passive public; such messages are processed by individuals who accept or reject them, depending in part on the messages' perceived credibility (Sniderman, Brody, and Tetlock 1991; Kuklinski and Hurley 1994; Druckman 2001, "On the Limits"). One source of credibility is the belief that the speaker and listener have common interests (Crawford and Sobel 1982). This suggests that consumers will regard statements by their own party as more credible than those of the opposing party, all else equal. From this Partisan Credibility conjecture we derive the following hypothesis:

HYPOTHESIS 4: PARTISAN CREDIBILITY
    Presidential evaluations by an individual's fellow partisans will more strongly influence that individual's approval of the president than will evaluations by members of the other party.

Another important source of credibility derives from the interaction of source and message: whether the message is costly to the speaker (Spence 1973). Typical individuals regard messages that are harmful to the interests of the speaker as more credible than those that are self-serving and

---

[18]Of course, other characteristics of these stories might also systematically vary. In our empirical tests of this hypothesis in chapters 3, 6, and 8, we therefore carefully control for other systematic differences in newsworthiness across the parties. Similarly, in chapter 4, we explicitly control for the possibility that the underlying population of stories might systematically vary across parties.

so impose no costs (so-called cheap talk).[19] In the context of partisan communication, it follows that typical individuals will regard messages by partisan speakers that damage their party or help the other party as more credible than messages that help their party or damage the other party. We term this the Costly Credibility conjecture. Such costly messages should be at least somewhat credible, regardless of the party affiliation of the listener. Our fifth hypothesis follows:

HYPOTHESIS 5: COSTLY CREDIBILITY
    Evaluations that impose a cost on the speaker's own party will have a stronger effect on individuals' propensity to support the president than will equivalent "cheap talk" evaluations that impose no cost on the speaker's party.

Part C of table 2.1 summarizes the relative credibility of different partisan messages about the president based on their partisan credibility and costly credibility for viewers of each party. It demonstrates the relatively weak persuasive power of "politics as usual" statements (that is, intra-party praise or cross-party attacks). Such statements by members of each party serve only to rally their own followers, who probably already agreed with the speaker prior to the statement (Baum 2002).

In contrast, NPP praise should be exceptionally persuasive and beneficial to the president, especially among members of the NPP. Similarly, if members of the president's own party attack him, the effects on public opinion should be dramatic and damaging, especially among the president's fellow partisans. In both cases, the media demand for such statements virtually ensures they will receive coverage, further magnifying their potential impact on opinion. We thus predict:

HYPOTHESIS 6: COMBINED CREDIBILITY
    Positive evaluations by NPP elites and negative evaluations by PP elites will have the strongest effects on presidential approval among their fellow partisan identifiers.

Credible Messages and Partisan Control of Government

Returning to the top of table 2.1, and briefly to the *supply* side of our theory (that is, media coverage), we see that the newsworthiness of the two most credible types of partisan evaluations noted in the Costly Credibility hypothesis (H5), PP criticism and NPP praise, is systematically related to the partisan makeup of government. Because the PP is *more* (and

---

[19]Two related lines of inquiry are research in social psychology into the influence of "incongruous" (Walster, Aronson, and Abrahams, 1966; Koeske and Crano 1968) or "disconfirming" (Eagly, Wood, and Chaiken 1978) messages.

the opposition party *less*) authoritative in unified government, shifting from unified to divided government decreases the newsworthiness of the most damaging type of message (PP criticism) while increasing the newsworthiness of the most helpful messages (NPP praise). After all, in unified government, PP criticism is not only novel and conflictual but also authoritative, thereby making it exceptionally attractive to journalists. In contrast, in divided government, NPP praise is not only novel and balance enhancing but also more authoritative than in unified government (since the NPP controls at least one house of Congress), making it exceptionally newsworthy. A hypothesis follows:

HYPOTHESIS 7: DIVIDED GOVERNMENT MEDIA
The proportion of credible praise to credible criticism in the media will be greater in divided than in unified government.

This pattern, in turn, seems likely to influence the propensity of the public to support the president when he leads the nation's military forces into harm's way. A final *demand*-side (that is, public opinion) hypothesis follows:

HYPOTHESIS 8: DIVIDED GOVERNMENT OPINION
The president will receive greater overall public support in times of foreign crises during divided government than during unified government.

Salient Foreign Crises as Special Cases for Public Opinion

As previously noted, criticizing the president during a high-profile foreign crisis is especially risky for MCs. This assessment stems from a political calculation that the public holds the president, as commander in chief, far more accountable than Congress for the outcome of a military conflict. Hence, MCs have little to gain and potentially much to lose from opposing the president early in a crisis. An MC who supports a policy that subsequently fails will likely pay at least some political price, such as emboldened opposition at the next election, but the cost of opposing a successful policy is likely to be greater. After all, a victorious commander in chief (along with his party in Congress) will be more likely to possess both the motive (political retribution) and opportunity (in the form of enhanced political capital) to punish recalcitrant MCs. As one senior congressional foreign policy aide commented with regard to the congressional vote to support President George H. W. Bush on the eve of the 1991 Persian Gulf War, "Why not support the president when he stands up for American interests? You can always withdraw your support later if you want to. In the meantime, go along" (quoted in Zaller 1994, 256). Consequently, if political circumstances necessitate taking a position early in a conflict, MCs are likely to view support as relatively less risky than opposition, all else equal.[20]

Scholars continue to debate whether (e.g., Mueller 1973; Gartner and Segura 2000) or not (e.g., Gelpi, Feaver, and Refler 2005) rising casualties depress public support for a conflict over time. Regardless, we do not believe this logic typically applies in the earliest stages of a crisis (which we refer to here and throughout the book as the *rally period*). Schwartz (1994), for instance, argues that in the short term, casualties usually harden the public's resolve, consequently *strengthening* public support for the use of force (see also Kull and Destler 1999).[21] This raises the costly credibility of negative comments by either party during rally periods involving U.S. casualties (in the short run). Conversely, like journalists, the public is likely to anticipate initial elite support for the president during salient rally periods (e.g., those involving U.S. casualties). This reduces the costly credibility associated with supportive comments by the opposition party (NPP), thereby mitigating their persuasive impact. For the PP, however, comments supporting the president nearly always lack costly credibility. Thus, such comments have little credibility to lose and should produce similar, limited effects on opinion both during and outside of salient rally periods. An additional hypothesis follows:

HYPOTHESIS 9: SALIENT RALLY PRAISE AND CRITICISM
  Negative evaluations by either party, which are most costly during rally periods with U.S. casualties, will have a larger negative effect on approval ratings during rally periods than during other periods, especially among the speaker's fellow partisans and independents. Conversely, positive evaluations during such rally periods by the NPP will produce smaller effects on approval ratings than similar comments during other periods. Because they always lack costly credibility, positive comments by the PP should be similarly unpersuasive in periods with and without casualties.

The Mediating Effect of the Outlet Reputation on Opinion

Recent research (Baum and Gussin 2008) suggests that media outlet labels, and the ideological reputations their brand names carry, serve as

---

[20]President Obama appears to represent a clear example of how taking a politically "risky" position, such as opposition to the Iraq War, can sometimes prove politically beneficial in subsequent elections. Indeed, Obama's stance stood in marked contrast to most of his major 2008 primary election competitors, who had cast "safer" votes in favor of the war, and arguably helped cement his support with the antiwar Left in the Democratic Party.

[21]We nonetheless seek to isolate the *salience* component of the effects of casualties in our statistical models by separately controlling for expert assessments of whether each U.S. use of force was "successful" and "worthwhile."

important judgmental heuristic cues, which consumers employ to help interpret both the meanings and implications of partisan messages in the media. As a consequence, we argue that the nature of the media's influence on policy has evolved from what scholars often refer to as the "CNN effect," which emphasized the importance of the 24-hour news cycle and live coverage of events, to what we refer to as an emerging "Fox effect."[22] The latter effect concerns the implications of perceived partisan favoritism by news outlets, combined with the effects of audience self-selection (that is, audiences sorting into ideologically "friendly" news environments) and credibility-based discounting of information from outlets perceived as ideologically hostile.

Table 2.2 disaggregates the expected credibility of messages attacking and praising a Republican president (like President George W. Bush) based on the perceived partisan leanings of the network airing the story. Assuming Republicans believe they have common interests with networks they perceive as conservative, while Democrats believe that liberal networks share their interests, the patterns in table 2.2 suggest the following hypothesis:

HYPOTHESIS 10: PARTISAN MEDIA OPINION
Statements critical of a president will be more credible to viewers when they appear on a news source perceived as aligned with the president's political ideology. Conversely, statements praising a president will be more credible on a news source perceived as opposed to the president's political ideology.

If, as predicted by the Costly Credibility hypothesis (H5), viewers find rhetoric perceived as costly (that is, contrary to the outlet's perceived partisan leaning) to be more valuable and credible than other rhetoric, one empirical manifestation ought to be a relatively greater propensity to discount, or counterargue (e.g., criticize as biased), "cheap talk" rhetoric from news outlets (that is, rhetoric supportive of the outlet's perceived ideological leaning). This suggests another hypothesis:

HYPOTHESIS 11: SELECTIVE ACCEPTANCE
Individuals will be more critical of statements supporting president from sources they perceive as aligned with the president's political ideology, relative to the same news from sources they perceive as opposed to the president's political ideology.

[22]In its original formulation, the so-called "CNN effect" hypothesis held that dramatic television images of human suffering could move democratic citizens to demand that their leaders take action to alleviate the situation. This could create sufficient pressure to induce a leader to launch a humanitarian intervention, such as the U.S.-led intervention in Somalia in 1992, known as Operation Restore Hope (see, e.g., Livingston and Eachus 1995; Mermin 1997; Baum 2004, "How Public Opinion . . .").

TABLE 2.2
Credibility Impact of Outlet Attribution

	Congressional Democrats Attack Republican President	*Congressional Republicans Attack Republican President*
Conservative Outlet	More credible	More credible
Liberal Outlet	Less credible	Less credible
	Praise Republican President	*Praise Republican President*
Conservative Outlet	Less credible	Less credible
Liberal Outlet	More credible	More credible

Note: We use the "more" and "less" credible values here to help indicate that these credibility impacts are presumably in addition to those stemming from our base model, shown in table 2.1. For viewers who see the networks as ideologically neutral, the effects should reduce to our basic model's predictions. For a Democratic president, the effects would be reversed, with criticism on liberal and praise on conservative networks gaining credibility, and praise on liberal and criticism on conservative networks losing credibility.

RHETORIC AND REALITY

Journalists do not cease exercising their judgments regarding the newsworthiness of stories with the expiration of a rally period. Nor is there any reason to believe that as a conflict continues, citizens cease employing credibility assessments in determining whether and to what extent a given story is persuasive. Consequently, we anticipate that the previously described independent effects of elite rhetoric regarding foreign policy crises—that is, those that are independent of objective indicators of reality—are likely to persist well beyond the initial rally period. We therefore anticipate, contrary to the (often implicit) prevailing view in the literature on public opinion and foreign policy (see chapter 1), continued support for our hypotheses concerning journalists' preferences and the persuasiveness of stories both *during* and *beyond* rally periods, albeit to varying degrees.

Nonetheless, the qualities that make a given story interesting to journalists and persuasive to the public are unlikely to remain constant over time. In the former case, for instance, a story, or type of story, that is highly novel today (time t) may be somewhat less so tomorrow (time $t + 1$) if similar stories have become commonplace. Stated more generally, the perceived novelty of a given story type (e.g., PP criticism or NPP praise) is likely to vary with the prior frequency of that story type. Novelty in turn influences perceptions of newsworthiness; stories perceived as novel are more likely to be covered than stories perceived as routine. Robin Sproul reinforced this point through a hypothetical scenario, noting that what is novel, and hence newsworthy, "depends on what point we are in the story. If we are at the point in the story in which the Republicans have held firm, and suddenly you have a conservative Republican who by all expectations would be expected to be holding firm who has broken away, it's a big story to us." She added that in determining a story's newsworthiness, questions she considers include, "Is it different than what we saw yesterday? Does it change the story in any way? And will it have impact?"[23] A hypothesis follows:

Hypothesis 12: Novelty over Time
   The more common a given story type is in the media prior to a given point in time t, the less novel it will be perceived to be and hence the less coverage it will receive at time t. Conversely, the less common a story is prior to time t, the more novel it will be perceived to be and hence the more coverage it will receive at time t.

The logic underlying the Media Indexing hypothesis described in chapter 1 rests in large measure on an assumption that journalists are dependent on government officials for information about foreign policy events. The information advantage of government officials, especially those from the administration and majority party in Congress, makes them appealing to journalists seeking authoritative sources. This advantage is particularly acute in the early stages of an overseas conflict or crisis, when an administration possesses a near monopoly on high-quality information about the event. Speaking with respect to the early stages of the 2003 Iraq invasion, Sproul explained the dominance of the Bush administration's preferred framing of war coverage as follows:

Number one is the relative dearth of information that would allow you to [challenge the President's claims]. . . . Number two would be [that] . . . we usually have in the political universe of Washington a very powerful opposing point of view or opposition party or interest groups that speak out with powerful opposition and/or evidence and/or something that is independent. . . . That really wasn't there to the extent that certainly [it] is now [in 2007].[24]

Over time, as information diffuses, journalists will both gather an increasing store of information about the event and develop alternative

[23]Interview with author (M.B.), October 10, 2007, Cambridge, Mass.
[24]Interview with author (M.B.), October 10, 2007, Cambridge, Mass.

information sources. Hence, while an administration conducting a war will always have *some* informational advantage, its extent is almost certain to recede with time.

Regardless of how events on the ground actually unfold, any administration has a powerful incentive to cast them in the most favorable light. Journalists in turn can be expected to challenge this attempt at framing and to seek to highlight any evaluations that depart from the party line (Zaller 1999).[25] However, in the early stages of a conflict, the administration's substantial informational advantage will likely limit the ability of journalists to effectively challenge the administration's preferred frame. Over time, as journalists are better able to discern for themselves what is actually happening on the ground, and as any prior discrepancies between administration framing and reality come to light, the administration's advantage recedes, and the discrepancy between reality and coverage should diminish. In the case of the Iraq War, for instance, Sproul commented that

> [T]he tone of the story changed as the facts on the ground changed. . . . It wasn't that we had the same set of facts and we suddenly looked at it through a different prism. It was that it became a more transparent view of what the facts actually were, had been all along. . . . Some of the inspectors started speaking out and then Colin Powell. Over a period of time it became clear that . . . there weren't people celebrating in the streets and this wasn't hailed as a great victory, and that it wasn't as billed, that the things they said would happen didn't happen, and then it started to get worse and worse.[26]

Stated differently, in the words of one political blogger, "Reality asserted itself."[27] If things are, in fact, going well, then an administration may be able to continue framing the conflict as a success. Such was mostly the case in the first Persian Gulf War in 1991 (Page and Entman 1994, Iyengar and Simon 1993). However, if the state of the conflict is more ambiguous, or if events are not going well, a negative frame becomes increasingly likely to predominate. Either way, media coverage seems likely to converge on the actual valence of events over time. The greater the initial gap between reality and the administration's frame, the larger the likely change, over time, in the tenor of coverage.

[25]Zaller (1999) shows how journalists actively seek to maintain "voice" in their coverage.

[26]Interview with author (M.B.), October 10, 2007, Cambridge, Mass.

[27]Quotation from blogger offered in response to an open-ended follow-up question asking why he indicated, in a prior question, that the Bush administration's influence on public opinion regarding Iraq had receded since the start of the war. (From author survey; see chapter 8.)

Hypothesis 13: Elasticity of Reality

Over time, the tenor of media coverage of a conflict will increasingly parallel objective indicators of reality (relative to administration framing of reality), so long as such indicators remain consistent.[28]

Of course, over time, as reporters settle on a particular narrative for a conflict that is continually reinforced by subsequent events and reporting of those events, the narrative frame should become increasingly resistant to change. Scholars (Mendelsohn and Crespi 1970; Kovach and Rosenstiel 2001; Jamieson and Waldman 2003; Rosenstiel 2004; Jamieson, Hall, and Waldman 2007; PEJ 2008) have long recognized that journalists tend to cue off one another in their coverage, producing "pack journalism" and "meta-narratives." Once the media settle on a particular narrative regarding a candidate, such as "Al Gore is dishonest" or "George W. Bush is unintelligent," this meta-narrative tends to be continually referenced and thereby reinforced. Over time, it becomes increasingly resistant to challenges, even if it is based on faulty assumptions (as many believe is the case with both of the aforementioned examples from the 2000 presidential campaign). In the context of a military conflict, once a given narrative frame becomes entrenched, only large and sustained changes in events on the ground are likely to influence it.

Such dominant frames in turn can take hold fairly rapidly, as the media repeatedly exposes citizens to them. In the context of the Iraq War, retired U.S. Army Lieutenant General Ricardo S. Sanchez complained to military reporters and editors, "Once reported, your assessments become conventional wisdom and nearly impossible to change. . . . [I]n your business 'the first report' gives Americans who rely on the snippets of CNN . . . their 'truths' and perspectives on an issue" (Sanchez 2007). A hypothesis follows:

Hypothesis 14: Framing Stickiness over Time

Over time, as the prevailing media framing of a conflict grows increasingly entrenched, the marginal change in objective indicators of reality required to induce a given change in media framing will increase.

The dynamics in public opinion over time are likely to track those in the media, although at different rates among different partisan groups. After all, typical individuals largely depend on the news media—either directly, through their own consumption, or indirectly, by talking to individuals

---

[28]See hypothesis 15b (Event-Shift Effects corollary) for our predictions regarding situations involving a sustained change in the reality of a conflict that diverges from the dominant prior narrative regarding the conflict.

who have gained *their* information through the media—for their information about an overseas conflict. As one newspaper reporter observed
with respect to the relationship between media reporting on Iraq and
public attitudes regarding the conflict, "War reporting and public opinion entered an echo chamber: one rebounded off the other."[29]

In addition, for typical individuals, a given piece of information is
likely to exert less influence as that individual collects and retains more
information over time. To understand why, it is useful to review Zaller
and Feldman's (1992) "top-of-the-head" model of public opinion. According to this model, typical individuals possess a range of considerations on any issue. Zaller and Feldman argue that when asked their
opinion, individuals average across those considerations that are accessible at the time they are asked. They then respond probabilistically,
based on the mix of accessible considerations on the pertinent issue. For
instance, the greater the proportion of accessible considerations that
point toward supporting the conflict in Iraq, the greater the probability
that they will express support for the conflict.[30]

Now consider an individual who at some time t possesses, say, five
considerations regarding Iraq. Suppose three of the five considerations
are favorable. If we assume that each consideration is equally accessible,
then, if asked her opinion of the conflict, the individual has a 60% probability of expressing support for the conflict. If that individual accepts
two additional pieces of negative information about the conflict, her
probability of expressing support for the war if queried would, all else
held equal, decline from 60% to 43%. If, however, that same individual
possessed 50 considerations, then an additional two negative pieces of
information would have a much smaller effect (that is, a decline from
60% to 58%).[31]

Presumably, as the U.S. engagement in Iraq has continued—approaching seven years as of this writing—typical citizens have, to varying degrees,
increased their store of information about the conflict. As a consequence,
attitudes regarding the war have likely solidified relative to early in the
conflict, when elites and journalists enjoyed a substantial informational
advantage over the public. That informational advantage had afforded

[29]Comment offered in response to an open-ended question regarding media influence on
public opinion (from author survey of professional journalists; see chapter 3).

[30]One implication of Zaller and Feldman's theory is that because politically attentive
individuals tend to possess more and more consistent considerations about political issues
than inattentive individuals, they are likely to be more consistent in their responses over
time than their less attentive counterparts.

[31]This logic is consistent with Bayesian updating. That is, the higher the probability assigned to one's prior belief, the greater the weight (that is, probability) assigned to that belief in calculating the posterior probability, and hence the larger the influence of that prior
belief on an individual's posterior belief (that is, probability assessment) (Zalta 2008).

them substantial leeway in the initial framing of events. The public was thus far more inclined to accept information as reliable relatively uncritically in the early stages of the conflict.

The public is especially vulnerable to this sort of influence early in a conflict, when political elites and journalists enjoy a substantial informational advantage over typical citizens, thereby granting them considerable leeway in the framing of events. Because news is in many ways an experience good—that is, one whose value cannot be observed prior to consuming it (Hamilton 2003)—individuals can, over time, retrospectively evaluate the reliability of information they consumed in the past.[32] In other words, one must generally consume news before determining its quality. For instance, when pundits predicted in 2007 that Rudy Giuliani and Hillary Clinton had a "lock" on the nominations of their respective parties in the 2008 presidential election, the public had relatively little reason to doubt that prediction. However, it became clear with the passage of time that such stories were, in fact, incorrect.

Such retrospective updating may lead to a shift in the balance of previously stored considerations as individuals retag some negatively or positively tagged information based on a retrospective revision of the their reliability assessment, as well as a coloring of assumptions regarding the reliability of new information. While inattentive citizens might be expected to have difficulty retroactively retrieving and updating their assessed valuation of information consumed in the murky past, and may be relatively unmotivated to do so, prominent initial efforts by an administration to gain publicity for a desired frame should help citizens recall it later. For example, the Bush administration's rhetorical reliance on Saddam Hussein's alleged weapons of mass destruction (WMDs) program to justify the war made it easier for critics to dredge up such claims later to undermine the administration's credibility in future claims.[33]

As this process unfolds, and as elites' informational advantage recedes over time, the influence of new information inconsistent with the (updated) prevailing media representation of reality presumably recedes. In other words, as individuals gather additional considerations and update their beliefs about the reliability of those considerations (in large part based on the weight of prior coverage), they are less influenced (proportionately) by subsequent considerations, especially those deemed likely to be unreliable. Consequently, the elasticity of reality—that is, elites' capacity to frame events distinctly from their true status—declines over time. Only

---

[32]McManus (1992) notes that in some conditions, news might actually qualify as a credence good, in which consumers are uncertain about the quality of the good even after consuming it.

[33]See http://www.publicintegrity.org/WarCard/ for a comprehensive listing of the Bush administration's allegedly deceptive statements on Iraq.

a fairly dramatic and sustained change in the valence of information would foster significant change in opinion once the prevailing narrative is firmly established, and even then only after some lag period during which citizens would continue to discount the credibility of the new information.

Figure 2.1 illustrates this process. It traces the typical path of the foreign policy informational advantage leaders enjoy relative to the public (that is, the trend in the elasticity of reality). Specifically, figure 2.1 focuses on the effects of reality (that is, the true nature of events on the ground) relative to the representation of that reality offered by elites, via the mass media. The Communication/Elite Rhetoric Effects curve represents the framing of events (e.g., positive, negative, or neutral valence, offensive vs. defensive foreign policy goals) embedded in media reporting of elite rhetoric about the conflict. The Reality Effects curve in turn represents the influence of actual events on the ground. The gap between the two curves represents the elasticity of reality—that is, the range of frames of events, with varying degrees of distance from those events' true tenor, that the public will accept as reliable.

At the outset of the conflict (at time t_0), the public has little or no independent information about the situation on the ground. At this stage the public depends on a representation of events provided by elites, the construction of which in turn depends on media framing. Absent any capacity on the part of the public to retrospectively assess the reliability of this information, the elasticity of reality is extremely large, approaching infinity (though presumably bounded in some manner by longer-term public attitudes, values, and perhaps experience gleaned from prior conflicts).[34] After a little time passes, but still relatively early in a conflict, say at time t_1, the true tenor of events should still matter relatively less than the media framing of elite rhetoric regarding those events. If media coverage diverges from reality, the former is likely to exert greater influence than the latter, as shown by the gap between C_1 (Communication/Rhetoric Effects at time t_1) and R_1 (Reality Effects at time t_1), which represents the elasticity of reality at time t_1. The two are likely to converge over time, with news increasingly reflecting actual events, as shown in figure 2.1 at time t_2, where $R_2 = C_2$. If one allows that some media outlets might favor a particular party in their coverage, such outlets should be expected to resist or accelerate this convergence, depending on the degree to which it

---

[34]Note that figure 2.1 attempts to represent the range of possible effects of rhetoric and reality—controlling for each other. If politicians choose not to make any statements at all early in a conflict, the impact of their rhetoric would presumably be minimal. Conversely, if the conflict is relatively uneventful or if there is no consistent pattern in the events surrounding it, reality should have marginally less influence on opinion. Iraq represents a particularly compelling case in part because it provoked intense elite debate and followed reasonably clear trends in its trajectory over much of the course of the conflict.

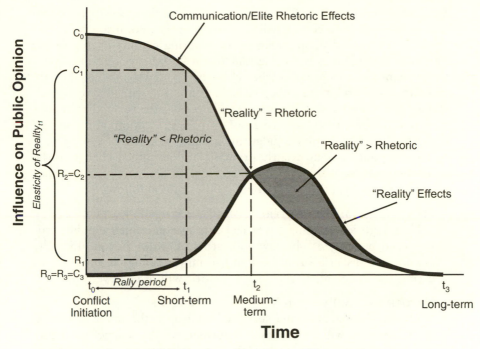

FIGURE 2.1. Elasticity of Reality for a Given State of Events

favors their preferred party. However, in the face of continued impingement by contrary real-world data, partisan media are likely to converge as well, though at a different rate than nonpartisan media (more gradually if they perceive the real-world data as *harmful* to their preferred party, more rapidly if they perceive it as *beneficial* to their preferred party). Eventually, however, as the public's store of information about the conflict increases, and as the public retrospectively updates its reliability assessments, the marginal influence of new information will recede. This decline is likely to be more rapid for communication effects, which exerted a disproportionate influence early on and consequently have more room to fall. Typical individuals will tend to be skeptical of information that diverges from their updated assessments regarding reality. Consequently, as the elasticity of reality collapses, the capacity of news coverage to influence opinion independent of actual events diminishes. At the same time, actual developments on the ground continue to contribute, although presumably at a reduced marginal rate, to net public assessments. This period is represented by the shaded area between times t_2 and t_3, where reality exerts a greater influence on public opinion than does news coverage, at least for a time.

Of course, the precise rate of convergence shown in figure 2.1 is arbitrary; the figure is intended solely to illustrate the theoretical point.

Presumably the actual rates of convergence, as well as the slopes of and gaps between the two curves, will vary across events. For instance, all else equal, given journalists' preferences for covering conflict over covering harmony among elites (Groeling and Baum 2008), the rate of convergence seems likely to be faster when elites are divided than when they are unified in support of the policy (which, consistent with Brody [1991], Zaller [1992], and others, we believe will decrease the variability of public opinion). Nonetheless, regardless of the precise locations and slopes of the curves, eventually public judgment becomes relatively fixed, by time t_3. At this point, absent a fairly dramatic and sustained change in the tenor of events, neither events nor rhetoric seem likely to exert much influence. Several hypotheses regarding public opinion follow:

HYPOTHESIS 15: LONGER-TERM COMMUNICATION EFFECTS
Elite rhetoric regarding a war will continue to influence public attitudes independent of objective indicators of reality beyond the rally period, but absent a substantial and sustained change in the tenor of events, the marginal effects of such rhetoric will recede over time.

HYPOTHESIS 16: PARTISAN MEDIA CONVERGENCE
Absent a substantial and sustained change in the tenor of events, news coverage will more closely approximate the valence of reality over time, but partisan media will be slower than nonpartisan media to converge when such coverage is damaging to their preferred party and faster when such coverage is helpful to their preferred party.

HYPOTHESIS 17: LONGER-TERM "REALITY" EFFECTS
Over time, absent a substantial and sustained change in the tenor of events, the marginal influence of objective indicators of a war's progress on public attitudes will first increase and then eventually recede.

HYPOTHESIS 18: RHETORIC VERSUS REALITY
Over time, the marginal influence of elite rhetoric will decline more than the marginal influence of objective indicators of a war's progress.

These declines are unlikely to be uniform throughout the public. Consistent with the Partisan Credibility hypothesis (H4), we anticipate that such declines should be more precipitous for the NPP relative to the PP. After all, due to their partisan affinity, statements by a president should be more credible to his fellow partisans than to opposition partisans or independents, and should remain so for a longer period of time, all else equal (Groeling and Baum 2008).[35] This suggests a corollary to the Longer-term Communication Effects hypothesis (H15):

[35] Also potentially contributing to partisan differences in responses to "new" information about a conflict is the possibility that individuals may simply be disproportionately inclined (or "biased") to believe whatever news frame makes them feel better (Caplan 2007).

HYPOTHESIS 15A: PARTISAN LONG-TERM EFFECTS

After the initial rally period following initiation of a conflict, negative events or elite rhetoric will tend to decrease the support of NPP partisans in the electorate more quickly and sharply than that of independents, who in turn will be more affected than PP partisans. Conversely, positive events or elite rhetoric will increase the support of PP partisans more quickly and sharply than that of independents, who will be more affected than NPP partisans.

Figure 2.1 and its corresponding hypotheses rest on an important assumption: that the fundamental nature of reality remains relatively constant. In other words, our discussion thus far presumes that war-related events follow a consistent, reinforcing path, while the media and the public gradually recognize that path and converge toward an accurate understanding of it. But what if reality changes? It is always possible that the tenor of events might swing substantially in a different direction. If so, depending in large measure on where along the elasticity timeline in figure 2.1 the prior state of events lies, we anticipate at least a resurgence of the influence of rhetoric relative to reality. In other words, a major, sustained change in reality seems likely to reopen the elasticity of reality, at least to some extent. Following such a change, this reopening consists of journalists and much of the public initially discounting rhetoric or other information inconsistent with the state of affairs prior to the change as they seek to determine whether it is real or illusory. Figure 2.2 graphically illustrates the effects of such a shift in events.

Figure 2.2 presents three curves separately tracking the effects of a fundamental shift in the tenor of events for PP and NPP partisans and independents. On the left side of the graph, events are uniformly negative for an extended period of time. As the true, bleak nature of events becomes clearer over time, all three groups grow less susceptible to positive pronouncements about the conflict. However, PP partisans are far slower than NPP partisans or independents to lose faith in the president. NPP partisans are particularly quick to begin discounting presidential rhetoric.

If events begin improving substantially, PP partisans will relatively quickly regain confidence in the president's positive rhetoric, while NPP partisans will remain skeptical for a considerable period of time before beginning to recognize and accept the change in reality and consequently reassessing. Independents will again fall in between. Eventually, all three groups will renew at least some of their initial confidence in the credibility of the administration's positive rhetoric. However, depending on how long the prior, negative tenor of events persisted—and hence how firmly public opinion is entrenched—such responsiveness may not return to levels comparable to the outset of the conflict.

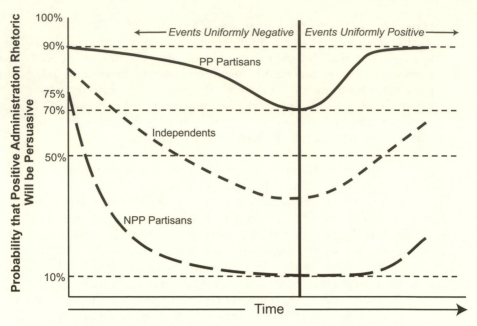

FIGURE 2.2. Persuasiveness of Presidential Rhetoric over Time, by Party

The media's response to the decline in military and civilian casualties in Iraq during the late summer and early fall of 2007, following the widely publicized surge in the U.S. troop presence in Iraq, illustrates this process. Initial reports of declining casualties received little attention from the media, were mentioned only in passing on network newscasts, and were relegated to pages 10, 14, 16, and 4 ("a couple of paragraphs") in the *New York Times, Washington Post, USA Today*, and *Los Angeles Times*, respectively (Kurtz 2007). Asked why the story had not received more coverage, *Washington Post* columnist Robin Wright commented, "The fact is we're at the beginning of a trend–and it's not even sure that it is a trend yet. . . . There is also an enormous dispute over how to count the numbers." CNN correspondent Barbara Starr added:

> [W]e don't know whether it is a trend about specifically the decline in the number of U.S. troops being killed in Iraq. This is not enduring progress. . . . We've had five years of the Pentagon telling us there is progress, there is progress. Forgive me for being skeptical, I need to see a little bit more than one month before I get too excited about all of this. (Kurtz 2007)

Later in the fall of 2007, as the trend in declining casualty rates persisted, the media gradually began offering more prominent coverage of the decline, as well as beginning to grapple with the possibility that the situation in Iraq may have taken a meaningful turn for the better. The title of an opinion article appearing in *Newsweek*'s December 3, 2007, issue illustrates the tentative nature of this turnaround: "The Case for Facing Facts: Why We Need to Acknowledge That the News from Iraq Has Been Getting Better" (Peters 2007). On this point, Sproul explained the "stickiness" of the prevalent negative frame as follows: "We finally could get some [independent] observation, and then I think probably we were more skeptical about good news stories because . . . in retrospect . . . we were all burned." She went on to note that "there is a little sense of skepticism that we turned a corner [in Iraq], because every time the language goes in that direction we fall back ten steps. So I do think, and it looks like, some news organizations were a little . . . skeptical . . . about using it [declining casualty numbers following the "surge"] with a weight that would make it a lead story."[36] Indeed, the very fact that this *partial* reassessment did not emerge until after about five months of consistently declining casualty levels demonstrates the stickiness of the media's core framing of the Iraq conflict as a failed policy. As Sproul observed, "I think earlier on [in the conflict], if you had a dramatic drop [in casualties] it would have probably been more of a story . . . a lead story."[37]

After more than three years of seemingly unwavering bad news from Iraq, the "failed policy" frame proved highly resistant, though not completely impervious, to reappraisal. Increasingly, news organizations possessed both the motive and opportunity to independently verify the president's assertions. As Sproul commented, "You would go [for a] reality check to our national security correspondent, and then you go to your correspondent in Baghdad or you probably send a bigger contingent to Iraq to try to report further . . . it's our job to say if we really thought there was no basis in fact on [administration claims]."[38]

Even after journalists did begin to partially reassess the state of events in Iraq, the opposition party predictably remained far more skeptical than the president's fellow partisans. For instance, House Speaker Nancy Pelosi (D-CA) declared on February 10, 2008—nearly a year after the start of the surge—that the war "is a failure." She also criticized the surge itself, noting that, on the one hand, "the troops have succeeded, God bless them," but on the other, "the purpose of the surge was to create a secure time for the government of Iraq to make the political change to bring reconciliation to Iraq. They have not done that" (Allen 2008). Senator Hillary Clinton (D-NY) offered a similarly skeptical assessment of the surge in her response to testimony from General David Petraeus,

[36]Interview with author (M.B.), October 10, 2007, Cambridge, Mass.
[37]Interview with author (M.B.), October 10, 2007, Cambridge, Mass.
[38]Interview with author (M.B.), October 10, 2007, Cambridge, Mass.

commander of U.S. forces in Iraq: "I think that the reports that you provide to us really require the willing suspension of disbelief" (Clinton 2007). Senate Majority Leader Harry Reid, in turn, echoed Senator Clinton, stating: "I believe . . . that this war is lost, and this surge is not accomplishing anything" (Associated Press 2007).

One can easily imagine the opposing case, in which events are proceeding well and public confidence in the administration is high, followed by a significant turn for the worse. The U.S. intervention in Somalia in 1992–1993 appears to have been such a case (Baum 2004, "How Public Opinion . . ."). In Somalia, most observers regarded the initial U.S. humanitarian mission as an overwhelming success, resulting in public euphoria and support. However, in the wake of a seemingly unsuccessful nation-building effort in the spring and summer of 1993, including a failed military campaign against Somali warlord Mohamed Farah Aideed, frustration and disappointment replaced this euphoria. Eventually, both partisans and independents lost confidence in presidential claims contrary to the declining state of affairs. However, consistent with figure 2.2, the rate at which the loss of confidence occurred, and the lag between the change in events and the onset of declining confidence, varied with partisan affiliation. Most notably, in fall 1993 Republicans predictably (given a Democratic commander in chief) began advocating a U.S. withdrawal from Somalia well before Democrats did (Koppelman 2006).

This discussion suggests an additional corollary to the Longer-term Communication Effects (H15) and Reality Effects (H17) hypotheses. The hypothesis addresses how the public processes a change in reality that is not matched by a change in elite rhetoric—that is, rhetoric consistent with the prior state of the world but not with a recent shift in events—as well as the predicted variations in such processes across partisan subgroups.

Hypothesis 15b: Event-Shift Effects Corollary

Following a significant and sustained change of events, the public will initially be more susceptible to influence by elite rhetoric in the media consistent with prior events, relative to the "new" reality or rhetoric consistent with it. Only later will the public become more responsive to the current true tenor of events (as represented by media coverage) and to rhetoric consistent with it. Given a *positive* change of events, the president's fellow partisans will respond *more* quickly and positively to rhetoric and events consistent with the new positive situation relative to NPP partisans and independents. Conversely, given a *negative* change of events, they will be *less* susceptible to such influence than NPP partisans and independents.

Conclusion

The following excerpt from a 2007 report on trends in public opinion regarding Iraq, appearing on pollster.com, summarizes several core aspects of our argument:

> [C]itizens don't shift their opinion based on quantified measures of progress. . . . For most citizens, opinions are driven more by the messages they hear from partisan leaders, with some sifting for credibility of the claims and filtering by predispositions. And, it must be added, by some effects of "reality," whatever that is. (Franklin 2007)

In some respects our theoretical representation of the relationship between elites, the press, and the public is, like the above quotation, at once both parsimonious and complex. It is parsimonious in that our core theoretical assumptions are few in number and relatively straightforward. Indeed, most of our assumptions are widely employed in the literatures on political communication, American politics, and political psychology. However, employed in combination, these relatively unproblematic assumptions lead to a wide range of nontrivial—and in many instances novel—predictions concerning which stories journalists will choose to cover and what effects such stories will have on public attitudes regarding presidents' foreign policy initiatives. These predictions are, however, highly contingent, depending on a wide range of factors, including the characteristics of those sending the message (politicians), those receiving the message (the public), and those transmitting it (the media), as well as on political circumstances (e.g., partisan control of government). Each of these factors can profoundly affect the incentives of journalists, the public, and partisan elites.

The complex and contingent nature of our predictions, while daunting in some respects, offers an important benefit: it affords us the ability to test a wide range of observable implications of our theory. To the extent that we are able to support these diverse predictions, the case for our theory will be far stronger than is typically possible with a narrower range of hypothesis tests. After all, the more diverse the range of phenomena a theory successfully predicts, the more improbable any alternative explanations for those phenomena become. In the remaining chapters of the book, we turn to this task, undertaking a wide range of empirical tests of the hypotheses derived in this chapter, wherever possible against multiple data environments and contexts.

CHAPTER 3

Elite Rhetoric, Media Coverage, and Rallying 'Round the Flag

IN THE 1930s, Senator Arthur Vandenberg (R-MI) was one of the most consistent and powerful foreign policy isolationists in the Senate. Prior to the attack on Pearl Harbor that prompted America to enter the Second World War, Vandenberg steadfastly opposed President Franklin Roosevelt's attempts to increase American involvement in the conflict and actively worked to constrain Roosevelt's foreign policy through legislation, including the Neutrality Acts. In contrast Vandenberg increasingly came to advocate "bipartisanship" in the conduct of foreign policy during and after the war, by which he meant "mutual effort, under our indispensable two-Party system, to unite our official voice at the water's edge so that America speaks with maximum authority against those who would divide and conquer us and the free world" (Vandenberg 1952).

For Vandenberg, this united voice did not preclude free debate and the frank exchange of views in the derivation of the policy. Rather, he argued that, at its core, this unity "simply seeks national security ahead of partisan advantage" (Vandenberg 1952). Speaking nearly 50 years after Vandenberg, Representative Lee Hamilton (D-IN) echoed Vandenberg's famous sentiment, arguing that "foreign policy always has more force and punch when the nation speaks with one voice. . . . A foreign policy of unity is essential if the United States is to promote its values and interests effectively and help to build a safer, freer, and more prosperous world" (Hamilton 2001).

In this chapter, we examine the degree to which American politicians have in fact spoken with one voice on foreign policy issues, and whether such unity truly matters for public opinion. To do so, we analyze network news coverage of congressional evaluations of the president and his administration in periods surrounding the initiation of all major U.S. uses of military force between 1979 and 2003. We propose to demonstrate that even after accounting for a wide range of indicators of empirical reality, *communication* still plays a crucial, independent role in influencing public support for the president during foreign crises. We further show that, rather than simply parroting the statements of Washington elites, public opinion in these crises varies systematically with the credibility of those statements, as well as with the institutional context in which political communication takes place and the characteristics of the receivers—that is, depending on who the president is at the time of a crisis, who is speaking about it, and who is listening to their rhetoric.

To accomplish these tasks, we undertake a series of statistical analyses testing nine media and opinion hypotheses derived in chapter 2, as well as several of the theoretical assumptions underlying the hypotheses. The first set of tests include three media-focused hypotheses: Oversampled Presidential Party Criticism (H1: *the media will present more negative than positive evaluations of the president by his own party*), Salient Crisis Novelty (H2: *the amount of criticism, relative to praise, will increase during high-salience rally periods*), and Divided Government Media (H7: *the proportion of credible praise relative to credible criticism will be greater in divided than in unified government*).

In the second part of the analysis, we test six opinion-related hypotheses: Partisan Credibility (H4: *evaluations of the president will have a stronger effect on members of the same party as the evaluator*), Costly Credibility (H5: *net of party affiliation, costly evaluations will have a stronger effect than cheap talk*), Combined Credibility (H6: *positive evaluations of the president by elites in the nonpresidential party [NPP] and negative evaluations by members of the president's own party [PP] will have the strongest effects on their fellow partisans*), Divided Government Opinion (H8: *aggregate public opinion rallies will be more positive in divided government*), and Salient Rally Praise and Criticism (H9: *during rally periods with U.S. casualties, positive evaluations by members of the NPP will produce smaller effects than during other periods, positive comments by members of the PP should be similarly unpersuasive in periods with or without casualties, and negative evaluations by either party will have a bigger negative effect than during other periods*).

Finally, as a validity check on several of our theoretical assumptions, we surveyed national samples of citizens and professional journalists on their news preferences. Before turning to our empirical tests, however, we first describe the data set we employ as the basis for our statistical testing in this chapter, as well as our methodological approach.

DATA AND METHODS

Mueller (1973, 209) defines rally events as issues that are international, directly involve the president, and are "specific, dramatic and sharply focused." Oneal, Lian, and Joyner (1996, 265) further restrict their definition of rally events to "major uses of force during a crisis," ensuring that they are "considering only cases that were truly consequential for the U.S. and salient to the public, necessary conditions for a rally." Following Oneal and colleagues, we restrict our analysis to major uses of force during foreign policy crises.[1] Our data include a total of 42 such events between 1979 and 2003 (hereafter "rally events"). Appendix 3.1 lists all 42 rally events.

We collected data on all congressional comments on the president and the executive branch during the 61-day window surrounding each rally event, from 30 days before to 30 days after the announcement or initiation of the major U.S. force deployment associated with each event. Evaluations by members of Congress (MCs) arguably represent the most consequential subset of all partisan rhetoric (Hallin 1986; Bennett 1990; Althaus et al. 1996; Oneal, Lian, and Joyner 1996; Zaller and Chiu 2000).[2] While presidential rhetoric is vital to the conduct of modern American politics (Kernell 1997), presidents tend to uniformly support their own initiatives, leading to almost no variation in our key variables of interest. For instance, in a multiyear content analysis of presidential rhetoric, Groeling (2001) found that more than 90% of presidential self-evaluations are positive. In addition, for the reasons already noted in our discussion of partisan message credibility, such self-serving statements are cheap talk, and so should generally be far less persuasive to typical voters than messages of support from across the aisle.

We also focus on congressional rhetoric because the news media often attempt to cover Congress as an "institutional counterweight" to the president (Hess 1991). The congressional contingent of the NPP represents the most important federal officeholders of that party, especially during divided government. Legislators are also among the best-known national politicians available to the media. By using such well-known figures in stories, reporters can substantially reduce the effort devoted to providing background to viewers.

[1]We employ an updated version of Baum's (2002) data set, which in turn represents an update of Blechman and Kaplan's (1978) data set on political uses of force (see also Oneal, Lian, and Joyner 1996; Fordham and Sarver 2001). Again following Oneal, Lian, and Joyner (1996), we code all uses of force measuring levels 1–3 on Blechman and Kaplan's (1978) scale as "major uses of force." Following Baum (2002), we exclude several events inconsistent with these definitions, such as long-scheduled military exercises, the cancellation of previously scheduled withdrawals of forces, or events that clearly were not major uses of force during a U.S. foreign policy crisis (e.g., U.S. support for withdrawal of UN forces from Somalia in January to March 1995, long after the United States withdrew its forces).

[2]While we would prefer to have gathered comprehensive measures of *all* sources of partisan rhetoric, the exceptional costliness of this content analysis work, representing many thousands of hours of research assistant labor, forced us to limit ourselves to the most important subset of these data.

Content Analysis

For each 61-day window, we first searched the Vanderbilt Television News Abstracts to locate every appearance by a senator or representative on the evening newscasts of ABC, CBS, and NBC.[3] Our research assistants watched recordings or read verbatim transcripts of each selected story, coding the statement's valence (positive, negative, or neutral) along a number of issue dimensions (e.g., foreign policy, budget, taxation), as well as the characteristics of the speaker (e.g., party, leadership status).[4] All coded statements were direct quotations of an identifiable MC pertaining directly to the president. Each observation consists of a summary of the content of a statement by a single MC in a single story. Although each statement might contain multiple distinct instances of praise or criticism of the president, we code all statements dichotomously on both dimensions, separately recording whether or not a given statement included praise and whether or not it included criticism.[5] We assigned each story to two coders, who worked independently. Two experienced graduate students then reviewed and arbitrated any disagreements in the coding. Prior to arbitration, inter-coder agreement on praise and criticism of the president was 95% and 88% for CBS and 86% and 96% for NBC, respectively.[6] The arbitration process further increased the reliability of our coding. In a random sample of our data, our two arbitrators agreed on more than 98% of all arbitration decisions.[7] We identified a total of 5,302 pertinent congressional appearances on network evening newscasts during the 2,115 days falling within the 61-day windows surround-

[3]Vanderbilt and UCLA archives supplied videotapes, Lexis-Nexis provided transcripts.

[4]Before coding, students attended an orientation with one of the principal investigators or their two graduate research assistants, then practiced using a series of five online interactive practice sessions.

[5]Any additional utility from coding each individual critique within a member statement would be outweighed by the exponential increase in complexity for our coding scheme. Our MC Appearances variable also accounts for news appearances by MCs that did not include codable evaluations.

[6]Prearbitration kappa scores for these variables were .44 and .51, respectively, for CBS and .52 and .48, respectively, for NBC. Altman (1991, 404) characterizes this as "moderate" agreement. Our inter-coder agreement for ABC was 80%. (Owing to differences in coding procedures, we were unable to calculate a kappa score for ABC.)

[7]The resulting postarbitration kappa score for our key causal variables was .86. While the coding form has remained constant (see http://www.sscnet.ucla.edu/comm/groeling/warstories/ch3form.html for the coding form), we implemented some improvements in the coding process over time. For example, for a subset of ABC data, students hand-coded the stories, met to compare their coding, and submitted their consensus results to a graduate research assistant for further examination. Students submitted all of the NBC and CBS data, and the remainder of the ABC data, online, and were unaware of the identity of their coding partner, prior to arbitration. We excluded a small subset of observations where the corresponding tapes or transcripts were damaged or unavailable.

ing our 42 rally events.[8] (Appendix 3.2 presents the instructions we gave to coders.)

Dependent Variables

For our analyses of MC rhetoric, our dependent variable is positive rhetoric by either party as a proportion of all rhetoric, both positive and negative. For the dependent variables in our public opinion analyses, in turn, we employ as our units of analysis individual Gallup presidential approval polls appearing within our 61-day windows. We aggregate all causal variables to this same unit level (that is, values, sums or averages, as appropriate, for a given period between individual Gallup polls). This yields an average of 4.1 unique observations per event, of which over half (2.7), on average, took place *after* a major deployment was initiated or announced. We transform our public opinion dependent variables into *differences* between approval in the polls conducted at poll period (or time) $t + 1$ and at poll period t for each partisan subgroup.[9]

Independent Variables

Many of our causal variables mirror those employed in previous studies of presidential approval and the rally phenomenon (e.g., Oneal, Lian, and Joyner 1996; Gartner and Segura 2000; Baum 2002; Nicholson et al. 2002; Chapman and Reiter 2004). They are intended to account for the domestic political circumstances surrounding each rally event as well as the characteristics of the speaker evaluating the president, of the adversary nation, of the rally event itself, and of the international environment at the time of the event. For speaker characteristics, in addition to party affiliation, we include a dummy variable measuring whether MCs are identified in a given story as leaders of the House or Senate, their party, or a committee. For domestic political variables, we include the number of mentions per poll period of the adversary nation on the front page of the *New York Times*, the monthly change in consumer sentiment (lagged one month),[10] as well as dummies for presidential and midterm election years, unified government, presidential transition periods, second-term

---

[8]About 8.6% of our coded evaluations (457 out of 5,302) occur less than 30 days before one rally *and* less than 30 days after another rally. In all cases where sequence matters in our analysis, we count any overlapping days as "after" the prior event, rather than "before" the next event.

[9]Because the several observations associated with each rally event are clearly not independent of one another, we cluster the standard errors by event. We tested our models with event-specific fixed effects. The results were in many respects comparable to those with clustered errors. Given our limited number of observations, however, we have insufficient statistical leverage to be confident in the reliability of a fixed-effects specification.

[10]Changes in consumer sentiment outperformed a variety of other macroeconomic indicators.

presidents, and Democratic presidents. We also account for the number of days between consecutive approval polls and the number of appearances by MCs on network evening newscasts during each poll period.

For adversary characteristics, we control for U.S. trade dependence and relative material capabilities (that is, capability ratio) vis-à-vis the adversary, and whether the adversary was a U.S. ally. For the international environment, we include variables measuring the number of U.S. foreign policy crises in the year of each event and whether the event took place during the cold war.[11] Finally, for event characteristics, we include dummies for whether an observation took place before or after the start dates of major U.S. force deployments (or announcements of such), whether the U.S. goal was imposing "foreign policy restraint" (FPR), "internal political change" (IPC), or "humanitarian intervention" (HI) (as defined by Jentleson 1992 and Jentleson and Britton 1998), and whether the event was terrorism-related, involved a significant ground invasion by U.S. troops,[12] or lasted only one day. We also account for whether the United States suffered any fatalities in a given conflict during each pertinent poll period.[13]

To increase our confidence that we are fully accounting for the unique characteristics of each event, we polled 38 scholars with expertise in American foreign policy, asking them to separately evaluate (on scales of 0–10) the extent to which, in their judgment, the events were "successful" and "worthwhile" (based on their own cost-benefit assessment) for the United States.[14] Figure 3.1 summarizes the results of this survey. We added the two items together to form a single *expert assessment* scale. We then regressed all of our control variables on this summary indicator and saved the residuals. The R^2 was .72, indicating that our control variables, *excluding* partisan rhetoric and lagged presidential approval, account for 72% of the variance in our experts' summary assessments of our 42 rally events. We employ the residual of our experts' summary assessments— that is, the exogenous portion—as a causal variable.

Finally, to mitigate serial autocorrelation, we include the appropriate partisan presidential approval poll lagged one period. This also accounts for the possibility that MCs may base their decisions to rhetorically oppose or support the president on their assessments of his ex ante political capital, or on anticipated public reactions. In table 3.1 we provide summary statistics for all causal variables, including our rhetoric indicators. (See appendix 3.3 for definitions and coding of all control variables.)

---

[11] A post-9/11 dummy proved insignificant and had no material effect on our results.

[12] Events meeting this definition include Grenada, Panama, Afghanistan, and Iraq (1991 and 2003).

[13] A similar variable, measuring the logged number of U.S. casualties per poll period, produced similar effects in our models. However, because we anticipate a *threshold*, rather than cumulative, short-term effect of casualties, we prefer the dichotomous specification.

[14] We contacted 96 foreign policy experts via e-mail; our response rate was thus 40%.

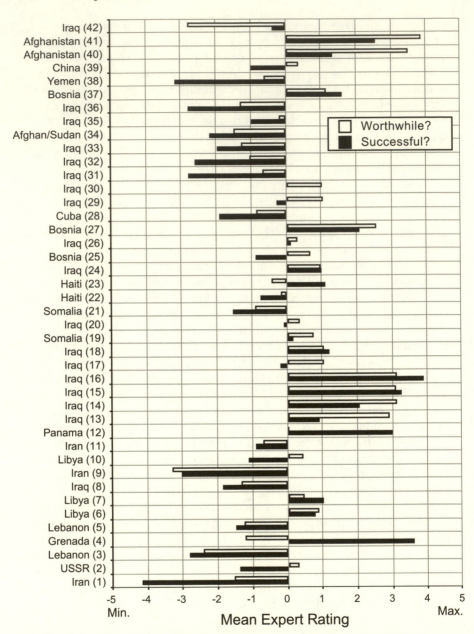

FIGURE 3.1. Mean Expert Ratings of Whether U.S. Military Actions Were
Successful or Worthwhile (N = 38; Event ID Number in Parentheses)

TABLE 3.1
Summary Statistics

Variable	Mean Frequency per Poll Period (Std. Dev.)	
Type of MC Rhetoric	*Overall*	*Ground Invasions*
Presidential party praise	0.95 (1.58)	0.53 (.86)
Presidential party criticism	1.44 (2.69)	0.39 (.89)
Nonpresidential party praise	0.67 (1.32)	0.74 (1.43)
Nonpresidential party criticism	4.42 (6.11)	2.71 (4.20)
Dichotomous Causal Variables	*Proportion of Total Observations*	
Divided government	0.74	
Democratic president	0.55	
Presidential election year	0.21	
Midterm election year	0.28	
Second-term president	0.34	
During presidential transition	0.02	
Any casualties	0.12	
U.S. ground invasion	0.22	
Post-cold war	0.83	
Terrorism related	0.20	
U.S ally	0.09	
Post event initiation	0.66	
Foreign policy restraint goal	0.90	
Internal political change goal	0.31	
Humanitarian intervention goal	0.12	
One-day event	0.25	
Other Causal Variables	*Mean (Std. Dev.)*	
(Consumer sentiment)	0.18 (4.61)	
Days between polls	10.23 (9.55)	
Party leader	6.13 (8.50)	
Total MC network news appearances per poll period	31.76 (34.96)	
Expert assessment of whether event was successful/worthwhile ($\times$10 to +10 scale)	−0.13 (3.67)	
New York Times front-page mentions of adversary-per-poll-period	0.12 (0.16)	
U.S. crises per year	1.02 (0.72)	
U.S. trade dependence vis-à-vis adversary	0.003 (0.01)	
U.S. capability ratio vis-à-vis adversary	0.94 (0.11)	

Testing Key Assumptions

To test our assumptions concerning the qualities that make news stories appealing to citizens and journalists, we conducted parallel surveys of citizens and national journalists. In the former case, we surveyed a nationally representative sample of 1,000 U.S. adults.[15] In the latter, we contacted 126 local and national journalists working in either print or broadcast media, asking them to participate in a web-based survey.[16] We received 40 responses, representing a response rate of about 32%. Among other questions, both surveys asked respondents to rate their degree of interest in eight stylized categories of news stories (on −2 to +2 scales for the journalists and on 0–100 scales for the national population sample): (1) congressional Republicans criticize President Bush, (2) congressional Republicans praise President Bush, (3) congressional Democrats criticize President Bush, (4) congressional Democrats praise President Bush, (5) congressional Republicans praise congressional Democrats, (6) congressional Republicans criticize congressional Democrats, (7) congressional Democrats criticize fellow congressional Democrats, and (8) congressional Democrats praise fellow congressional Democrats.[17]

RESULTS

Assumptions Regarding Journalist and Citizen Preferences

Our theory depends in part on an assumption that both journalists and citizens will prefer costly rhetoric to cheap talk (that is, they will prefer rhetoric that is contrary to the speaker's perceived interests over self-serving rhetoric that either bolsters the speaker's own interests or harms a political opponent's interests), and that journalists look for stories embodying novelty, conflict, balance, and authority. One implication, noted in chapter 2, is that the most appealing type of story for both journalists and citizens entails PP elites criticizing their fellow partisan president. Such

---

[15]Polimetrix provided the sample.

[16]We provided them with a link to the survey and a unique identification number.

[17]For the journalist survey, we gave a response option two points if a journalist selected it as the most interesting story type, one point if they selected it is the second-most interesting story type, −1 point if they selected it as the second-least interesting story type and −2 points if they selected it as the least interesting story type. This produces a scale running from −2 to +2, where −2 represents the least interesting story and +2 the most interesting story. For the Polimetrix survey, respondents were asked to rate each story type on a 0–100 scale, where 0 represented lowest level of personal interest and 100 represented highest level of interest. For the national population survey, we employ the population weight provided by Polimetrix (using "pweight" in Stata).

rhetoric possesses three of the four characteristics that appeal to journalists: novelty, authority (especially in unified government), and conflict. It is also costly, which should make it interesting to citizens.

Conversely, the least appealing story type should be one in which the president's party praises him. Such rhetoric lacks novelty, conflict, or balance and is self-serving (that is, cheap talk) as well. While individual journalists we interviewed or cited in chapter 2 anecdotally supported these assumptions, here we present the results of our systematic surveys of journalists and the general population. Figure 3.2 graphically illustrates the results of both surveys, with the top graphic presenting the results for journalists and the bottom graphic the results for citizens. Looking across the two graphics, we see that in both instances the results mirror our expectations, with respondents selecting "congressional Republicans criticize President Bush" and "congressional Republicans praise President Bush" as the *most* and *least* interesting story types, respectively.

Beginning with the general public (the top graphic), we find that the four types of rhetoric rated as *most* interesting are costly speech (partisans criticizing their fellow partisans or praising the opposition party), while the four story types rated as *least* interesting are cheap talk (that is, partisans praising themselves or criticizing the other party). Moreover, within the cheap talk categories, and consistent with the conflict assumption, respondents uniformly prefer criticism over praise.

Turning to journalists (the bottom graphic), the patterns are nearly identical, with only one difference: again consistent with the conflict assumption, journalists prefer "congressional Democrats criticize fellow congressional Democrats" over "congressional Republicans praise congressional Democrats." As with the general public, journalists prefer all costly rhetoric types over all cheap talk types, and in this instance, even more so than typical citizens, journalists prefer criticism to praise, all else equal. Taken together, these results offer clear and consistent support for our core theoretical assumptions concerning the story characteristic preferences of journalists and citizens.[18]

Media Coverage Hypotheses

In figure 3.3, we summarize the daily aggregate totals of praise and criticism during our 61-day windows. The most noteworthy pattern is the overwhelming predominance of negative or critical coverage, which varies

[18]We replicated the journalist survey results with a question asking respondents to rank the stories in terms of their newsworthiness (as opposed to personal interest). The results are nearly identical to those reported herein based on journalists' perceptions of story interest. Because the story interest question more closely parallels the Polimetrix survey, we focus our discussion on those results.

Journalists
(For each respondent: most preferred story type=2 points; second most
preferred=1 point; least preferred = -2 points; second least preferred =-1 point)

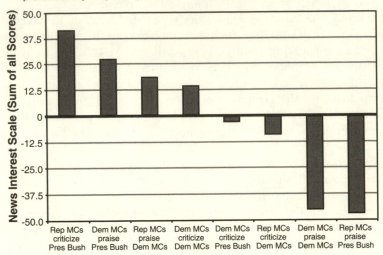

Citizens
(Overall Average on 0-100 News Interest Scale)

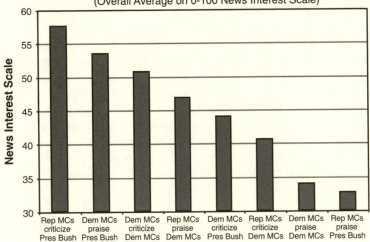

FIGURE 3.2. Journalist and Citizen Ratings of Interest in News, by Different
Types of News Stories

Abbreviations: MCs, members of Congress; Rep, Republican(s); Dem, Democrat(s).

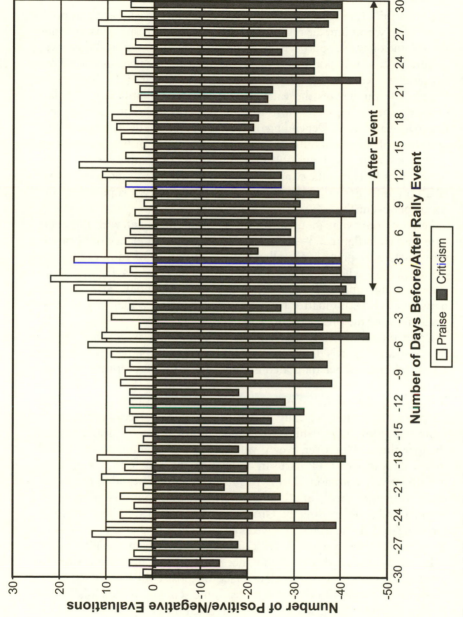

Figure 3.3. Trend in Positive and Negative Foreign Policy Evaluations ±30 Days from Rally Event Onset

hardly at all from before to after the initiation of a rally event. Though the relative volume of critical rhetoric does appear to subside somewhat following event initiations, this decline is small and short-lived, lasting approximately two weeks into the rally period. More important, in no instance does the volume of praise approach, let alone surpass, that of critical rhetoric.

Turning to our hypothesis tests, we begin with our Oversampled Presidential Party Criticism (H1) and Salient Crisis Novelty (H2) hypotheses. Figure 3.4 summarizes the valence of partisan evaluations in our data. Once again, perhaps the most striking pattern is the predominance of negative evaluations. Depending on how we parse the data, between 55% and 90% of all evaluations are negative. This pattern holds across networks, and also if we focus only on evaluations concerning the president's handling of foreign policy. Indeed, we find an average of more than seven MC criticisms per rally event, compared to about two supportive comments per event.[19]

Perhaps somewhat more surprisingly—and consistent with the aggregate pattern in figure 3.3—the overwhelming predominance of negativity remains largely unchanged following the initiation of rally events, and during periods where the United States suffered casualties. Figure 3.4 also offers strong support for the Oversampled Presidential Party Criticism hypothesis (H1): no matter how we parse the data, a majority of all PP evaluations of the president are negative.

Unfortunately, within the confines of these data we cannot directly demonstrate that this dramatically skewed distribution results from journalists' choices rather than a conscious choice by PP partisans to attack their leader nearly twice as often as they praise him in the news. However, if one accepts what we consider an extremely modest assumption—that PP partisans do not typically attack their fellow partisan president far more than they support him—then our empirical results clearly support the hypothesis. Moreover, even if we exclude the one noteworthy episode in our data in which PP partisan attacks on their own party's president were relatively common, during the 1998 Lewinsky scandal, the overall pattern changes hardly at all. In chapter 4 we confront this "unobserved population" problem directly (Groeling and Kernell 1998; Groeling 2008; Groeling and Baum 2009). As we shall see, we find that the news media do in fact heavily oversample criticism, particularly from the PP.

It is possible that this predominance of negativity may result from the disproportionate weight our data place on post-cold war years, which account for a majority of our sample. Some scholars (e.g., Holsti 2004) have speculated that absent the unifying threat posed by the Soviet Union,

---

[19]The precise figures are 7.14 MC criticisms of the president (1.57 and 5.57 critical comments by PP and NPP MCs, with standard deviations of 1.90 and 5.23, respectively), and 2.05 supportive comments (1.26 and .79 by the PP and NPP, with standard deviations of 1.65 and .89, respectively).

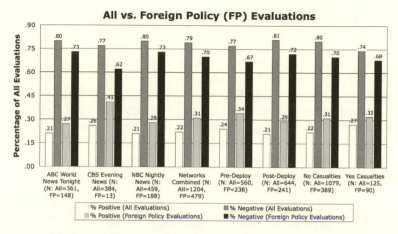

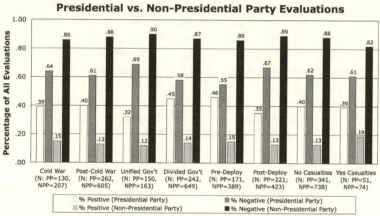

FIGURE 3.4. Summary of Valence in Congressional Evaluations of President (Percent of All MC Messages, by Type)

Note: Sums exceed 100% because some evaluations include both praise and criticism.

domestic politics may wield a stronger influence on U.S. foreign policy in the post–cold war era. Our results, also shown in figure 3.4, do not support this conjecture, as we observe no statistically significant differences between the cold war and post–cold war periods for either party's MCs.

Figure 3.4 also tests our Salient Crisis Novelty hypothesis (H2). Contrary to the conventional wisdom, the results support our prediction. As a result of their exceptional novelty, PP criticism in the news actually increases by 12 percentage points (from 55% to 67% of all PP evaluations, $p < .01$) following U.S. military deployments (or announcements of such) during rally events. Conversely, positive rhetoric by PP MCs declines by 11 points (from 46% to 35%, $p < .05$). Also as predicted, criticism of the president by NPP MCs increases and NPP praise decreases following the onset of a rally event, although these latter changes are small and statistically insignificant.[20] However, when we raise the bar and focus only on periods where it would be *most* politically risky for MCs to criticize the president—that is, rally periods in which the United States suffers casualties—we find, inconsistent with the predictions of H2, modest declines in criticism, although these declines are statistically insignificant.

Table 3.2, in turn, provides strong support for the Divided Government Media hypothesis (H7), which predicts that the proportion of credible praise to credible criticism will be greater in unified than in divided government. Here, we break down the relative proportion of all partisan messages in unified and divided government according to their partisan and costly credibility (keeping in mind that, all else equal, PP criticism and NPP praise of the president are costly, while NPP criticism and PP praise are cheap talk). As predicted, the most damaging PP evaluations (PP criticism) drop proportionately by more than half from unified to divided government (33% vs. 16% of all evaluations in unified vs. divided government, $p < .001$). Also as predicted, the most costly and hence credible praise of the president (NPP praise) nearly doubles proportionately in unified relative to divided government (6% vs. 10% of evaluations, $p < .02$).

In sum, figure 3.4 and table 3.2 offer clear support for our media predictions, including strong support for our Oversampled Presidential Party Criticism (H1) and Divided Government Media (H7) hypotheses, as well as qualified support for the Salient Crisis Novelty hypothesis (H2), supporting it when we compare pre- versus postdeployment periods, but (perhaps unsurprisingly) less so when we compare periods in which the United States suffered casualties with periods in which it did not.

While cross-tabulations offer the most straightforward tests of our media hypotheses, they do not allow us to account for potential alternative explanations for these relationships. Hence, we retest the Salient Crisis Novelty (H2) and Divided Government Media (H7) hypotheses under a more extensive set of controls. In this instance, we present our detailed regression results in the main text so that the reader will have a clear understanding of the nature of the statistical investigations undertaken throughout the book. However, to maintain a focus on the explicit tests of our predictions and avoid excessively technical discussions, for subsequent statistical analyses throughout the remainder of the book we present only the substantive results of theoretical interest in the main text.

[20]Baum (2003) reports a trend between 1953 and 1998 toward larger rallies among the least educated Americans, but not among their highly educated counterparts. At first glance, this appears inconsistent with our findings of overwhelmingly critical rhetoric and its strong effects on public opinion. However, the least educated segment of the population has constricted proportionately since the 1950s, and these citizens might be less able to distinguish between credible and noncredible rhetoric. Also, Baum's time series extends far longer than our data, making it difficult to draw direct comparisons between the studies.

TABLE 3.2
Proportional Distributions of Rhetoric by
Credibility and Party, Unified versus Divided
Government

Costly Credibility	Partisan Credibility	
	High	Low
Presidential Party Viewers		
Unified Government (n = 313)		
High	(PP−) 33%	(NPP+) 6%
Low	(PP+) 15%	(NPP−) 47%
Divided Government (n = 891)		
High	(PP−) 16%	(NPP+) 10%
Low	(PP+) 12%	(NPP−) 63%
Nonpresidential Party Viewers		
Unified Government (n = 313)		
High	(NPP+) 6%	(PP−) 33%
Low	(NPP−) 47%	(PP+) 15%
Divided Government (n = 891)		
High	(NPP+) 10%	(PP−) 16%
Low	(NPP−) 63%	(PP+) 12%

Note: PP+ denotes praise by presidential party MCs,
PP− denotes criticism by presidential party MCs, NPP+
denotes praise by nonpresidential party MCs, and NPP−
denotes criticism by non-presidential party MCs.

(For interested readers, we present complete statistical results in a series of appendix tables at the end of each empirical chapter.)

Additionally, to emphasize our hypothesis testing and for purposes of brevity, we do not discuss the substantive interpretations of the control variables except where pertinent to our theory. Instead, we concentrate on the key causal relationships that test our hypotheses. Along similar lines, in many instances we employ comparable (though, depending on availability, not always identical) sets of socioeconomic, domestic and international political and economic controls. Hence, for subsequent investigations, except where important differences in model specification arise, we do not discuss in detail in the main text the specific control variables employed in each model. Interested readers are invited to consult the appropriate appendices for presentation of the full model specifications, variable definitions and coding, and statistical results from which we derive the substantive findings reported throughout the remainder of the book.

Table 3.3 reports the results from three ordinary least squares (OLS) models testing the Salient Crisis Novelty (H2) and Divided Government

TABLE 3.3
Results of OLS Investigations of Correlates of MC Rhetoric and Changes in Approval

	Base Models				
	(1) Praise/ Crit. Ratio	(2) PP Approve	(3) NPP Approve	(4) Ind. Approve	(5) Praise/ Crit. Ratio
Independent variable					
Approval$_t$	—	−0.215 (0.053)***	−0.082 (0.036)*	−0.185 (0.059)**	—
PP criticism	—	−0.404 (0.149)**	−0.194 (0.132)	−0.469 (0.200)*	—
NPP criticism	—	0.061 (0.105)	−0.175 (0.121)	−0.186 (0.157)	—
PP praise	—	0.001 (0.329)	−0.120 (0.325)	−0.207 (0.382)	—
NPP praise	—	0.618 (0.356)^	1.220 (0.369)**	1.124 (0.351)**	—
Any KIA	−0.081 (0.049)	—	—	—	−0.099 (0.046)*
PP crit. × any KIA	—	—	—	—	—
NPP crit. × any KIA	—	—	—	—	—
PP praise × any KIA	—	—	—	—	—
NPP praise × any KIA	—	—	—	—	—
Any KIA × post-deployment	—	—	—	—	—
Evaluations-per-period	—	−0.026 (0.030)	0.016 (0.029)	0.025 (0.032)	0.000 (0.001)
Days between polls	—	—	—	—	0.000 (0.003)
Post-deployment	—	—	—	—	−0.063 (0.054)
Pre- and post-deployment	—	—	—	—	0.015 (0.055)
Major war	—	—	—	—	0.071 (0.054)
Pres. election year	−0.144 (0.034)***	—	—	—	−0.120 (0.052)*
Midterm election year	—	—	—	—	0.060 (0.039)

Fully Specified Models			Fully Specified Interaction Models			
(6) PP Approve	(7) NPP Approve	(8) Ind. Approve	(9) Praise/ Crit. Ratio	(10) PP Approve	(11) NPP Approve	(12) Ind. Approve
−0.663 (0.112)***	−0.400 (0.143)**	−0.492 (0.091)***	—	−0.661 (0.113)***	−0.406 (0.146)**	−0.514 (0.092)***
−0.515 (0.216)*	−0.226 (0.257)	−0.510 (0.274)^	—	−0.508 (0.285)^	−0.013 (0.228)	−0.309 (0.295)
0.093 (0.101)	−0.244 (0.124)^	−0.193 (0.182)	—	0.092 (0.104)	−0.266 (0.133)^	−0.201 (0.189)
0.079 (0.354)	−0.399 (0.509)	−0.448 (0.516)	—	0.199 (0.441)	−0.536 (0.594)	−0.298 (0.599)
0.934 (0.465)^	1.166 (0.409)**	1.050 (0.448)*	—	0.987 (0.485)*	1.167 (0.429)**	1.228 (0.490)*
1.319 (1.549)	1.253 (2.538)	4.314 (2.090)*	0.049 (0.061)	2.621 (2.810)	5.122 (4.516)	9.146 (3.593)*
—	—	—	—	−0.052 (0.294)	−0.419 (0.234)^	−0.329 (0.333)
—	—	—	—	−0.210 (0.512)	−1.428 (0.960)	−1.123 (0.762)
—	—	—	—	−0.091 (0.902)	1.334 (1.473)	0.821 (1.057)
—	—	—	—	−0.343 (0.975)	0.961 (1.098)	−0.416 (0.805)
—	—	—	−0.179 (0.083)*	—	—	—
0.010 (0.029)	0.056 (0.036)	0.058 (0.042)	−0.000 (0.001)	0.007 (0.030)	0.058 (0.037)	0.045 (0.043)
−0.017 (0.052)	0.007 (0.037)	0.010 (0.063)	0.000 (0.003)	−0.014 (0.053)	0.026 (0.045)	0.029 (0.065)
2.232 (1.088)*	2.448 (1.404)^	1.470 (1.557)	−0.049 (0.054)	2.079 (1.052)^	2.198 (1.363)	1.184 (1.557)
−2.585 (0.901)**	−1.775 (2.514)	−0.549 (1.735)	0.015 (0.055)	−2.479 (0.899)**	−1.474 (2.344)	−0.155 (1.649)
5.319 (1.809)**	11.370 (3.088)***	10.346 (2.149)***	0.066 (0.055)	5.401 (1.881)**	11.922 (3.532)**	11.198 (2.217)***
0.376 (1.426)	−2.891 (1.782)	−2.104 (1.871)	−0.116 (0.052)*	0.392 (1.494)	−2.886 (1.836)	−2.000 (1.936)
−0.343 (1.012)	−0.003 (0.974)	−1.821 (1.487)	0.057 (0.039)	−0.236 (1.083)	−0.083 (1.100)	−1.825 (1.723)

(continued)

TABLE 3.3 (*continued*)

	Base Models				
	(1) *Praise/* *Crit. Ratio*	(2) *PP* *Approve*	(3) *NPP* *Approve*	(4) *Ind.* *Approve*	(5) *Praise/* *Crit. Ratio*
Party leader	—	—	—	—	0.002 (0.002)
Second term	−0.109 (0.043)*	—	—	—	−0.118 (0.052)*
Consumer sentiment	—	—	—	—	−0.007 (0.003)*
Unified government	−0.089 (0.042)*	—	—	—	−0.098 (0.045)*
Transition	—	—	—	—	0.193 (0.089)*
Democratic president	—	—	—	—	0.054 (0.073)
Post-cold war	−0.107 (0.039)**	—	—	—	−0.127 (0.073)^
NY *Times* coverage	—	—	—	—	0.338 (0.123)**
Expert assessment	—	—	—	—	0.014 (0.005)**
One-day event	—	—	—	—	−0.002 (0.039)
Capability ratio	—	—	—	—	−0.070 (0.220)
Terrorism related	—	—	—	—	0.061 (0.040)
US crises-per-year	—	—	—	—	−0.014 (0.045)
US ally	—	—	—	—	−0.027 (0.067)
Trade dependence	—	—	—	—	−0.286 (2.584)
FPR	—	—	—	—	−0.167 (0.068)*
IPC	—	—	—	—	−0.158 (0.049)**
HI	—	—	—	—	0.096 (0.085)
Constant	0.370 (0.050)***	19.056 (4.703)***	3.405 (1.675)*	11.353 (3.894)**	0.564 (0.140)***
No. of Obs.	170	166	166	164	169
R^2	0.08	0.16	0.08	0.13	0.19

$^p \leq .10$, $^*p \leq .05$, $^{**}p \leq .01$, $^{***}p \leq .001$. Robust standard errors in parentheses. Dependent variables are shown in column headings.

Fully Specified Models			Fully Specified Interaction Models			
(6) PP Approve	(7) NPP Approve	(8) Ind. Approve	(9) Praise/ Crit. Ratio	(10) PP Approve	(11) NPP Approve	(12) Ind. Approve
-0.113 (0.067)^	-0.079 (0.111)	-0.005 (0.126)	0.002 (0.002)	-0.113 (0.075)	-0.086 (0.118)	-0.002 (0.126)
3.818 (1.319)**	-0.240 (1.370)	2.031 (1.607)	-0.112 (0.052)*	3.796 (1.251)**	-0.702 (1.317)	1.767 (1.578)
-0.070 (0.088)	-0.262 (0.198)	-0.361 (0.169)*	-0.007 (0.003)*	-0.083 (0.095)	-0.329 (0.223)	-0.442 (0.186)*
-6.429 (1.708)***	-6.675 (2.909)*	-6.475 (2.548)*	-0.091 (0.044)*	-6.592 (1.980)**	-7.497 (3.453)*	-8.250 (3.031)**
-1.732 (3.044)	0.860 (2.704)	0.776 (5.513)	0.205 (0.085)*	-2.122 (3.192)	0.794 (2.668)	0.518 (5.923)
0.618 (2.102)	-2.607 (2.459)	0.844 (2.613)	0.049 (0.074)	0.710 (2.085)	-2.203 (2.461)	1.497 (2.770)
3.903 (2.520)	0.145 (1.935)	2.353 (2.747)	-0.112 (0.075)	3.554 (2.618)	-0.584 (1.991)	1.160 (2.983)
8.306 (3.637)*	10.628 (4.293)*	8.755 (4.951)^	0.334 (0.113)**	7.650 (3.967)^	8.093 (4.940)	6.153 (5.349)
0.384 (0.166)*	0.442 (0.323)	0.504 (0.250)*	0.013 (0.006)*	0.389 (0.165)*	0.464 (0.328)	0.558 (0.258)*
0.535 (0.961)	-1.396 (1.673)	-0.218 (1.690)	-0.004 (0.040)	0.460 (0.963)	-1.437 (1.674)	-0.900 (1.774)
-3.815 (5.296)	-31.354 (12.755)*	-26.964 (9.939)**	-0.103 (0.220)	-3.402 (5.764)	-32.939 (13.702)*	-27.239 (10.722)*
-0.732 (1.323)	2.839 (1.446)^	2.817 (1.803)	0.058 (0.040)	-0.683 (1.314)	2.749 (1.505)^	3.092 (1.885)
1.505 (1.025)	2.948 (1.104)**	4.082 (1.316)**	-0.015 (0.045)	1.501 (1.087)	3.348 (1.212)**	4.511 (1.488)**
-10.414 (2.587)***	5.156 (2.168)*	0.687 (2.782)	-0.020 (0.068)	-10.489 (2.541)***	4.408 (2.206)^	-0.376 (3.015)
186.478 (62.218)**	-173.946 (106.455)	-120.597 (101.435)	-0.682 (2.587)	195.234 (66.927)**	-170.170 (105.332)	-83.598 (109.031)
-5.962 (2.720)*	-2.068 (1.938)	-3.232 (2.145)	-0.166 (0.068)*	-6.177 (2.732)*	-2.774 (2.224)	-4.496 (2.341)^
3.862 (1.987)^	-6.437 (1.720)***	-3.866 (2.307)^	-0.153 (0.049)**	3.748 (1.950)^	-6.508 (1.700)***	-4.638 (2.155)*
-4.180 (2.356)^	7.908 (2.257)***	4.274 (2.841)	0.094 (0.086)	-4.035 (2.393)^	7.980 (2.310)***	4.865 (2.925)^
56.598 (10.815)***	42.623 (16.622)**	47.789 (12.294)***	0.577 (0.133)***	56.628 (11.552)***	45.342 (18.253)*	51.093 (13.316)***
165	165	163	169	165	165	163
0.44	0.34	0.41	0.19	0.44	0.36	0.43

Abbreviations: PP, presidential party; NPP, nonpresidental parties; Crit., criticism; KIA, U.S. troops killed in action; FPR, foreign policy restraint; IPC, internal political change; HI, humanitarian intervention.

Media (H7) hypotheses (models 1, 5, and 9), as well as nine models testing our public opinion hypotheses (models 2–4, 6–8, and 10–12).[21] In order to investigate the sensitivity of our results to model specification, we present three versions of each model. The first version (models 1–4) excludes most of the controls. The second version (models 5–8) adds the control variables, while the third version (models 9–12) adds interactions with dummies for whether the observation took place before or after the initiation of a given event (model 9) or for whether the United States suffered any casualties in a given poll period (models 10–12). (In table 3.A1, appendix 3.4, we replicate all models using only the domestic political and economic controls, as well as using only the actor- and event-characteristic controls, with comparable results.)

The first noteworthy pattern in table 3.3 is the impressive consistency of the results on our key causal variables across model specifications: throwing the proverbial kitchen sink at our rhetoric indicators produces surprisingly modest changes in their effects. While many of the controls are statistically significant, their effects appear mostly orthogonal to our key causal variables. We can therefore proceed more confidently to interpreting our results from the fully specified models.

Model 5 in table 3.3 presents our fully specified OLS model testing the Salient Crisis Novelty (H2) and Divided Government Media (H7) hypotheses. Recall that the dependent variable for this analysis is positive evaluations (from either party) as a proportion of all valenced (that is, positive or negative) evaluations. The key causal variables are dummies for unified government and for whether a given event produced U.S. casualties (our primary indicator of salient rally events). The results indicate that, consistent with the Divided Government Media hypothesis (H7), MC rhetoric in the news is about 10 percentage points more positive during divided government ($p < .05$), while, consistent with the Salient Crisis Novelty hypothesis (H2), the presence of casualties is associated with about a 10-point *decline* in praise relative to criticism ($p < .05$). Recall that this latter pattern failed to emerge in our simple cross-tabulations, thereby demonstrating the importance of accounting for potentially confounding influential factors through multiple regression analysis.

Of course, the predicted effects of casualties in the early stages of a rally event are conditional on the existence of a U.S. military action that the public *could* rally behind. In fact, our data include several instances where casualties took place prior to the apparent start date of an event (such as the beating death of Marine Lt. Robert Paz by Panamanian forces four days before the U.S. invasion of Panama in December 1989).

---

[21] All models exclude one to two extreme outlier observations, the inclusion of which modestly weakens but does not fundamentally alter the reported results.

Consequently, in model 9 we isolate the post-event-initiation effects of casualties by interacting the casualty indicator with a post-event-initiation dummy.

It is difficult to interpret the results from interaction models based on the coefficients on individual causal variables or interaction terms.[22] (See appendix 3.5 for further discussion of this point.) Hence, for ease of interpretation, in figure 3.5 we employ Clarify (King, Tomz, and Wittenberg 2000), a statistical simulation procedure that allows us to calculate the expected values of our dependent variables as the key causal variables vary, as well as to determine whether the differences in the effects of the causal variables, separately or in interaction, are themselves statistically significant.[23] We return to this technique throughout the book, in most cases presenting the calculated values in the text and relegating the raw regression results to appendices.

The results indicate that, as anticipated, the criticism-enhancing effect of salience (with salience measured by the presence of U.S. casualties) is considerably stronger after the initiation of an event. As shown in figure 3.5, prior to the initiation of an event, casualties are associated with a relatively small and statistically insignificant 4.9-percentage-point increase in relative praise (from .225 to .274). In contrast, following event initiation the presence of one or more casualties is associated with a nearly 13-percentage-point relative decline in praise (from .18 to .05, $p < .05$). Indeed, for events involving no U.S. casualties, the onset of an event (that is, moving from the pre-event period to the post-event-initiation period) is associated with only about a 5-percentage-point decline in relative praise (.225 pre-event vs. .176 post-event, insig.). Conversely, for events in which the U.S. suffers casualties, the onset of the event is associated with a far larger 23-percentage-point decline in relative praise (from .274 pre-event to .046 post-event, $p < .01$). These results strongly support our Salient Crisis Novelty hypothesis (H2). Far from the popular stereotype of Congress reflexively rallying 'round the president when the nation is at war and lives are on the line, our data indicate that the news media typically offer the public a representation of Congress in conflict with the

[22]The *combined* effects of interaction terms and their constituent variables, upon summing the coefficients on the interaction term and key base category, are frequently associated with statistically significant effects on dependent variables even when the individual coefficient on either variable by itself is insignificant. Hence, evaluating the substantive importance of such effects requires assessing the significance of the differences in the dependent variable(s) produced by the combined variations in the key causal variables and interaction terms.

[23]We are able to calculate the significance of the differences in the predicted effects of the key causal variables on the dependent variable because Clarify simulations produce confidence intervals surrounding the expected values of the dependent variable.

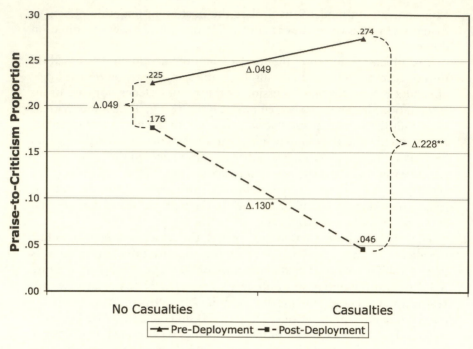

FIGURE 3.5. Praise as Estimated Proportion of Valenced Rhetoric (Praise and Criticism) as Casualties Vary, Pre- versus Postdeployment Periods
*p < .05, **p < .01.

president on foreign policy, whether or not such a representation accurately reflects the relative mix of opinions in the legislative branch.

Public Opinion Hypotheses

We turn next to the Partisan (H4), Costly (H5), and Combined Credibility (H6) hypotheses, as well as our Divided Government Opinion hypothesis (H8). The dependent variables for these analyses are differences across polls in PP, NPP, and independent approval ratings, while the key causal variables measure the number of instances of praise or criticism of the president by either party during a poll period. Figure 3.6 presents the results from our simulations testing these hypotheses. (We present the data underlying figure 3.6 in table 3.A2 in appendix 3.6.)

Beginning with party identifiers, models 6 and 7 in table 3.3 investigate the effects of MC rhetoric on PP and NPP partisans in the electorate, respectively. The top left graphic in figure 3.6 illustrates the substantive effects of a two-standard-deviation increase in each type of MC rhetoric. (Here and throughout the remainder of this discussion, whenever we

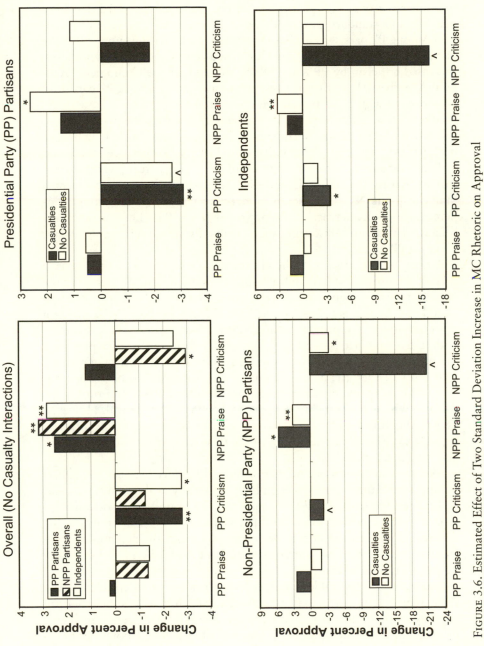

FIGURE 3.6. Estimated Effect of Two Standard Deviation Increase in MC Rhetoric on Approval $p < .10$, $^{*}p < .05$, $^{**}p < .01$.

note a simulated increase in a particular type of rhetoric, we are referring to an increase of *two standard deviations*, from one standard deviation below to one standard deviation above the mean for that type of rhetoric.) Among PP partisans in the electorate, we find strong support for the Partisan (H4), Costly (H5), and Combined (H6) Credibility hypotheses. Increased criticism by PP MCs, which should (per the Combined Credibility hypothesis) have the strongest persuasive impact among PP partisans, is associated with a 2.8-percentage-point drop in approval ($p < .01$). As predicted, this is the largest substantive effect across the four types of rhetoric for PP partisans. In contrast, criticism by NPP MCs, which lacks both partisan and costly credibility for PP partisans, produces small and insignificant effects. Increased high-cost NPP praise, in turn, which should (per the Costly Credibility hypothesis) have a greater persuasive impact than cheap talk NPP criticism, is in fact associated with a far larger, 2.5-percentage-point increase in PP approval ($p < .05$). Last, presumably because it is cheap talk during such events, PP praise has no significant effect on PP partisans.

Among NPP partisans in the electorate, consistent with the Partisan (H4) and Costly (H5) Credibility hypotheses, cheap talk PP praise of the president has no significant effect, while, consistent with the Partisan Credibility hypothesis (H4), increased criticism by NPP MCs yields a 2.9-point drop in approval among NPP partisans ($p < .05$). Consistent with the Combined Credibility hypothesis (H6), increased praise of the president by NPP MCs is associated with the largest effect across the four types of rhetoric: a 3.1-percentage-point increase in NPP approval ($p < .01$). Increased criticism of the president by PP MCs in turn is associated with a 1.2-percentage-point decline in NPP approval. However, presumably because of its low partisan credibility, despite being correctly signed and relatively large in magnitude this latter relationship is statistically insignificant.

Also consistent with our predictions, the difference between the effects on approval ratings of increases in high-credibility evaluation types (that is, between increases in PP criticism and NPP praise) is statistically significant among both PP and NPP partisans ($p < .01$). In contrast, the difference between the effects on approval ratings of increases in low-credibility evaluation types (that is, between increased NPP criticism and PP praise) is insignificant.

Finally, model 8 in table 3.3 presents the results for independents. The substantive results shown in figure 3.6 (again, the top left graphic), in turn, strongly support the Costly Credibility hypothesis (H5). Increased high-cost PP criticism of the president yields about a 2.8-percentage-point decline in approval ($p < .05$), while an equivalent increase in high-cost NPP praise yields the mirror opposite: about a 2.8-point increase in approval ($p < .01$).

Comparable increases in cheap talk PP praise or NPP criticism of the president yield smaller and insignificant effects. Hence, consistent with the Costly Credibility hypothesis (H5), increases in both high-credibility evaluation types, PP criticism and NPP praise, produce significant effects in the predicted directions, while increases in both low-credibility evaluation types, PP praise and NPP criticism, do not. Moreover, as with party identifiers, the difference between the effects of high-credibility positive and negative evaluations (again, criticism of the president by PP MCs and praise by NPP MCs) is itself significant ($p < .01$), while that between low-credibility positive and negative evaluation types (again, PP praise of the president and NPP criticism) is far smaller and insignificant.

Next, we test the Divided Government Opinion (H8) hypothesis. To do so, we again employ models 6–8 in table 3.3 to determine the marginal predicted change in presidential approval, given the actual observed flows of partisan rhetoric in both unified and divided government across our 42 events. Consistent with the Divided Government Opinion hypothesis (H8), our results predict that, on average, the actual partisan evaluations of the president in divided government would add 1.22 approval points, while the flows in unified government would actually cost the president .15 approval points. This 1.37-percentage-point difference from divided to unified government is significant at $p < .01$. Even though our model explicitly controls for divided government, these changes track fairly closely the average aggregate opinion changes across our 42 rally events, particularly during divided government (increases of .85 approval points overall and of .93 and .55 approval points during divided and unified government, respectively).

This pattern is consistent with prior research (e.g., Meernik and Waterman 1996) that has found that typical rallies (with the exception of major wars: Chapman and Reiter 2004) tend to be relatively small and ephemeral.[24] Examples of the former type of event include several U.S. interventions in the 1990s, including Haiti, Bosnia, and Kosovo. Averaging across several surveys conducted just before and immediately after these interventions, President Bill Clinton's approval ratings actually declined by two and three percentage points following the initiation of the U.S.-led multinational peacekeeping intervention in Bosnia in December 1995 and the launch of NATO's Kosovo air war in March 1999, respectively, while remaining unchanged following the dispatch of U.S. troops to Haiti

---

[24]The marginal aggregate opinion change for each event represents an equally weighted average of the predicted change for independents, PP, and NPP partisans. The average observed change in approval across all of our events was an increase of .85 for PP members, 1.06 for NPP members, and .87 for independents. If we include all controls, set at their mean values, the model predicts somewhat larger (slightly positive) rallies in divided (unified) government.

in September 1994. In contrast, following the larger-scale U.S. invasions of Panama in December 1989 and Iraq in March 2003—two examples of the latter type of rally event (that is, relatively major wars)—Presidents George H.W. Bush and George W. Bush saw their approval ratings spike by 9 and 13 percentage points, respectively.

We turn finally to our Salient Rally Praise and Criticism (H9) hypothesis, which predicts that criticism of the president by either party's MCs during rally periods with U.S. casualties will have a bigger effect than criticism in other periods, while praise of the president from NPP MCs (but *not* PP MCs) will have a smaller effect relative to non-casualty periods. To test these predictions we interact each type of rhetoric with our casualty dummy. The results for PP partisans, NPP partisans, and independents are shown in models 10, 11, and 12, respectively, of table 3.3. The top right, bottom left, and bottom right graphics in figure 3.6, in turn, compare the substantive effects of increases in each type of rhetoric during casualty periods with the effects during periods without casualties among PP partisans, NPP partisans, and independents, respectively.

Beginning with PP partisans, the top right graphic in figure 3.6 indicates that, consistent with our hypothesis, increased high-cost criticism of the president by PP MCs is associated with larger (-3.1 vs. -2.7) and more significant ($p < .01$ vs. $p < .10$) effects during casualty periods, while variations in criticism of the president by NPP MCs do not significantly influence approval ratings among PP partisans. Also consistent with our hypothesis, increased high-cost NPP praise yields considerably larger (2.6 vs. 1.5) and more significant ($p < .05$ vs. insig.) effects during non-casualty periods, while increases in cheap talk PP praise do not produce significant effects during either casualty or non-casualty periods.

Turning next to approval ratings among NPP partisans in the electorate, the bottom left graphic in figure 3.6 indicates that, consistent with our hypothesis, criticism of the president by either party's MCs exerts a far larger effect during periods in which the United States suffers casualties (-2.4 for PP, $p < .10$; -20.8 for NPP, $p < .10$) relative to periods without casualties ($-.07$ for PP, insig.; 3.3 for NPP, $p < .05$). Also consistent with the hypothesis, increased praise of the president by PP MCs has no significant effect on approval among NPP partisans during either periods with or without U.S. casualties, while the corresponding increase in criticism of the president by NPP MCs produces a more highly significant increase in approval during periods without U.S. casualties ($p < .01$ vs. $p < .05$). However, contrary to the hypothesis, the effect is somewhat larger during periods in which the U.S. suffers casualties (3.0 vs. 5.5 percentage points). Nonetheless, with this one partial exception, the results for PP and NPP partisans offer strong support for the Salient Rally Praise and Criticism hypothesis (H9).

Finally, among independents, the bottom right graphic in figure 3.6 indicates that, as predicted by the Salient Rally Praise and Criticism hypothesis (H9), increased high-cost criticism of the president by PP MCs is associated with larger (-3.4 vs. -1.8) and more significant ($p < .05$ vs. insig.) drops in presidential approval during periods in which the United States suffers casualties. Similarly, and also consistent with this hypothesis, increased criticism of the president by NPP MCs is also associated with much larger (-16.0 vs. -2.5) and more significant ($p < .10$ vs. insig.) declines in approval during periods with U.S. casualties. Also consistent with H9, an increase in costly NPP praise of the president yields larger (3.2 vs. 2.0) and more significant ($p < .01$ vs. insig.) increases in approval during periods without U.S. casualties, while cheap talk praise by PP MCs is not associated with significant effects in either periods with or without casualties. Overall, the data support the Salient Rally Praise and Criticism hypothesis (H9) fairly unambiguously in 11 of 12 possible comparisons, and at least partially in every instance. Once again, this represents strong support for our theory. Indeed, overall approximately 90% of the hypothesis tests in this chapter support the theory.

A Few Words on Potential Counterarguments

We briefly address four potential criticisms, including (1) reverse causality; (2) that the intrinsic characteristics of the events may drive both elite rhetoric and public opinion; (3) that MC criticism is intrinsically more significant than praise as a signal to voters of the merits of a president's foreign policy activities—who, absent a signal to the contrary, might assume the president is competent in foreign policy (Baum 2004, "Going Private")—and so journalists *should* cover it and the public *should* value it more; and (4) that differences in elite rhetoric in the news could reflect the *actual* mix of elite rhetoric rather than journalists' preferences.

Beginning with reverse causality, we believe the concern that the changing patterns of evaluations could *reflect*, rather than cause, changes in presidential popularity is unfounded, for at least three reasons. First, approval ratings at the time of the evaluation are directly factored into our models through inclusion of approval at time t as a lag term. In other words, we are directly accounting for the president's prior popularity, which would presumably form the basis for any potential MC evaluations based on anticipated future presidential political capital. Second, because we employ the difference between approval at time (that is, poll period) $t + 1$ and at time t as our dependent variable, a president's unknown future approval logically cannot *cause* present actions. Of course, in some cases MCs might be able to accurately forecast future presidential approval. In the case of rally events such as the September 11 attacks, it was probably clear to most politicians that the public would rally around George W. Bush. But in most cases it seems unlikely an MC could predict a president's future popularity with enough certainty to affect his or her present actions, especially given the comparatively safe option of reserving comment until the implications of a policy are known.

Last, and most important, if one assumes that anticipated future increases in presidential approval cause politicians to increase their support for the president, this should affect the political calculations of both PP and NPP MCs. Yet in most cases we observe significant effects only for praise from NPP MCs, while PP praise is insignificant in every case. Similarly, there would be no reason to expect that criticism by the PP, but not by the NPP, would be *caused* by anticipated future drops in PP partisan approval, with NPP partisans in the electorate responding only to criticism from *their* fellow partisan elites.

The second potential concern is that differences in the intrinsic characteristics of the events rather than in media coverage may drive differences in MC rhetoric, and thus in public reactions. Yet our fully specified models include controls for a wide array of the unique characteristics of the events, including the adversary's military capabilities, whether it was a U.S. ally, U.S. trade relations with the adversary, the U.S. "principal policy objectives" in the conflict, the presence of U.S. casualties, the number of U.S. foreign policy crises under way at the time, as well as whether the event involved a large-scale U.S. ground invasion or terrorism, took place during the cold war, or lasted one day. Moreover, wherever possible, we gathered data based on the poll period, giving us an average of about four distinct observations per event. This allows us to account for evolving circumstances as events unfold. Inclusion of our expert assessments further enhances our confidence. The fact that our other controls explain well over 70% of the variance in our experts' summary assessments suggests that we have included a fairly comprehensive set of controls. In the presence of all of these controls (including the exogenous portion of our expert assessments), it seems improbable that some additional, unknown "unique" characteristics of the events are driving our results.

With respect to possible greater intrinsic value of critical evaluations, as also noted, our results clearly show that *praise* by NPP MCs is strongly persuasive to all but PP partisans. Similarly, if negative evaluations were more intrinsically important, it seems likely that this would apply to *all* critical statements by MCs of both parties and not, as we find, just the subsets that are most credible to their own partisans or independents. After all, criticizing a president in foreign policy can be politically risky, even for the opposition party.

Finally, we turn to the possibility that variations in actual elite rhetoric rather than in journalists' preferences could be driving the differences we observe in elite rhetoric presented in the news. As noted earlier, we believe it would be a truly heroic assumption to presume that, all else equal, elites *prefer* to criticize their fellow partisan presidents far more than support them—which is the pattern we found in our data. Still, because our data set does not account for the complete universe of elite rhetoric offered to the media, we cannot determine with certainty whether the observed patterns of coverage accurately reflect the available population of potential evaluations.

While we cannot systematically resolve this concern within the confines of the data presented here, in chapter 4 we address precisely this issue. There, to isolate the media's independent effect, we investigate a class of stories for which we *can* observe a full population of potential elite rhetoric: all interviews with MCs on the network Sunday morning political roundtable programs. Examining which statements out of the complete universe of available MC rhetoric on the Sunday morning political talk shows the networks actually selected for broadcast on the evening news provides us with greater leverage than in the present chapter to divine journalists' preferences. In chapter 4, we find that relative to the Sunday morning talk shows, the evening news heavily overrepresents criticism of the president by PP MCs while underrepresenting PP praise, especially during unified government. Consequently, we remain confident that, consistent with our theory, the rhetorical patterns we observe likely reflect the preferences of journalists more than the actual population of statements offered by political elites (particularly elites in the presidential party).

Conclusion

The findings presented here hold potentially important implications for future leaders. While the data appear to bear out Brody's (1991) hypothesis concerning the link between elite debate and the magnitude of rallies, the process through which the content of this debate is selected and influences opinion is substantially more complex and nuanced than previously assumed. Whether a given member of the public rallies to support the president following the use of force is not simply a function of the overall tenor of elite debate but rather of at least four considerations: (1) one's own partisan affiliation, (2) the partisan affiliations of the elite debaters selected to appear in the media, (3) the costliness of the messages communicated to the public, and (4) journalists' decisions to cover or ignore particular speakers and messages.

We find little evidence that presidents can consistently anticipate substantial rallies when they use force abroad, especially during unified government and at least to the extent that the magnitude of a rally does follow from the nature and extent of elite debate presented in the media, as our evidence suggests. Indeed, one of the most striking patterns in our data is the seemingly unyielding wave of negativity in media coverage of elite discussion concerning the president and his policies. Most U.S. deployments of military force fail to alter the unrelenting negative tone of elite rhetoric featured in the media.

Major conflicts may be a partial exception. When we limit our data to U.S. invasions involving substantial incursions of ground forces (Grenada, Panama, Afghanistan, and Iraq in 1991 and 2003), we find less credible criticism and more credible praise relative to the other events in our data. During postdeployment periods surrounding ground invasions, highly credible praise of the president by NPP MCs nearly doubles proportionately (from 12% to 22% of all NPP evaluations), while highly credible criticism by PP MCs falls from 69% to 42% of all PP evaluations. Applying the calculus employed earlier to predict average rally size across our 42 events thus unsurprisingly yields larger predicted rallies during ground invasions—an average increase of about 3.3 approval points—with, as before, larger rallies (about 4.4 points on average) during divided government. This is consistent with the aforementioned prior research (Chapman and Reiter 2004) indicating that substantial rallies are mostly limited to major wars and may help reconcile our finding of an overwhelming overall negativity bias with the occasional emergence of substantial rally effects.

In addition to offering support for our theory concerning the effects of individual and institutional factors in shaping the nature and extent of post-use-of-force rallies, our findings also hold an important implication for diversionary war theory (Levy 1989). If presidents cannot be confident of receiving favorable treatment in the media when they employ military force abroad—at least short of a full-scale war like Operation Desert Storm or Operation Iraqi Freedom—it seems highly unlikely that they would do so for purely domestic political purposes. Our data suggest that, at least from a domestic political perspective, using military force abroad, whether or not the goal is to divert public attention from domestic difficulties, is a high-risk strategy with at best an uncertain payoff.

Prior to the midterm elections of 2002, President George W. Bush crisscrossed the nation in what was described as a "tireless campaign blitz" to win back Republican control of Congress. In relentlessly campaigning for his fellow Republicans, Bush was gambling with the bipartisan prestige he had accumulated following the 9/11 attacks and the war in Afghanistan. But perhaps more important for our story, Bush also worked to ensure that his rapidly approaching confrontation with Iraq would take place under unified Republican control of government.

Ironically, our study suggests that while the midterm election results may have made it easier for Bush to win the congressional vote authorizing the war, the subsequent absence of credible praise from authoritative

Democratic sources made it far more difficult for him later to rally Democrats and independents in the electorate to his side. In addition, despite continuing support by the majority of Republican elites, the news media's elevation of highly credible criticism from fellow Republicans such as Senator Chuck Hagel (R-NE) (see chapter 1) helped push Bush's approval ratings to historic lows. Viewed in this light, unified government appears to be a mixed blessing, at least with respect to the president's conduct of foreign affairs.

APPENDIX 3.1 EVENT LIST

1. Hostage crisis in Iran, November 1979
2. Soviet invasion of Afghanistan: Carter Doctrine, January 1980
3. Marine barracks bombing, October 1983
4. Invasion of Grenada, October 1983
5. Further attacks on/by U.S. troops in Lebanon, December 1983
6. Operation El Dorado Canyon: U.S. air strikes against Libya in response to Berlin disco bombing, April 1986
7. Operation Prairie Fire: the United States engages Libyan aircraft, ships, and missile sites around the Gulf of Sidra, April 1986
8. U.S.S. *Stark* attacked by a missile, May 1987
9. U.S.S. *Vincennes* shoots down Iranian civilian airliner, July 1988
10. Response to Pan Am flight 103 destruction, December 1988
11. Two carriers, battleship groups moved to eastern Mediterranean, Persian Gulf, and Arabian Sea after killing of Colonel William Higgins in Lebanon, August 1989
12. Invasion of Panama, December 1989
13. Immediate U.S. response to Iraqi invasion of Kuwait, August 1990
14. Larger U.S. deployment to Middle East in response to Iraqi invasion of Kuwait, August 1990
15. First Gulf War begins (air war), January 1991
16. First Gulf War begins (ground war), February 1991
17. Military exercises conducted in Kuwait and the Persian Gulf to get Iraqi compliance with weapons inspections, July 1992
18. 200 U.S. Air Force and Navy aircraft used to enforce "no-fly zone" in southern Iraq, September 1992
19. 30,000 American troops, carrier group deployed in Somalia to facilitate famine relief, December 1992
20. Troops deployed in Kuwait and aircraft and missiles used to attack Iraqi military installations in January 1993
21. Additional troops, aircraft carrier deployed to Somalia in October and November after U.S. soldiers killed in October 1993 clash with Somalis

22. Military exercises in Caribbean simulate an invasion of Haiti, July 1994
23. 20,000 troops occupy Haiti after agreement with military regime on September 1994
24. Large ground force, ships, aircraft sent to Persian Gulf region in response to Iraqi threats to Kuwait, October 1994
25. Carrier task force, Marine contingent, attack submarine, and other ships move into Adriatic on May 29–30 after UN observers taken hostage by Serbs in Bosnia, May 1995
26. Troops, ships deployed to Persian Gulf region in response to Iraqi threats in August 1995
27. Troop deployment to Bosnia as part of Dayton Accords begins in December 1995
28. Cuba shoots down American civilian plane, February 1996
29. The U.S. military launches cruise missile attacks against 14 Iraqi air-defense bases following Iraq's invasion of the Kurdish "safe haven," September 1996
30. Troops mobilized; B-52s, Patriot missiles deployed near Iraq in response to Kurdish-area invasion and inspection violations, September 1996
31. Iraq ceases cooperation with UN inspectors, October 1997
32. Iraq expels UN inspectors, November 1997
33. Clinton threatens major attack on Iraq, February 1998
34. Operation Infinite Reach (OBL retaliation): cruise missile strikes against Afghanistan and Sudan in response to bombings of two U.S. embassies in Africa, August 1998
35. Operation Desert Fox: attacks on Iraq for inspections violations, November 1998
36. Iraq orders UN inspectors to leave (again), December 1998
37. Kosovo air campaign, March 1999
38. Bombing of U.S.S. *Cole* in Yemen, October 2000
39. Chinese air force forces down U.S. reconnaissance plane, April 2001
40. Initial deployment of troops to Afghanistan, September 2001
41. Afghanistan invasion, October 2001
42. Second Gulf War, March 2003

APPENDIX 3.2. CODING INSTRUCTIONS

(*Note that this coding scheme is adapted from that of the Center for Media and Public Affairs.*)

Praise and criticism of the president must be unambiguous, and should be defensible (you should be able to point out the statement containing the praise or criticism to a reasonable person and have him or her agree that it's praise or criticism). Neutral statements raise the issue without making any judgment.

It's possible for a member's statement to contain lots of different types of praise and criticism of the president, and also neutral information. Something like, "The president made the right decision regarding Afghanistan, but has erred tremendously in his handling of Iraq," contains both praise and criticism of the president's handling of foreign policy/ military, so you would mark all that apply. If you have doubts about coding a statement a particular way, you should err on the side of caution (when in doubt, leave it out).

Here are some guidelines (adapted from the Center for Media and Public Affairs) about what exactly counts as praise or criticism:

Praise/Positive/Supportive/In Defense of—

A positive evaluation would include direct praise of the official, as in, "Clinton has really mastered dealing with Congress," or positive evaluations of what the individual has done, such as, "Bush has impressed Western leaders with his latest plan on Liberia."

IMPORTANT NOTE: Positive evaluations of future political status are only coded here if they are not qualified based on any condition, as in, "Gore will be the Democratic nominee if he avoids incidents such as the one on last Thursday." This also applies to criticism, as we'll see below. Oh, and as another wrinkle, if they said something like, "Bush's popularity will fall if he continues to mismanage the economy," the implication that he is currently mismanaging the economy is built-in criticism, so you would count that part as criticism despite it being embedded in the hypothetical "if."

We'll also be counting self-defensive statements as praise. For instance, if a source is reported to have panned a policy of an official, and that official then presents a defense of their own policy, that would be coded as a positive evaluation. For instance, if Daschle claims that Bush's tax plan is only for the rich, and Bush is then shown saying, "That's not true." You would code a positive evaluation on Bush from Bush on the issue of Government Budget/Deficit/Spending/Taxation.

Criticism/Negative/Attacking—

A negative evaluation would include direct criticisms of the president, as in, "Bush has failed to grasp the fact that the defense budget will be between one-third and one-half smaller in the next five years," or negative evaluations of the president's policies, as in, "Clinton's antagonistic attitude toward business has made him a political liability for the Democratic Party."

As with positive evaluations, negative evaluations of the future political status of the President cannot be coded here if they are qualified on a hypothetical condition, such as "Clinton will face a strong backlash in the United States if he attempts to impose rationing of health care services."

APPENDIX 3.3. CONTROL VARIABLE DEFINITION AND CODING

Days between Polls—Number of days between Gallup polls at time t and $t + 1$.

MC Appearances—Number of appearances—with or without explicit evaluations of the president/administration—by MCs on network newscasts during poll period.

Pres. Election Year—Coded 1 for cases occurring within 365 days of a presidential election (including the election date), 0 otherwise.

Midterm Election Year—Coded 1 for observations occurring within 365 days of a midterm election (including the election date), 0 otherwise.

Party Leader—Number of observations per poll period in which MC evaluator was a party leader. Party leaders were coded as members of the chamberwide party leadership (that is, not committee chairs), including the majority/minority leaders in the Senate, their assistants/whips, and the president pro tempore. In the House, we counted the Speaker, Majority Leader, Majority Whip, Minority Leader, Minority Whip, and the heads of the party caucus/conference.

Second Term—Coded 1 if a president was in second term in office, 0 otherwise.

Consumer Sentiment—Subtracts prior month's consumer sentiment score from the current month's score as measured by the University of Michigan's Index of Consumer Sentiment.

Unified Government—Coded 1 if presidential party had majority control of both chambers of Congress, 0 otherwise. Control is assumed to pass with the election of a new speaker or majority leader.

Transition—Coded 1 if observation occurred after election but prior to inauguration day, 0 otherwise.

Democratic President—Coded 1 if a Democrat was in office at the time of a given poll, 0 otherwise.

Any KIA—Coded 1 if the United States suffered any combat deaths during a given poll period, 0 otherwise.

Postdeployment—Coded 1 if the statement was made on the day of the major U.S. force deployment, or within 30 days after such an event, 0 otherwise.

Pre+Postdeployment—Coded 1 if statement was made both within 30 days *after* a force deployment and within 30 days *before* another deployment, 0 otherwise.

Major War—Coded 1 for U.S. invasions of Grenada, Panama, Iraq (1991 and 2003), and Afghanistan, 0 otherwise.

Post-Cold War—Coded 1 if observation occurred after fall of Berlin Wall (November 9, 1989), 0 otherwise.

NY Times Coverage—Count of the number of mentions of the adversary nation on the front page of the *New York Times* during a given poll period, divided by the average number of front-page stories in the *New York Times* during the same poll period.

One-Day Event—Coded 1 if a given rally event lasted only one day, 0 otherwise.

Capability Ratio—Correlates of War (COW) National Material Capabilities summary statistic (Singer and Small 1993). It takes the form of $C_A/(C_A + C_B)$, where C_A = U.S. capabilities and C_B = adversary capabilities.

Terrorism—Coded 1 if the event involved international terrorism, 0 otherwise.

U.S. Crises per Year—Count of the number of foreign policy crises (Brecher and Wilkenfeld 2006) in the same calendar year as a given event, in which the United States was the crisis actor. (This variable consistently outperformed the number of rally events per year, drawn from the data set employed in this study.)

U.S. Ally—Coded 1 if the adversary was involved in a formal alliance relationship with the United States at the time of a rally event, 0 otherwise. These data are derived from the Correlates of War Interstate Alliance data set, version 3.03 (Gibler and Sarkees, 2004).

Trade Dependence—This indicator is derived from the U.N. World Trade Flows data set (Feenstra et al. 2005). It represents the sum of U.S. exports to the adversary, as a proportion of all U.S. exports, plus U.S. imports from the adversary, as a proportion of all U.S. imports.

Foreign Policy Restraint (FPR), Internal Political Change (IPC), Humanitarian Intervention (HI)—Coded 1 if a U.S. goal in conflict was imposing FPR, IPC, or HI, respectively (Jentleson 1992; Jentleson and Britton 1998).

Expert Assessment—Scale measuring extent to which, on average, 38 foreign policy experts considered each event "successful" and "worthwhile" for the United States. The scale runs from -5 to $+5$, with -5 ($+5$) indicating least (most) successful or worthwhile ($\mu = 5.57$; $\sigma = 3.67$).

APPENDIX 3.4. VARYING SPECIFICATION OF TABLE 3.3 MODELS

TABLE 3.A1
Base, Political Control, and International Environment/Adversary
Characteristic Control Models

	Base Models				
	(1) Praise/ Crit. Ratio	(2) PP Approve	(3) NPP Approve	(4) Ind. Approve	(5) Praise/ Crit. Ratio
Approval$_t$	—	−0.215*** (0.053)	−0.082* (0.036)	−0.185** (0.059)	—
PP criticism	—	−0.404** (0.149)	−0.194 (0.132)	−0.469* (0.200)	—
NPP criticism	—	0.061 (0.105)	−0.175 (0.121)	−0.186 (0.157)	—
PP praise	—	0.001 (0.329)	−0.120 (0.325)	−0.207 (0.382)	—
NPP praise	—	0.618^ (0.356)	1.220** (0.369)	1.124** (0.351)	—
Any KIA	−0.081 (0.049)	—	—	—	−0.037 (0.042)
Evaluations per period	—	−0.026 (0.030)	0.016 (0.029)	0.025 (0.032)	0.0002 (0.001)
Days between polls	—	—	—	—	−0.001 (0.002)
Post deployment	—	—	—	—	—
Pre- and post- deployment	—	—	—	—	—
Major war	—	—	—	—	—
Pres. election year	−0.144*** (0.034)	—	—	—	−0.115** (0.038)
Midterm election year	—	—	—	—	0.067^ (0.036)
Party leader	—	—	—	—	0.001 (0.002)
Second term	−0.109* (0.043)	—	—	—	−0.143** (0.047)
Consumer sentiment	—	—	—	−0.006* (0.003)	−0.063 (0.094)
Unified government	−0.089* (0.042)	—	—	—	−0.103* (0.043)
Transition	—	—	—	—	0.262** (0.081)

Political Models			International/Adversary Trait Models			
(6) PP *Approve*	*(7)* NPP *Approve*	*(8)* Ind. *Approve*	*(9)* Praise/ Crit. Ratio	*(10)* PP *Approve*	*(11)* NPP *Approve*	*(12)* Ind. *Approve*
−0.317*** (0.081)	−0.200* (0.075)	−0.286*** (0.078)	—	−0.395*** (0.100)	−0.269* (0.130)	−0.401*** (0.100)
−0.364* (0.170)	−0.040 (0.130)	−0.400 (0.240)	—	−0.440* (0.210)	−0.305 (0.210)	−0.512^ (0.260)
0.065 (0.098)	−0.151 (0.090)	−0.198 (0.200)	—	0.088 (0.110)	−0.195^ (0.110)	−0.111 (0.160)
0.001 (0.350)	−0.250 (0.340)	−0.291 (0.360)	—	−0.029 (0.340)	−0.335 (0.490)	−0.571 (0.510)
0.672 (0.410)	1.282*** (0.350)	0.964* (0.380)	—	0.668 (0.470)	1.273* (0.480)	1.077* (0.480)
—	—	—	−.114* (.0480)	0.418 (1.410)	0.433 (1.620)	3.167* (1.540)
−0.019 (0.031)	0.043 (0.028)	0.050 (0.033)	.001 (.001)	−0.016 (0.030)	0.031 (0.024)	0.041 (0.037)
−0.038 (0.033)	−0.001 (0.035)	−0.020 (0.051)	.002 (.003)	−0.077 (0.052)	−0.053 (0.041)	−0.030 (0.062)
—	—	—	−.083 (.055)	1.980* (0.910)	2.707* (1.270)	1.209 (1.150)
—	—	—	.024 (.059)	−1.393 (1.010)	−0.607 (2.290)	0.740 (1.670)
—	—	—	.024 (.076)	4.870** (1.560)	11.03** (3.550)	10.24*** (2.110)
−1.337 (1.010)	−1.436 (1.620)	−2.206 (1.810)	−.142** (.053)	0.120 (1.230)	−1.865 (1.680)	−1.717 (1.570)
−0.588 (0.640)	0.376 (0.840)	−0.292 (1.260)	—	—	—	—
−0.005 (0.067)	−0.139 (0.092)	−0.042 (0.120)	—	—	—	—
1.532^ (0.770)	−0.059 (1.150)	1.013 (1.350)	−.115 (.050)*	—	—	—
−0.201 (0.200)	−0.328 (0.220)	—	—	—	—	—
−1.766* (0.870)	−2.528 (1.600)	−2.288 (1.930)	−.092^ (.049)	—	—	—
−7.552** (2.180)	−1.176 (1.190)	−1.563 (4.490)	—	—	—	—

(continued)

TABLE 3.A1 (*continued*)

	Base Models				
	(1) *Praise/* *Crit. Ratio*	*(2)* *PP* *Approve*	*(3)* *NPP* *Approve*	*(4)* *Ind.* *Approve*	*(5)* *Praise/* *Crit. Ratio*
Democratic president	—	—	—	—	0.025 (0.040)
Post-cold war	−0.107** (0.039)	—	—	—	−0.110** (0.039)
NY *Times* coverage	—	—	—	—	—
Expert assessment	—	—	—	—	—
One-day event	—	—	—	—	—
Capability ratio	—	—	—	—	—
Terrorism related	—	—	—	—	—
U.S. Crises per year	—	—	—	—	—
U.S. ally	—	—	—	—	—
Trade dependence	—	—	—	—	—
FPR	—	—	—	—	—
IPC	—	—	—	—	—
HI	—	—	—	—	—
Constant	0.370*** (0.050)	19.06*** (4.700)	3.405* (1.680)	11.35** (3.890)	0.339*** (0.059)
No. of obs.	170	166	166	164	170
R^2	0.08	0.16	0.08	0.13	0.13

^$p < 0.10$, *$p < 0.05$, **$p < 0.01$, ***$p < 0.001$. Robust standard errors in parentheses. Dependent variables are shown in column headings.

Abbreviations: PP, presidential party; NPP, nonpresidential party; Crit., criticism; KIA, U.S. troops killed in action; FPR, foreign policy restraint; IPC, internal political change; HI, humanitarian intervention.

Note: In table 3.A1, we first reproduce the base models from table 3 in the main text. We then present a model that adds only the domestic political/economic control variables, followed by a model that adds to the base model only the characteristics

Political Models			International/Adversary Trait Models			
(6) PP Approve	(7) NPP Approve	(8) Ind. Approve	(9) Praise/ Crit. Ratio	(10) PP Approve	(11) NPP Approve	(12) Ind. Approve
−1.050 (1.02)	−1.456 (1.22)	0.326 (1.31)	—	—	—	—
—	—	—	−.064 (.044)	1.022 (1.310)	−1.479 (1.060)	1.726 (1.570)
6.898** (2.09)	13.85** (4.06)	14.26*** (2.72)	.359** (.127)	—	—	—
—	—	—	.014* (.006)	0.216 (0.220)	0.226 (0.350)	0.451 (0.290)
—	—	—	.020 (.039)	0.743 (0.980)	−0.780 (1.330)	0.657 (1.360)
—	—	—	−.221^ (.129)	3.979 (4.670)	−9.584 (6.920)	−13.59^ (7.370)
—	—	—	.087* (.042)	0.255 (1.030)	2.530 (1.950)	3.741* (1.770)
—	—	—	.012 (.038)	1.233 (0.780)	1.305^ (0.750)	3.168** (1.110)
—	—	—	.037 (.056)	−5.653^ (3.350)	3.493 (2.090)	1.865 (2.110)
—	—	—	−2.527* (.999)	75.53^ (39.700)	−59.76 (63.700)	−118.9^ (63.900)
—	—	—	−.131* (.058)	−1.507 (3.170)	0.265 (2.160)	1.561 (2.290)
—	—	—	−.165** (.053)	−0.783 (1.680)	−6.154** (2.140)	−5.424** (1.780)
—	—	—	.121* (.059)	0.881 (2.370)	5.926* (2.250)	6.532* (2.500)
27.95*** (7.750)	7.452^ (4.260)	15.93* (6.050)	.637*** (.122)	28.07** (8.550)	16.38 (10.900)	27.30** (9.810)
165	165	163	169	165	165	163
0.27	0.19	0.24	0.16	0.28	0.23	0.33

of the international environment, rally event, and adversary. The results are strikingly similar across the three model specifications, suggesting that our results are highly robust. The sole partial exception concerns the "Praise/Crit. Ratio" model, where "Any Casualties" is somewhat smaller in magnitude (although similarly signed) and statistically insignificant in the political model specification. As it happens, this is attributable to the absence of a single variable, *New York Times* coverage, which captures the intensity of media (and presumably also public) interest in a given event. Adding this single variable to the political model brings the "Any Casualties" indicator in line with its effects in the other two models.

APPENDIX 3.5. INTERPRETING INTERACTIVE RELATIONSHIPS

In interpreting our results, it is important to bear in mind that in the presence of interaction terms, we cannot test our hypotheses by observing magnitudes or significance levels on individual coefficients, or even by comparing pairs of coefficients, for two primary reasons. First, interaction terms necessarily produce colinearity between causal variables, thereby frequently dampening the significance of individual coefficients. Second, and more important, evaluating the substantive implications of interactive relationships requires comparisons across *combinations* of variables (e.g., whether the sum of base category w plus interaction term v is statistically distinguishable from the sum of base category y plus interaction term z). Consequently, we cannot evaluate our hypotheses by comparing any two individual coefficients in our models.

To embed this general discussion within the context of our particular analysis, in our models we interact several distinct indicators of partisan rhetoric with a dummy for the presence of any U.S. fatalities during a given poll period. For purposes of this example, assume variable w represents one type of partisan rhetoric, while variable z represents the casualty dummy. When z equals zero, the effects of rhetoric are given by the coefficient on w alone. In that case, one can assess the statistical significance of effects of the rhetoric causal variable on the dependent variable by looking solely at the coefficient on w. However, when y takes a value of 1, indicating that the United States did suffer casualties in a given poll period, then to determine the effects of rhetoric on the dependent variable (approval), it becomes necessary to add the coefficient on w to that on the interaction term ($w \times z$). The key significance test thus becomes whether the *combined* (that is, sum total) effect of the coefficients on w and on $w \times z$ together is statistically distinguishable from zero effect. This cannot be easily determined by reviewing the significance levels on the separate coefficients on w and/or $w \times z$. We therefore employ Clarify (King, Tomz, and Wittenberg 2000) to simulate the expected values of the dependent variable as the key causal variables vary *in combination*. These results, presented in figure 3.6, represent the key tests of our predictions concerning the effects of rhetoric on approval during periods involving U.S. casualties. In fact, it is frequently the case that individually insignificant variables combine to produce statistically significant effects on a given dependent variable, at least at certain values of one or both of the interacted causal variables. This is the case in several of our results shown in figure 3.6.

Finally, to offer one concrete example, we take the case of the effects of PP criticism on independents, shown in model 12 of table 3.3. The coefficient on PP criticism is −.309, with a standard error of .295. The coefficient (standard error) on the interaction term (PP criticism × Any KIA) is −.329 (.333). Obviously, neither approaches statistical significance. However, the combined effect, representing the effect of PP criticism on independents for cases involving casualties, is much larger (−.309 + −.329 = −.638). Figure 3.6 indicates that this latter, combined effect is, in fact, significant at the .05 level (to be specific, given a two standard deviation change in PP criticism during rally events with at least one U.S. casualty).

APPENDIX 3.6. DATA UNDERLYING FIGURE 3.6 IN MAIN TEXT

TABLE 3.A2
Effect of Different Types of Rhetoric on Presidential Approval

Evaluation Type	Marginal Effect of Evaluation[a]	Difference from No Evaluation
Presidential Party Approval (No evaluation = 0.096)		
PP praise	0.311	0.214
PP criticism	−2.676	−2.772**
NPP praise	2.586	2.489*
NPP criticism	1.244	1.238
Nonpresidential Party Approval (No evaluation = 1.564)		
PP praise	0.231	−1.333
PP criticism	0.344	−1.220
NPP praise	4.690	3.126**
NPP criticism	−1.363	−2.927*
Independents' Approval (No evaluation = 1.881)		
PP praise	0.500	−1.382
PP criticism	−0.876	−2.757*
NPP praise	4.713	2.832**
NPP criticism	−0.526	−2.407

(continued)

TABLE 3.A2 (*continued*)

Casualty (KIA) vs. Noncasualty (No KIA) Period Interaction Models

	No KIA		KIA	
	Marginal Effect of Evaluation	Difference from No Evaluation	Marginal Effect of Evaluation	Difference from No Evaluation

Presidential Party Approval (No evaluation or KIA = −.637; No evaluation with KIA = 2.573)

PP praise	−.059	0.577	3.074	0.501
PP criticism	−3.299	−2.663^	−0.503	−3.076**
NPP praise	1.981	2.617*	4.064	1.491
NPP criticism	0.505	1.142	0.762	−1.811

Nonpresidential Party Approval (No evaluation or KIA = 1.276; No evaluation with KIA = 6.435)

PP praise	−.477	−1.753	8.999	2.564
PP criticism	1.206	−0.069	4.070	−2.365^
NPP praise	4.302	3.026**	11.983	5.547*
NPP criticism	−2.026	−3.298*	−14.373	−20.808^

Independents' Approval (No evaluation or KIA = .685; No evaluation with KIA = 9.639)

PP praise	−0.176	−0.861	11.322	1.683
PP criticism	−1.094	−1.779	6.253	−3.386*
NPP praise	3.865	3.180**	11.635	1.996
NPP criticism	−1.835	−2.521	−6.356	−15.995^

^$p < .10$, *$p < .05$, **$p < .01$.

[a]Based on two standard deviation increase in type of rhetoric, with other types of rhetoric held constant at zero.

CHAPTER 4

War Meets the Press

STRATEGIC MEDIA BIAS AND ELITE
FOREIGN POLICY EVALUATIONS

WHAT MAKES IT INTO THE NEWS? Longtime CBS anchor Walter Cronkite neatly summarized the widely shared perspective of journalists when he said, "Our job is only to hold up the mirror—to tell and show the public what has happened."[1] In sharp contrast, journalist Walter Lippmann (1922) famously said the press was "like the beam of a searchlight that moves restlessly about, bringing one episode and then another out of darkness into vision."

Chapter 1 began with an anecdote in which the media offered tremendously different coverage of the remarks by two seemingly similar Republican senators who appeared together on an interview program. In chapter 2 we challenged Cronkite's assertion that journalists simply passed along a representative sample of elite rhetoric, and modeled the characteristics that would tend to cause journalists to bring a story "out of darkness into vision"—that is, to view a story as more or less newsworthy. We argued that, far from serving as passive conduits of information, journalists actively prefer stories embodying novelty, conflict, balance, and authority. In chapter 3 we tested a series of implications of these assumptions by looking at the characteristics of elite rhetoric regarding rally events that appeared on the evening news.

Unfortunately, there is a potential problem with stopping there; even when we find evidence that news coverage tends to correspond to our predictions, as we did in chapter 3, it remains unclear whether that coverage results from the mix of stories journalists *chose* to cover, or from the mix of stories *available* to cover. In other words, if one observes that elites from the presidential party (PP) criticize the president in 90% of their statements on the evening news, that *could* reflect the news choices of journalists, or it may accurately reflect a reality in which 90% of all statements by such elites in the pertinent time frame were critical of the president. Anecdotal evidence like the Hagel-Allen appearance on ABC's

---

[1]Cronkite continues by saying, "Then it is the job of the people to decide whether they have faith in their leaders or governments" (quoted in Alan and Lane 2003).

This Week described in chapter 1 appears to suggest that the media are not presenting the public with a random, unbiased sample of all available political rhetoric. However, absent more comprehensive data showing the universe of rhetoric from which evening news producers might potentially have selected the statements that ultimately appeared on the news, we cannot be entirely confident.

Socrates defined wisdom as knowing "what I do not know" (Plato, *The Apology*, Section 6). In 2002, former Secretary of Defense Donald Rumsfeld echoed this sentiment when he responded to a reporter's question about the links between Iraq, terrorists, and weapons of mass destruction thusly:

> As we know, there are known knowns; there are things we know we know. We also know there are known unknowns; that is to say we know there are some things we do not know. But there are also unknown unknowns—the ones we don't know we don't know. . . . [P]eople who have the omniscience that they can say with high certainty that something has not happened . . . can do things I can't do. (Department of Defense [DoD], February 12, 2002)

In Rumsfeld's parlance, if the content of the evening news is a "known known," then the potential stories that *could* have been aired, yet were not, represent "unknown unknowns." To address this "unobserved population" problem (Hofstetter 1976; Harrington 1993; Groeling and Kernell 1998; Niven 2002; Groeling 2008), we extend our analysis from chapter 3 by investigating a class of stories for which we *can* observe the full population of potential elite praise and criticism of the president. Specifically, we analyze content from all interviews with members of Congress (MCs) on three Sunday morning political interview shows, NBC's *Meet the Press*, ABC's *This Week*, and CBS's *Face the Nation*, for the identical 61-day periods surrounding rally events across the same 25-year time span investigated in chapter 3 (1979–2003).

Of course, Sunday morning political interview shows clearly do not account for the full universe of potential MC commentary from which network news producers might select. Nor are they necessarily a random sample of elite rhetoric. After all, Sunday morning talk show producers presumably select guests in part based on their expectations regarding the newsworthiness of what they anticipate those guests will say. However, once on such a show, the guests essentially enjoy an extended open mic forum in which they are free to say whatever they like, with minimal editing and at most limited interjection from the interviewers. Such interviews thus afford elites a chance to present their views to a relatively small, politically attentive audience in an unfiltered format. Most important, because we have gathered *all* such rhetoric, we employ these data as representative of *one* complete subuniverse of rhetoric from which network newscasters might select elements for their broadcasts.

Sunday morning talk shows are a particularly appropriate subuniverse of rhetoric because the networks themselves produce them. This affords evening news producers unfettered access to a relatively wide range of elite political rhetoric in a prepackaged, readily accessible format. More important for our purposes, all three broadcast networks' evening news programs routinely comb these interviews for fodder.

This chapter conceptually focuses on the second of the three questions motivating the book: does media coverage of foreign policy debates in Washington accurately reflect the intensity, substance, or variance of those debates? To conduct our investigation, we determine which comments journalists select for inclusion on the evening news and compare their characteristics with the characteristics of comments *not* selected. Wherever possible, we compare rally periods (immediately following rally event initiation) with pre-event time periods (prior to event initiation). By doing so, we identify which types of comments, covering which types of topics, and under which types of external circumstances, the news media are most likely to feature in larger patterns of coverage.[2]

Empirically, we substantiate three of our core assumptions and retest two of our hypotheses in a distinct, and arguably more challenging, context. In the former case, we test four implications of the assumptions underlying our theory.[3] We begin by testing our Negativity assumption, which implies that negative rhetoric on Sunday morning talk shows will be more likely than positive rhetoric to be selected to appear on the evening news. Second, our Novelty assumption implies that the evening news will be more likely to select praise of the president by nonpresidential party (NPP) MCs appearing on Sunday morning talk shows for broadcast than criticism by such MCs. Conversely, the same logic implies that evening news broadcasters will be more likely to select criticism by PP MCs appearing on morning talk shows than praise by those same MCs.

Third, our Authority assumption implies that proportionately more PP rhetoric will appear on Sunday morning talk shows during unified than during divided government. Finally, the Authority assumption also suggests a fourth testable implication; namely, relative to the available universe of rhetoric on Sunday morning talk shows, the evening news will be

---

[2]To provide a baseline for our analysis, we also code any MC appearances on these programs for the month *prior* to the initiation of each rally event.

[3]Because our coding scheme does not capture rhetoric by members of the administration, we cannot directly test the balance assumption.

more likely to select for broadcast PP rhetoric during unified than during divided government.

We also test corollaries of two hypotheses introduced in chapter 2. The first, the Divided Government Media hypothesis (H7), predicts a higher proportion of credible praise relative to credible criticism in the media in divided than in unified government. In the context of the present chapter, the implication is that the impact of our Novelty assumption is likely to be strongest for the NPP and weakest for the PP during divided government.

The second, the Salient Crisis Novelty hypothesis (H2), predicts a higher criticism-to-praise ratio for stories selected to appear on the news during high-salience rally periods relative to other periods. As noted previously, we derive our data from periods surrounding the initiation of rally events (±30 days). Thus, the primary empirical prediction for these data is simply that the differential between criticism and praise on the evening news—that is, the extent to which criticism will exceed praise—relative to Sunday morning talk shows will be greater for foreign policy rhetoric than for rhetoric pertaining to other topics. Nonetheless, we do anticipate that foreign-policy-related rhetoric ought, all else equal, to be more appealing to evening newscasts *after* the initiation of a rally event than *before* event initiation. We also test this second empirical implication of the Salient Crisis Novelty hypothesis (H2).

The remainder of this chapter proceeds as follows. In the next section, we discuss our data and methodology. We then present the results of our statistical investigations. We first compare the aggregate mixes of rhetoric on evening newscasts and Sunday morning talk shows. We then analyze the probability that a given statement by an MC on a Sunday morning talk show will be picked up for broadcast by the evening news, depending on the characteristics of the statement, speaker, and political environment at the time of the show. The final section summarizes our findings and sets the stage for chapter 5, in which we employ experiments and survey data to determine how the speaker, message, and media outlet influence the persuasiveness of these several types of messages.

DATA AND METHODS

For our evening news data, we employ the same content analysis dataset as in chapter 3. Our content analysis of the three Sunday morning talk shows closely mirrors the evening news methodology, coding shows appearing during the identical 61-day time periods (that is, centered on the start date of 42 major U.S. uses of military force between 1979 and

2003).[4] We analyzed the content of all congressional evaluations of the president and the executive branch of government on the three interview programs during these periods.

Dependent Variables

For our aggregate-level investigation, we quantify all incidents of praise and criticism of the president by MCs from both parties. Our tallies separately account for all such comments on interviews from the Sunday morning talk shows, as well as those appearing on the evening newscasts of the three broadcast networks. The aggregate analysis also tracks net evaluations of the president, which we calculate by subtracting negative from positive evaluations for each record, yielding a score of -1, 0, or 1 for each evaluation.[5]

For our individual-statement-level investigation, we employ two binary dependent variables. The first (cross-network) measures whether a statement from a Sunday morning talk show subsequently appeared on the evening newscast of *any* of the three major networks. The second (within-network) measures whether the statement appeared on the evening broadcast of the *same* network as the morning show on which it originally appeared. We replicate all of our analyses with both dependent variables. Our coders collected these data by manually comparing all MC speakers and statements on the Sunday morning talk shows with MC statements on the evening news over the subsequent month.

---

[4]There were, however, several noteworthy differences between the evening news and Sunday morning talk show coding. First, there exists no central index comparable to the Vanderbilt Television News abstracts that lists congressional appearances on Sunday morning political roundtable talk shows. To locate relevant MC appearances on the evening news prior to the availability of online transcripts, we reviewed archival newspapers for program and guest listings or news stories following such appearances. We then ordered the videotapes from the UCLA News and Public Affairs video archive (if they were available). Students then transcribed the videotaped interviews, noting both the interviewer's question and the source's response, and broke them up into individual records. To ensure like-sized observations, we limited each answer to no more than 10 sentences. We treated any (relatively rare) answers longer than 10 sentences as separate observations. Next, we randomly assigned the individual records to a second set of students, who coded both the question and the answer along a variety of dimensions, including our original evening news measures of issue area and valence. As with the evening news coding, our main variables of interest consist of praise and criticism of the president, although unlike the evening news dataset, here we also code the reporter's questions along a variety of dimensions. (Our content analysis coding form is available at http://www.sscnet.ucla.edu/comm/groeling/warstories/form.html.) We were unable to locate many early broadcasts (especially prior to late 1980) in the UCLA News and Public Affairs video archive. In addition, Sunday broadcast schedules seemed particularly vulnerable to preemption by sports events.

[5]We exclude comments lacking any evaluations.

Key Causal Variables

Our key causal variables for the individual statement level of analysis encapsulate the partisan content of each MC comment. Specifically, we created a set of variables separately measuring whether and to what extent the PP and NPP praised or criticized the president. Because our units of analysis in this chapter are paragraphs no longer than 10 sentences, rather than sound bites (as in chapter 3) or entire interviews, each answer potentially includes several sentences that might be usable by news producers as sound bites. Thus, our rhetoric variables in this chapter reflect the number of different dimensions (that is, topics) of praise or criticism within a given paragraph, and can also account for both praise and criticism along the same issue dimension. For example, below is an exchange between *This Week*'s Sam Donaldson and Senator John McCain (R-AZ) in November 1998, as the United States was threatening military action against Iraq for impeding United Nations weapons inspections. The comment by Senator McCain includes both foreign-policy-related praise and foreign-policy-related criticism of the president (noted in italics).

> SAM DONALDSON: All right, you've heard President Clinton talk about standing down in a sense. Do you think he made the right decision?
> JOHN McCAIN: I think given his demands and the response that the Iraqis gave, that he really *did the right thing by not launching* [*foreign policy praise of Clinton*]. But number one, we never should have been in this position to start with, of constantly reacting. As we all know, this is the fourth or fifth time that Saddam Hussein has done this to us. And he should have said next time there's a place you don't allow us to inspect, stand by, because it will be destroyed [*foreign policy criticism of Clinton*]. (*This Week*, November 15, 1998)

Throughout the remainder of this chapter we refer to individual observations, defined as paragraphs of up to 10 sentences spoken by an individual MC in response to a question or comment by an interviewer, as *statements*. For each statement, we coded for the presence of evaluations along eight possible issue dimensions: economic, international trade/finance, budget and taxation, other domestic policy, foreign policy/military, scandal, character or leadership, and other. Hence, unlike our analysis of network news content in chapter 3, for our analysis of Sunday morning talk shows the *overall* rhetoric indicators are not limited to one total occurrence of praise or criticism per observation. Instead, they tally up to one occurrence per issue dimension within a given statement. To test whether evening news programs were disproportionately likely to select rhetoric addressing a particular issue dimension (foreign policy obviously being the most relevant category for our purposes), these data allow us to compare the probability that evening news shows selected similar evaluations (e.g., those with the same source and valence, such as praise by the NPP or criticism by the PP) on *any* issue dimension (e.g., foreign policy or domestic policy).[6]

CONTROL VARIABLES

Our statistical models include dummies for the network that broadcast a given statement, whether the president was a Democrat, whether the interview took place during unified or divided government, whether the observation took place before or after the initiation of a rally event, and for the party affiliation of the speaker. In addition, we control for presidential approval rating, the number of days between approval polls, the state of the economy (measured by monthly changes in consumer sentiment and GDP), and specific characteristics of each of the rally events, including whether the event was terrorism-related, whether it constituted a major war, whether any Americans were killed in action during the conflict, whether it involved a U.S. ally or occurred after the end of the cold war, and whether the event was an instance of foreign policy restraint, internal political change, or humanitarian intervention (see Jentleson 1992 and Jentleson and Britton 1998 for a discussion of this typology). Finally, we controlled for the material capabilities of the adversary in the conflict relative to the United States and the degree of trade dependence between the United States and the adversary (see chapter 3 for detailed descriptions of these variables).[7] Finally, the aggregate evening news coding includes statements taken from the evening newscasts of all three networks.[8]

The overall probability of a particular statement by an MC appearing (in whole or in part) on a network newscast is quite low: about 1.4% in our data set. This figure is small, but probably not unsurprisingly so. Because each MC is interviewed for a considerable length of time on such

[6]More detailed explanations and definitions are available in the content analysis codebook, which, as noted above, can be viewed online at http://www.sscnet.ucla.edu/comm/groeling/warstories/ codebook.html.

[7]For a variety of reasons unrelated to our research question (e.g., preemption for sports events), *Meet the Press*, *This Week*, or *Face the Nation* broadcasts were sometimes unavailable (particularly in the late 1970s and early 1980s). Our aggregate-level analysis examines only those evening news broadcasts occurring during a rally event for which we have coded at least one Sunday morning talk show interview with an MC (two of our rally events had no interviews with MCs available). Additionally, we tested a variety of additional controls, including dummies for different presidential administrations and political circumstances (e.g., election years, party of the president or source). Because they did not materially affect our results, we exclude them from the final models.

[8]We undertook extensive testing to determine if the three networks differed in any significant ways. No materially significant differences emerged.

shows, they provide multiple answers during each visit. Our data set includes segments from 465 different stories, each of which averages around 20 paragraphs of interview answers. If the evening news selected one sound bite from every interview, this would translate into networks selecting only 5% of records—reasonably close to the 1.4% observed. In addition, the coded sound bites by MCs must compete with those offered by other figures, including administration sources, further driving down the likelihood that any individual statement will be selected. Researchers have developed specialized estimation procedures to address the particular statistical problems associated with data sets in which positive occurrences on the dependent variable are relatively rare. In our case, for our individual-statement-level statistical analyses we employ *Rare-event Logit* (or ReLogit) (Tomz, King, and Zeng 2003).[9]

RESULTS

Wherever possible, throughout this section we undertake multiple tests of each hypothesis, first investigating our data aggregated across programs, and then disaggregated to the level of individual statements by MCs. In doing so, we present both cross-tabulations and graphical illustrations clearly highlighting the key relationships, as well as more rigorous multivariate analyses, which allow us to better control for potential alternative explanations for the relationships.

DESCRIPTIVE ANALYSIS

Before turning to hypothesis testing, we briefly summarize the overall tallies of our content analyses across the two data sets. As shown in table 4.1, our data set includes 9,309 statements by MCs on *Meet the Press, This Week,* or *Face the Nation,* of which 1,162 statements explicitly praised and/or criticized the president. Of the 9,309 total statements, approximately 58% originated from the NPP, three-fourths took place in divided

---

[9]ReLogit is specifically designed to correct for the bias introduced by either small sample case selection on the dependent variable or, more important for our purposes, rare positive occurrences in the overall population. While we believe this is the most appropriate estimator, given our data, it is worth pointing out that all of the results reported below remain comparable if we employ a standard logit estimator with heteroskedasticity-consistent standard errors (which ReLogit employs by default). As a robustness test, we re-ran all models three additional ways, clustering the standard errors by rally event (as we did in our analyses in chapter 3), as well as by date and by story number. In this instance, however, doing so did not substantively affect the results. Consequently, in the interest of minimizing the restrictions placed on the data, we do not cluster the errors in the reported results.

TABLE 4.1
Descriptive Statistics, Sunday Morning Talk Show Data

Type of Observation	N
Total observations coded	9,309
Presidential/nonpresidential party source	3,913/5,361
Unified/divided government	2,223/6,998
Before/after rally event	4,937/5,103[a]
Republican/Democratic president	3,075/6,146
Statements selected to appear on *any* network newscast/*same* network's newscast	129/84
Observations in stories with at least one statement on evening news	2,749
Negative/positive evaluations of the president	869/331[b]
Negative/positive foreign policy evaluations of the president	117/105[c]

[a]731 observations took place before one event and after another, within our 61-day windows.

[b]Another 38 statements had both praise and criticism of the president, so there were 1,162 total statements containing evaluations of the president.

[c]Two statements included both praise and criticism of the president regarding foreign policy.

government, 55% took place in the 30 days after (rather than before) the initiation of major U.S. uses of military force (that is, during rally events), and two-thirds took place during Democratic presidencies.

As previously noted, only about 1.4% (129) of the 9,309 statements by MCs were actually selected to appear on a network evening newscast. However, 2,749 statements came from shows in which the evening news selected at least one statement for broadcast. Of the 1,162 statements that evaluated the president, three out of four were negative. Of the 220 evaluations specifically directed at the president's handling of foreign policy, just over half (53%) were negative.

AGGREGATE-LEVEL ANALYSIS

We begin our statistical investigations with a series of basic, aggregate-level comparisons. For this analysis, we assume that the unfiltered MC statements on Sunday morning talk shows will more closely approximate MC preferences than the highly edited MC rhetoric selected for broadcast on the evening news. Similarly, rhetoric appearing on the evening news should presumably reflect journalists' preferences more closely than that appearing on Sunday morning interview shows. By comparing the two aggregate populations for similar time periods, we can infer some differences in news values across the programs.

Of course, a variety of uncontrolled factors may affect these relationships. For instance, Sunday morning interviewers might select guests who they know have a desired point of view. For example, journalists and politicians regarded Senator Joe Lieberman (I-CT) as a consistent proponent of the George W. Bush administration's policies in the Middle East who could reasonably be expected to support those policies as a guest on such programs. Nonetheless, such bivariate aggregate-level comparisons are a useful validity check before we move on to a more rigorously controlled analysis of individual statements.

Beginning with our Negativity assumption, in table 4.2 we see that for nearly every type of congressional rhetoric targeting the president (15 of 16 comparisons shown in the table), the heavily edited evening news rhetoric is more negative than that appearing on Sunday morning interviews for the same period. (Note that for comparing the morning and evening news shows, the relevant cells in the top part of table 4.2, examining unified versus divided government, are located in the same rows—that is, left to right—while in the second part of the table, before versus after rally events, the relevant morning and evening news comparisons are arrayed in different rows within the same columns—that is, top to bottom.)

Our Divided Government Media hypothesis (H7) anticipates that the evening news representation of PP rhetoric during unified government will be especially hostile to the president, and that in divided government we should observe somewhat more favorable evaluations from NPP sources. Table 4.2 provides substantial support for this hypothesis, especially with regard to foreign policy evaluations. In particular, we see that in unified government relative to divided government, criticism of the president by his own party rises substantially on both the morning and evening news programs for every comparison except non-foreign policy evaluations on the Sunday interview shows.

For the NPP, again for unified government relative to divided government, we see a slight rise in the relatively unfiltered Sunday interview show foreign policy rhetoric, but a large 17.1-percentage-point spike in negativity on the evening news for that same type of rhetoric. On the other hand, for non-foreign policy evaluations by the NPP, the tallies are overwhelmingly negative in both unified and divided government. However, because foreign policy evaluations are likely to be especially salient during these crisis periods, it appears that the president is more likely to face a favorable rhetorical environment for rallies occurring in divided government relative to unified government. Further buttressing this conclusion, it is important to note that, consistent with our theory. the most striking variations in foreign policy rhetoric across unified and divided government consist of relative *declines* during divided government in the most damaging type of rhetoric for the president (criticism from his own party) and relative *increases* in the most helpful rhetoric (praise from the opposition party).

TABLE 4.2
Aggregate Percentage of *Valenced* Congressional Evaluations of the President That Are Negative[a]

| | Unified vs. Divided Government | | | | |
| | Sunday Morning | | Evening News | | |
Party Source	% Negative	n	% Negative	n	Diff.
Foreign Policy Evaluations					
Unified Government					
Presidential party	50.0	28	68.8	64	18.8^
Nonpresidential party	65.1	83	91.8	61	26.7***
Divided Government					
Presidential party	29.5	61	46.4	97	16.9*
Nonpresidential party	64.6	48	74.7	253	10.1
Non-Foreign Policy Evaluations					
Unified Government					
Presidential party	34.4	64	65.3	72	30.9***
Nonpresidential party	88.7	124	90.6	96	1.9
Divided Government					
Presidential party	53.8	143	50.0	100	−3.8
Nonpresidential party	89.1	321	92.2	245	3.1

| | Before vs. After Rally Events | | | | |
| | Before Event | | After Event[b] | | |
Party Source	% Negative	n	% Negative	n	Diff.
Foreign Policy Evaluations					
Sunday Morning					
Presidential party	40.0	40	33.3	36	−6.7
Nonpresidential party	72.0	59	57.3	62	−14.8*
Evening News					
Presidential party	49.4	77	64.6	82	15.2*
Nonpresidential party	75.2	161	85.6	125	10.4*
Non-Foreign Policy Evaluations					
Sunday Morning					
Presidential party	36.3	113	59.0	105	22.8***
Nonpresidential party	86.2	185	86.1	263	−0.1
Evening News					
Presidential party	54.8	84	63.4	82	8.6
Nonpresidential party	92.3	169	92.1	151	−0.2

^p < .10, *p < .05, ***p < .001.

[a]Excludes 1,998 evaluations on the topic of Monica Lewinsky.

[b]Excludes cases where evaluations occurred within 30 days after one event and before the next.

Somewhat (if imperfectly) consistent with the Novelty assumption, in five of the eight comparisons between PP and NPP rhetoric shown in table 4.2 (unified vs. divided government and before vs. after rally event initiation), the negativity bias in the evening news is larger for PP rhetoric. Consistent with our Authority assumption, we see that in unified government, the PP accounts for about 31% of evaluations of the president on the Sunday interview shows, compared to nearly half on the evening news programs. In contrast, in divided government PP evaluations account for about 36% of all presidential evaluations on the Sunday interview shows but only about one in four (25.3%) on the evening news.

Finally, the bottom portion of table 4.2 divides the data according to whether the evaluations took place before or after the start of a foreign policy rally event. Recall that our Salient Crisis Novelty hypothesis (H2) predicts that the greater novelty associated with criticism of the president during rally periods should make such criticism even more novel and newsworthy during a rally event. Consequently, we expected to find evening news rhetoric skewed even more negatively against the president during rally event periods relative to non-rally periods, especially for foreign policy evaluations.

The results shown in table 4.2 provide considerable support for these predictions. On the Sunday morning interview shows (which should represent less-filtered rhetoric from MCs), foreign policy evaluations actually become significantly less critical of the president during rally events relative to pre-event periods. Consistent with the Salient Crisis Novelty hypothesis (H2), however, significantly more foreign policy MC evaluations from both parties that are critical of the president are broadcast on the evening news after the onset of a rally event. In contrast, for evaluations unrelated to foreign policy, PP rhetoric is actually substantially and significantly more negative following initiation of a rally event on the relatively unfiltered Sunday morning programs but varies insignificantly on the evening news. NPP rhetoric unrelated to foreign policy is essentially unchanged before and after a rally event begins. Taken together, these results appear mostly, though imperfectly, consistent with our predictions. With this in mind, we now turn to a more systematic, multivariate analysis of our individual statement-level data.

Individual-Level Analysis

In this analysis, each MC statement appearing on Sunday morning talk show represents a separate observation. We begin by testing our Negativity and Novelty assumptions. (Table 4.A1 in appendix 4.1 presents a series of ReLogit models intended to test the empirical implications of these assumptions, as well as of the Salient Crisis Novelty hypothesis [H2].)

The Novelty assumption holds that evening newscasts will select costly rhetoric (which is potentially harmful to the speaker's perceived interests) more frequently than cheap talk (which is self-serving for the speaker), while the Negativity assumption predicts that, all else equal, negative rhetoric on Sunday morning talk shows will be more likely than positive rhetoric to appear on the evening news. The previously described empirical implication of the Salient Crisis Novelty hypothesis (H2) in turn holds that there will be a larger criticism-to-praise ratio in foreign-policy-related evaluations selected for broadcast on the evening news than for other evaluations.[10] We test each prediction against both of the previously described variants of our dependent variable (cross-network and same-network).[11] In figure 4.1, we once again employ Clarify to transform the coefficients from our fully specified models into probabilities that the evening news selected a given evaluation for broadcast.

Figure 4.1 offers fairly strong support for the Novelty assumption. Recall that the cross-network dependent variable takes a value of 1 when an evaluative statement appears on *any* network evening newscast, while the same-network dependent variable only does so when a statement appeared on the evening newscast of the *same* network as the morning talk show. Beginning with the top two graphics, which incorporate *all* rhetoric on all topics across both dependent variables, we find that variations in cheap talk PP praise have no discernable effect on the probability that a statement will be selected for broadcast. In contrast, a maximum increase in PP criticism of the president (from zero to three occurrences within a statement) is associated with a 5.1-percentage-point increase (from .011 to .062, $p < .10$) in the probability that *at least one* network will broadcast a statement, and a 6.1-percentage-point increase (from .012 to .073, $p < .05$) in the probability that the same network as the talk show on which the statement appeared (that is, the originating network) will broadcast some portion of it. A comparable increase in NPP praise of the president (again, from zero to three occurrences) is associated with a 17.3-percentage-point increase (from .012 to .185, $p < .01$) in the probability that at least one network will broadcast a statement and a

---

[10]As a robustness test, the top half of table 4.A1 presents a basic set of models, excluding all control variables. The results are strikingly similar to the fully specified models, shown in the bottom half of table 4.A1. Incrementally layering in individual control variables or subgroups of variables (e.g., international crisis characteristics, domestic politics, adversary characteristics) makes little difference. This increases our confidence that our results are not artifacts of model specification. Consequently, we focus the remainder of our discussion on interpreting the results from our fully specified models and report only basic and fully specified variants of the models.

[11]Models 1 and 3 in the bottom half of table 4.A1 test our Novelty assumption, with the former employing the cross-network dependent variable and the latter employing the same-network dependent variable.

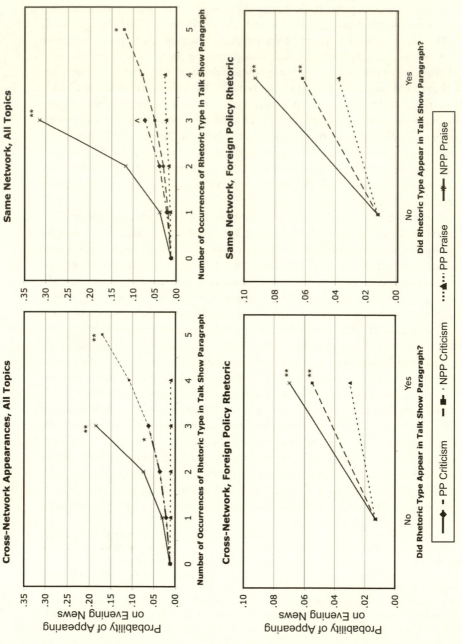

FIGURE 4.1. Estimated Probability That Sunday Morning Talk Show Evaluation Appears on Evening News
$p < .10, *p < .05, **p < .01.$

30.2-percentage-point increase (from .012 to .314, $p < .01$) in the probability that the originating network will broadcast some portion of it.

Additionally, a maximum increase in NPP criticism (in this instance, from zero to five occurrences) is associated with a 16-point increase (from .012 to .185, $p < .01$) in the probability that *at least one* network will broadcast a statement and an 11-point increase (from .012 to .121, $p < .05$) in the probability that the originating network will broadcast some portion of it.[12] In this case, though smaller in magnitude than the effects of costly NPP praise, the effects of NPP criticism are nonetheless substantial and statistically significant. This may be attributable, at least in part, to the relatively greater costliness of NPP criticism during foreign policy crises (the periods from which our data are drawn).

It is also worth noting that, as is apparent in the top two graphics in figure 4.1, across both dependent variables the marginal effect of one incidence of relatively more costly NPP praise is considerably larger than that for NPP criticism. In the case of PP rhetoric, costly rhetoric trumps cheap talk in terms of both marginal and total effects. Consequently, on balance, these results are largely consistent with our Novelty assumption.

Turning to foreign policy rhetoric (shown in the bottom two graphics in figure 4.1), we again see that across both dependent variables, the network evening news programs are more likely to select for broadcast a statement including NPP praise or NPP criticism than one lacking these types of rhetoric. In this instance, because of the relatively lower frequencies of each type of rhetoric when we limited the data to one domain (foreign policy), we focus on only the presence or absence of a given type of rhetoric in a statement, rather than counting the number of occurrences of each type of rhetoric within a statement.

In the former case, the presence of NPP praise increases the probability that *at least one* network will broadcast a given statement by 5.7 percentage points (from .013 to .07, $p < .01$), while increasing the probability that the originating network will broadcast it by 8.1 points (from .012 to .093, $p < .01$). In the latter case, the presence of NPP criticism increases

---

[12]Senator John Edwards (D-NC) provided an example of a single statement that touched on five different dimensions on August 26, 2001, when he offered the following criticism of President George W. Bush:

> There are two serious problems going on. Number one: The president has said all along to the American people, "You can have everything. You can have a huge tax cut, you can have an increase in defense spending. We can pay for privatizing Social Security, we can have additional education spending." The list goes on and on. And, "We won't touch Medicare and Social Security, and we'll pay down the debt." That's not the truth. I mean, the—the government is like every American family. We have to make choices. We have to make decisions.

Edwards's criticism touched on the budget, economy, foreign policy and military issues, domestic policy, and Bush's character.

the likelihood that *at least one* network will broadcast a given foreign policy statement by 4.2 percentage points (from .013 to .055, $p < .01$), while increasing the probability that the originating network will broadcast it by 5 points (from .012 to .062, $p < .01$). Moreover, as before, across both dependent variables the effect of relatively more costly NPP praise is larger than that for NPP criticism. These results are again consistent with the Novelty assumption.

Figure 4.1 also tests the Negativity assumption. Because the Negativity and Novelty assumptions can offset one another, we cannot test the former merely by comparing the overall amount of negative rhetoric appearing on the two venues. After all, novel positive rhetoric (from the NPP) will be highly appealing to journalists, and most likely more so than cheap talk negative rhetoric (again, from the NPP). Consequently, a relatively pure test of the Negativity assumption requires isolating the novelty component of MC rhetoric. To do so, we explicitly compare the two types of cheap talk, PP praise and NPP criticism. Neither is novel. Consequently, after controlling for authority (which we do by including a divided government dummy in our models), the Negativity assumption clearly implies that NPP criticism ought to be preferred by evening news broadcasters over PP praise.

In fact, looking over the four graphics composing figure 4.1, this is precisely what we find in every instance. As noted previously, the PP praise curves are relatively flat and statistically insignificant across both dependent variables, both for overall rhetoric and when (in the bottom two graphics) we focus only on foreign policy rhetoric. In contrast, again in every instance, increases in NPP criticism are associated with large (always larger than that associated with PP praise) and statistically significant ($p < .05$ or $p < .01$) increases in the probability that journalists will select a statement to appear on the evening news. These results are clearly consistent with our Negativity assumption.[13]

Turning to our Salient Crisis Novelty hypothesis (H2), here we compare the patterns of story selection for foreign-policy-related rhetoric with the corresponding patterns for non-foreign-policy-related rhetoric. (Models 7 and 8 in the bottom half of table 4.A1 present the results of this analysis for the cross-network and same-network dependent variables, respectively.) In this instance, we include a set of dummies that take positive values when a given type of rhetoric appears in a statement, separately accounting for foreign policy and non-foreign policy rhetoric.

---

[13]One potential criticism might be that journalists might be less likely to select PP praise to appear on the evening news because the president or his representatives will often appear supporting their own position. The balance assumption (see chapter 2) thus anticipates that journalists will seek a counterbalance to PP self-praise. However, this is likely to be true both on the morning talk shows and on the evening news. Hence, we effectively hold constant the presence of administration self-praise across the two venues and so this alternative cannot account for the disparity in selection.

The first thing to note (as is apparent in the bottom two graphs in figure 4.1) is that foreign-policy-related criticism of the president by his own party drops out of the two statistical models, indicating either that network newscasts picked up *no* such criticism offered on Sunday morning talk shows or that little or none was offered in the first place. A review of the data supports the latter explanation. In our individual-level sample, we find a total of only four foreign-policy-related criticisms of the president by PP members on Sunday morning talk shows that subsequently aired on the evening news. Overall, we found significantly fewer instances of PP criticism than any other type of rhetoric on the morning talk shows. Consequently, we are unable to test the Salient Crisis Novelty hypothesis (H2) with respect to PP MCs.

Despite these limitations, we *are* able to test the hypothesis with respect to rhetoric from the NPP. In figure 4.2, we again transform the results into probabilities that journalists will select a given type of rhetoric appearing on a morning talk show to appear on the evening news. As figure 4.2 indicates, the raw predicted probabilities reveal a substantially larger criticism-to-praise ratio for non-foreign policy rhetoric than for foreign policy rhetoric. This appears directly counter to our prediction. However, these unweighted probabilities are deceiving in a key respect. Recall from our descriptive analysis that the NPP rarely ever praises the president except in foreign policy, while being substantially more prone to criticize in non-foreign policy issue areas. Approximately 88% of all non-foreign-policy-related NPP evaluations directed at the president are negative, compared to 64% of evaluations on foreign policy. This means that when journalists are combing the morning talk shows for rhetoric to include in the evening news, they are not encountering a level playing field. That is, they are not equally likely to encounter all types of rhetoric. Rather, they have a much larger (relative) likelihood of encountering NPP criticism on non-foreign policy issues and of encountering NPP praise on foreign-policy-related issues. This presumably influences the net likelihood of selecting one form of rhetoric or another, independent of journalists' preferences. Consequently, in order to level the playing field—that is, to equalize the probability that a given type of rhetoric appears in the overall population of evaluations on Sunday morning talk shows—we weight the predicted probabilities of praise and criticism by the proportions of praise and criticism, respectively, appearing in the overall population of rhetoric.[14]

[14]So, while the unweighted proportions are given by equation (1) $\frac{c}{p+c}$ (where p = probability of selection given praise and c = probability of selection given criticism), the weighted proportions are given by equation (2) $\frac{c/\%C}{c/\%C + c/\%P}$ (where $\%P$ and $\%C$ represent the proportions of praise and criticism in the underlying population that are positive [P] and negative [C], respectively).

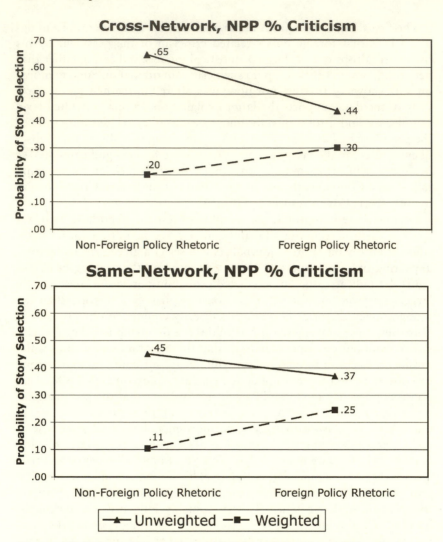

FIGURE 4.2. Estimated Proportion of All Valenced (Positive and Negative) Morning Talk Show Evaluations Appearing on Evening News That Are Negative, Foreign versus Non-Foreign Policy Rhetoric

Beginning with the unweighted probabilities, the presence of NPP criticism or praise on a foreign policy topic is associated with 4.4- and 5.9-percentage-point increases, respectively, in the probability of selection by any network newscast ($p < .01$ in both cases) and 3.8- and 5.8-point increases, respectively, in the probability of selection by the same network as the morning talk show ($p < .01$ in both cases). The corresponding effects of non-foreign-policy-related NPP criticism and praise are increases of 1.9 ($p < .05$) and 0.4 (insig.) points, respectively, for the cross-network dependent variable and 1.0 ($p < .10$) and 1.0 (insig.) percentage points, respectively, for the same-network dependent variable. Based on the unweighted probabilities, the solid curves in figure 4.2 indicate that 65% and 45%, respectively, of valenced (positive or negative) cross- and same-network non-foreign policy rhetoric selected for the evening news was critical, compared to 44% and 37%, respectively, of foreign policy rhetoric. In both instances, we thus see more relative criticism for non-foreign policy issues.

However, after weighting the probabilities of praise and criticism by their overall proportions in the underlying population of valenced rhetoric on the morning talk shows (as shown in the dashed curves in figure 4.2), the directions of the curves reverse. In this instance, 20% and 11%, respectively, of valenced cross- and same-network non-foreign policy evaluations selected for the evening news were critical, compared to 30% and 25%, respectively, of foreign policy evaluations. In other words, once we level the playing field by accounting for the underlying propensity of each type of rhetoric to be available for selection, we find a substantially greater likelihood—by 1.5 to 1 and 2.3 to 1 for the cross-network and same-network models, respectively—that the networks will select a given instance of criticism when it involves foreign policy than when it does not. These results support our Salient Crisis Novelty hypothesis (H2).

Finally, we turn to the more basic empirical implication of the Salient Crisis Novelty hypothesis (H2). (Models 5 and 6 in the bottom half of table 4.A1 test this prediction.) In this instance, we compare the probability of story selection for foreign-policy-related rhetoric *prior* to the start date of each rally event with that for comparable rhetoric appearing *after* the start date of each event. After transforming the coefficients into probabilities, the results indicate that prior to a use of force, a foreign-policy-related MC statement on a Sunday morning talk show is not statistically significantly more likely than any other type of statement to appear on the evening news. However, following uses of force, foreign-policy-related statements are significantly more likely than other types of statements to appear on the evening news, either across networks ($+1.4$ percentage points, $p < .05$) or on the same network ($+2.1$ points, $p < .01$). This result further supports the Salient Crisis Novelty hypothesis (H2).

CONCLUSION

In this chapter we investigated an aspect of the relationship between public opinion and foreign policy that, perhaps because of data limitations, most previous scholars have overlooked. We sought to determine whether the preferences of journalists play a meaningful independent intervening role between elites and the public in the context of foreign policy crises or whether, as assumed by most variants of indexing theory, press coverage merely reflects the true nature and extent of elite rhetoric.

The results from our individual- and aggregate-level analyses largely if imperfectly support our theory, not the implicit passive media assumption underlying indexing theory. This suggests that whether or not the public will rally behind a president when he takes the nation to war turns, at least in part, on the strategic interests and preferences of the news media.

Of course, there are several limitations to the results presented here, most notably the relatively small number of Sunday morning talk show statements selected for evening news broadcast during the time frame covered by our data. Moreover, as previously noted, since MCs are invited guests on Sunday morning talk shows, it seems likely that the journalists involved in these programs might, in at least some circumstances, select guests likely to say particular things. In other words, taking the talk show interview as a proxy for the actual preferred statements by MCs might be at least somewhat misleading if specific guests are invited based on their likelihood of providing "good" stories. Nonetheless, because we have *all* such interviews, we can reasonably employ them as *one* complete subuniverse of potential story fodder for network newscasts; and one that is particularly accessible to them.[15]

Despite these limitations, we find clear and substantial differences between the valence of unedited MC rhetoric on Sunday morning talk shows and that appearing on the heavily edited network evening newscasts. As figures 4.1 and 4.2 decisively demonstrate, and as our theory predicts, PP rhetoric on the evening news strongly overrepresents criticism of the president. This is especially the case with respect to foreign policy and in situations where the president's party controls the legislature. According to these data, if the press were the mirror described by Cronkite, rather than the "beam of a searchlight" described by Lippmann, most comments by PP MCs regarding foreign policy on the evening news would be supportive of the president, as is in fact the case on the Sunday morning talk shows. Yet the majority of such rhetoric on the evening news is *critical* of the president.

---

[15]In addition, there have been many changes over time to the Sunday morning programs, such as the expansion of *Meet the Press* from 30 minutes during the 1980s to a full hour under former host Tim Russert. This likely weights our data disproportionately toward events occurring after the expansion of the show. Finally, the sound bites selected for evening news broadcast seldom match up precisely with our talk show transcripts, meaning that some of the characteristics coded in the talk show record might not actually apply entirely to the smaller portion shown on the evening news.

As we saw in chapter 2 and will return to later, the sight of the president's own partisans turning against him (or of the opposing party rallying to his side) should be particularly consequential for moving public support. In contrast, for statements from the NPP, we actually find journalists assigning greater newsworthiness to *praise* relative to criticism. Indeed, overall, across our measures it seems clear that the evening news provides its audience with a heavily biased representation of elite views concerning presidential foreign policy initiatives.

It is nonetheless important to keep in mind that our findings in this and the previous chapter primarily focus on the preferences of traditional journalists and citizens' consumption of traditional news sources. Yet we argued in chapter 2 that the preferences and incentives of news suppliers in the so-called new media, as well as citizens' reactions to new media content, may differ in important ways from journalist preferences and citizen evaluations in the context of traditional news sources. In the next several chapters, we thus explore the incentives of new media content providers and of citizens consuming new media content, as well as the implications of this interaction for public opinion and presidential leadership in foreign policy.

APPENDIX 4.1. REGRESSION ANALYSIS TABLES

TABLE 4.A1
Relogit Investigations of Probability of Story Selection as Rhetoric Characteristics Vary

I. Basic Models

Independent Variable	(1) Cross-Network	(2) Cross-Network	(3) Same Network	(4) Same Network	(5) Cross-Network	(6) Same Network	(7) Cross-Network	(8) Same Network
PP criticism	0.568^ (0.291)	—	0.683* (0.313)	—	—	—	0.931* (0.428)	1.189* (0.475)
NPP criticism	0.497*** (0.136)	—	0.458** (0.177)	—	—	—	0.825** (0.286)	0.588 (0.392)
PP praise	-0.098 (0.528)	—	0.217 (0.476)	—	—	—	-0.232 (1.016)	0.167 (1.025)
NPP praise	0.858* (0.352)	—	1.155*** (0.337)	—	—	—	0.257 (0.998)	0.779 (0.997)
NPP criticism (FP)	—	1.560*** (0.461)	—	1.763*** (0.513)	—	—	1.643*** (0.463)	1.827*** (0.516)
PP praise (FP)	—	0.776 (1.013)	—	1.232 (1.015)	—	—	0.815 (1.015)	1.245 (1.020)
NPP praise (FP)	—	1.661** (0.586)	—	2.091*** (0.590)	—	—	1.735** (0.587)	2.162*** (0.592)
Foreign policy related	—	—	—	—	0.026 (0.600)	0.096 (0.712)	—	—
Postdeployment	—	—	—	—	-0.379* (0.185)	-0.411^ (0.232)	—	—
Foreign policy × postdeployment	—	—	—	—	1.001 (0.697)	1.141 (0.813)	—	—

	(1) Cross-Network	(2) Cross-Network	(3) Same Network	(4) Same Network	(5) Cross-Network	(6) Same Network	(7) Cross-Network	(8) Same Network
Praise	—	—	—	—	0.144 (0.287)	0.352 (0.270)	—	—
Criticism	—	—	—	—	0.495*** (0.134)	0.496** (0.166)	—	—
PP source	—	—	—	—	-0.007 (0.184)	0.148 (0.227)	—	—
Constant	-4.363*** (0.097)	-4.310*** (0.0919)	-4.816*** (0.120)	-4.766*** (0.115)	-4.175*** (0.153)	-4.681*** (0.196)	-4.395*** (0.101)	-4.846*** (0.126)
No. of obs.	9,309	9,309	9,309	9,309	9,221	9,221	9,309	9,309

II. Fully Specified Models

	(1) Cross-Network	(2) Cross-Network	(3) Same Network	(4) Same Network	(5) Cross-Network	(6) Same Network	(7) Cross-Network	(8) Same Network
PP criticism	0.586* (0.295)	—	0.636^ (0.327)	—	—	—	1.027* (0.435)	1.180* (0.479)
NPP criticism	0.575*** (0.144)	—	0.492* (0.195)	—	—	—	0.975*** (0.294)	0.667 (0.408)
PP praise	-0.036 (0.521)	—	0.212 (0.485)	—	—	—	-0.162 (1.016)	0.173 (1.026)
NPP praise	0.965** (0.365)	—	1.232*** (0.357)	—	—	—	0.312 (1.013)	0.753 (1.009)
NPP criticism (FP)	—	1.499** (0.470)	—	1.647** (0.538)	—	—	1.589*** (0.476)	1.691** (0.548)
PP praise (FP)	—	0.859 (1.020)	—	1.169 (1.041)	—	—	0.908 (1.022)	1.185 (1.043)
NPP praise (FP)	—	1.729** (0.633)	—	2.126** (0.671)	—	—	1.806** (0.640)	2.194** (0.680)

TABLE 4.A1 (continued)

Independent Variable	(1) Cross-Network	(2) Cross-Network	(3) Same Network	(4) Same Network	(5) Cross-Network	(6) Same Network	(7) Cross-Network	(8) Same Network
Foreign policy related	—	—	—	—	-0.293 (0.710)	-0.028 (0.723)	—	—
Postdeployment	-0.433^ (0.224)	-0.402^ (0.224)	-0.417 (0.269)	-0.390 (0.270)	-0.502* (0.226)	-0.499^ (0.275)	-0.455* (0.227)	-0.435 (0.274)
Foreign policy × postdeployment	—	—	—	—	1.218 (0.805)	1.188 (0.830)	—	—
Praise	—	—	—	—	0.259 (0.278)	0.397 (0.263)	—	—
Criticism	—	—	—	—	0.552*** (0.144)	0.499** (0.188)	—	—
PP source	—	—	—	—	-0.092 (0.194)	0.080 (0.238)	—	—
Meet the Press	0.079 (0.246)	-0.000 (0.239)	0.105 (0.280)	0.007 (0.273)	0.069 (0.244)	0.083 (0.276)	0.012 (0.239)	0.014 (0.271)
This Week	0.330 (0.255)	0.253 (0.250)	-0.143 (0.341)	-0.238 (0.330)	0.318 (0.255)	-0.145 (0.338)	0.281 (0.250)	-0.216 (0.331)
Days between polls	0.013 (0.009)	0.013 (0.009)	0.015 (0.012)	0.015 (0.012)	0.014 (0.009)	0.016 (0.012)	0.013 (0.009)	0.015 (0.012)
Presidential election year	-0.363 (0.341)	-0.381 (0.338)	-0.844^ (0.473)	-0.873^ (0.468)	-0.357 (0.339)	-0.815^ (0.475)	-0.372 (0.342)	-0.847^ (0.471)
Presidential approval	0.009 (0.014)	0.007 (0.014)	-0.005 (0.017)	-0.008 (0.017)	0.010 (0.014)	-0.004 (0.017)	0.008 (0.014)	-0.006 (0.017)
Divided government	-0.765 (0.483)	-0.730 (0.479)	-0.518 (0.615)	-0.478 (0.610)	-0.746 (0.483)	-0.535 (0.622)	-0.776 (0.485)	-0.539 (0.619)
Post-cold war	-0.643 (0.534)	-0.612 (0.540)	-0.019 (0.693)	0.006 (0.698)	-0.678 (0.535)	-0.089 (0.672)	-0.702 (0.543)	-0.094 (0.691)
Democratic president	-0.626^ (0.371)	-0.595 (0.377)	-0.947^ (0.499)	-0.890^ (0.508)	-0.625^ (0.375)	-0.962^ (0.504)	-0.594 (0.379)	-0.904^ (0.507)

	(1)	(2)	(3)	(4)	(5)	(6)	(7)	(8)
Consumer sentiment	-0.053** (0.017)	-0.052** (0.018)	-0.074*** (0.020)	-0.073*** (0.021)	-0.055** (0.017)	-0.075*** (0.020)	-0.052** (0.018)	-0.072*** (0.021)
Change in GNP	6.277 (6.795)	6.566 (6.861)	13.684^ (8.130)	13.779^ (8.123)	5.756 (6.788)	12.725 (8.040)	5.579 (6.841)	12.673 (8.078)
U.S. ally	0.810 (0.842)	0.640 (0.847)	1.033 (1.050)	0.849 (1.066)	0.800 (0.847)	0.993 (1.060)	0.658 (0.852)	0.847 (1.075)
Capability ratio	-0.025 (2.399)	-0.187 (2.528)	-4.269^ (2.519)	-4.766^ (2.577)	0.054 (2.477)	-4.393^ (2.633)	-0.135 (2.475)	-4.608^ (2.576)
Terrorism related	-0.265 (0.329)	-0.218 (0.336)	-0.003 (0.440)	0.096 (0.446)	-0.287 (0.330)	-0.049 (0.435)	-0.256 (0.328)	0.022 (0.431)
Major war	0.277 (0.181)	0.327^ (0.182)	0.375 (0.246)	0.429^ (0.249)	0.296 (0.182)	0.421^ (0.248)	0.300 (0.185)	0.411^ (0.250)
Trade dependence	-23.818 (21.088)	-24.174 (21.856)	-54.678* (26.231)	-57.048* (26.619)	-22.731 (22.025)	-56.346* (27.559)	-24.038 (21.552)	-56.627* (26.640)
Foreign policy restraint	0.022 (0.582)	-0.022 (0.584)	-0.023 (0.728)	-0.070 (0.732)	0.012 (0.577)	0.010 (0.728)	0.002 (0.586)	-0.039 (0.734)
Internal political change	-0.725 (0.446)	-0.724 (0.455)	-0.419 (0.530)	-0.403 (0.534)	-0.682 (0.447)	-0.351 (0.541)	-0.658 (0.450)	-0.330 (0.542)
Humanitarian intervention	1.060^ (0.632)	1.042 (0.642)	1.397^ (0.810)	1.385^ (0.816)	1.028 (0.635)	1.354 (0.824)	0.983 (0.637)	1.326 (0.822)
Pre- and post-deployment	0.232 (0.362)	0.298 (0.355)	-0.045 (0.506)	0.024 (0.490)	0.203 (0.364)	-0.092 (0.511)	0.250 (0.358)	-0.016 (0.499)
Any KIA	-0.112 (0.806)	-0.139 (0.801)	0.088 (1.060)	0.067 (1.059)	-0.111 (0.811)	0.095 (1.065)	-0.067 (0.806)	0.106 (1.063)
Constant	-4.317^ (2.613)	-4.089 (2.706)	-0.586 (2.879)	-0.050 (2.897)	-4.388 (2.674)	-0.989 (2.984)	-4.119 (2.667)	-0.594 (2.917)
No. of obs.	8479	8479	8479	8479	8479	8479	8479	8479

^$p < .10$, *$p < .05$, **$p < .01$, ***$p < .001$. Robust standard errors in parentheses.

Abbreviations: PP, presidential party; NPP, nonpresidential party; FP, foreign policy; KIA, U.S. troops killed in action. Unless otherwise noted, the party rhetoric variables in this table exclude foreign policy evaluations.

CHAPTER 5

Shot by the Messenger

AN EXPERIMENTAL EXAMINATION OF THE EFFECTS
OF PARTY CUES ON PUBLIC OPINION REGARDING
NATIONAL SECURITY AND WAR

REPUBLICAN CANDIDATES have famously argued that the media are biased against their candidates, perhaps best exemplified by a popular 1992 bumper sticker reading, "Annoy the Media: Re-elect George Bush." However, with the rise of the Fox News Channel, Democrats have mounted specific, targeted attempts to marginalize and delegitimize what they argue is a pro-Republican news outlet. For instance, in early 2007, liberal activists pressured the Nevada Democratic Party to cancel a Fox-sponsored Democratic candidate debate. In launching the successful campaign to drop Fox as a debate sponsor, liberal blogger Chris Bowers of MyDD. com argued that "instead of giving [Fox] a golden opportunity to further distort the image of Democratic presidential candidates, and instead of providing them with credibility for all of their past and future attacks against Democrats, it would be best if the Nevada Democratic Party chose a different media partner to broadcast this debate" (Bowers 2007).[1] Shortly before the 2008 presidential election, in turn, then-Democratic nominee Barack Obama offered the following speculation:

> I am convinced that if there were no Fox News, I might be two or three points higher in the polls. If I were watching Fox News, I wouldn't vote for me, right? Because the way I'm portrayed 24/7 is as a freak! I am the latte-sipping, *New York Times*-reading, Volvo-driving, no-gun-owning, effete, politically correct, arrogant liberal. Who wants somebody like that? I guess the point I'm making is that there is an entire

[1] The cited cause for the cancellation was a joke by Fox News chairman Roger Ailes conflating Barack Obama with Osama Bin Laden. Ailes responded to the boycott by complaining that pressure groups were now urging candidates to "only appear on those networks and venues that give them favorable coverage" (Whitcomb 2007). While Fox and the Congressional Black Caucus (CBC) later agreed to co-sponsor one Republican and one Democratic candidate debate, activist groups immediately sought to pressure both the CBC and Democratic candidates to withdraw from the debate (Phillips 2007). The Democratic National Committee subsequently declined to sanction it, and the three major Democratic candidates also declined to participate, leading to the indefinite postponement of the debate.

industry now, an entire apparatus, designed to perpetuate this cultural schism, and it's powerful. (Bai 2008)

In this chapter, we test Obama's conjecture regarding the influence of media outlets perceived as having partisan interests, and in doing so begin to systematically address the third major research question motivating this book: to what extent do the new media alter the relationships between media content and public opinion regarding foreign policy? To do so, we examine how different types of elite messages regarding national security and war, appearing in media outlets with distinct partisan reputations, affect the attitudes of different types of individuals. While prior research (including our own in chapter 3 and other studies cited therein) provides some intuition about the potential effects of elite messages, in this chapter we employ national survey data and a media exposure experiment to determine exactly *when* and *how* public opinion is influenced by various partisan messages emanating from different sources and media outlets. As we have previously noted, our core assumptions concerning the factors contributing to the persuasiveness of information are not novel. However, in this chapter we offer more systematic tests than prior studies of several implications of these assumptions, at least some of which (e.g., with respect to partisan support for Iraq) are counterintuitive.

The present chapter tests four of the hypotheses derived in chapter 2, beginning with the Partisan (H4) and Costly (H5) Credibility hypotheses. Recall that the former predicts that presidential evaluations will have a greater influence on partisans from the speaker's own party, while the latter predicts that evaluations that impose a cost on a speaker's own party will have a stronger effect than self-serving, or *cheap talk*, evaluations. We previously tested these hypotheses in chapter 3; however, those tests focused on short-term relationships emerging during rally periods. They also relied on aggregate survey data, making causal inferences difficult. In this chapter we employ both survey data and a media exposure experiment to more directly test our opinion hypotheses. Both were conducted several (two to four) years after the initiation of the Iraq War. This allows us to begin testing our core argument that communication influences the relationship between public opinion and foreign policy beyond the rally period at the outset of a military conflict.

We also test the Partisan Media Opinion (H10) and Selective Acceptance (H11) hypotheses. The Partisan Media Opinion hypothesis (H10) predicts that statements critical of a president will be more credible to viewers coming from a news source perceived as sharing the president's ideological orientation relative to one perceived as opposed to the president's ideology. Conversely, statements praising a president will be more credible coming from a news source perceived as opposed to the president's ideology relative to a news source perceived as sharing the president's ideological orientation. The Selective Acceptance hypothesis (H11) in turn predicts that typical individuals will be more critical of statements opposing a president coming from sources they perceive as opposing the president's ideological orientation, relative to the same news from sources perceived as supporting the president's ideology. In contrast, individuals will be more critical of statements supporting a president from sources they perceive as supporting the president's ideology, relative to the same news from sources perceived as opposing the president's ideological orientation.

To test for these effects, we first conducted an experiment in which we exposed participants to a series of distinct partisan messages embedded in video and web text versions of edited news stories attributed to either CNN or Fox. We subsequently investigated the treatments' effects on our participants' opinions regarding the president and the news stories they consumed. Finally, to bolster confidence in the external validity of our experimental results, we applied our analysis to national survey data examining public opinion related to the war in Iraq several years after the beginning of the conflict. As we will see, the results of both investigations support our theoretical argument.

EXPERIMENTAL EXAMINATION OF MESSAGE EFFECTS

Design

We first test our hypotheses through an online experiment designed to explore the effects of intra- and interparty attacks on and praise of the president attributed to either Fox or CNN.[2] The treatments consist of a streaming video regarding the National Security Agency's (NSA) domestic spying scandal, followed by a static web text report on the war in Iraq.[3]

---

[2]Our treatment conditions include two evaluation sources × two evaluation types × two networks, for a total of eight possible treatments. Moreover, our predictions vary depending on respondents' partisan affiliations (Democrats, Republicans, and independents). Hence, we actually have 24 distinct "cells" of interest in this experiment (eight treatments × three partisan subgroups). Given the complexity of this comparison and the limited number of participants, we adopted a randomized comparative experimental structure, rather than incorporating an additional control group that would be unexposed to any treatment. For similar reasons, we interpret our statistical results through a combination of ordinal logit analyses and simulations intended to help the reader more easily interpret and visualize the impact of the treatment conditions across respondent and treatment groups.

[3]We anticipated that, on average, viewers would rate CNN as relatively less ideologically extreme than Fox, while locating CNN to the ideological left of Fox. The data support both expectations. However, the latter, *relative* differential is more important for our analysis than respondents' views concerning the absolute locations of the two outlets.

As with any media exposure experiment, we faced a trade-off between external validity (that is, the generalizability of our findings to the "real world") and greater control (that is, accounting for potential alternative factors that could potentially account for our observed results). For our comparisons of the effects of network reputations, we were able to maximize control—that is, isolate the effects of the networks' partisan reputations—by testing the effects of treatments that were precisely identical across networks except for the relevant network-identifying information.[4] However, because we have already demonstrated the opinion effects of partisan rhetoric (see chapter 3), we elected to sacrifice some degree of experimental control in testing our rhetoric hypotheses in favor of enhancing realism and external validity in our video treatments—that is, applicability to the "real world"—by varying the politicians appearing in the videos across rhetorical treatment categories. That said, in a separate pilot study, we investigated participants' attitudes toward the political figures appearing in our various treatments. We found no significant differences in mean thermometer scores for the figures cited in each party's praise and criticism treatments (video or text).[5] This implies that the re-

---

[4]Owing to a paucity of actual Democratic praise of the president, we were forced to misattribute positive remarks by Senator Charles Grassley (R-IA) to Senator Herb Kohl (D-WI), and take other remarks by actual Democrats out of context. We selected Grassley to stand in as Kohl because of their relatively low name recognition. For instance, according to one survey, 62% of Americans outside of Iowa had never heard of Grassley (Beaumont 2005). Presumably, only a subset of the remaining 38% would recognize his face or voice. Kohl, by most accounts, has an even lower national profile. In a separate pilot study, only 11% and 21% of our Democratic and Republican participants, respectively, were willing to rate Grassley on a thermometer scale. The corresponding percentages for Kohl were 21% and 23%. The remaining categories of partisan rhetoric were readily available. Hence, we were able to employ correctly attributed real-world comments in all other instances. Still, by using real-world comments, we were forced to vary somewhat both the individual speakers and the precise content of their statements, rendering the conclusions we are able to draw from our rhetorical comparisons somewhat more tentative than would be the case with greater control. This trade-off applies only to the video treatments. For the static web pages, we were able to achieve far greater control, as statements attributed to MCs were constant within the praise and criticism categories, and only the identities were changed to reflect the known stances of existing MCs.

[5]In appendix 5.2, table 5.A1, we present the mean thermometer rating for each senator appearing in our treatment videos and web page stories, broken out by the treatment condition within which they appeared. As one would expect, respondents from each party rated their own partisans more highly than figures from the other party, but these differences were symmetric across the parties. In other words, Republican identifiers rated Republican MCs at about the same level as Democrats rated Democratic MCs, while Republicans rated Democratic MCs about the same as Democrats rated Republican MCs. It is also possible that differences in the stature or notoriety of individual MCs featured in our treatments could influence their persuasiveness. Our data do not allow a direct test of this conjecture, but they do allow an indirect test. More senior or noteworthy MCs ought, all else equal, to

ported differences are *not* artifacts of differences in participants' attitudes toward particular politicians, net of party affiliation.

After watching and reading the video and text stories, participants filled out a survey asking them to indicate which aspect of the news reports they found most interesting, and answered some questions about their political attitudes. (For the full text of all treatments, see appendix 5.1.)

Our experiment included 1,610 participants drawn from UCLA communication studies (55%) and political science (45%) courses taught between spring 2006 and winter 2007.[6] Twenty-one percent identified themselves as Republicans (including leaners), while 53% identified themselves as Democrats (again, including leaners). Independents and third-party identifiers accounted for the remaining 24% of our participants. Table 5.1 presents population characteristics for the overall sample, as well as for Republican and Democratic subsamples.[7]

Key Variables

The main dependent variable for this experiment is participants' approval of President Bush's handling of national security ("Do you approve or disapprove of the way George W. Bush is handling national security?"), which we employ to test the Partisan Credibility (H4) and Costly Credi-

---

engender more intense, and less neutral, feelings among respondents. After all, such MCs should be more familiar to them. If so, all else equal, we would anticipate finding systematic differences between MCs in the mean distance from the neutral points of their thermometer ratings. Yet the overall average distance from the neutral point across all MCs appearing in our treatments, and across partisan respondents rating them is less than half of one point (.42 points) on the 0–10 scale, the largest gap across treatments by a given partisan group is about .4 points and the largest gap across partisan respondents' ratings of the identical treatment is about .31 points. These represent gaps of 3.8%, 3.6%, and 2.8%. This suggests that our participants had similarly intense feelings toward the MCs featured in each treatment condition, and that these relative intensities were similar across partisan subgroups. This represents at least some suggestive evidence that variations in the stature or notoriety of the MCs in our treatments are not driving our results. (See http://www.sscnet .ucla.edu/comm/groeling/warstories/Treatment_videos.html for all video treatments.)

[6] We offered modest extra credit to participants.

[7] Of course, some research (Sears 1986) has famously called into question the generalizeability of experimental findings based on student population samples. We are cognizant of this concern and have sought to enhance our confidence in the generalizeability of our findings by subsequently applying our analysis to a national survey. It is also worth noting that we have successfully replicated several variants of this experiment across numerous distinct student population samples between 1999 and 2007, drawn from eight different universities that, in total, cover every region of the country. Consequently, while we cannot entirely discount the possibility that *any* student sample is inherently biased, we *can* confidently conclude that our results are highly robust across numerous distinct student population samples with quite distinct characteristics. Additionally, recent research has called into at least some question this often cited critique of experimental results derived from student subject pools. Most notably, Kuhberger (1998) reviewed 136 studies of framing effects and

bility (H5) hypotheses, as well as the Partisan Media Opinion hypothesis (H10). To test the Selective Acceptance hypothesis (H11), we measure whether participants criticized the balance of the stories they viewed in response to an open-ended question asking, "What did you find most interesting about either or both of the news reports you just watched and read?"

We employ national security approval rather than overall presidential approval for two reasons. First, we specifically selected our treatments to target the national security domain of politics. Consequently, we anticipate that the treatment conditions should primarily influence participants' attitudes in this area. Second, at the time of the experiment, President Bush's approval ratings were well below 40%. Among Democrats in our data, less than 5% indicated that they approved of the president's overall job performance. This creates a significant floor effect. In other words, criticism of the president, however credible, could not significantly erode the president's approval among our Democratic participants, nearly all of whom already disapproved. While most Democrats also disapproved of the president's handling of national security, his approval rating in this area among Democrats was nonetheless over twice as high, at about 10%.[8] This leaves more room for any potential negative effects of credible criticism to emerge.

For a similar reason, we also employ an expanded version of the approval question that distinguishes between "strongly" and "somewhat" approving or disapproving, as well as permitting a response of "neither approve nor disapprove." This allows us to observe treatment effects that a more blunt "approve vs. disapprove" question might obscure. The Criticize Balance dependent variable in turn is binary, coded 1 if respondents explicitly criticized the ideological balance of the treatment to which they were exposed (in the aforementioned open-ended question), and 0 otherwise.

Our main independent variables account for which of the eight treatment conditions participants viewed. The categories are based on the tone of the story (supportive or critical of the Bush administration), the

---

found no significant differences between student and target samples. Our research, though not directly addressing framing, focuses on similar types of cognitive processes. Hence, while it is important to remain cautious in generalizing from a single experimental result based on a single population sample, and especially one drawn from a nonrepresentative subject pool, by the same token, the evidence of a particular systematic bias associated with student population samples, at least in experimental contexts relatively comparable to ours, remains ambiguous.

[8] These figures set responses of "neither approve nor disapprove" to zero. If these responses are set at the midpoint between disapproval and approval (that is, halfway between 0 and 1, or .5), overall and national security approval rise to about 7% and 15%, respectively. (Note that the y-axis in Figure 5.1 is the probability of *disapproving*, not the probability of approving.)

TABLE 5.1
Summary of Participant Characteristics (Means and Standard Deviations)

Participant Characteristic	Overall	Democrats	Republicans
Total no. of participants	1,610[a]	861	343
% Leaners	27 (45)	34 (47)	22 (42)
% African American	2 (15)	2 (16)	2 (15)
% White	46 (50)	40 (49)	62 (49)
% Hispanic	13 (34)	16 (37)	9 (29)
% Middle Eastern	6 (23)	6 (23)	6 (23)
% Asian	35 (48)	36 (48)	24 (43)
% Native American	0.7 (8)	0.6 (08)	0.9 (9)
% Liberal	60 (49)	89 (32)	6 (23)
% Conservative	23 (42)	3 (18)	85 (36)
Mean age	20.6 (3.75)	20.5 (3.36)	20.6 (4.06)
Mean annual family income	~$100,000	$75,000–100,000	$100,000–150,000
Mean % correct of 10 factual political knowledge questions	51 (26)	52 (24)	54 (24)
% Republicans (including leaners)	21 (41)	n/a	n/a
% Democrats (including leaners)	54 (50)	n/a	n/a
% Independents (excluding leaners)	25 (43)	n/a	n/a

[a]Owing to missing data, the total N in our statistical analysis varies from 1,235 to 1,461.

Note: Standard deviations shown in parentheses.

party affiliation of the members of Congress (MCs) appearing in the story (Republican or Democrat), and the participants' partisan affiliations (Republican, Democrat, or independent).[9]

While random assignment ought, at least in theory, to account for many potentially confounding causal factors, our student population sample differs systematically from a truly random population sample in

[9]Specifically, we modeled these relationships as interactions between three variables: Negative (scored 1 if the treatment criticized the Bush administration), Republican Source (scored 1 if the MCs who appeared in the stories were Republicans), and, to allow us to test

several important ways. For instance, our students are more liberal and Democratic, as well as more likely to be of Asian descent, than the overall national population. Moreover, it is always possible to draw a systematically biased sample even when drawing at random, especially given relatively small treatment groups. For both reasons, we add several control variables intended to account for these systematic differences. These include ideology, campaign interest, whether participants were enrolled in a communication or political science course, ethnicity, a 10-point index of political knowledge (defined in appendix 5.3), age, and participants' assessments of the ideological orientations of Fox and CNN on a liberal to conservative scale (from the pretest).[10]

Results

We begin with tests of the Partisan Credibility (H4) and Costly Credibility (H5) hypotheses. (Model 1 of table 5.A2, in appendix 5.2 presents an ordered logit analysis testing these hypotheses.[11]) To simplify the presentation of our substantive findings (after all, our analysis examines the impact of *four* different types of rhetoric on *three* different types of partisan viewers' decisions to approve or disapprove on a *five*-point scale), in figure 5.1 we transform the key coefficients into probabilities of disapproving of President Bush's handling of national security and chart the effects of moving from one type of treatment message to the next.[12]

Beginning with the Partisan Credibility hypothesis (H4), we first compare the effects of moving from the Democratic criticism to Democratic praise treatments among Democratic identifiers with the corresponding changes associated with the same rhetoric from Republican sources. Because both parties' rhetoric includes both cheap and costly evaluations, the Partisan Credibility hypothesis (H4) would predict that the effect

---

differences in partisan credibility, the participant's own party affiliation. In the latter case we created dummy variables for Republicans and Democrats, including leaners, and also for nonleaning independents, including third-party members. We remap "Other" and "None" responses into the independents category. The inclusion of the "other" partisans has no material effect on the ideological orientation of participants in this category.

[10]Most of the controls only modestly affect our results. Yet, given that many are statistically significant—suggesting that, as anticipated, random assignment did not eliminate all bias in our data—we elected to retain them in our final models.

[11]Model 1 excludes four influential outlier observations (0.2% of our cases). Including these cases modestly weakens several results and modestly strengthens several others, but does not materially alter the results. We also exclude 16 observations (0.9% of our cases) where participants clearly indicated in open-ended questions that they had recognized the treatment manipulations.

[12]As in prior chapters, we employ Clarify (King, Tomz, and Wittenberg 2000) to derive the probabilities and statistical significance estimates in figure 5.1 and throughout the remainder of this chapter.

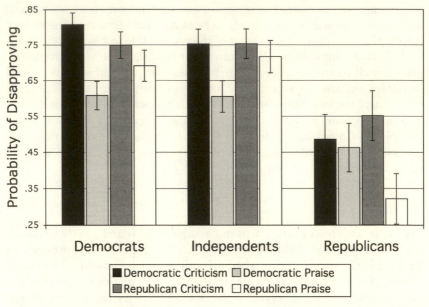

FIGURE 5.1. Estimated Probability of Disapproving of President Bush's Handling of National Security, as Message Source and Valence Vary
Note: Error bars denote standard errors.

associated with Democratic sources should be larger and more significant than that for Republicans, which is in fact what we find. In the former case, moving from criticism of the administration to praise by Democratic MCs yields a 16.2-percentage-point decline in the probability of disapproving of President Bush's handling of national security (combining "strongly" and "somewhat" disapprove, $p < .01$).[13] The corresponding decline among Democrats from the equivalent shift in Republican rhetoric is a far smaller and (as predicted) statistically insignificant 6 points.[14]

Figure 5.1 also indicates that, as predicted by the Partisan Credibility hypothesis (H4), shifting from Republican criticism to Republican praise of the Bush administration affects the disapproval of Republicans far

[13]For clarity (and brevity) of exposition, we collapse the "strongly" and "somewhat" categories in our reported results and focus specifically on disapproval. Disaggregating the other results for this simulation, we find a 6.7-point increase in the probability of neither approving nor disapproving and a 9.1-point increase in the probability of approving (also $p < .01$). Fully disaggregated results are available from the authors.

[14]Conversely, we found a 6.7-percentage-point increase in the probability of neither approving nor disapproving and a 9.1-percentage-point increase in the probability of approving ($p < .01$ in each case). Once again, to facilitate clarity and brevity of exposition, we collapse the "strong" and "somewhat" categories in our reported results. Fully disaggregated results are available from the authors.

more than Democrats. For Republicans, this shift is associated with a highly significant ($p < .01$) 22-percentage-point drop in the probability of disapproving. The corresponding decline among Democrats is a far smaller and (as predicted) statistically insignificant six points.

Turning next to the Costly Credibility hypothesis (H5), we compare the effects of moving from cheap, self-serving (Democratic) criticism to similarly cheap (Republican) praise with the effects of moving from costly (Republican) criticism to costly (Democratic) praise. To isolate the effects of costly credibility, in this instance we focus our analysis on independents, for whom partisan credibility presumably plays no offsetting role in credibility assessments.

The results (as noted, shown in model 1 of table 5.A2 and summarized in figure 5.1) once again strongly support our prediction. Among independents, moving from costly (Republican) criticism to costly (Democratic) praise is associated with about a 14-percentage-point decrease in the probability of disapproving of the president's handling of national security ($p < .01$).[15] Conversely, moving from cheap (Democratic) criticism to cheap (Republican) praise is associated with a small and statistically insignificant effect on approval ratings. In short, consistent with the Costly Credibility hypothesis (H5), among respondents without clear partisan interests, costly (and hence credible) rhetoric moves opinion, while cheap talk does not.

We next investigate our media outlet hypotheses, where, as noted, variations in our treatment conditions are more precisely controlled. We begin with the Partisan Media Opinion hypothesis (H10), which predicts that, because of its relatively greater costly credibility, viewers will find criticism of President Bush more credible when it appears on a news source they perceive as conservative, while finding praise more credible on outlets they perceive as liberal. (Model 2 in table 5.A2 presents an ordered logit analysis testing this hypothesis.) Table 5.2 summarizes the substantive difference in support for President Bush's handling of national security as a given message moves from a liberal to a conservative network. In the top half of figure 5.2 we separately plot the probabilities of disapproving (strongly or weakly) among participants exposed to costly or cheap rhetoric.

The results in table 5.2 and figure 5.2 strongly support the Partisan Media Opinion hypothesis (H10). Costly outlet communication matters far more than cheap talk. Among participants exposed to cheap talk (any praise of President Bush on a conservative network or any criticism on a liberal network), moving from the praise to criticism conditions has no significant effect on disapproval of the president's handling of national security. In sharp contrast, the corresponding effect among participants ex-

---

[15]The probability of *approving*, in turn, increases by 8 percentage points ($p < .10$).

TABLE 5.2
Effects of Perceived Outlet Ideology on Probability of Approving of President's Handling of National Security, as Treatment Varies from Liberal to Conservative Network

National Security Approval Type	Conservative Network	Liberal Network	Difference (Praise − Criticism)
	Costly Talk		
	Criticism	Praise	
Strongly disapprove	0.362	0.133	0.229**
Disapprove	0.403	0.334	0.069**
Neither approve nor disapprove	0.110	0.186	−0.076**
Approve	0.104	0.274	−0.170**
Strongly approve	0.021	0.074	−0.053**
	Cheap Talk		
	Praise	Criticism	
Strongly disapprove	0.303	0.238	0.065
Disapprove	0.411	0.403	0.008
Neither approve nor disapprove	0.129	0.153	−0.024
Approve	0.130	0.169	−0.039
Strongly approve	0.027	0.037	−0.010

**$p < .01$.

posed to costly communication (moving from praise on a liberal network to criticism on a conservative network) is a highly significant ($p < .01$), 30-percentage-point increase in the probability of disapproving (strongly or weakly), from .47 to .77. In other words, as predicted, the ideological reputations of the networks mediate the persuasive power of the information they present to consumers. Messages perceived by our participants as running counter to the presumed ideological interests of the outlets to which we exposed them had a far greater effect on their attitudes toward the president than messages perceived as self-serving for the networks, again given their presumed ideological orientations.

Finally, we turn to the Selective Acceptance hypothesis (H11), which holds that, all else equal, people are more prone to critically assess, or counterargue, information perceived as supportive of a news outlet's presumed ideological orientation (cheap talk) relative to information that challenges an outlet's presumed orientation (costly talk). (Model 3 in table 5.A2 presents a logit analysis testing this hypothesis.) In the bottom half of figure 5.2, we again transform the key coefficients into predicted probabilities that participants criticized the experiment's news stories as unbalanced or biased.

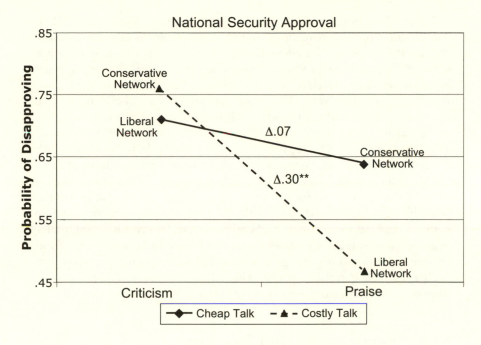

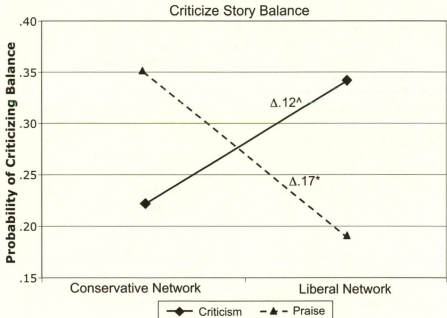

Figure 5.2. Estimated Probability of Disapproving of President Bush's Handling of National Security, as News Source and Message Valence Vary
$\hat{p} < .10$, *$p < .05$, **$p < .01$.

The results strongly support the Selective Acceptance hypothesis (H11). Participants were 12 percentage points *more* likely to criticize rhetoric *critical* of Republican President George W. Bush when it appeared on a network they considered liberal, relative to the identical rhetoric appearing on a network perceived as conservative (.34 vs. .22, $p < .10$). Conversely, participants were 17 percentage points *less* likely to criticize rhetoric *supportive* of the president when it appeared on a network they perceived as liberal, relative to the same rhetoric on a network perceived as conservative (.18 vs. .35, $p < .05$). Interestingly, looking across both the criticism and praise treatments, we see that the probabilities of criticizing both types of cheap talk are nearly identical, .34 for criticism on a liberal network and .35 for praise on a conservative network, as are the probabilities of criticizing costly talk, .22 for criticism on a conservative network and .19 for praise on a liberal network. This result strongly suggests that viewer credibility assessments derive in significant measure from ex ante assumptions regarding the ideological orientations of news outlets. Such assessments, in turn, appear to heavily influence consumers' propensities to counterargue different types of rhetoric (cheap vs. costly talk).

NEWS CONSUMPTION AND ATTITUDES TOWARD IRAQ

We turn next to national public opinion regarding the Iraq War. Our goal is to determine whether the patterns that emerged in our experiment generalize to a real-world context. Specifically, we investigate the effects of the credibility assessments of different types of consumers (Democrats and Republicans) vis-à-vis different media outlets (Fox vs. CNN) on attitudes toward the war. This investigation tests the external validity of our theoretical framework, and in particular, given the distinct perceived partisan leanings of Fox and CNN, the effects of the Partisan Media hypothesis (H10) and the Selective Acceptance hypothesis (H11).

For our dependent variable in this analysis, we employ the following question from a June 2005 Pew Research Center survey (Pew 2005): "How well is the U.S. military effort in Iraq going?" (coded 1 = very or fairly well, or 0 = not too well or not at all well).[16] We compare responses to this question across individuals with different partisan affiliations who claim to get most of their news about politics and international affairs from CNN or Fox.[17]

Unlike our experiment, in this survey we have no way to determine precisely what information Fox or CNN viewers actually consumed. For-

[16]We code 54 responses of "don't know" or refusals to answer as missing data.

[17]This represents about 35% of the sample. Among CNN viewers, 104, 66, and 93 respondents identified themselves as Democrats, Republicans, and independents, respectively. Among Fox viewers, the corresponding numbers are 46, 131, and 66.

tunately, we can derive some insight from a Project for Excellence in Journalism (PEJ) study (PEJ 2005), which content analyzed cable news coverage of the war in Iraq in the year preceding the Pew survey. PEJ found that Fox was nearly twice as likely as CNN to air stories with an "overwhelmingly" positive tone (38% of war-related stories for Fox, vs. 20% for CNN). Conversely, CNN aired nearly twice as many segments as Fox with negative tones (23% vs. 14%). Overall, CNN aired slightly more negative than positive segments, while Fox aired more than twice as many positive as negative segments.[18] The overtly pro-conservative Media Research Center similarly found, in its own study, that between May 15 and July 21, 2006, Fox aired nearly twice as many stories about successes in Iraq as CNN and MSNBC combined (McCormack, Whitlock, and Noyes 2006). In short, circa 2005, regular Fox viewers were in all likelihood exposed to a substantially more positive version of events in Iraq than their counterparts who relied primarily on CNN for news about the conflict.

The implications of these coverage patterns for our theoretical model depend also on consumer perceptions. In fact, evidence suggests Americans are polarized in their opinions regarding the ideological slant of Fox to a greater extent than with respect to CNN. For instance, one survey (Pew 2006) found a much larger gap between liberals and conservatives in rating the believability of Fox, relative to CNN. Liberal and conservative respondents differed by only three percentage points in their probabilities of saying they believe "all or most" of the news on CNN (28% vs. 25%, respectively). The gap for Fox was over five times larger (16% vs. 32%). In other words, liberals rate CNN as being similarly believable as conservatives rate Fox (28% vs. 32%), yet liberals rate Fox as considerably less believable than conservatives rate CNN (16% vs. 25%).

If Fox indeed presents more positive coverage of the war than CNN, respondents with different partisan affiliations should tend to differ in their responses. Democrats will likely dismiss pro-war news on Fox as non-credible, while being relatively more likely to accept equivalent information on CNN as reliable. Conversely, Republicans exposed to the relatively more positive war news on Fox will be more likely to believe things are going well in Iraq than their counterparts exposed to CNN's near-equal mix of praise and criticism. Moreover, liberals (most of whom are Democrats) are more skeptical of Fox than conservatives (most of whom are Republicans) are of CNN. The implication is that liberals (and Democrats) are more likely to discount pro-war content on Fox than conservatives (and Republicans) are to dismiss anti-war content on CNN.

---

[18]PEJ reports that 41% and 39% of Fox and CNN stories, respectively, were neutral, while 15% and 9%, respectively, were categorized as multisubject and were not coded for tone.

This suggests two Iraq-specific corollary hypotheses, both of which follow from our more general Partisan Media Opinion (H10) and Selective Acceptance (H11) hypotheses:

HYPOTHESIS 10A: IRAQ DEMOCRATIC COROLLARY:
    Democrats who rely on CNN are *more* likely than Fox-watching Democrats to believe the war in Iraq is going well.

HYPOTHESIS 10B: IRAQ REPUBLICAN COROLLARY
    Republicans who rely on Fox are *more* likely than CNN-watching Republicans to believe the war in Iraq is going well.

Of course, differences in the characteristics of respondents who choose to watch Fox and CNN, rather than—or in addition to—the content of news to which they are exposed, could be driving any observed relationship between outlet preferences and war attitudes. To some extent, we anticipate this is the case; after all, our model presumes that partisans will take advantage of the opportunity to self-select into friendly environments. In fact, there is evidence of such a pattern. Democratic and Republican Fox watchers in this survey are more conservative than their counterparts who prefer CNN (by .42 and .46 points on the five-point ideology scale, for Democrats and Republicans, respectively). To further assess this possibility, we investigated the factors influencing respondents' choices to rely on Fox or CNN for news about national and international politics.[19] (In appendix 5.5, we discuss at length our empirical approach to investigating this potential confounding causal factor, and present the results of our tests.) The key question is whether and to what extent knowledge about or attitudes toward the war, net of other factors, influence the decision to watch either network. The answer (as shown in appendix 5.5) is that despite our best efforts, we find no evidence suggesting that differences in the internal characteristics of Democratic and Republican respondents can adequately account for the relationships reported herein between news consumption preferences and attitudes toward the Iraq War.

In light of these results, we tentatively conclude that preexisting attitudes toward Iraq, the key potential selection effect for our purposes, do not appear to be fundamentally driving the decision to consume Fox or CNN. However, the question remains as to whether the information encountered by viewers, in interaction with their partisan predispositions,

---

[19]An alternative means of addressing endogeneity concerns would be an instrumental variable approach. While this has some conceptual advantages, we were unable to derive a persuasive instrument for media consumption preferences. This is less of a concern for our approach, as we are less interested in predicting preferences for Fox or CNN than in determining the extent to which attitudes toward Iraq do or do not predict such preferences.

does influence their attitudes toward Iraq. To test the Iraq Democratic (H10a) and Republican (H10b) corollary hypotheses, we interact respondents' partisan affiliations with their preferred sources of news about politics and international affairs. We also include a standard battery of demographic and political control variables, as well as controls for overall trust in the news media and interest in the war.[20] (Table 5.A4 in appendix 5.2 reports the results of a logit model testing the effects of news preferences and partisan affiliation on attitudes toward the Iraq War.)[21] In figure 5.3 we illustrate the probabilities that respondents believe things are "going well" in Iraq as their primary source of news about politics and international affairs varies from CNN to Fox.

Consistent with most polling data (Jacobson 2006), Republicans in this survey are far more supportive of the war than are Democrats. However, after controlling for a variety of correlates of attitudes toward Iraq, no statistically significant difference emerges between Democrats and Republicans who prefer CNN. In contrast, Republican Fox viewers are 54 percentage points more likely than Democratic Fox viewers to believe the Iraq War is going well (.83 vs. .29, $p < .01$).

That said, testing the Iraq Democratic (H10a) and Republican (H10b) corollary hypotheses requires comparing differences *within* partisan groups. These results indicate that Democrats watching mostly positive coverage of the war on Fox (recall the aforementioned PEJ analysis of Fox and CNN news coverage) actually *decreased* their assessment of the war's progress by a highly significant 28 percentage points relative to their peers who consumed relatively balanced coverage on CNN (from .52 to .24 for CNN and Fox viewers, respectively, $p < .01$). This supports the Iraq Democratic corollary hypothesis (H10a). Republicans, on the other hand, were more strongly influenced by Fox's relatively positive coverage, enhancing their assessment of the war's progress by 24 points (from .57 to .81 for CNN and Fox viewers, respectively, $p < .05$). These results support the Iraq Republican corollary hypothesis (H10b).

Notwithstanding our previously discussed exploration of the correlates of preferring Fox and CNN, we cannot rule out entirely the possibility that the moderate ideological difference between Republican CNN and Fox watchers might help account for at least part of the greater optimism regarding the war among Republican Fox watchers. However, self-selection based on ideological affinity cannot account for *lower* optimism

[20] We include controls for preferring network newscasts or the Internet as sources for national and international political news. Other media outlets (newspapers, magazines, radio) were insignificant and did not affect our results. Hence, they are excluded.

[21] The reported results exclude four influential outlier observations (or 0.3% of our cases). Including these outliers modestly weakens but does not materially alter the reported results.

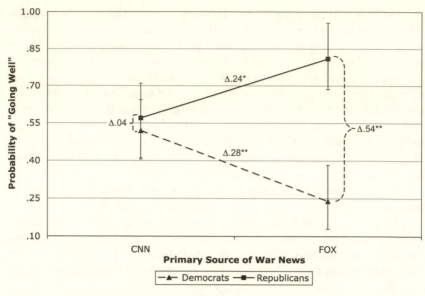

FIGURE 5.3. Estimated Probability of Believing the Iraq Conflict Is "Going Well," as Source of War News and Party Identification Vary

*$p < .05$, **$p < .01$. Error bars denote 95% confidence intervals.

among the somewhat more conservative (relative to their CNN-watching counterparts) Democratic Fox watchers. This latter pattern is precisely the opposite of what one would predict if differences in the ideological preferences of CNN and Fox viewers were driving our results. Yet it is precisely what one would predict as a consequence of partisan credibility and selective acceptance. We thus conclude that while self-selection matters, so too do differences in the substantive information to which viewers of Fox and CNN are exposed, mediated by their partisan predispositions to accept or reject messages with particular (pro- or anti-war) valences.[22]

---

[22]Note that our empirical results suggest the possibility that credibility effects might vary across categories of actors. In our experiment, we found stronger support for our partisan credibility predictions when the speakers were themselves partisan, and stronger support for the costly credibility predictions when we vary news organizations. While some of these differences might be artifacts of the statistical modeling required to test the predictions, it also seems plausible that the shared interest assumption underlying partisan credibility would apply more strongly to people publicly labeling themselves as fellow partisans, relative to media outlets that are merely viewed as sympathetic to the party (especially if those outlets deny such sympathies). Similarly, it seems possible that the public would place somewhat less weight on the credibility of statements made by office-seeking politicians relative to those of media outlets, for whom credibility can literally be a matter of corporate life and

CONCLUSION

Scholars have a clear understanding of the concept and implications of party with respect to legislative and voting behavior. Increasingly, however, parties have become more concerned about the collective image they present to the public through the media. As a consequence, parties are growing increasingly aggressive in their attempts to foster or enforce such unity. Our findings suggest that politicians are justified in being concerned not just about what they do, but also what they say and where they say it. While much rhetoric in the public domain is rightly characterized as cheap talk, a party's messages (and those of the opposing party) do have tremendous potential to affect public opinion. In many cases politicians' messages will be lost in the modern media maelstrom. Yet we find that relatively subtle partisan messages can have large effects on opinion, even in high-salience issue areas like war and national security and among well-informed, politically attentive partisans on the lookout for political manipulation and bias.

However, the news media environment itself is clearly changing, with the so-called new media in the vanguard. Indeed, regardless of whether CNN or Fox actually favors a particular party, the public's increasing belief that they—particularly Fox—do so has important implications for partisan communication. As we saw throughout our empirical investigations, ascriptions of partisanship on the part of news media strongly influence which partisan messages citizens regard as credible to those media. For instance, in a 2008 Republican primary debate, Mitt Romney skewered John McCain by asserting, "If you get endorsed by the *New York Times*, you're probably not a conservative" (Reuters 2008). Less than a month later, donations to John McCain's presidential campaign increased among conservatives following publication of a *New York Times* article questioning his ties to lobbyists, reportedly because "For a lot of conservatives, being attacked by the *New York Times* is a badge of honor" (Bumiller 2008). In the same article, Fox News anchor Chris Wallace commented: "I think they [conservatives] must figure, 'Well, if John McCain's being bashed by the *Times*, he must not be all bad.'" On the Democratic side, Barack Obama attempted to refute a claim advanced by John McCain in the final debate of the 2008 presidential campaign, saying, "Even Fox News disputes [this claim] . . . and that doesn't happen very often when it comes to accusations about me" (CNN 2008).

---

death in the news marketplace. Finally, our focus on the war in Iraq, the subject of one of the most bitter and contentious partisan struggles in recent memory, may have reduced the likelihood that partisans in the electorate would attend to any statements from the opposing party, even if those statements were supportive of their personal views.

These findings have clear implications for our third research question (noted at the outset of this chapter). Clearly, the new media hold the potential to alter the relationship between politicians, the press, and the public. For politicians attempting to influence public opinion, the contrast to most of the television era could not be clearer: new media perceived as siding with a particular party will actually be less persuasive for all, save members of the same party, in communicating anything short of attacks against that same party. Conversely, stories communicating bipartisan support reported by a "hostile" media outlet should be one of the few positive messages that remain credible to partisans from *both* parties.

Ironically, the bipartisanship that sprang more easily from cross-cutting cleavages and overlapping party issue areas has become that much more crucial for parties and politicians striving to rally public support at precisely the moment the parties are becoming more ideologically polarized at the national level. Similarly, news outlets with independent reserves of credibility and prestige have themselves become less influential, or have squandered their remaining credibility in well-publicized reporting failures (e.g., election night 2000, WMDs in Iraq) or scandals (Jayson Blair, "Rathergate," and Reuters's doctored photographs of the Israeli-Hezbollah conflict are but a few examples). Without being able to draw on these reservoirs of credibility, American parties will likely find their opportunities to actually *persuade* the public increasingly few and far between.

This, to return to a theme we stress repeatedly throughout the book, will almost certainly complicate efforts to forge a bipartisan consensus behind major presidential or congressional policy initiatives. For instance, Baum (2002) finds that the rally-'round-the-flag effect occurs mostly among opposition identifiers, the very individuals who are increasingly likely to discount, if not avoid altogether, elite messages supporting a president's actions abroad. As retired U.S. Army Lt. General Ricardo S. Sanchez observed in prepared comments to a group of military reporters and editors regarding the conflict in Iraq, "Since 2003, the politics of war have been characterized by partisanship as the Republican and Democratic parties struggled for power in Washington" (Sanchez 2007). As a consequence, it seems likely that future presidents will find the American public, other than their fellow partisans, less willing than in prior decades to rally behind their president when he or she sends the nation to war.

In the next two chapters we explore General Sanchez's assertion and its implications, while testing our dynamic media coverage and opinion hypotheses, through a case study of the U.S. invasion and subsequent occupation of Iraq.

APPENDIX 5.1. TREATMENT CONDITION TRANSCRIPTS

Republican Criticism Video Transcript

GONZALEZ: The terrorist surveillance program is necessary, it is lawful.

REPORTER: That's been the administration's line since the secret program was exposed and the Attorney General stuck with it, backing his boss all the way.

GONZALEZ: He is absolutely determined to do everything that he can, under the Constitution and the laws of this country, to prevent another September 11th from happening again.

REPORTER: Surprisingly, some of the administration's harshest criticism in the hearings came from members of the president's own party as Republicans took the gloves off, questioning whether the eavesdropping overextended the president's war authority

SPECTER: You think you're right. But there are a lot of people who think you're wrong. As a matter of public confidence, why not take it to the FISA Court? What do you have to lose if you're right?

DEWINE: This country would be stronger and the president would be stronger—if he did so, if he did come to the Congress

GRAHAM: Taken to its logical conclusion, it concerns me that it could basically neuter the Congress and weaken the courts.

GONZALES: I don't believe that's where we're at right now.

GRAHAM: That's where you're at with me.

SPECTER: I hope you will give weighty thought to taking this issue to the Foreign Intelligence Surveillance Court. And the Al Qaida threat is very weighty, but so is the equilibrium of our constitutional system.

GONZALES: I agree, Senator.

SPECTER: And security is very weighty, but so are civil rights.

REPORTER: That hearing was just the warm-up, Terry; there are at least two more hearings to come.

Democratic Criticism Video Transcript

GONZALEZ: The terrorist surveillance program is necessary, it is lawful.

REPORTER: That's been the administration's line since the secret program was exposed and the Attorney General stuck with it, backing his boss all the way.

GONZALEZ: He is absolutely determined to do everything that he can, under the Constitution and the laws of this country, to prevent another September 11th from happening again.

REPORTER: It came as no surprise that some of the administration's harshest criticism came from across the aisle as Democrats took the gloves off, questioning whether the eavesdropping overextended the president's war authority.

LEAHY: And you're saying that you were told by members of Congress we couldn't write a law that would fit it, and now you tell us that the committee that has to write the law never was asked.

GONZALES: We had—

LEAHY: Does this sound like a CYA on your part? It does to me.

FEINGOLD: You wanted this committee and the American people to think that this kind of program was not going on. But it was and you knew that. And I think that's unacceptable.

BIDEN: What's really at stake here is the administration's made assertions in the past where their credibility has somewhat been questioned. And so it's not merely the constitutional reach you have; it is: What is actually happening, what is actually going on?

FEINSTEIN: This program is much bigger and much broader than you want anyone to know.

REPORTER: That hearing was just the warm-up, Terry; there are at least two more hearings to come.

Republican Praise Video Transcript

GONZALEZ: The terrorist surveillance program is necessary, it is lawful.

REPORTER: That's been the administration's line since the secret program was exposed and the Attorney General stuck with it, backing his boss all the way.

GONZALEZ: The president is duty-bound to do everything he can to protect the American people. He took an oath to preserve, protect and defend the Constitution. In the wake of 9/11, he told the American people that to carry out this solemn responsibility, he would use every lawful means at his disposal to prevent another attack.

GRASSLEY: If that is true, is it in some sense incredible to you that we're sitting here having this discussion today about whether the president acted lawfully and appropriately in authorizing a program narrowly targeted at communication that could well lead to a disruption or prevention of such an attack?

REPORTER: It came as no surprise that members of the president's own party were among his strongest supporters, defending the program as vital in the struggle to prevent another terrorist attack on American soil.

SESSIONS: I think there's been a remarkable unanimity of support for the inherent power of the president to do these kind of things in the interest of national security.

GRASSLEY: I always want to remind people in the United States that what we're talking about here today is to make sure that September the 11th doesn't happen again. We ought to remember that it happened in Madrid, it happened in London, it happened in Amman, it happened in a resort in Egypt, it happened in Bali twice. And it has happened here; it can happen again. And it seems to me that what you're trying to tell us is the president's determined to make sure that it doesn't happen in the United States again and that's what this surveillance is all about.

GONZALES: Senator, he is absolutely determined to do everything that he can, under the Constitution and the laws of this country, to prevent another September 11 from happening again.

REPORTER: That hearing was just the warm-up, Terry; there are at least two more hearings to come.

Democratic Praise Video Transcript

GONZALEZ: The terrorist surveillance program is necessary, it is lawful.

REPORTER: That's been the administration's line since the secret program was exposed and the Attorney General stuck with it, backing his boss all the way.

GONZALEZ: The president is duty-bound to do everything he can to protect the American people. He took an oath to preserve, protect and defend the Constitution. In the wake of 9/11, he told the American people that to carry out this solemn responsibility, he would use every lawful means at his disposal to prevent another attack.

GRASSLEY [Identified as Kohl]: If that is true, is it in some sense incredible to you that we're sitting here having this discussion today about whether the president acted lawfully and appropriately in authorizing a program narrowly targeted at communication that could well lead to a disruption or prevention of such an attack?

REPORTER: Surprisingly, some of the administration's strongest support in the hearings came from across the aisle as Democrats defended the program as vital in the struggle to prevent another terrorist attack on American soil.

SCHUMER: Like everyone else in this room, I want the president to have all the legal tools he needs as we work together to keep our nation safe and free, including wiretapping.

GRASSLEY [Identified as Kohl]: I always want to remind people in the United States that what we're talking about here today is to make sure that September the 11th doesn't happen again. We ought to remember that it happened in Madrid, it happened in London, it happened in Amman, it happened in a resort in Egypt, it happened in

Bali twice. And it has happened here; it can happen again. And it seems to me that what you're trying to tell us is the president's determined to make sure that it doesn't happen in the United States again and that's what this surveillance is all about.

GONZALES: Senator, he is absolutely determined to do everything that he can, under the Constitution and the laws of this country, to prevent another September 11 from happening again.

REPORTER: That hearing was just the warm-up, Terry; there are at least two more hearings to come.

Republican/Democratic Web Page Criticism

SUNDAY TALK SHOW ROUNDUP—FOCUS IRAQ

WASHINGTON—Jan. 23, 2006, by Timothy G. McCaughan

President Bush (SEARCH) is preparing separate speeches this week to update the nation on Iraqi efforts to train its security forces while its leaders build a democratic government. The move comes as Iraqi Army soldiers and about 1,000 U.S. troops began conducting counterterrorism operations targeting insurgents in Iraq's volatile Anbar province, which has been a hotbed for insurgency.

Anticipating the Bush Administration's renewed public focus on Iraq, the future of that nation was the primary topic on the Sunday morning political talk shows. [Republican/Democratic] senators appearing on Sunday news shows advocated getting U.S. forces out of Iraq to avoid a Vietnam-like quagmire.

[Nebraska Sen. Chuck Hagel/Delaware Senator Joseph Biden] (SEARCH) argued that the United States needs to develop a strategy to leave Iraq. [Hagel/Biden] scoffed at the idea that U.S. troops could be in Iraq four years from now at levels above 100,000, a contingency for which the Pentagon is preparing. "We should start figuring out how we get out of there," [Hagel/Biden] said on *This Week* on ABC. "I think our involvement there has destabilized the Middle East. And the longer we stay there, I think the further destabilization will occur." [Hagel/Biden] said "stay the course" is not a policy. "By any standard, when you analyze almost three years in Iraq . . . we're not winning," he said.

Appearing on NBC's *Meet the Press*, [Sen. Richard Lugar/Sen. Evan Bayh] (SEARCH), an Indiana [Republican/Democrat], said "What I think the White House does not yet understand—and some of my colleagues— the dam has broke on this policy." Echoing [Hagel/Biden], [Lugar/Bayh] added, "The longer we stay there, the more similarities (to Vietnam) are going to come together."

Republican/Democratic Web Page Praise

SUNDAY TALK SHOW ROUNDUP—FOCUS IRAQ

WASHINGTON—Jan. 16, 2006, by Timothy G. McCaughan

President Bush (SEARCH) is preparing separate speeches this week to update the nation on Iraqi efforts to train its security forces while its leaders build a democratic government. The move comes as Iraqi Army soldiers and about 1,000 U.S. troops began conducting counterterrorism operations targeting insurgents in Iraq's volatile Anbar province, which has been a hotbed for insurgency.

Anticipating the Bush Administration's renewed public focus on Iraq, the future of that nation was the primary topic on the Sunday morning political talk shows. [Republican/Democratic] senators appearing on Sunday news shows advocated remaining in Iraq until the mission set by Bush is completed.

[Sen. George Allen/Sen. Joe Biden (SEARCH), R-Virginia/D-Delaware], appearing on ABC's *This Week*, said a constitution guaranteeing basic freedoms would provide a rallying point for Iraqis. "I think this is a very crucial time for the future of Iraq," said [Allen/Biden], also on ABC. "The terrorists don't have anything to win the hearts and minds of the people of Iraq. All they care to do is disrupt." [Allen/Biden] added that unlike the communist-guided North Vietnamese who fought the U.S., the insurgents in Iraq have no guiding political philosophy or organization.

Speaking on NBC's *Meet the Press*, Indiana [Republican Sen. Richard Lugar/Democratic Senator Evan Bayh] (SEARCH) said the U.S. is winning in Iraq but has "a way to go" before it meets its goals there. "I do think we, the president, all of us need to remind people why we have made this commitment, what is being done now, what progress we are making," [Lugar/Biden] said. "The mission is not an easy one, but few worthwhile things are easy."

Appendix 5.2. Regression Tables

Table 5.A1
Pretest Thermometer Ratings of Senators, by Party (Based on 0–10 Scales)

Criticism or Praise, by Member of Congress	Independents (N = 115)		Republicans (N = 107)		Democrats (N = 228)	
	Mean	Std. Dev.	Mean	Std. Dev.	Mean	Std. Dev.
Republican Criticism Video						
Arlen Specter (R)	4.626	1.181	4.897	1.324	4.504	1.462
Mike DeWine (R)	4.730	0.958	5.084	0.802	4.684	1.125
Lindsey Graham (R)	4.722	1.005	4.991	0.863	4.750	0.954
Democratic Criticism Video						
Joseph Biden (D)	4.896	1.012	4.579	1.221	5.377	1.172
Patrick Leahy (D)	4.896	0.931	4.748	1.133	5.075	1.102
Russell Feingold (D)	5.130	1.380	4.598	1.359	5.583	1.561
Republican Praise Video						
Charles Grassley (R)	4.870	0.538	4.981	0.777	4.855	0.876
Jeff Sessions (R)	4.826	0.787	5.121	0.809	4.732	1.038
Democratic Praise Video						
Charles Schumer (D)	4.948	0.747	4.682	1.256	5.360	1.239
Herb Kohl (D)[a]	5.009	0.682	4.916	0.992	5.281	1.119
Web Page Text Treatments						
Richard Lugar (R)—praise/criticism	4.922	0.580	5.028	0.906	4.917	0.894
Chuck Hagel (R)—criticism	4.974	0.668	4.832	1.193	4.974	0.929
George Allen (R)—praise	4.696	1.156	5.047	0.635	4.461	1.514
Joseph Biden (D)—praise/criticism	4.896	1.012	4.579	1.221	5.377	1.172
Evan Bayh (D)—praise/criticism	5.009	0.656	4.766	0.917	5.219	0.908
Max. within-party % gap	4.6%		4.9%		7.9%	

[a]Grassley is identified as Kohl in Democratic praise video treatment.

Note: Thermometer rating is unavailable for Diane Feinstein (D-CA), who appears in Democratic criticism video treatment.

TABLE 5.A2
Ordered Logit and Logit Analyses of the Correlates of Approving the President's
Handling of National Security and Criticizing the Ideological Balance in News
Story Content

Independent Variable	(1) Approval (Message Source)	(2) Approval (Outlet Credibility)	(3) Criticize Balance (Outlet Credibility)
Democrat × Rep. criticism	−0.071 (0.245)	—	—
Democrat × Rep. praise	0.216 (0.244)	—	—
Democrat × Dem. criticism	−0.267 (0.243)	—	—
Democrat × Dem. praise	0.512 (0.244)*	—	—
Republican × Rep. criticism	0.754 (0.339)*	—	—
Republican × Rep. praise	1.787 (0.345)***	—	—
Republican × Dem. criticism	1.257 (0.336)***	—	—
Republican × Dem. praise	1.301 (0.323)***	—	—
Independent × Rep. criticism	−0.116 (0.260)	—	—
Independent × Rep. praise	−0.088 (0.275)	—	—
Independent × Dem. criticism	0.541 (0.250)*	—	—
Ideology of treatment outlet	—	0.167 (0.053)***	−0.148 (0.066)*
Criticism	—	−0.466 (0.111)***	0.055 (0.139)
Outlet ideology × criticism	—	−0.066 (0.069)	0.252 (0.084)**
Fox treatment	0.080 (0.099)	0.319 (0.128)*	0.313 (0.153)*
Communication class	−0.092 (0.121)	−0.083 (0.129)	−0.753 (0.155)***
Campaign interest	−0.285 (0.076)***	−0.244 (0.086)**	0.229 (0.100)*
Age	−0.037 (0.017)*	−0.031 (0.019)	−0.041 (0.021)*
African American	−0.929 (0.427)*	−0.626 (0.422)	−1.107 (0.631)^
Asian	−0.011 (0.156)	−0.093 (0.172)	0.218 (0.219)
White	0.281 (0.153)^	0.195 (0.167)	0.139 (0.205)
Hispanic	−0.407 (0.193)*	−0.397 (0.205)^	0.076 (0.232)
Middle Eastern	0.453 (0.248)^	0.371 (0.258)	0.294 (0.282)
Self ideology rating	−0.624 (0.061)***	−0.596 (0.068)***	−0.016 (0.073)
CNN ideology rating	0.136 (0.046)**	—	—
Fox ideology rating	0.158 (0.037)***	—	—
Political knowledge	0.012 (0.027)	0.030 (0.029)	0.074 (0.035)*
Republican message source	—	−0.057 (0.110)	−0.105 (0.132)
Party ID	—	−0.284 (0.052)***	−0.084 (0.058)
Constant 1	−4.925 (0.562)	−6.277 (0.554)	−0.477 (0.600)
Constant 2	−3.215 (0.551)	−4.519 (0.541)	—
Constant 3	−2.240 (0.545)	−3.745 (0.535)	—
Constant 4	−0.228 (0.550)	−1.831 (0.535)	—
Pseudo-R^2 (N)	.16 (N = 1,461)	.16 (N = 1,235)	.07 (N = 1,244)

^$p < .10$; *$p < .05$; **$p < .01$. ***$p < .001$. Robust standard errors in parentheses.

TABLE 5.A3
Logit Analyses of Correlates of Relying on Fox or CNN as Primary Source of Political and International News

Independent Variable	(1)	(2)	(3)	(4)
Fox				
Democrat	-0.242 (0.235)	-0.050 (0.240)	0.024 (0.251)	0.032 (0.256)
Republican	0.657 (0.203)***	0.402 (0.221)^	0.338 (0.238)	0.251 (0.232)
Conservative	0.562 (0.190)**	0.452 (0.194)*	0.324 (0.201)	0.405 (0.282)
Liberal	0.235 (0.261)	0.357 (0.271)	0.413 (0.280)	0.329 (0.203)
Republicans more correct on national security	—	0.211 (0.144)	0.112 (0.151)	0.065 (0.156)
Republicans more correct on taxes and spending	—	0.306 (0.141)*	0.148 (0.145)	0.123 (0.142)
Republicans more correct on social policy	—	0.206 (0.132)	0.126 (0.136)	0.118 (0.136)
Network TV news favorability	—	—	-0.548 (0.128)***	-0.521 (0.132)***
Local newspaper favorability	—	—	-0.145 (0.118)	-0.146 (0.119)
National newspaper favorability	—	—	-0.239 (0.133)^	-0.239 (0.133)^
Local TV news favorability	—	—	0.265 (0.123)*	0.255 (0.123)*
Cable news favorability	—	—	0.690 (0.139)***	0.685 (0.138)***
Media too critical of president	—	—	0.163 (0.134)	0.099 (0.146)
News quality scale	—	—	-0.021 (0.088)	—
Know U.S. casualty level in Iraq	—	—	—	0.166 (0.180)
Follow Iraq War	—	—	—	0.103 (0.114)
Iraq War right	—	—	—	0.365 (0.259)
Constant	-2.072 (0.185)***	-2.050 (0.186)***	-2.629 (0.564)***	-3.137 (0.704)***
Pseudo-R^2 (N)	0.04 (N = 1,406)	0.05 (N = 1,406)	0.10 (N = 1,380)	0.10 (N = 1,376)

CNN	(5)	(6)	(7)	(8)
Democrat	0.206 (0.184)	0.126 (0.187)	0.030 (0.192)	-0.040 (0.199)
Republican	-0.165 (0.222)	-0.064 (0.239)	0.205 (0.233)	0.150 (0.236)
Conservative	-0.390 (0.201)*	-0.303 (0.206)	-0.296 (0.203)	-0.394 (0.201)*
Liberal	-0.341 (0.197)^	-0.390 (0.196)*	-0.416 (0.197)*	-0.271 (0.203)
Republicans more correct on national security	—	0.106 (0.137)	0.097 (0.140)	0.074 (0.141)
Republicans more correct on taxes and spending	—	-0.139 (0.142)	-0.068 (0.144)	-0.082 (0.144)
Republicans more correct on social policy	—	-0.245 (0.124)*	-0.204 (0.130)	-0.201 (0.128)
Network TV news favorability	—	—	0.054 (0.129)	0.109 (0.126)
Local newspaper favorability	—	—	0.066 (0.110)	0.086 (0.110)
National newspaper favorability	—	—	0.106 (0.115)	0.124 (0.113)
Local TV news favorability	—	—	-0.112 (0.129)	-0.095 (0.129)
Cable news favorability	—	—	0.476 (0.135)***	0.469 (0.130)***
Media too critical of president	—	—	-0.289 (0.127)*	-0.281 (0.132)*
News quality scale	—	—	0.139 (0.073)^	0.042 (0.168)
Know U.S. casualty level in Iraq	—	—	—	0.359 (0.105)***
Follow Iraq War	—	—	—	-0.026 (0.205)
Iraq War right	—	—	—	—
Constant	-1.324 (0.151)***	-1.374 (0.156)***	-2.786 (0.576)***	-4.069 (0.693)***
Pseudo-R^2 (N)	0.01 (N = 1,406)	0.01 (N = 1,406)	0.04 (N = 1,380)	0.05 (N = 1,376)

^$p < .10$; *$p < .05$; **$p < .01$. ***$p < .001$. Robust standard errors in parentheses. All models employ probability weighting ("pweight" in Stata).

TABLE 5.A4
Logit Analysis of Likelihood of Believing the Conflict in Iraq is "Going Well,"
as News Source and Party Identification Vary

Independent Variable	Coefficient (Stat. Err.)
Democrat	−0.366 (0.231)
Republican	0.294 (0.237)
Fox primary news source	0.870 (0.385)*
CNN primary news source	−0.527 (0.318)^
Democrat × Fox primary news source	−1.464 (0.589)*
Democrat. × CNN primary news source	1.195 (0.461)**
Republican × Fox primary news source	0.552 (0.577)
Republican × CNN primary news source	0.728 (0.464)
Know U.S. casualty level in Iraq	−0.017 (0.169)
Follow Iraq War	0.097 (0.092)
Iraq right	1.720 (0.188)***
Network news primary news source	−0.175 (0.186)
Internet news primary news source	0.252 (0.184)
Media too critical of president	0.604 (0.118)***
News quality scale	0.167 (0.070)*
Age	−0.006 (0.005)
Education	−0.330 (0.079)***
Male	−0.013 (0.165)
Family income	0.024 (0.041)
Hispanic	−0.305 (0.300)
White	−0.547 (0.358)
African American	−0.657 (0.429)
Asian	−0.701 (0.607)
Ideology	−0.244 (0.093)**
Voted in 2004	0.107 (0.225)
Constant	−0.047 (0.736)
Pseudo-R^2 (N)	0.30 (N = 1,382)

$^p < .10$; $*p < .05$; $**p < .01$. $***p < .001$. Robust standard errors in parentheses. Reported results employ probability weighting ("pweight" in Stata).

APPENDIX 5.3. SURVEY EXPERIMENT QUESTIONS

Ethnicity: What is your race/ethnicity? (Check all that apply): African American/Black, Asian American/Asian, Caucasian/White, Hispanic/Latino, Middle Eastern, Native American, Other.

Campaign Interest: Some people don't pay much attention to political campaigns. How about you? Would you say that you are very much interested (4), somewhat interested (3), not much interested (2), or not at all interested (1) in the political campaigns this year?

Self Ideology Rating: Many people describe their political views as liberal, conservative or centrist. How would you describe your political views, or haven't you given it much thought?: Extremely Conservative (-3), Conservative (-2), Centrist, but leaning conservative (-1), Centrist (0), Centrist, but leaning liberal (1), Liberal (2), Extremely liberal (3), or haven't give it much thought (recoded to 0)?

Ideology of Treatment Outlet: How would you characterize the political orientation (if any) of [CNN]/[Fox] (*separate questions*), or haven't you given it much thought?: Extremely Conservative, Conservative, Centrist, but leaning conservative, Centrist, Centrist, but leaning liberal, Liberal, Extremely liberal, or haven't give it much thought? (Same coding as above.) (Note: for the combined indicator, we employ the ideology rating of the outlet to which participants were exposed.)

Party ID: What do you consider to be your party affiliation? Strong Democrat (7), Weak Democrat (6), Independent—Lean Democrat (5), Independent (4), Independent—Lean Republican (3), Weak Republican (2), Strong Republican (1), Other Political Party (recoded to 4), No Political Affiliation (recoded to 4).

Political Knowledge Scale: The scale includes responses to 10 questions: (1) Who has the final responsibility to decide if a law is constitutional or not?; (2/3) Which political party has the most members in the United States [House of Representatives]/[Senate]?; (4) In order for an international treaty to become law in the United States, who, other than the President, must approve it?; (5) What percentage of members of the U.S. Senate and House are necessary to override a presidential veto?; (6) What are the first ten amendments to the Constitution called?; (7)Who is the Speaker of the U.S. House of Representatives?; (8) Who is the majority leader of the U.S. Senate?; (9) Who is the Chief Justice of the Supreme Court?; (10) Who was Vice-president of the United States when Bill Clinton was President? Each respondent's score represents the number of questions answered correctly, with the resulting scale running from 0 to 10 ($\mu = 5.59$, $\sigma = 2.30$).

Appendix 5.4. Key Pew Survey Questions

Fox, CNN, Network News, or Internet Primary News Source: How have you been getting most of your news about national and international issues. . . . From television, from newspapers, from radio, from magazines, or from the Internet? IF 'TELEVISION' AS EITHER 1ST OR 2ND RESPONSE, ASK: Do you get most of your news about national and international issues from: Local news programming, ABC Network news, CBS Network news; NBC Network news; CNN Cable news, The Fox News Cable Channel, DK/Refused.

Party ID: In politics today, do you consider yourself a Republican, Democrat, or independent?

Ideology: In general, would you describe your political views as. . . Very conservative, Conservative, Moderate, Liberal, or Very liberal?

Voted in 2004: In last year's presidential election between George W. Bush and John Kerry, did things come up that kept you from voting, or did you happen to vote?

Family Income: Last year, that is, in 2004, what was your total family income from all sources, before taxes? Just stop me when I get to the right category: < $10,000, $10,000–$20,000, $20,000–$30,000, $30,000–$40,000, $40,000–$50,000, $50,000–$75,000, $75,000–$100,000, $100,000–$150,000, > $150,000.

Education: What is the last grade or class that you completed in school? Coded: 1 = None, or grade 1–8, 2 = High school incomplete (Grades 9–11), 3 = High school graduate (Grade 12 or GED certificate or technical, trade, or vocational school AFTER high school), 4 = Some college, no 4-year degree (including associate degree), 5 = College graduate (B.S., B.A., or other 4-year degree), 6 = Postgraduate training or professional schooling after college (e.g., toward a master's degree or Ph.D.; law or medical school)

Ethnicity: Are you, yourself, of Hispanic origin or descent, such as Mexican, Puerto Rican, Cuban, or some other Spanish background? IF NOT HISPANIC, ASK: What is your race? Are you white, black, Asian, or some other?

Iraq War Right: Do you think the U.S. made the right decision or the wrong decision in using military force against Iraq? Recoding: 0 = wrong decision, .5 = don't know, 1 = right decision.

Follow Iraq War: Now I will read a list of some stories covered by news organizations this past month. As I read each item, tell me if you happened to follow this news story very closely, fairly closely, not too closely, or not at all closely: News about the current situation in Iraq.

Know U.S. Casualty Level in Iraq: Since the start of military action in Iraq, about how many U.S. soldiers have been killed? To the best of your knowledge, has it been under 500, 500–1,000, 1,000–2,000, or more than 2,000?: Under 500, 500–1,000, 1,000–2,000, More than 2,000, Don't know/Refused. Recoding: 1 = 1,000–2,000 (correct response), 0 = all other responses.

News Quality Scale: Constructed from four questions: (1) In general, do you think news organizations get the facts straight, or do you think that their stories and reports are often inaccurate? Coded: 1 = get the facts straight, 0 = stories often inaccurate, .5 = "don't know"; (2) In presenting the news dealing with political and social issues, do you think that news organizations deal fairly with all sides, or do they tend to favor one side? Coded: 1 = Deal fairly with all sides, 0 = Tend to favor one side, .5 = Don't know/Refused; (3) In general, do you think news organizations are pretty independent, or are they often influenced by powerful people and organizations? Coded: 1 = Pretty independent, 0 = Often influenced by powerful people and organizations, .5 = Don't know/Refused; and (4) In general, do you think news organizations pay too much attention to GOOD NEWS, too much attention to BAD NEWS, or do they mostly report the kinds of stories they should be covering? Coded: 1 = Report the kinds of stories they should be covering, 0 = Too much attention to [good or bad] news, 5 = Don't know/Refused. The elements were combined to form a 0–4 scale (μ = 1.14, σ = 1.13).

"Republicans More Correct" Questions: (1) Has the [Republican/ Democratic Party] become too conservative, too liberal, or is it about right on social issues such as homosexuality and abortion? (2) [D]o you think the [Republican/ Democratic Party] has become too conservative, too liberal, or is it about right on economic issues such as taxes and government programs? (3) [D]o you think the [Republican/ Democratic Party] is too tough, not tough enough, or about right in its approach to foreign policy and national security issues? Recoded (each question): 1 = about right, 0 = all other responses. Summary scales created by subtracting Democratic score from Republican score, yielding three variables running from −1 to 1, where −1 = Democrats more right, 0 = both parties equal, and 1 = Republicans more right.

News Outlet Favorability Questions: Now I'd like your opinion of some groups and organizations in the news. (First,) would you say your overall opinion of . . . (INSERT ITEM) is very favorable, mostly favorable, mostly unfavorable, or very unfavorable?: (1) Network television news such as ABC, NBC and CBS, (2) The daily newspaper you are most familiar with, (3) Large nationally influential newspapers such as the *New York Times* and the Washington Post, (4) Local television news, (5) Cable news networks such as CNN, Fox News Channel and MSNBC. Recoding (for each question): 1 = very unfavorable, 2 = mostly unfavorable, 2.5 = never heard of/can't rate, 3 = mostly favorable, 4 = very favorable.

Media Too Critical of President: Do you think the press has been too critical of the Bush Administration policies and performance so far, not critical enough or do you think that the press has handled this about right? Recoding: 1 = not critical enough, 2 = about right or don't know/refused, 3 = press too critical.

Appendix 5.5. Investigating the Correlates of News Outlet Preferences

In this appendix, we investigate the correlates of choosing to rely on Fox or CNN for news about politics and international affairs. We begin with preferences for watching Fox (see logit analyses in models 1–4 in table 5.A3 in appendix 5.2). Our first analysis (model 1 in table 5.A3) investigates the effects on network preferences of being liberal, conservative, Republican or Democrat. The results indicate that Republicans and conservatives are significantly more likely to rely on Fox, while being liberal or a Democrat has no significant effect on Fox watching. We next (in model 2) add three binary causal variables to our base model, derived from questions asking respondents about the appropriateness of the Democratic and Republican party positions on (1) national security and foreign policy, (2) economic policies (e.g., government spending and taxes), and (3) social issues (e.g., abortion and gay rights).[23] The results indicate that only attitudes regarding the relative appropriateness of the two parties' economic policy positions significantly influence the tendency to prefer Fox.[24]

---

[23]For each issue area, we subtracted the Democratic from the Republican "appropriateness" variable, to yield a scale (running from −1 to 1) measuring whether the respondent thinks one or the other party has a relatively more correct position on the issue. (See appendix 5.4 for question wording and coding of key casual variables employed in our survey analyses.)

[24]We replicated model 2 (not shown), first adding a battery of demographic controls (age, education, income, ethnicity, gender) and then a battery of media consumption preference controls (network TV news, internet news, local TV news, newspapers, CNN). The demographic variables had no discernable effect on respondents' propensity to watch Fox, or on the three relative correctness indicators. As one might expect, each of the media consumption preference indicators was highly significant and negatively correlated with propensity to rely on Fox. However, none mediated the effect of the issue correctness measures.

Next (in model 3 of table 5.A3), we add several indicators of attitudes toward the media. Perhaps unsurprisingly, while attitudes regarding the overall quality of the news media have no effect, nearly all of the specific media outlet favorability indicators included in this analysis significantly affect news consumption preferences. Believing the news media are too critical of President Bush also positively influences the propensity to prefer Fox, though the coefficient is insignificant. *None* of the aforementioned relative partisan issue correctness variables remains significant.

Finally (in model 4), we drop the highly insignificant news quality scale and add several indicators of knowledge about and attitudes toward the war in Iraq. These include dummies measuring whether the respondent: (1) reports following the Iraq conflict (fairly or very) closely (2) knows the approximate number of U.S. casualties, and (3) believes invading Iraq was the right thing to do. The latter question represents the best available indicator of retrospective evaluations of the conflict, as distinct from contemporaneous estimates of the war's progress.[25] In fact, none of these indicators significantly influences respondents' propensity to prefer Fox; as before, neither does preferring the Republican Party's policies regarding national security and foreign affairs.

We replicated model 4 (not shown) without the Iraq and foreign policy variables, except whether or not invading Iraq was the right thing to do. The Iraq attitude indicator remained insignificant. In other words, once general partisanship, ideology, and attitudes toward the news media are controlled, neither a general preference for Republican policies on national security or foreign affairs nor knowledge of and attitudes toward the war significantly predict respondents' propensities to prefer Fox for news about politics and international affairs. These results indicate that attitudes toward the mainstream news media and partisan or ideological predispositions mediate respondents' propensity to prefer Fox far more than do attitudes regarding Iraq.

Turning to CNN (see logit analyses in models 5–8 in table 5.A3, which replicate models 1–4 with preference for CNN as the dependent variable), the key results are similar to those for Fox. Hence, we do not discuss the CNN results in similar detail. There are, however, several differences. Most notably, interest in Iraq is positively associated with preferring CNN, while being liberal is negatively related to a preference for CNN. Attitudes about the overall quality of the mainstream news media here matter more than specific outlet favorability ratings. However, factual knowledge about and attitudes toward Iraq have no discernable effect on propensity to watch CNN. Overall, the pseudo-R^2 values on the fully

---

[25]Of course, contemporaneous estimates influence post hoc retrospective evaluations. The two indicators correlate at .57, indicating that while reasonably strongly related to one another, they are not substitutes.

specified models (4 and 8) suggest that the causal variables offer only about half as much predictive power for CNN as for Fox. Finally, comparing pseudo-R^2 values across models 3 and 4 for Fox and models 7 and 8 for CNN indicates that the Iraq knowledge and attitudes items add little explanatory power to the models (about +.005 for Fox and +.01 for CNN).

CHAPTER 6

Tidings of Battle

POLARIZING MEDIA AND PUBLIC
SUPPORT FOR THE IRAQ WAR

JUST BEFORE THE 2004 presidential election, the *New York Times Magazine* published an article by veteran reporter Ron Suskind titled "Faith, Certainty and the Presidency of George W. Bush." In it, the author recounted being criticized by an unnamed member of the Bush administration for overvaluing "judicious study of discernible reality" in the evaluation of policy options. The administration source argued, "That's not the way the world really works anymore. . . . We're an empire now, and when we act, we create our own reality. And while you're studying that reality—judiciously, as you will—we'll act again, creating other new realities, which you can study too, and that's how things will sort out" (Suskind 2004).

Scholars too have often disagreed about the impact of "reality" on government policy, particularly in the arena of foreign policy. As noted in chapter 1, scholars have long debated whether public support for the overseas use of military force is shaped more by political rhetoric and wrangling or by the ebb and flow of actual events (e.g., Lippmann 1934; Almond 1950; Rosenau 1961; Brody 1991; Baum 2003; Feaver and Gelpi 2004; Holsti 2004).

In chapter 3, we investigated U.S. uses of military force between 1979 and 2003. We found that communication effects on public attitudes emerge independently from, or at least in addition to, the "facts on the ground." However, because those data were limited to 60-day windows surrounding each use of force, we were only able to observe the short-term effects of communication and actual events.

In this chapter we investigate the effects of political rhetoric and real world events over a considerably longer time frame, well beyond the initial "rally period" of a military conflict. We begin with a narrative discussion of media coverage and public opinion regarding a series of high-profile events during the Iraq War. The primary purpose is to provide some context to the issues and events pertinent to the hypothesis testing that we undertake throughout the rest of the chapter. Nonetheless, in many instances, the events described in these narratives hold clear implications for our theory and hypotheses. We highlight such patterns and their implications as they arise.

Following our narrative discussion, we test a series of hypotheses concerning longer-term patterns of media coverage, elite rhetoric, and public opinion regarding U.S. foreign policy. To do so, we gathered a daily time series of rhetoric regarding military issues in general, and the war in Iraq in particular. Our data include rhetoric by members of both political parties, including members of Congress (MCs) and the Bush administration, appearing on *CBS Evening News, NBC Nightly News*, and the Fox News Channel's *Special Report with Brit Hume*, from August 2004 through February 2007.[1]

To complement this analysis, we assembled a parallel weekly time series on public attitudes toward the conflict in Iraq. These data allow us to investigate longer-term patterns in news coverage and their effects on public opinion, as well as to more directly compare communication effects with the effects of actual events on the ground over a relatively long time period. Doing so allows us to pit our theory against so-called "reality-based" explanations on the traditional turf of the latter arguments. This makes finding independent communication effects a particularly challenging test for our theory.

These data allow an additional set of tests of several of our media and opinion hypotheses. On the media side, this includes Iraq War–specific variants of several of our core predictions. Because the war in Iraq is closely associated with the Bush administration, we equate rhetorical support for the conflict with support for the administration, and vice versa. So, in applying the general hypotheses from chapter 2 to the Iraq War case, praise of the war or the administration's handling of it by a Democrat would represent *cross*-party praise, while criticism by those same Democrats would represent cross-party criticism. Similarly, praise of the war by a Republican would represent *intraparty* praise, while Republican criticism would constitute intraparty criticism. Consequently, we test the Oversampled Presidential Party Criticism hypothesis (H1), as well as derive a war-specific corollary, termed the Negativity hypothesis (H1a), which predicts that net of their actual valence (positive or negative), the onset of major events in Iraq will be associated with relatively larger increases in negative than in positive coverage of the war.

We also test the Media Partisanship hypothesis (H3), which predicts that coverage on Fox will be significantly more pro-war and anti-Democratic, and significantly less anti-Republican, than coverage on the other networks. On the opinion side, we test the Partisan (H4), Costly (H5), and Combined (H6) Credibility hypotheses. Through these predictions, we seek to bridge the theoretical divide that frequently separates

---

[1] We were unable to acquire equivalent data for CNN and ABC.

research on the short- and longer-term relationships between media coverage of and public support for war.

A Review of Several Major Events in Iraq

Data and Methods

We begin by providing some of the context within which the movements in elite rhetoric, media reporting, and public opinion documented throughout this chapter took place. Hence, we briefly review a series of major substantive developments in the Iraq War beginning in summer 2004, as well as patterns of rhetoric and opinion surrounding them. We selected these developments based on a review of major events during the Iraq conflict (henceforth the "Iraq event" series). To generate the Iraq event series, we conducted a search of timelines of the Iraq War assembled by the Department of Defense, news organizations like the BBC, and online sites like Wikipedia, and selected the most important events from each. After culling these listings, we assembled a list of 45 major battles and military operations, mass casualty events, diplomatic or political developments, arrests, trials, or executions.[2] We then asked a group of 39 scholars with expertise in American foreign policy to rate each event on a scale ranging from −10 (disaster) to 10 (great success), taking into account both the valence of the event (positive vs. negative) and its importance to the overall status of the conflict.[3] (In appendix 6.1 we present the

[2]In the vast majority of instances, media and public attention to major events in Iraq took place in close proximity to the unfolding of the events. However, in several cases (e.g., Haditha) there were substantial delays between the time an event took place and the onset of substantial media and public attention to it. Because there is no clear ex ante means of predicting the nature or duration of such delays, for our empirical analyses we have elected to treat the actual date an event took place as the "start date" for purposes of investigating media and public opinion reactions. To the extent that the media and opinion responses are delayed for several events, this should weaken rather than strengthen our results. We therefore consider this the most conservative alternative available.

[3]We solicited responses from 125 individuals. Our response rate was thus 31%. The exact instructions were as follows:

> For each of the events below, please indicate on the −10 to 10 scale whether, from the U.S. perspective, the event was harmful or beneficial to the prospects of a successful outcome to the situation in Iraq (as you yourself define "success"). Scores of −10 should indicate that the event was particularly disastrous, with serious harm to the prospects of success; scores of −5 should be moderately harmful; scores of 0 are neutral; scores of +5 are moderately helpful, while scores of +10 should indicate a particularly beneficial event that substantially increased the prospects for a successful outcome in Iraq. If you would like to look up more information about the incident before answering, we have

complete list of events, as well as the average expert appraisal of each event.)

For the following narrative discussion, we focus on those incidents the experts identified as particularly significant in helping or hindering American prospects for victory in Iraq. Specifically, we selected all events receiving an average score of *at least* plus or minus four on the −10 to +10 impact scale (that is, −10 to −4 or +4 to +10). In each instance, we summarize the event in question and review the nature and extent of elite rhetoric surrounding it.

We draw the primary news content data for this and all subsequent analyses in the present chapter from an extensive analysis of media content conducted by Media Tenor.[4] As noted, the data extend from August 2004 through February 2007 and include every valenced (positive, negative, or neutral) statement about partisan figures that appeared on Fox's *Special Report with Brit Hume*, NBC *Nightly News*, and CBS *Evening News*. These data also allow us to categorize the evaluations by topic area, including whether or not the evaluation concerns Iraq. For our analyses, we employ all evaluations of and by partisans—that is, individuals identifiable as Democrats or Republicans—that either explicitly address Iraq or concern issues involving U.S. military activities.[5]

Event 1: Iraqi National Elections

One of the events our experts rated most positively occurs near the beginning of our sample, on January 30, 2005, when millions of Iraqis voted in their first free elections. Despite the specter of violence at the polls and a boycott by Sunni groups within Iraq, our experts gave the elections an average score of +4, indicating they viewed it as one of the

---

included links to external web pages (note that reading this supplemental material is optional).

As a validity check, we also submitted the survey to the readers of the online military affairs blog Intel Dump, run by Phil Carter. The results were highly correlated, giving us greater confidence that we have good measures of the impact of these events.

[4]Media Tenor is a German firm, founded in 1994, that describes itself as "the first international institute specializing in continuous and comprehensive media evaluation." Media Tenor codes the source, target, subject, explicit evaluation, and other related information for each evaluative statement on the programs. Data were unavailable for NBC from May 17 through June 7, 2005, for CBS from April 7 through 8, 2005, and for Fox from September 1 through 3, 2005, and May 29 through June 8, 2006. In the narrative section, we also include verbatim quotes taken from the UCLA Communication Studies Archive.

[5]We include the latter category because most discussion of U.S. military actions appearing in the media during this period dealt with Iraq or related subjects, either directly or indirectly. Omitting these observations would thus exclude a great deal of pertinent media coverage.

two most helpful events in the entire time series for the future prospects of Iraq.

News accounts immediately surrounding the election were also hopeful and generally upbeat, although normally with cautions attached along the lines of "much work remains. . . ." For example, that evening's report on ABC's *World News with Charles Gibson* acknowledged the high drama of the moment: "Not since they tore down that famous statue of Saddam Hussein has Iraq experienced something so powerful, so dramatic." However, Gibson cautioned against expecting any large changes quickly: "But today it is beginning to dawn on people here that things are not going to change overnight."

Following the election, continued insurgent attacks appear to have diminished the optimism expressed by reporters. For instance, a commentator on a Los Angeles local TV newscast (KABC *Eyewitness News at 11*, February 12, 2005) observed: "In Iraq the election process may be drawing to a close. But insurgents are continuing their relentless campaign of violence. Today a suicide car bombing near Baghdad left 17 Iraqis dead and more than 20 injured." Later that week (KNBC *Early Today*, February 14, 2005) another report observed: "Today, we begin with Iraq where the winners of the country's historic democratic elections now face the task of forming a government as the daily cycle of violence there continues."

In figures 6.1 and 6.2, we attempt to embed these anecdotes within the broader context of news coverage of the election. The graphics, drawn from the core Media Tenor data set employed in this chapter, plot overtime trends in Iraq- and military-related evaluations of each political party from the evening newscasts of CBS and NBC (henceforth "the networks") and from the Fox News Channel's *Special Report with Brit Hume* (henceforth "Fox"), respectively.[6] While not strictly measuring evaluations of the situation in Iraq itself, these evaluations do indicate the degree to which the parties were being praised or criticized for their actions or statements related to the war.

Reviewing figures 6.1 and 6.2 for the January–February 2005 period, it is apparent that the elections had far less impact on the mix of elite rhetoric appearing on either the networks or Fox than the preceding year's elections in the United States, when we observe far larger spikes in both positive and negative—but especially negative—coverage of rhetoric from both parties. Nonetheless, comparing coverage in January 2005 with that in the following month, we do see evidence of a shift from highly negative evaluations in January to a relatively larger proportion of

[6]Note that our data set has several gaps where Media Tenor data were unavailable, particularly in 2007 for Fox. Because of these gaps, we were unable to include the late 2007 data shown here for the networks and for Fox in the time-series analysis reported later in this chapter.

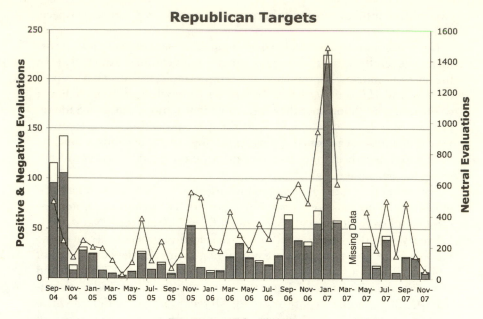

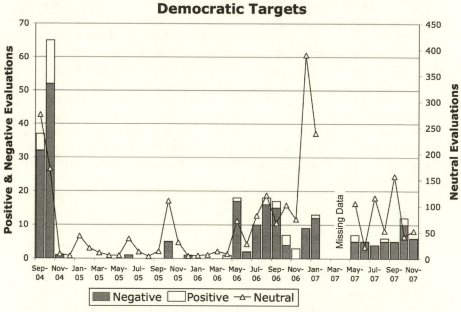

FIGURE 6.1. Network Iraq- and Military-Related Evaluations from All Sources

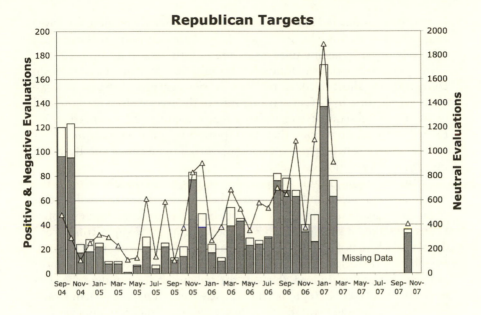

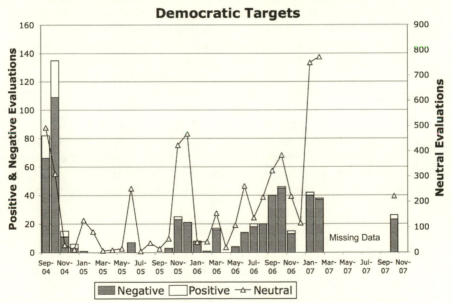

FIGURE 6.2. Fox Iraq- and Military-Related Evaluations from All Sources

neutral evaluations in February. Indeed, in February we observe far fewer evaluations with any valence at all. This change appears to have been relatively durable, lasting until a spike in negativity around June 2005.

In Congress, optimism following the election appears to have been comparatively short-lived. In the bottom right graphic in figure 6.3, we chart the rhetoric by MCs regarding Iraq in the week before the vote and in the three subsequent weeks. This figure includes all valenced, Iraq-related congressional floor rhetoric reported in the *Congressional Record*, coded for whether the speaker supported or opposed the Bush administration's position on the war.[7]

As the top right graphic in figure 6.3 shows, immediately prior to the elections, Republican and Democratic rhetoric was polarized, with Democrats offering a large number of highly negative speeches, while Republicans presented a smaller number of speeches strongly supporting President Bush's Iraq policies. In the week immediately following the elections, Republican rhetoric in Congress spiked dramatically and became almost universally positive. Indeed, this was the only week surrounding the election in which *positive* Republican rhetoric exceeded *negative* Democratic rhetoric. The change was fleeting, however, as Democrats appeared to redouble their rhetorical assault on the president's position in subsequent weeks, with their critiques far surpassing Republican support for the president, in terms of both the number of speeches and their negative valence.

In sum, media reaction to the Iraqi elections is best characterized as positive yet moderate. Rather than reversing valence, the primary media response to this event was a shift from overwhelmingly negative coverage to somewhat more neutral coverage (recall the patterns in figures 6.1 and 6.2). This shift was relatively short-lived, however, with congressional rhetoric gradually returning to, and eventually exceeding, prior levels of criticism. The Iraq election appears to have exerted a larger yet considerably more fleeting effect on rhetoric by MCs, who within two weeks had returned to their pre-election patterns of partisan polarization on the war.

Event 2: Fall 2005 Suicide Bombing Campaign

In mid-September 2005, Al Qaeda in Iraq initiated a surge of violence beginning with a suicide car bombing in Baghdad's Oruba Square that killed 114 people. Many other attacks followed in rapid succession. The bombings came on the heels of a panic two weeks earlier in which rumors of impending suicide bombings caused a stampede among Shia pilgrims, killing more than 1,000.

---

[7]These data are from Howell and Kriner (2008). We thank Will Howell and Doug Kriner for graciously sharing their data with us.

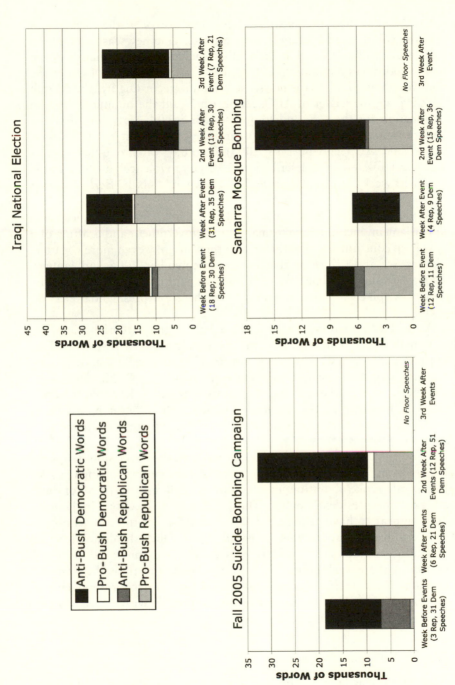

FIGURE 6.3. Floor Rhetoric by Members of Congress Regarding Major Events in Iraq

Coverage of these events stressed not only horror at the carnage but also the volume and brutality of the attacks. One newscast decried the "wave of deadly violence in Iraq" that included "more than a dozen highly-coordinated bombings in Baghdad . . . killing at least 177 people, and wounding 570." In the newscast, an audio recording by Abu Musab Al-Zarqawi, the leader of Al Qaeda in Iraq, said the bombings were in "retaliation for the U.S. and Iraqi offensive in Tal Afar" and declared "all-out war on Shiites, Iraqi troops, and the government" (KABC Channel 4 *News at 5*, September 14, 2005). Two days later, one Los Angeles area local TV newscast described the "surge of violence" as "one of the bloodiest weeks in Baghdad since the war began" (KNBC *Early Today* at 4:30 a.m., September 16, 2005).

As violence in Iraq appeared to escalate despite political advancements in Parliament, including the formation of a government and drafting of a new Iraqi constitution, elite rhetoric on the war grew even more negative. Figures 6.1 and 6.2 show that between September 2005 and January 2006, the volume and negativity of Iraq evaluations on both Fox and the networks spiked to levels not seen since the 2004 presidential election cycle.

As the bottom left graphic in figure 6.3 illustrates, MC rhetoric in the aftermath of the bombings (and the tragic stampede two weeks earlier) appears consistent with an environment characterized by a tightening elasticity of reality (recall the discussion in chapter 2). Within the halls of Congress, we saw the first serious instance in which Republicans criticized the president on the war more frequently than they supported him (although subsequent weeks reverted to the prior pattern of Republican support).

The Democrats, on the other hand, increased their cohesion in opposing the war. Two weeks after the start of the bombing campaign, 51 Democrats spoke about Iraq on the floor of Congress; nearly all of them attacked the president's policy. Thus, if the Iraqi elections in January 2005 appear to have produced a lull in criticism of the war as people waited to see if democracy might assuage the conflict, the dramatic spike in violence in late summer 2005 appears to have convinced critics of the war that any such hopes had been in vain. By this time, the elasticity of reality had constricted considerably, making it easier for opponents of the war to frame events in a negative light, especially with regard to statements actually appearing on the news.

Event 3: Samarra Bombing

As noted, Al Qaeda in Iraq declared "all-out war on Shiites, Iraqi troops, and the government" in fall 2005. That campaign scored perhaps its

greatest success on February 22, 2006, with a bomb attack on the important Shia shrine in Samarra (the Al Askari Mosque). The attack unleashed
waves of sectarian violence and pushed the country to (and perhaps past)
the brink of civil war. This event received the single largest and most
negative score in our expert survey, indicating that our experts believed it
was the most ominous occurrence in our entire time frame.

The tone of coverage following the blast reflected the perceived seri-
ousness of the threat of civil war. As one commentator put it on the PBS
Newshour the day after the attack, "What happened in Samarra has been
a major turning point for the war in Iraq, and now going back to the
situation even before yesterday is a very tall order . . . " (February 23,
2006). By the weekend, commentators on Fox were also decrying the
situation, saying, for instance, "I think we'd all agree it has been a terri-
ble week in Iraq," and asking, "[A]re we going down the road to civil
war?" (*Sunday with Chris Wallace*, 8 a.m., February 26, 2006).

Somewhat surprisingly, such concerns did not immediately translate
into larger volumes of negative news coverage of the war. As we see in
figures 6.1 and 6.2, neither the volume nor the negativity of coverage
spiked in the immediate aftermath of the attacks. Rather, both continued
at similar levels as in prior months. Perhaps because the Shiite response
to the attacks did not immediately seem to deliver on the threat of civil
war (with levels of internecine violence instead gradually escalating over
the next several months), this event produced relatively little direct impact
on aggregate news coverage, despite its apparent severity in retrospect.

The story in Congress, shown in the top right graphic in figure 6.3, was
similar, with members actually reducing their praise and criticism of the
president on Iraq the week immediately after the attack, before returning
to their prior pattern of Republican support and Democratic opposition
the subsequent week (although with substantially increased volume).

Events 4–6: 2006 Troop Misconduct Allegations

In March 2006, *Time* magazine published its bombshell report of an alleged November 19, 2005 massacre of 24 Iraqi civilians in the town of
Haditha. The military's initial account of the massacre, which had actually
occurred the prior November, attributed 15 of the civilian deaths to an
insurgent bomb blast, and a further eight "insurgent" deaths to the U.S.
Marines returning fire. The explosive *Time* account, on the other hand,
alleged that according to eyewitnesses and local officials, "the civilians
who died in Haditha on Nov. 19 were killed not by a roadside bomb but
by the Marines themselves, who went on a rampage in the village after the
attack, killing 15 unarmed Iraqis in their homes, including seven women
and three children" (McGirk 2006). The killings were widely condemned,

particularly in the international media, and soon drew comparisons to U.S. military actions in Vietnam, and particularly the infamous March 1968 My Lai massacre of civilians (Pyle 2006). An AP reporter explicitly made the comparison, saying, "Nearly four decades later, the notorious name of that hamlet—My Lai—has been summoned from memory again, as the U.S. military investigates allegations of mass civilian killings by a group of Marines in the western Iraqi town of Haditha" (Pyle 2006).

The story rhetorically reopened earlier wounds related to military misconduct and abuse of prisoners at the Abu Ghraib prison in Iraq. Much as with that story, reporters questioned whether the Pentagon had perpetrated a cover-up in the case, and the degree to which the chain of command had failed. As figures 6.1 and 6.2 show, the stories coincided with a large spike in negative Iraq coverage in March 2006.

In Congress, the most newsworthy response came in May 2006, when Representative John Murtha (D-OH), himself a former Marine, disputed the official account at a news conference, stating, "There was no firefight, there was no IED [improvised explosive device] that killed these innocent people. Our troops overreacted because of the pressure on them, and they killed innocent civilians in cold blood" (McIntyre 2006).[8] Charges were officially pressed against eight Marines in December 2006. However, seven of the eight were either acquitted or saw the charges against them dropped.[9] Similar allegations of misbehavior by American troops surfaced in April (Hamdania) and March (Al-Mahmudiyah) 2006, which critics seized on as evidence of a pattern of misbehavior by U.S. forces in Iraq. In the Hamdania case, U.S. Marines allegedly abducted an Iraqi civilian from his house, killed him, and then placed components and spent AK-47 cartridges near his body to make it appear he was planting an IED. In the Al-Mahmudiyah case, a squad of U.S. soldiers allegedly gang-raped a 14-year-old Iraqi girl, then murdered her and most of the members of her family to cover up the crime. Figure 6.4 tracks the volume of media coverage of each scandal over time.[10]

Interestingly, in all three instances, the largest media impact occurred literally months after the actual scandalous behavior occurred. This lag in coverage helps demonstrate, writ small, a similar elasticity of reality pattern as observed in the overall war. In each case, early, "official" accounts were taken at face value by reporters and relayed to the public as

---

[8]Unfortunately, the Howell and Kriner data employed in our discussions of the first three events do not include the time period when the media publicized them (see discussion below), or the period surrounding the 2006 midterm election (event 7).

[9]The final Marine, Staff Sgt. Frank Wuterich, pled not guilty to charges of voluntary manslaughter. Wuterich and another accused Marine, Lance Corporal Justin Sharratt, subsequently sued Murtha for defamation (Ganassi 2008).

[10]We retrieved these data from Lexis-Nexis archives of wire-service content.

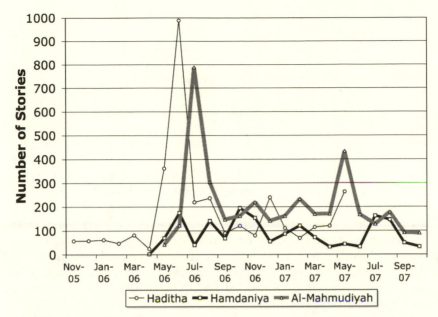

FIGURE 6.4. Monthly Wire Service Stories Mentioning Haditha, Hamdaniya, or Al-Mahmudiyah Scandals

Note: Data are derived from searches of Lexis-Nexis news wire services index for 18 months after the approximate date of event. Because the scandals were often referred to specifically using the geographic area in which the event occurred, the tallies include some stories unrelated to the scandalous occurrences. Because the city names are transliterated, we used several alternative spellings of each scandal as search terms.

an accurate portrayal of events on the ground. Also in each case, before reporters could challenge the initial account and break the story, they needed to invest additional time and resources, as well as identify outside sources. However, once the media publicized the new, more critical version of the story, coverage expanded exponentially.

These patterns are also consistent with one of the core assumptions underlying our theory. That is, the objective reality of these events mattered little for elite rhetoric or public attitudes until the media challenged the official versions of the stories, offering far more negatively framed narratives. In each case, as noted, this took place several months after the event occurred. In other words, the public had no capacity to respond to reality—indeed, it was either unaware of it or in some cases aware yet mollified by the unchallenged and relatively benign official versions of the stories—until the media offered a framed representation of events that challenged the official version. As shown in figure 6.4, coverage of all three cases subsequently continued for months as formal charges were filed and as developments unfolded in the resulting court cases.

Such coverage clearly contributed to the solidifying of the "failed war" narrative that appears to have predominated among journalists and the public. As we will see, this narrative proved difficult to challenge, thereby presumably slowing the media's recognition of the success of the surge (at a minimum in reducing casualties) later in the conflict.

Event 7: Regime Change in Washington

Figures 6.1 and 6.2 reveal that in the months leading up to the 2006 congressional midterm elections, the partisan attacks and criticism regarding Iraq appearing in the news reached levels unseen since the 2004 presidential election. As Democrats aggressively campaigned to retake control of Congress for the first time since the 1994 "Republican Revolution," they used the Republican handling of the war in Iraq as a centerpiece of their national message strategy. In the words of future Speaker of the House Nancy Pelosi (D-CA), "This election is about Iraq. If indeed it turns out the way that people expect it to turn out, the American people will have spoken, and they will have rejected the course of action the president is on" (quoted in Sandlow 2006).

In the aftermath of the Republican loss of both houses of Congress, most analysts attributed the outcome to public dissatisfaction with Republican management of the war. As MSNBC commentator Tucker Carlson observed in his post-election summation, "Things could not have been worse for the Republican Party and the reason for that can be summed up in a single word: Iraq" (Tucker Carlson, November 13, 2006). According to the 2006 General Exit Poll, 89% of voters said that Iraq was at least "somewhat" important in their congressional vote.[11]

Following the election, President Bush immediately signaled a shift in U.S. policy when he announced the resignation of Secretary of Defense Donald Rumsfeld. The resignation was surprising in part because "Democrats had been calling . . . for Rumsfeld to resign for months upon months; some of them for years" (CNN Newsroom November 8, 2006). As Democrats took over the reins of power, they made it clear to the Republican administration that they were expecting a change in Iraq policy, and particularly an acceleration of American troop withdrawal from the troubled country.

To their great consternation, President Bush instead announced that he was increasing, not decreasing, U.S. troop strength in Iraq as part of a larger counterinsurgency strategy that became known as "the surge," de-

[11]Twenty-one percent said "somewhat important," 32% said "very important," and 36% said "extremely important." Majorities disapproved of the war (56%) and thought the United States should withdraw some (25%) or all (29%) U.S. troops from Iraq (Exit Poll 2006).

spite critics' efforts to describe it as an escalation. As figures 6.1 and 6.2 show, the reaction to Bush's January announcement was swift and over-whelmingly negative. In fact, the volume and tone of reaction that month represented the single most negative month of evaluations in our entire 2004–2007 series, surpassing in negativity even the rhetoric surrounding the 2004 general election. However, unlike in 2004, the reaction was overwhelmingly negative on both Fox and the networks.

Moreover, even after it became clear that the surge had succeeded in improving the security situation in Iraq, television news outlets responded by decreasing overall Iraq coverage, rather than by increasing positive coverage. However, figures 6.1 and 6.2 show that the decrease in volume of coverage appears to have been greater on the networks than on Fox. The overall decline in coverage is consistent with our negativity assumption (see chapter 2), according to which journalists prefer stories involv-ing partisans attacking each other to those in which they praise each other. Consistent with this conclusion, in a separate analysis presented in figure 6.5, we see that as U.S. casualties dropped precipitously through-out 2007, Iraq coverage on the networks dropped to about one-fifth of its initial volume, while on Fox coverage dropped by half.

As noted in our discussion of the surge in chapter 2, this partisan and journalistic skepticism continued even after several months of apparent gains on the ground in Iraq. Interestingly, skepticism about the surge extended to our panel of foreign policy experts. When polled about the surge's impact on the prospects for a coalition victory in Iraq several months following its implementation (in July and August 2007), the ex-perts gave the strategy an average score of 0.14 (on a -10 to $+10$ scale), indicating they viewed it as slightly positive, but largely inconsequential or neutral in impact. Their skepticism paled in comparison to that of anti-war politicians and interest groups responding to a favorable report on the surge delivered by General David Petraeus in September 2007. Democratic Representative Rahm Emmanuel (D-IL) criticized Petraeus's report before it came out, complaining, "the Bush administration is cherry-picking the data to support their political objectives. . . . We don't need a report that wins the Nobel Prize for creative statistics or the Pulitzer for fiction." The Democrats' leader in the Senate, Harry Reid (D-NV), delivered a similar pre-trial verdict on the report, saying, "be-fore the report arrives in Congress, it will pass through the White House spin machine, where facts are often ignored or twisted" (quoted in Jaffe 2007).

Some Democrats explicitly based their argument on prior optimistic statements about Iraq that had, they believed, proven inaccurate time after time. As Senator Dick Durbin (D-IL) observed, "President Bush is preparing

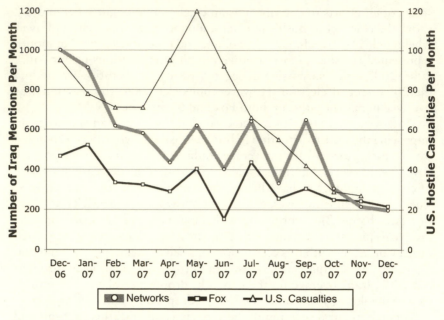

FIGURE 6.5. U.S. Military Casualties in Iraq and Mentions of Iraq on Fox and
Network Evening News Programs

    Note: We conducted searches on transcripts from UCLA's Communication Studies
Archive for keyword "Iraq" on the weekday and weekend evening news programs for
each network and Fox. For Fox, we conducted searches for the program *Special Report
with Brit Hume*. For the networks, we conducted searches for evening news broadcasts of
ABC, CBS, and NBC.

to tell the nation, *once again* [emphasis added], that his strategy in Iraq is
succeeding. . . . The reality is despite heroic efforts by U.S. troops, the
Bush surge is not working. . . . By carefully manipulating the statistics,
the Bush-Petraeus report will try to persuade us that violence in Iraq is
decreasing and thus the surge is working. Even if the figures were right,
the conclusion is wrong" (quoted in Jaffe 2007).

    While some of this rhetoric can undoubtedly be attributed to tempo-
rary partisan expediency, the refusal of these members to acknowledge
evidence of the surge's positive impact on the Iraqi security situation
nonetheless represents strong anecdotal evidence in support of our Event-
Shift Effects corollary hypothesis (H15b). The fact that members explicitly complained about prior misleading frames by the White House in
their dismissal of fresh evidence further illustrates how squandered ex
ante credibility proved difficult for the administration to reclaim, particularly among partisans of the other party.

LONGER-TERM PATTERNS OF ELITE RHETORIC, NEWS COVERAGE, AND EVENTS IN IRAQ

Data and Methods

In this section, we again employ the aforementioned Media Tenor data set. Our public opinion series in turn aggregates results from over 200 different polling questions regarding support for the war in Iraq. We selected questions from 15 different polling organizations, including whether removing Hussein or the result of the war was worth the loss of lives, whether the respondents approved of military action in Iraq, whether the United States did the right thing in going to war, whether respondents supported or opposed the current U.S. military presence in Iraq, whether they favored or opposed having gone to war; whether it was the right decision despite the CIA report on WMDs, whether the war was a mistake, and whether their view of the war was favorable (see Jacobson 2006 for details about the surveys included in this analysis, including question wording and sponsors). The series—which, following Jacobson (2006), we smooth to account for random variations across survey organizations and question formats—includes separate values for Democrats, Republicans and independents.[12] For our dependent variables, we employ the difference in average Iraq support between weeks (or *time* periods) t and $t + 1$. To account for the impact of current support of the war on future support (that is, serial correlation), we include the lagged Iraq support value (at week t) as a control variable.

[12]The aggregated series uses LOESS (that is, locally weighted polynomial regression) smoothing with a bandwidth of .05 to account for variation across survey wordings and organizations. This process fits a series of simple models to localized subsets of the data to build up a function that describes the deterministic part of the variation in the data, point by point. The National Institute of Standards and Technology (NIST 2006) defines the LOESS smoothing process as follows:

> At each point in the data set a low-degree polynomial is fit to a subset of the data, with explanatory variable values near the point whose response is being estimated. The polynomial is fit using weighted least squares, giving more weight to points near the point whose response is being estimated and less weight to points further away. The value of the regression function for the point is then obtained by evaluating the local polynomial using the explanatory variable values for that data point. The LOESS fit is complete after regression function values have been computed for each of the n data points.

We also include as a control a dummy variable, coded 1 during weeks in which one particular form of the question appeared: whether or not the respondent supported going/having gone to war. This is the only question format dummy that proved statistically significant across a series of tests for each individual question format included in the aggregate series.

We employ three main measurements of reality on the ground in Iraq. The first two are U.S. combat deaths, as provided by the Department of Defense, and non-U.S. casualties in Iraq, as reported by Iraqbodycount .org.[13] Our third and most important measure of the objective state of affairs in Iraq is the expert assessment of our aforementioned Iraq event series. Unlike the casualty series, which can only represent "bad" values in differing degrees, with this indicator—which, as noted, consists of a unique rating for each event on a −10 to +10 scale based on its tenor (negative to positive) and importance (low to high)—we attempt to measure both progress and setbacks in Iraq.

In modeling the impact of rhetoric, casualties, and events on public opinion, we faced a difficult modeling decision: how to account for the impacts of these factors over time. On the one hand, they each presumably have some lingering impact beyond the day or week in which they originally occur. On the other, it seems unreasonable to expect that an event or statement will have exactly the same marginal impact two years later as it did initially. To model this process of gradually declining marginal influence, we explicitly incorporate a nonlinear decay function into our indicators. The decay function carries forward 99% of the prior day's value of each variable, and then adds any new value for that day on top of the existing tally. The following day carries forward 99% of the prior day's total and adds on any new value for the next day, and so on. Figure 6.6 illustrates how a hypothetical 10-unit value (representing the cumulative weight of rhetoric or casualties at a given point in time) would decay over the course of a year with no further new values added.

Because we anticipate that news organizations are likely to be relatively more concerned about present developments in choosing their news, we use a slightly different specification for our news selection tests. In these cases, the Iraq event series includes the decay function of only the most recent events. In other words, it does not carry forward the residual value of the prior events when a new event occurs.[14]

To control for general media salience related to the war, we include a daily tally of every mention of "Iraq" in the headline or citation of front-page *New York Times* articles. To control for the state of the economy, we include controls for both the level of consumer sentiment (lagged one period) and inflation (measured as the change in consumer prices). Fi-

---

[13]We use the "minimum" tally from the site, rather than their higher estimate. While estimating non-U.S. casualties in Iraq is a controversial and undoubtedly imprecise exercise, by using the same estimator for the entire series, inflated or deflated levels should cancel out, leaving the relevant change effects intact.

[14]Note that we experimented with a variety of decay functions but selected the 1% daily decay because it outperforms the alternatives in our models and also has compelling face validity.

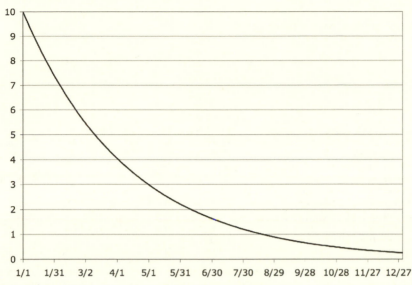

FIGURE 6.6. Illustration of 1/100th Daily Decay Function

nally, we also include dummy variables for the 61 days preceding the 2004 presidential election (which extends back to the first date in our series) and the six months preceding the 2006 midterm elections, as well as for periods of divided government.[15]

RESULTS

Media Coverage Hypotheses

In table 6.1 we begin our analysis by briefly exploring the contours of the data across different actors, outlets, and issue areas. In the first row of the table, we see a surprising discrepancy in the number of evaluations across outlets. Perhaps because of its hour long format and more heavily political focus, during every year in our sample Fox News *Special Report* airs considerably more evaluations of partisans than CBS and NBC combined. On all three outlets, Democrats outnumber Republicans as sources of evaluations, while Republicans outnumber Democrats as the targets of those evaluations. In both cases, Fox is an outlier, with the smallest proportion of Republican sources (perhaps somewhat surprisingly, given

[15]For the midterm election dummy, we experimented with specifications controlling for two through six months prior to the election. The results were strongest for the six-month dummy, which we employ in the final models.

TABLE 6.1
Descriptive Statistics, Media Tenor Data

Type of Observation	CBS	Fox	NBC
Total evaluations[a]	2,519	12,548	3,787
2004[b]	755	3,024	1,164
2005	621	3,249	995
2006	863	4,926	1,217
2007[c]	280	1,349	411
Republican vs. Democratic Party source[d]	48.4% (1,129)	41.2% (6,258)	44.6% (1,920)
Republican vs. Democratic Party targeted	74.9% (2,518)	64.5% (12,544)	74.9% (3,784)
Negative evaluations	72.9% (2,519)	70.2% (12,548)	73.9% (3,787)
Negative evaluations of Republicans	80.4% (1,885)	69.4% (8,096)	79.1% (2,834)
Negative evaluations of Democrats	50.7% (633)	71.7% (4,448)	58.5% (950)
Negative evaluations by Republicans	66.4% (547)	62.2% (2,577)	64.1% (858)
Negative evaluations by Democrats	80.2% (582)	87.2% (3,683)	86.7% (1,064)
Negative evaluations regarding Iraq or U.S. military	88.5% (558)	83.8% (1,923)	89.4% (775)
Negative evaluations by partisans regarding Iraq or U.S. military	88.1% (293)	88.0% (1,175)	88.5% (513)

[a]Whereas Media Tenor's coding also included a substantial number of mentions without an explicit positive or negative evaluation, those nonevaluative statements are excluded from this analysis. For values shown as percentages, corresponding Ns are shown in parentheses.
[b]August–December 2004 only.
[c]January–February 2007 only.
[d]Our data set includes evaluations of Democrats and Republicans by nonpartisan figures.

Fox's conservative reputation) and the highest proportion of Democratic targets (perhaps less surprising).

All three outlets feature similar overall levels of negativity (between 70% and 74% of evaluations). However, consistent with our Media Partisanship hypothesis (H3), Fox and the networks differ significantly ($p < .001$) in the targets of those negative evaluations. Whereas the networks present roughly four times more negative than positive evaluations of Republicans, on Fox the ratio is about seven negative evaluations for every three positive ones. Similarly, evaluations of Democrats are significantly more likely to be negative on Fox than on the networks ($p < .001$), although again, each outlet presents more negative than positive evaluations.

Evaluations by the parties across the outlets are also mostly negative, including more than 60% of evaluations by Republicans and more than 80% of evaluations by Democrats. Somewhat surprisingly—again, given Fox's conservative reputation—Republican rhetoric was less negative ($p < .10$) and Democratic rhetoric more negative ($p < .01$) on Fox. Finally, while evaluations related to Iraq or the U.S. military were overwhelmingly negative on all three outlets, they were significantly less so ($p < .001$) on Fox. Because Fox clearly differs from the networks in its patterns of coverage while the networks largely parallel each other, and in order to simplify the analysis, for the remainder of this chapter we collapse observations from CBS and NBC into a single indicator of network news coverage.

In figure 6.7, we continue exploring the differences between the coverage of Fox and the networks across parties. Beginning with the upper left graphic in the figure, we see that in both venues, the Democrats are nearly uniformly negative in their assessments of President Bush. However, consistent with the Media Partisanship hypothesis (H3), Republican criticism of Bush is significantly less prevalent (proportionately) on Fox relative to the networks, which air nearly identical levels of Republican praise and Republican criticism of the president. The upper right graphic, which repeats this analysis for congressional Democratic targets, is a virtual partisan mirror image of the results for President Bush. Here, Republicans are nearly unanimous in their criticism of Democrats on both Fox and the networks (although slightly more critical on Fox). However, again consistent with the Media Partisanship hypothesis (H3), damaging internal party criticism among Democrats appears more than twice as frequently on Fox (again, proportionately) relative to the networks ($p < .001$).

The middle two graphics in figure 6.7 present evaluations of the administration and president, respectively (excluding self-evaluations). As before, and consistent with the Media Partisanship hypothesis (H3), the networks air a significantly greater proportion of criticism than Fox ($p < .001$). Repeating the analysis for evaluations pertaining to the Iraq War yields a similar though even more sharply negative pattern. In strong support of the Oversampled Presidential Party Criticism hypothesis (H1), nearly three out of every four Iraq-related evaluations of President Bush by his fellow Republicans appearing on the networks are negative. Consistent with the Media Partisanship hypothesis (H3), in turn, Fox presents significantly fewer of these damaging evaluations. Nonetheless, nearly half of all Republican evaluations of President Bush appearing on Fox are negative. Evaluations of Democratic congressional figures are again similar, though the differences are less significant, most likely because of the smaller number of war-related evaluations targeting Democrats.

Of course, thus far we have examined rhetoric in isolation, with relatively little consideration of the events to which the speakers might be responding. In figures 6.9 and 6.10 we test the Negativity hypothesis (H1a), which predicts that major events in Iraq will prompt relatively larger increases in negative than in positive coverage of the war, by examining the relationship between rhetoric and developments in Iraq. We do so through an evaluation-level logit analysis, employing the prior week's discounted expert assessment of the conditions in Iraq to predict whether the current broadcast is likely to air either supportive or critical evaluations

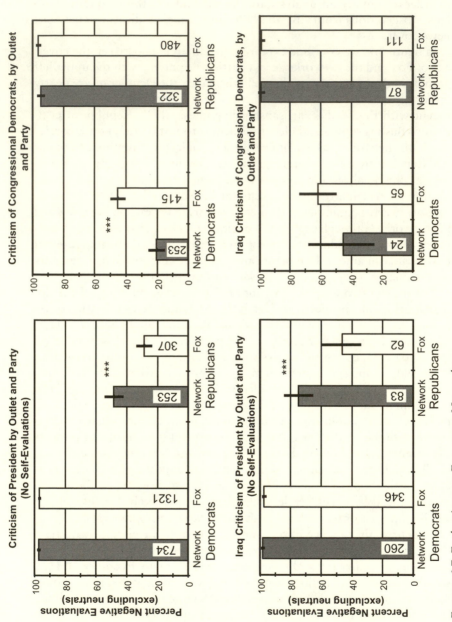

FIGURE 6.7. Evaluations on Fox versus Networks
***$p < .001$. Ns are shown within bars. Vertical black lines denote 95% confidence intervals.

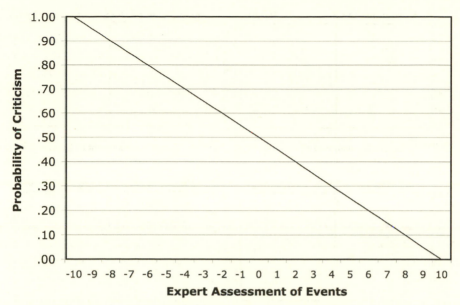

FIGURE 6.8. Predicted Curve If Rhetoric Perfectly Tracked Reality

related to the conflict. The dependent variable is coded 0 if the current broadcast airs praise of the president and 1 if it airs criticism.[16] To allow positive and negative developments in Iraq to vary independently from one another (that is, to have distinct slopes), we include a separate dummy variable accounting only for negative event values. For each of the curves plotted in the several figures, we transform the coefficients (shown in table 6.A1 in appendix 6.2) into probabilities and plot the predicted blend of criticism and praise that results from each positive or negative development in Iraq. Figure 6.8 presents a hypothetical downward-sloping curve illustrating how the curves *should* look if news coverage accurately reflects events in Iraq; that is, if bad news in Iraq yields relatively more criticism in the news, while good news yields relatively less criticism in the news. Figures 6.9 and 6.10 then present the *actual* patterns we found in our data for the networks and for Fox, respectively.

Consistent with the Negativity hypothesis (H1a), the actual network results generally show a strong, statistically significant positive relationship between criticism, on the one hand, and both negative *and* positive event outcomes in Iraq on the other. In other words, in most instances it is not the case that negative events are associated with more criticism and positive events are associated with less (which would be indicated by a downward-sloping line, as shown in figure 6.8). Nor do we see evidence

[16]We exclude nonevaluative statements or statements not about Iraq.

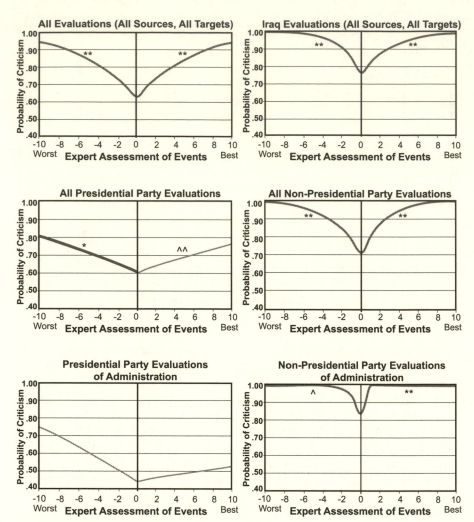

FIGURE 6.9: Estimated Effect of Events on Network Coverage of Elite Rhetoric, by Source, Target, and Topic

^^$p < .15$, ^$p < .10$, *$p < .05$, **$p < .01$. Thickened lines denote statistically significant curves ($p < .10$ or better).

of *no* relationship between event valence and criticism (which would produce a flat line). Rather, we find that in many cases, Fox and the networks respond to increases in the salience of major events with increased criticism, regardless of the tenor of those events. For instance, in the top left graphic in figure 6.9 (representing network rhetoric from all sources), as the curve moves away from zero in either a positive or negative direction (representing either an improving or a deteriorating situation in Iraq, re-

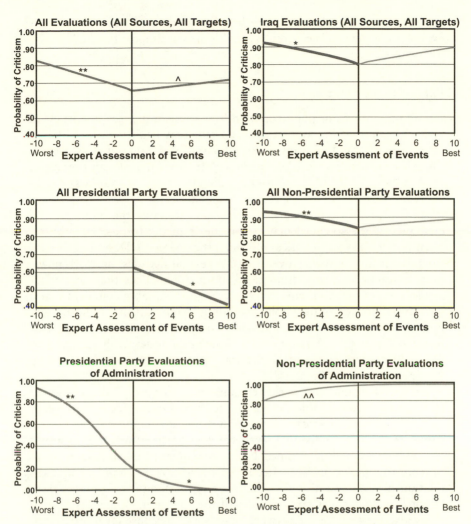

FIGURE 6.10. Estimated Effect of Events on Fox Coverage of Elite Rhetoric, by Source, Target, and Topic

^^$p < .15$, ^$p < .10$, *$p < .05$, **$p < .01$. Thickened lines denote statistically significant curves ($p < .10$ or better).

spectively), the curves trend upward from a low of about 62% to a high of about 95%, indicating an increase in the probability of criticism appearing in the news.

This trend is particularly pronounced on the networks, where improvements in Iraq are uniformly associated with increases in criticism on the air. Only in the case of Fox's coverage of Republican evaluations of the Bush administration (bottom left graphic in figure 6.10) does the curve indicate declining criticism when events in Iraq are going well (according to our expert assessments). These results provide strong support for the Negativity hypothesis (H1a).

Public Opinion Hypotheses

Before presenting our public opinion hypothesis tests, it is important to bear in mind that the average audience for network news (in 2006, an average of 18.3 million viewers for CBS and NBC combined) is over 13 times larger than that for Fox during prime time (in 2006, an average of 1.38 million viewers).[17] In addition to directly reaching a far larger audience, the major network newscasts are also more representative of the traditional national press. Indeed, they are arguably the quintessential examples of the so-called mainstream news media (or, as they are frequently referred to by political bloggers, the "MSM"). Despite their considerable loss of audience over the past several decades, network newscasts continue to reach dramatically larger audiences than any other single news outlet. Consequently, we can be reasonably confident that a substantial portion of the public, including Democrats, Republicans, and independents, regularly consumes either network news or something similar to it. In contrast, Fox remains a niche news outlet, with a disproportionately conservative and Republican audience (Baum and Groeling 2008; Baum and Gussin 2008).

It is therefore unclear whether changes in coverage on Fox are likely to be reflected in comparable changes in the overall mix of information consumed by typical Americans. Because our public opinion data are aggregated, rather than individual level, we cannot determine which survey respondents actually consumed Fox. Consequently, even if we were to observe significant opinion effects, we could not be confident that the relationship was causal, rather than merely masking some omitted third factor driving changes on both sides of the equation. While this is obviously also the case for the network news series, because far more Americans consume those outlets (or other outlets that follow or parallel the news choices they make) the conceptual leap between network news coverage and public opinion regarding the Iraq War is considerably smaller than that between Fox News coverage and public attitudes. Consequently, for our public opinion hypothesis tests, we focus on the network news rhetoric series.

It is also important to note that because we employ smoothed data for our dependent variables—which was necessary due to the previously

[17]Source: http://www.stateofthemedia.org/2007.

noted diverse question formats and wordings employed to construct the series as well as the limited number of questions available within each weekly observation (an average of about two Iraq-related questions per week)—it is especially difficult to isolate the marginal effects of causal variables on the remaining variance in the series. This is because the smoothing process by definition wipes away much of the variation in a series between weeks (or *times*) t and $t + 1$. (The top section of table 6.A2, in appendix 6.2, presents the actual range of variation for the differenced form of the smoothed Iraq approval series for Democrats, Republicans, and independents, respectively.)

In fact, the variation between any two weeks t and $t + 1$ in our data, as captured by our differenced dependent variables, ranges only from .89 to 1.2 percentage points (see the final column in the top section of table 6.A2). In other words, in our smoothed and differenced series, partisan approval of the Iraq War changes by no more than about .89, 1.2, and 1.2 percentage points in a given one-week period for Democrats, Republicans, and independents, respectively. With such a limited ceiling, when measured in absolute terms, the main effects we report are necessarily substantively modest. However, as we will see, measured as a proportion of the total *possible* variance given the maximum ranges in our data, the effects of rhetoric are frequently quite substantial despite the smoothed format of the dependent variables.

It is important in any comparative analysis to try, to the extent possible, to insure one is comparing apples to apples. In the present context, the challenge we face is that MCs offer, and journalists select for broadcast, different types of rhetoric (e.g., pro-war evaluations by Republican MCs versus pro-war evaluations by Democratic MCs) with widely varying frequencies. Hence, in order to "level the playing field," we adopt the convention of reporting the effects on public opinion of a shift from a complete absence of a given type of rhetoric to the 75th percentile level for that type of rhetoric. (This represents a level of such support equal to what we observe in the top quarter of the weekly values in our data, a fairly but not exceptionally high figure.)

With these important clarifications in mind, we turn to our statistical tests, beginning with retests of some of our core hypotheses derived in chapter 2, including the Partisan (H4), Costly (H5), and Combined (H6) Credibility hypotheses. The dependent variables for these analyses are changes in smoothed Democratic, Republican, and independent support for the Iraq War. The key causal variables measure the number of instances of praise of/support for or criticism of/opposition to the Iraq War or U.S. military policy by either party during a given week, employing cumulative values (from the start of the series) with the previously described 100-day decay process. (The bottom section of table 6.A2 presents the results from three OLS analyses testing these three hypotheses.)

Beginning with Democratic identifiers, the results (shown in the column labeled "Democrats" in the bottom section of table 6.A2) support all three hypotheses. At the 75th percentile, the cumulative level of Democratic support for the Iraq War in a given week in our data set is 65 positive evaluations (weighted by our 100-day decay process). With all other rhetoric types held constant at their mean values, an increase from 0 to 65 pro-war evaluations by Democratic MCs would be associated with about a .64-percentage-point increase in war support among Democratic partisans ($p < .05$). This figure, though quite small in absolute terms, represents about 72% of the maximum total actual variance in the smoothed Democratic war support dependent variable. As predicted by the Combined Credibility hypothesis (H6), this is the largest substantive effect across the four types of rhetoric. In contrast, consistent with Partisan (H4) and Costly (H5) Credibility hypotheses, increased pro-war rhetoric by Republican MCs (which lacks either partisan or costly credibility for Democratic partisans) actually depresses support for the war among Democratic partisans.

This suggests Democrats are alienated by Republican MCs support for the war, thereby producing a boomerang effect. At the 75th percentile, cumulative Republican MC war praise (again, discounted by the 100-day weight) totals 184 positive evaluations in a given observation. The predicted effect of an increase from zero to 184 such evaluations is about a .67-percentage-point decline in support for the war among Democratic partisans in the electorate ($p < .10$). This figure is equivalent to 76% of the actual maximum weekly variation in Democratic war support.

Negative evaluations by Republican MCs should, per the Costly Credibility hypothesis (H5), have a greater persuasive impact than cheap talk Republican praise. In this instance, the 75th percentile of (discounted cumulative) anti-war evaluations by Republican MCs for a given observation is about 541. All else equal, an increase from zero to this amount of anti-war rhetoric would be associated with about a .53-percentage-point decrease in war support among Democratic identifiers ($p < .01$), equivalent to about 60% of the maximum actual weekly variation in Democratic war support. As predicted by the Costly Credibility hypothesis (H5), this effect is in fact larger and more significant than the corresponding effect of pro-war rhetoric by Republican MCs on Democratic identifiers (which, as noted, actually depresses war support among Democrats).

Presumably because it is relatively cheap (that is, self-serving) talk, anti-war rhetoric by Democratic MCs has a small and insignificant effect on war support among Democratic partisans. Also consistent with the

Costly Credibility hypothesis (H5), the effect of cheap talk Democratic criticism of the Iraq conflict is smaller, if not quite significantly so ($p < .15$), than that of costly Democratic praise for the conflict. Finally, and more strongly consistent with the Costly Credibility hypothesis (H5), the difference between the effects of relatively costly praise and criticism (war praise by Democratic MCs vs. war criticism by Republican MCs) is itself statistically significant ($p < .01$), while that between relatively cheap talk praise and criticism (praise by Republican MCs vs. criticism by Democratic MCs) is about half as large in magnitude, and less significant ($p < .10$).

Turning to Republican identifiers (shown in the column labeled "Republicans" in the bottom section of table 6.A2), consistent with the Partisan Credibility hypothesis (H4), anti-war rhetoric by Republican MCs appearing on the network news is associated with reduced war support ($p < .05$). At the 75th percentile level of criticism, the predicted effect is nearly a .67 percentage point decrease in war support among Republican identifiers. This represents about 57% of the actual observed maximum weekly variance in the smoothed Republican war support dependent variable. Consistent with the Costly Credibility hypothesis (H5), this effect is larger in magnitude and far more significant than the corresponding effect of cheap talk pro-war Republican rhetoric, which does not significantly influence war support among Republican identifiers in the electorate.

Consistent with the Partisan Credibility hypothesis (H4), anti-war Democratic rhetoric exerts a small and insignificant effect on Republican identifiers. Consistent with the Costly Credibility hypothesis (H5), in turn, costly pro-war evaluations by Democratic MCs yield larger and statistically significant increases in war support among Republicans. An increase from 0 to the 75th percentile in pro-war Democratic evaluations (which, as noted, is 65 such evaluations) yields a predicted increase in war support of nearly three-quarters of one percentage point ($p < .001$). This represents 64% of the maximum total variance in smoothed Republican war support between any two weeks in our data set. Finally, as before, the difference between the effects of relatively costly praise by Democratic MCs and the effects of criticism by Republican MCs is statistically significant ($p < .001$), while that between cheap talk praise by Republican MCs and criticism by Democratic MCs is less than one-third as large in magnitude and statistically insignificant.

Turning to independents (shown in the column labeled "Independents" in the bottom section of table 6.A2), the results here are mixed, mostly but imperfectly supporting the Costly Credibility hypothesis (H5). The most noteworthy exception concerns pro-war evaluations by Democratic

MCs, which, despite their presumed costliness, do not appear to influence war support among independent identifiers. In contrast, (cheaper) anti-war rhetoric by Democratic MCs does yield significant declines in war support among independents ($p < .10$). At the 75th percentile (691 such evaluations), the predicted effect among independents of anti-war rhetoric by Democratic MCs is a decrease in war support of about .35 percentage points. This is equivalent to 29% of the maximum total weekly variance in independents' war support. The reason for this latter effect may be the relatively greater costliness of opposition party criticism in wartime. As discussed in chapter 2, criticizing the president—and, by extension, his policy—in wartime is more politically risky than during other periods. This makes such rhetoric costlier than in normal times, all else equal.

More clearly consistent with the Partisan Credibility hypothesis (H4), cheap talk pro-war evaluations by Republican MCs do not appear to influence war support among independents. In contrast, criticism of the conflict by Republican MCs *is* associated with reduced war support among independents ($p < .01$). Also consistent with the Costly Credibility hypothesis (H5), the latter marginal effect is over twice as large in magnitude and more highly significant ($p < .01$ vs. $p < .10$) than that associated with relatively less costly Democratic criticism. An increase from zero pro-war rhetoric by Republican MCs to the 75th percentile level (541 such evaluations) yields an increase in war support of about .69 percentage points. This represents 57% of the maximum weekly variation in smoothed war support among independents. In this instance, however, somewhat inconsistent with the Combined Credibility hypothesis (H6), the difference in the effects of relatively costly rhetoric (pro-war rhetoric by Democrats vs. anti-war rhetoric by Republicans) is somewhat smaller in magnitude (.50 vs. .84 at the 75th percentiles) and less significant ($p < .15$ vs. $p < .05$) than that for relatively cheap talk (pro-war rhetoric by Republicans vs. anti-war rhetoric by Democrats). Once again, the primary reason for this latter pattern appears to be the substantial negative effect of anti-war rhetoric by Democratic MCs, which typical individuals—especially independents, for whom partisan credibility is relatively less likely to mediate message persuasiveness—may for the previously discussed reasons perceive as somewhat costlier in wartime than in other periods.

Conclusion

In 2007, two MCs made important, unexpected, and countervailing statements about the war in Iraq. Senator John Warner (R-VA) made headlines across the country and the world by calling for American troops to begin withdrawing from Iraq by Christmas 2007. In contrast, the very next day an op-ed piece appeared in the *Seattle Times* in which Representative Brian Baird (D-WA), a longtime opponent of the war, praised the recent progress in Iraq and called for a continuation of the U.S. troop presence there. In the period following the public releases of the two statements, the news media devoted far more coverage to Warner's statement than to Baird's.[18] Some of the difference undoubtedly stems from Warner's relative prominence on the national stage and within his own party. Nonetheless, it appears from our results that there is also substantially more demand for and impact from criticism relative to praise, even on outlets like Fox that are reputed to be relatively sympathetic to the Bush administration.

Once again, far from revealing a world in which politics stops at the water's edge, our data suggest that partisanship and negativity dominate war coverage in contemporary America. Especially in the early stages of the Iraq War, the rhetoric passing through America's airwaves bore little resemblance to the situation on the ground in Iraq. We also observe relatively little similarity in the rhetoric devoted to the same topic flowing across competing television channels. It is therefore unsurprising that the Iraq War was so polarizing in the public sphere: each side consumed a steady diet of criticism targeting the other party, with relatively little positive news filtering through to the public.

Our analysis of the effects of this rhetoric on public opinion revealed patterns in most respects similar to overall patterns in public responses to elite rhetoric in general (Groeling 2001) and with respect to foreign policy (see chapter 3; see also Groeling and Baum 2008). They also call into question the longstanding scholarly practice of dividing the study of public opinion and American foreign policy into short-term (that is, rally-'round-the-flag) and longer-term (that is, everything else) studies, with research emphasizing distinct explanatory variables across the two time horizons. Media coverage of elite communication clearly matters in both the short *and* the longer terms of foreign policy crises. While the necessary smoothing of the opinion series clearly moderated the magnitudes of these effects in many instances, the overall patterns indicate that both partisan and costly credibility shaped public responses to the unfolding of events in Iraq, as well as to elite commentaries regarding those events.

---

[18] A Lexis-Nexis search for the member's name within 30 words of "Iraq" for the week of August 19–26 found 20 news wire reports and press releases for Baird, compared to 115 for Warner; 19 versus 480 news transcripts, 6 versus 36 newspaper stories, 0 versus 2 magazine articles, and 5 versus 13 indexed blog entries.

APPENDIX 6.1. EVENTS SERIES (EXPERT RATINGS IN PARENTHESES)

August 12, 2004: U.S., Iraqi forces prepare for major assaults in Najaf: Coalition forces launch offensive against outlaw militia loyal to radical cleric Muqtada al-Sadr in Kufa and Najaf. (0.54)

September 14, 2004: U.S., allies dispute Annan on Iraq War: Kofi Annan stated about the Iraq War, "From our point of view and the U.N. charter point of view, it was illegal." (−2.72)

September 16, 2004: Strike kills 60 terrorists near Fallujah: A strike on a compound near Fallujah kills approximately 60 terrorists in Operation Hurricane. (2.53)

October 1, 2004: "Scores die" in Samarra assault: U.S. and Iraqi government forces attack the insurgent-held city of Samarra in northern Iraq. United States says more than 100 militants killed and 37 captured; local doctors say at least 80 people died, and 100 were wounded, including civilians. (−0.51)

November 7, 2004: Major U.S.-led offensive against insurgents in Falluja: State of emergency is decreed on all the territory. More than 10,000 US soldiers and 2,000 Iraqi troops assault Fallujah in Operation al-Fajr, one of bloodiest battles of the war. (−0.06)

December 21, 2004: Experts investigating source of Mosul explosion: Attack on military dining facility in Mosul kills 22, wounds 78. (−2.54)

January 15, 2005: United States officially calls off search for Iraqi WMDs: U.S. inspectors end their search for WMDs in Iraq. (−3.41)

January 26, 2005: Deadliest day for U.S. in Iraq War: Helicopter crash in western Iraq claims the lives of 30 Marines and one sailor. (−3.08)

January 30, 2005: Millions of Iraqis vote in their first free elections: An estimated eight million people vote in elections for a Transitional National Assembly. The Shia United Iraqi Alliance wins a majority of assembly seats. (4)

February 28, 2005: Iraq suicide bomb kills at least 125: At least 125 people are killed by a massive car bomb in Hilla. It is the worst single such incident since the U.S.-led invasion. (−3.67)

March 4, 2005: Liberation of Italian journalist Giuliana Sgrena: Liberation of Italian journalist Giuliana Sgrena occurs, during which secret Italian agent Nicola Calipari is killed by U.S. fire. Berlusconi's government announces a partial withdrawal of Italian troops from the coalition forces. (−2.45)

March 16, 2005: Iraqi Assembly gets off to quiet start: First meeting of the transitional National Assembly is held. (1.28)

April 6, 2005: Jalal Talabani elected as Iraq's new president: Parliament selects Kurdish leader Jalal Talabani as president. Ibrahim Jaafari, a Shia, is named as prime minister. (2.23)

April 9, 2005: Iraqis protest on anniversary of Saddam's fall: Tens of thousands of demonstrators loyal to Shia cleric Muqtada Sadr march through Baghdad denouncing the U.S. occupation of Iraq. Also, insurgents kill 15 Iraqi soldiers. (−2.61)

April 28, 2005: Iraqi lawmakers OK Cabinet: In a milestone move, Iraq's National Assembly chose a new government Thursday following three months of political wrangling in the wake of historic elections. (3.05)

May 7, 2005: Hunt for insurgents near Syria ends: Marines said they "successfully completed Operation Matador," a weeklong hunt for insurgents along the Syrian border; nine Marines and more than 125 insurgents dead. (1.13)

May 15, 2005: Iraqi constitution panel formed: Formation of the parliamentary commission charged with drafting a new constitution. (2.23)

July 18, 2005: Death toll rises to 100 in suicide blast: The death toll in suicide bombing in the southern Iraqi town of Musayyib reaches 100. (−3)

August 22, 2005: Iraqi Parliament gets draft of constitution: Constitution's draft is presented to the Iraqi Parliament. (2.39)

August 31, 2005: More than 1,000 people are killed during a stampede in Shia ceremony: Rumors of a suicide bomber cause panic among pilgrims on the shrine of the Imam Musa al-Kazim–Tigris River bridge. (−2.63)

September 14, 2005: 182 people are killed in attacks: Weeklong surge of violence begins with suicide car bomb explosion in Baghdad's Oruba Square that kills 114, mostly Shia laborers. The same day, a suicide bomber attacks line of people waiting to fill gasoline cans, killing himself and 11 others. Al-Qaeda in Iraq announces a countrywide campaign of violence in response to the military attack on the northern town of Talafar. (−4.13)

October 15, 2005: Iraq draft constitution approved: Iraq's constitution is adopted by majority during the October 15 referendum, as Sunni Arab opponents fail to muster enough support to defeat it. Constitution aims to create an Islamic federal democracy. (2.45)

October 20, 2005: Defiant Hussein, lashing out at U.S., goes on trial: Saddam Hussein on trial; charges of crimes against humanity. (1.51)

November 19, 2005: Collateral damage or civilian massacre in Haditha? *Time* magazine publishes its initial report of an alleged November 19, 2005, U.S. massacre in Haditha in March of 2006. (−4.81)

December 15, 2005: Iraqi legislative election: Iraqis vote for the first, full-term government and parliament since the U.S.-led invasion. (3.69)

February 22, 2006: Samarra bombing: Bomb attack on an important Shia shrine in Samarra (Al-Askari Mosque) unleashes wave of sectarian violence. Iraqi government estimates 379 people killed in subsequent attacks; *Washington Post* reported over 1,300 people killed. (−6.79)

April 22, 2006: Iraqi compromise to end political deadlock: Newly reelected President Talabani asks Shia compromise candidate Jawad al-Maliki to form a new government. Move ends four months of political deadlock. (2.31)

April 24, 2006: Hamdania incident: Marines allegedly abduct Iraqi civilian from house, kill him, and place components and spent AK-47 cartridges near body to make it appear he was planting an IED. (−4.66)

June 1, 2006: Withdrawal of Japanese troops: Japan announces it will begin withdrawing its approximately 600 ground troops from Iraq, after two U.S. soldiers were kidnapped and tortured to death. (−1.97)

June 7, 2006: Abu Musab al-Zarqawi killed in bombing raid: Zarqawi, Al Qaeda in Iraq leader who led brutal campaign that included suicide bombings, kidnappings, and beheadings, killed. (3.03)

July 9, 2006: Mahmoudiya case: Five soldiers charged in Iraq rape-murder: Four U.S. soldiers are charged with participating in the "rape and murder of a young Iraqi woman and three members of her family." (−4.56)

July 25, 2006: Operation River Falcon: Operation aimed at denying terrorists use of Sayifiyeh as a safe haven, disrupting insurgent attacks and collecting and destroying insurgent munitions. (1.61)

August 20, 2006: Snipers kill 22: Sunni snipers kill at least 22 Shiites during a pilgrimage in Baghdad. (−3.17)

September 1, 2006: United States maintains operational control despite plans to transfer: A much-anticipated ceremony to transfer operational command from U.S.-led forces to Iraq's new army is postponed. (−1.92)

November 5, 2006: Saddam, co-defendants sentenced to hang: Hussein is found guilty of crimes against humanity and sentenced to death. Hussein and six subordinates are convicted and sentenced for the 1982 killings of 148 people in a Shiite town after an attempt on his life was made there. (1.74)

November 8, 2006: Democratic wins trigger Rumsfeld resignation: Secretary of Defense Donald Rumsfeld resigns one day later. Bush appoints former CIA chief Robert Gates to replace him. (4)

November 21, 2006: Iraq and Syria restore relations: Iraq and Syria restore diplomatic relations after nearly a quarter-century. (1.72)

November 23, 2006: Car bombings increase: More than 200 die in car bombings in mostly-Shia Sadr City. An indefinite curfew is imposed after the worst attack on the capital since the U.S.-led invasion began in 2003. (−3.64)

December 6, 2006: Iraq Study Group Report: Iraq Study Group report describes Iraq situation as grave and deteriorating; warns of prospect of slide toward chaos. (0.62)

December 30, 2006: Hussein executed by hanging: Executioners are videotaped taunting him, sparking protest. (−1.69)

January 7, 2007: Bush: "We need to change our strategy in Iraq"; Bush announces new Iraq strategy: troop surge. Thousands more US troops will be dispatched to shore up security. (0.14)

January 15, 2007: Head severed in botched hanging: Saddam Hussein's half-brother and the former head of Iraq's Revolutionary Court are both hanged. (−1.33)

February 12, 2007: Deadly bomb attacks in Iraq: Bomb in market kills more than 130 people. It is the worst single bombing since 2003. Twin car bombings explode in quick succession, killing at least 59 people and wounding 150. At least five others are killed in another bombing. (−3.74)

March 1, 2007: Hundreds injured in Falluja and Ramadi: Insurgents detonate three trucks with toxic chlorine gas, injuring hundreds. (−3.37)

March 20, 2007: Saddam's deputy hanged for crimes against humanity: Former Vice President Taha Yassin Ramadan is executed on the fourth anniversary of the U.S.-led invasion. (0.84)

TABLE 6.A1
Logit Analyses of Rhetoric Valence as Source and Target of Rhetoric Vary

Rhetoric Characteristics	Independent Variables			
	Negative Events	All Events	Constant	Pseudo-R² (N)
Networks				
All evaluations, all sources and targets	−0.466 (0.050)***	0.229 (0.032)***	0.538 (0.055)***	0.010 (N = 6,306)
Iraq evaluations, all sources and targets	−0.959 (0.198)***	0.383 (0.125)**	1.184 (0.170)***	0.040 (N = 1,333)
All PP evaluations	−0.175 (0.097)^	0.077 (0.061)	0.436 (0.108)***	0.002 (N = 1,405)
All NPP evaluations	−0.865 (0.133)***	0.481 (0.085)***	0.911 (0.128)***	0.030 (N = 1,646)
Admin. evaluations by presidential party	−0.165 (0.220)	0.033 (0.140)	−0.210 (0.284)	0.006 (N = 238)
Admin. evaluations by NPP	−77.137 (0.000)***	76.053 (0.723)***	1.655 (1.200)	0.150 (N = 363)
Fox				
All evaluations, all sources and targets	−0.117 (0.031)***	0.029 (0.021)	0.695 (0.038)***	0.003 (N = 12,548)
Iraq evaluations, all sources and targets	−0.184 (0.109)^	0.073 (0.075)	1.431 (0.116)***	0.003 (N = 1,923)
All PP evaluations	0.083 (0.064)	−0.085 (0.043)*	0.554 (0.080)***	0.002 (N = 2,577)
All NPP evaluations	−0.141 (0.080)^	0.041 (0.054)	1.737 (0.094)***	0.003 (N = 3,683)
Admin. evaluations by presidential party	0.003 (0.214)	−0.411 (0.165)*	−1.211 (0.243)***	0.160 (N = 380)
Admin. evaluations by NPP	0.094 (0.407)	0.086 (0.324)	4.037 (0.465)***	0.020 (N = 924)

Abbreviations: PP, presidential party; NPP, nonpresidential party.

TABLE 6.A2
Effects of Media Coverage of Elite Rhetoric on Public Support for Iraq War

I. Ranges of Variation in Dependent Variables (Change in Iraq War Support between Weeks t and t + 1)

Party	Mean	Std. Dev.	Minimum	Maximum	Max. Weekly Variance
Democrats	−0.050	0.167	−0.584	0.305	0.889
Republicans	−0.082	0.190	−0.709	0.454	1.163
Independents	−0.083	0.186	−0.685	0.525	1.210

II. OLS Investigations

Independent Variable	Democrats	Republicans	Independents
War support$_t$	−0.0349 (0.0282)	−0.0557 (0.0368)	0.0231 (0.0235)
Republican war support	−0.0037 (0.0020)^	−0.0030 (0.0024)	0.0026 (0.0017)
Democratic war support	0.0098 (0.0050)*	0.0114 (0.0061)^	−0.0030 (0.0045)
Republican war criticism	−0.0010 (0.0004)*	−0.0012 (0.0006)*	−0.0012 (0.0004)**
Democratic war criticism	0.0002 (0.0002)	−0.0003 (0.0004)	−0.0005 (0.0003)^
|ΔRepublican war praise|	0.0386 (0.0166)*	−0.0068 (0.0177)	0.0136 (0.0122)
|ΔDemocratic war praise|	0.0040 (0.0309)	0.0945 (0.0504)^	0.0598 (0.0289)*
|ΔRepublican war criticism|	−0.0010 (0.0055)	0.0079 (0.0068)	0.0091 (0.0067)
|ΔDemocratic war criticism|	−0.0068 (0.0049)	−0.0086 (0.0073)	−0.0144 (0.0070)*
"Other" war praise - criticism	−0.0010 (0.0002)***	−0.0014 (0.0004)***	−0.0014 (0.0002)***
Partisan presidential approval$_{t-1}$	−0.0001 (0.0043)	0.0116 (0.0056)*	0.0025 (0.0042)
Divided government	0.2904 (0.1205)*	0.4284 (0.1328)**	0.3790 (0.1320)**
Presidential election period	−0.6284 (0.1106)***	−0.1299 (0.1545)	−0.1260 (0.1407)
Midterm election period	0.1714 (0.0584)**	−0.0461 (0.0722)	0.0341 (0.0495)
No. of stories in *NY Times*	0.0017 (0.0262)	−0.0180 (0.0372)	0.0140 (0.0303)
% Change CPI	−0.0014 (0.0211)	0.0563 (0.0352)	0.0023 (0.0246)
Consumer sentiment$_{t-1}$	−0.0059 (0.0033)^	−0.0186 (0.0040)***	−0.0128 (0.0030)***
Missing network observations	0.0099 (0.0303)	−0.1173 (0.0714)^	−0.0943 (0.0485)^
Expert event assessment	−0.0019 (0.0050)	−0.0194 (0.0066)**	0.0028 (0.0057)
U.S. fatalities (decay)	−0.0002 (0.0008)	−0.0023 (0.0010)*	−0.0011 (0.0009)
Non-U.S. fatalities (decay)	0.0000 (0.0000)	0.0000 (0.0001)	0.0001 (0.0000)**
Change in U.S. fatalities$_{t-(t-1)}$	−0.0008 (0.0006)	−0.0014 (0.0009)	−0.0007 (0.0009)
Week counter	−0.0052 (0.0021)*	−0.0080 (0.0040)*	−0.0055 (0.0028)*
Support going/having gone to war	−0.0716 (0.0272)**	−0.0668 (0.0322)*	−0.0879 (0.0277)**
Constant	1.5241 (0.6080)*	5.6369 (2.9365)^	0.1343 (1.048)
R^2 (N)	0.63 (N = 130)	0.47 (N = 130)	0.62 (N = 130)

^ p<0.10; * p<0.05, ** p<0.01, *** p<0.001. Robust standard errors in parentheses.

CHAPTER 7

"Reality Asserted Itself"

THE ELASTICITY OF REALITY AND THE WAR IN IRAQ

MARSHALLING WHAT HE called "simple facts, plain arguments, and common sense," Thomas Paine once decried what he observed to be stubborn and wrongheaded resistance to the American war for independence: "A long habit of not thinking a thing wrong, gives it a superficial appearance of being right, and raises at first a formidable outcry in defense of custom." Paine, however, claimed to be optimistic that his cause would prevail in the fullness of time, as "Time makes more converts than reason" (Paine 1776).[1]

At the time of this writing, in winter 2008, it seems clear in retrospect that in 2007 an important shift took place in the situation on the ground in Iraq—a shift that checked and ultimately reversed what appeared to be an implacable slide into chaos and defeat. Whatever the ultimate outcome in Iraq, we demonstrate in this chapter that recognizing and articulating this substantial turn of events proved exceptionally difficult not only for entrenched politicians and partisans but also for journalists attempting to communicate the Iraq story to the public, and for citizens seeking to understand the status of the conflict.

Attempting to explain this dilemma, commentator Michael Yon complained, "No thinking person would look at last year's weather reports to judge whether it will rain today, yet we do something similar with Iraq news. The situation in Iraq has drastically changed, but the inertia of bad news leaves many convinced that the mission has failed beyond recovery . . . whether it is good news or bad, whether it is true or untrue, once information is widely circulated, it has such formidable inertia that public opinion seems impervious to the corrective balm of simple and clear facts" (Yon 2007).

The war in Iraq provides an exceptionally interesting case for testing our theory. The circumstances described by Yon suggest that at the time he made these observations, the elasticity of reality with respect to Iraq had effectively collapsed to such an extent that public opinion was al-

---

[1]Apropos of the topic of this book, Paine also observed, "There is something exceedingly ridiculous in the composition of monarchy; it first excludes a man from the means of information, yet empowers him to act in cases where the highest judgment is required."

most wholly unresponsive to incremental changes in events or in elite rhetoric, particularly on the part of the Bush administration. Subsequently, as the level of violence in Iraq continued to recede, a gap reopened in the relative and absolute influences of rhetoric and reality, such that most segments of the public seemed more responsive to negative rhetoric from the president's critics than to the increasingly positive reality of the situation on the ground in Iraq. In this chapter, we explain this perplexing shift in the relative influence of elite rhetoric and reality over the course of the conflict. In doing so, we test our argument that because the public largely views foreign conflicts through the mass media's distorted lens, the effects of elite communication on public opinion are likely to persist well beyond an initial rally period.[2] Such effects in turn are likely to be at least partly independent of the true state of events (that is, net of reality). However, as the public gathers more independent information over time, the potential gap between reality and its representation (or framing) in the mass media is likely to recede, as the influence of the former rises relative to that of the latter. In chapter 2, we referred to this change in relative responsiveness as the "elasticity of reality" (Baum and Potter 2008). As the elasticity of reality varies, so too, we anticipate, will the relative influence on public opinion of elite communication and objective indicators of reality. Eventually, absent a substantial and sustained change in the tenor of events, the public judgment about a conflict will begin to solidify, and citizens will grow increasingly unresponsive to fluctuations in either rhetoric or reality.

To test our predictions, we rely on a core time-series data set that begins in September 2004, about 17 months into the conflict, which originated on March 19, 2003. Hence, much (though not all) of our data represent only the medium to long term in the Iraq War. Because the elasticity of reality is presumably smaller later in the conflict than during the initial rally period, this should make it more difficult to find independent communication effects. We therefore supplement these data with additional analyses in which the available data do extend back to the beginning of the conflict, allowing us to more comprehensively investigate at least some elements of our theory.

[2]This is not to say that the media are the only route through which such information can flow. For instance, while relatively few Americans personally venture into war zones, many have familial or social ties to combatants who can serve as exceptionally credible sources of information about the true state of a conflict. Those same personal networks are also likely to highlight the costs of the conflict by increasing the knowledge and salience of casualties among linked service members. Moreover, Americans gain at least some independent information about the costs and benefits of a conflict through their daily lives. Increases (or decreases) in taxes, gas prices, deficits, or even terrorist attacks are examples of data Americans can easily track as by-products of their daily lives (Popkin 1994) and that they might, over time, employ in weighing the wisdom and success of a foreign policy venture.

Testing dynamic patterns in media coverage and public opinion poses a variety of substantive and methodological challenges. Any individual test can offer at best suggestive evidence in support of our theory. Many things vary over time, and it is difficult, if not impossible, to account for all potential causal factors within either a quantitative or qualitative analytic framework. Consequently, rather than relying on any single test, we undertake a range of empirical investigations, employing a variety of data sources and modeling techniques to build as strong a suggestive case for our theory as possible, given the limitations of each individual data source. Our hope is that, viewed in conjunction, our various tests will add up to considerably more than the sum of their parts. In other words, we believe the weight of the combined evidence makes a more persuasive case for the theory than would be possible based on any one, or even several, of our empirical investigations.

The remainder of the chapter consists of six distinct empirical investigations, through which we formally test our media- and opinion-related elasticity hypotheses (derived in chapter 2), as well as a key assumption underlying those hypotheses. Across these various empirical analyses, we exploit every opportunity to test our hypotheses against multiple, distinct data environments in order to build the most persuasive case possible for the theory.

The core assumption we test in this chapter concerns the dynamic nature of novelty; that is, what is novel today depends on what took place yesterday. We also test four of our media-related hypotheses. The first is the Novelty over Time hypothesis (H12), which predicts that the more frequently a given story type appeared in the media in the past (that is, prior to time t), the less it will be perceived as novel, and hence the less coverage it will receive in the present (that is, at time t). Conversely, stories that were relatively uncommon yesterday should be perceived as more novel today. Second, the Elasticity of Reality hypothesis (H13) predicts that over time (barring a major and sustained change in events), the tenor of media coverage of a conflict will increasingly parallel objective indicators of reality. Third, the Framing Stickiness over Time hypothesis (H14) predicts that, again over time, as the prevailing media framing of conflict grows increasingly entrenched, the marginal change in objective indicators of reality required to induce a given change in media framing will increase. Finally, the Partisan Media Convergence hypothesis (H16) predicts that coverage on news outlets will more closely approximate the valence of reality over time, but partisan media will be slower than nonpartisan media to converge when such coverage is damaging to their preferred party and quicker to converge when such coverage is helpful to their favored party.

Additionally, we test four of our opinion-related elasticity hypotheses and their corollaries. First, the Longer-term Communication Effects hypothesis (H15) predicts that elite rhetoric regarding a war will continue to influence public attitudes, independent of objective indicators of reality beyond the rally period, but absent a substantial and sustained change in the tenor of events, the marginal effects of such rhetoric will recede over time. Second, the Event-Shift Effects corollary hypothesis (H15b) predicts that following a significant and sustained change in the tenor of events, the public will be more susceptible to influence by elite rhetoric in the media and events on the ground than would otherwise be the case. The same corollary (H15b) also predicts that members of the president's party (PP) should be more responsive to such changes in rhetoric and events when they are favorable, and less responsive when they are unfavorable, than members of the opposing party (nonpresidential party, NPP) or independents. Third, the Longer-term Reality Effects hypothesis (H17) predicts that over time, absent a substantial and sustained change in the tenor of events, the marginal influence of objective indicators of a war's progress on public attitudes will first increase and then eventually recede. Finally, the Rhetoric versus Reality hypothesis (H18) predicts that the marginal influence of elite rhetoric will decline more than the marginal influence of objective indicators of the war's progress, over time. We conclude by considering the implications of our findings for the theory, and for future presidential leadership in foreign policy.

THE DYNAMICS OF NOVELTY

We begin by testing a key assumption underlying our theory (which is evident in figure 2.2 of chapter 2): that novelty, and hence the extent of journalists' and citizens' interest in stories, is dynamic. In other words, what is novel today depends on the prevailing storyline prior to today. After all, the essence of novelty is deviation from expectations, which is defined largely by inertia. That is, all else equal, we expect today to be like yesterday. It is therefore surprising and hence interesting when today turns out not to be like yesterday. Conversely, if today proves to be just like yesterday, we find that less surprising, and so less interesting, all else equal.

We included several questions in the previously discussed Polimetrix national population survey (see chapter 3) intended to evaluate the validity of this assumption vis-à-vis the conflict in Iraq. For our dependent variable, we asked respondents whether they would consider a 10% increase or a 10% decrease in casualties in Iraq to be a more interesting story, or whether they would consider the two stories equally interesting. We derive our key causal variable from a question asking respondents whether they believed the average rate of U.S. and Iraqi civilian casualties in Iraq was increasing, decreasing, or remaining relatively constant. Among respondents who believe casualties are on the rise, a story about declining casualty rates should be more novel and hence interesting. Conversely, among respondents who believe casualties are declining, a story about rising casualties should be of greater interest. (See appendix 7.2 for question wording and coding for all variables included in this analysis.)

Preliminary testing strongly suggested that respondents did not necessarily respond to the latter question purely based on a novelty calculus. Rather, some respondents appeared to factor their beliefs about the accuracy of the story into their assessment concerning its degree of interest to them. Such a calculus would lead to the exact opposite predictions: if you believe casualties are rising and you want the media to be accurate, you would prefer a story about rising casualties. Conversely, if you believe casualties are falling, you would consider the 10% decrease story more accurate, and hence would prefer it. To separate out these two factors, we included an interaction between respondents' beliefs regarding the casualty trend in Iraq and a dummy variable based on two questions asking respondents whether they believed the media had covered casualties and gains by coalition forces too much, too little, or about right. We coded the dummy equal to 1 if a respondent answered "about right" to both questions and 0 otherwise. Our expectation is that among respondents who believed the media had covered the conflict appropriately, perceptions of novelty would drive responses to the story interest question. Conversely, we anticipate that among respondents who believed the media had covered casualties or coalition gains too much or too little, the desire for accuracy in coverage would trump considerations of novelty. Part A of table 7.A1 in appendix 7.4 presents the results of a multinomial logit analysis testing these predictions. In figure 7.1 we once again employ Clarify to transform the results into probabilities of preferring a story about increases or decreases in casualties, or preferring either story about equally.

The results in figure 7.1 strongly support both predictions. Among respondents who believe the media have covered the Iraq story appropriately, moving from a belief that casualties are declining to a belief that they are rising is associated with a 14-percentage-point increase in the preference for a story about a 10% decline in casualties ($p < .05$), and no significant effect on the probability of preferring a story about a 10% increase in casualties.[3]

---

[3]Among the remaining respondents, the corresponding effect is an 18-percentage-point decline in the probability of believing the stories were equally interesting ($p < .05$).

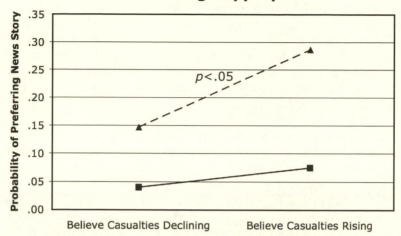

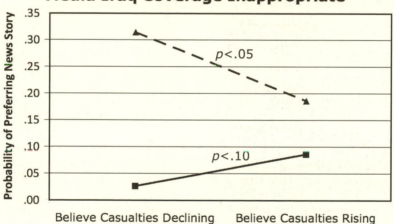

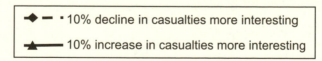

FIGURE 7.1. Estimated Interest in Stories Regarding Rising versus Declining Casualties, as Beliefs about Casualty Trends and Media Coverage Vary

In stark contrast, and as expected, respondents who believe the media have covered the Iraq story inappropriately—either over- or underemphasizing coalition gains or casualties—appear to prioritize accuracy in media coverage over novelty; that is, they prefer coverage that reflects their prior beliefs about the trend in casualties. Among these respondents, moving from a belief that casualties are declining to a belief that they are rising is associated with a 12-percentage-point decrease in the preference for a story about a 10% decline in casualties ($p < .05$) and a 6-percentage-point increase in the probability of preferring a story about a 10% increase in casualties ($p < .10$).[4]

Taken together, these results clearly support our assumption regarding the dynamic effects of novelty on public interest in news stories. All else equal, our respondents demonstrated a clear preference for the more novel story concerning casualties in Iraq. However, novelty is not the only consideration mediating interest in a given story. Our respondents, particularly those who believed prior news coverage was substantially inaccurate, also placed a premium on news stories consistent with their prior beliefs about the true state of affairs in the conflict.[5]

ALL COSTLINESS IS RELATIVE: THE CHANGING IMPACT OF PARTISAN REVERSALS ON IRAQ

To test the Novelty over Time hypothesis (H12), we search for instances in which the same sort of "surprising" or "novel" events or behavior recur, and then measure whether later instances receive proportionately different levels of coverage. As ABC's Robin Sproul noted (see chapter 2), what is novel, and hence newsworthy, "depends on what point we are in the story. If we are at the point in the story in which the Republicans have held firm [in support of the president's policy], and suddenly you have a conservative Republican who by all expectations would be expected to be holding firm who has broken away, it's a big story to us."

The war in Iraq allows us to test this prediction by reviewing several examples of exactly this scenario: members of Congress (MCs) who at one time strongly supported the Iraq War shifting their stance to oppose it. If the Novelty over Time hypothesis (H12) is correct, the changes in coverage should be greater for MCs who switched their position earlier,

---

[4]There was no statistically significant effect on the probability of considering the stories equally interesting.

[5]It should be noted that at the time of the survey, casualties in Iraq were in fact decreasing sharply from prior levels. U.S. military casualties from hostile fire, as well as Iraqi civilian casualties, had dropped by about 75% from their peak in early summer. Later, we separately address this misconception (and its significance) in figure 7.3.

relative to MCs who reversed course much later, especially if they did so after public perception of the war as a failure had begun to solidify.

In this case, we compare media coverage of four members whose shifts from support to opposition of the president's policy were regarded by reporters as surprising. The first two shifts, by Representative John Murtha (D-OH) and Senator Charles Hagel (R-NE), occurred in 2005, while the latter two, by Senators Richard Lugar (R-IN) and John Warner (R-VA), occurred in 2007. In all four cases reporters regarded the MCs as credible foreign policy leaders, and in all four cases the media interpreted their revised positions on the war as noteworthy shifts against the president's position.[6] Based on the Novelty over Time hypothesis (H12), we would predict that coverage of the MCs' statements announcing their changed views in 2005 should have increased more abruptly and the plateau should have lasted longer relative to coverage of the corresponding policy shifts in 2007. After all, the latter shifts took place well after a majority of the public had turned against the war. To test this prediction, in figure 7.2 we compare each MC's share of all TV news coverage mentioning both Congress and Iraq in the week before and the three weeks after their change in policy positions.[7]

As figure 7.2 shows, Hagel and Murtha (circa 2005) started out at a relatively lower prior level of coverage in the week before their statement, then saw their coverage spike to such an extent that they were mentioned in about half of *all* congressional coverage regarding Iraq during the weeks of their respective statements. A week later, Hagel and Murtha appeared in fewer than one in five congressional Iraq stories on television, further declining to a little more than one in ten such stories the following week.

In contrast, coverage of Warner and Lugar was already relatively prevalent before their reversals, likely because of their senior positions on Senate committees overseeing the war. Television coverage of the senators did increase in the week following their position reversals. However, the post-reversal increase was far smaller than in 2005. By the next week, the senators had returned to coverage levels comparable to their pre-policy-shift period. This again supports the Novelty over Time hypothesis (H12),

---

[6]According to the aforementioned (see chapter 6) data collected by Howell and Kriner (used with permission of the authors), whereas Lugar, Warner, and Hagel had all been strongly supportive of the president's position prior to their shifts, Murtha had actually already begun expressing reservations regarding the policy prior to his heavily covered "reversal." This, however, should bias the test *against* our prediction, as the Murtha case took place earlier, and hence should be more newsworthy, all else equal.

[7]The search term in each case entailed the appearance of the word "Iraq" within 30 words of the member's last name. The search term for the baseline congressional coverage of Iraq was "iraq and (senate or congress* or sen* or senator* or representative* or rep*)." We searched transcript databases for ABC, CBS, NBC, CNN, and Fox.

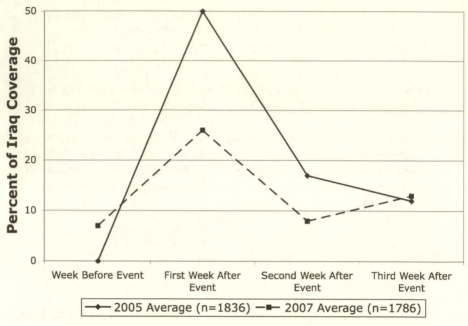

FIGURE 7.2. Comparison of Congressional Iraq Coverage Devoted to "Surprising" War Critics before and after Their Criticism, 2005 versus 2007

as the novelty of the story appears to have worn off more quickly in 2007 than in 2005. In sum, while certainly not a controlled test, this quasi-experimental comparison provides clear anecdotal support for our Novelty over Time hypothesis (H12).

INDIVIDUAL ATTITUDES AND THE ELASTICITY OF REALITY

Recall that the Longer-term Communication Effects (H15) and Longer-term Reality Effects (H17) hypotheses predict that the effect of rhetoric and events, respectively, on public opinion should recede over the course of a conflict after the initial rally period. The first corollary to H15, the Partisan Long-term Effects corollary hypothesis (H15a), then predicts that PP partisans will decrease from any initial support more slowly in response to negative events or rhetoric (and increase their support more rapidly in response to positive events or rhetoric) than will independents or NPP partisans. The second corollary to H15, the Event-Shift Effects corollary hypothesis (H15b), predicts that a substantial change in the tenor of events as a conflict unfolds will initially reinvigorate the effects of elite rhetoric in the media consistent with prior events, relative to the "new" reality or rhetoric consistent with it. Eventually, however, the public will become more responsive to the current true tenor of events (as represented by media coverage) and to rhetoric consistent with it. H15b further predicts that PP partisans will be quicker to respond to information consistent with a positive change in events, and slower to reassess when such information is unfavorable, relative to independents or members of the NPP.

To test these predictions at the individual-level, we revisit our national population survey conducted by Polimetrix. While one survey at a single point in time clearly cannot test the dynamic aspects of our theory, we nonetheless believe it is valuable for assessing the face validity of several of our assumptions and predictions. (See appendix 7.1 for the wording of all questions employed in this analysis.) The survey, in part, asked respondents about the trend in casualties and the prospects for a U.S. victory in Iraq, as well as about the ability of the Bush administration to influence public opinion on Iraq. Figure 7.3 presents four graphics that together summarize the results, broken out by respondents' party affiliations.

We begin with the top left and top right graphics in figure 7.3. These graphics indicate that as of December 2007 (when the survey was in the field), Democrats and independents believed that the U.S. prospect for victory in Iraq had remained largely unchanged over the preceding year (top left graphic) and that the troop surge had produced virtually no effect on the U.S. prospect for victory in Iraq (top right graphic), as both groups hover near the zero line (representing a response of "unchanged"). In sharp contrast, Republicans believed (perhaps correctly, in retrospect) by large margins that the prospects for victory had improved (top left graphic) and that the surge had improved the U.S. chances of victory (top right graphic). The differences between Democrats and independents on the one hand, and Republicans on the other are highly significant ($p <$ .001 in both cases).

The bottom left graphic presents the results from a question asking whether respondents believed the rate of U.S. military and Iraqi civilian casualties per month in Iraq had increased, decreased, or remained about the same since the start of the surge in March 2007. Once again, Democrats and independents believed (incorrectly) that casualty rates had remained roughly constant between March and December 2007, while Republicans, again by large margins, believed (correctly) that average monthly casualty levels had declined over that same time period. Once again, the differences between Democrats and independents, on the one hand, and Republicans on the other are highly significant ($p <$ .001 in both cases).

These results support our predictions, particularly those of the Event-Shift Effects corollary hypothesis (H15b). While opposition partisans

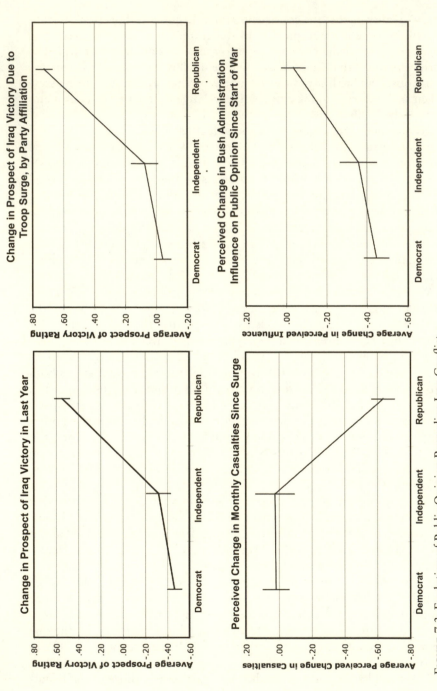

FIGURE 7.3. Evolution of Public Opinion Regarding Iraq Conflict

Note: Reported figures based on averages across respondents, coded: Increased = 1, About Same = 0, Decreased = −1.

and independents are slow to even *recognize* changes in events favorable to the president, let alone acknowledge their significance, the president's fellow partisans are substantially quicker to positively reassess, and more likely to do so in large numbers.

Additional national survey data provide more dynamic evidence of a partisan divide in perceptions following a shift in real-world events. According to a series of Pew Center surveys beginning in February 2007 (shortly after the announcement of the surge strategy in Iraq), members of the public differed starkly in their perceptions of the conflict in precisely the manner predicted by the Event-Shift Effects corollary hypothesis (H15b). As shown in figure 7.4, Republicans began to perceive progress in Iraq within months of the initiation of the surge, increasingly believing the U.S. was making progress in defeating Iraqi insurgents and preventing a civil war.

In contrast, and also consistent with the Event-Shift Effects corollary hypothesis (H15b), independents and especially Democrats remained skeptical, even as late as September 2007. Indeed, Democrats actually perceived a *deteriorating* situation with respect to the insurgency between February and September 2007. Only after several more months did Democrats and independents begin to join Republicans in believing that the United States was actually making progress in Iraq.[8]

Finally, returning to figure 7.3, the bottom right graphic tests the Longer-term Communication Effects (H15) and the Partisan Long-term Effects corollary (H15a) hypotheses, which predict that absent a major shift in the tenor of events, the effects of elite rhetoric on public attitudes will recede over time (H15), but that this pattern will be weakest among the president's fellow partisans (H15a). This graphic presents the results from a question asking whether the Bush administration's capacity to influence public opinion on the war had increased, decreased, or remained relatively constant since the start of the war. The results indicate, consistent with the predictions of the Longer-term Communication Effects hypothesis (H15), that on average, *all* respondents—Democrats, Republicans, and independents—agreed that the influence of the Bush administration on public support for the war had receded since the start of the conflict. Moreover, consistent with the predictions of the Partisan Long-term Effects corollary hypothesis (H15a), Democrats and independents

---

[8]Indeed, these partisan differences persisted well after the initiation of the surge. A Pew Research Center polling series on Iraq shows that in January 2008, around one in four Democrats thought the Iraq War was going very or fairly well, compared to 39% of independents and two-thirds of Republicans. By the end of 2008, however, the perception of progress in Iraq had become far more widespread, with 84% of Republicans, 55% of independents, and 42% of Democrats believing the war was going "very" or "fairly" well (Pew 2008, "Bush and Public Opinion").

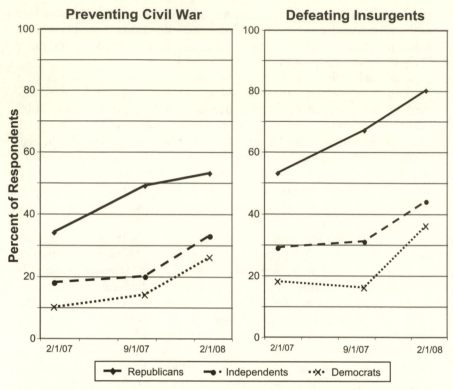

FIGURE 7.4. Perceived U.S. Progress in Iraq since Start of Surge, by Party

were far more likely than Republicans to hold this view. There are certainly multiple factors contributing to these assessments, and, as noted, self-reports at a single point in time concerning the influence of the Bush administration may be somewhat unreliable. Hence, these latter results represent only suggestive evidence. Nevertheless, they are precisely what our theory would predict.

TRENDS IN MEDIA COVERAGE AND PUBLIC OPINION

We next investigate whether and in what manner media framing of elite rhetoric influences public opinion over the longer term, independent of the true tenor of events in a conflict, as well as the influence of events themselves. Recall that the Longer-term Communication Effects hypothesis (H15) predicts that media representations of elite rhetoric regarding a war, here measured by *New York Times* coverage of casualties, will continue to influence public attitudes beyond the rally period, but that absent a substantial change in the true tenor of events, the extent of that influence will recede over time. The Longer-term Reality Effects hypothesis (H17) then predicts that the marginal influence of reality on public attitudes will first increase and then eventually recede.

The Event-Shift Effects corollary hypothesis (H15b), which we also test in this section, predicts that the public should thus grant disproportionate credibility to elite rhetoric, particularly media representations of that rhetoric, consistent with the prior state of reality. It should then gradually shift to recognize the new state of events on the ground, with the president's fellow partisans doing the latter more rapidly than opposition partisans or independents if the change in events is positive and more slowly if it is negative.[9] We also test the Rhetoric versus Reality hypothesis (H18), which predicts that over time, the marginal influence of elite rhetoric will decline more than the marginal influence of objective indicators of a war's progress. Finally, we test the Framing Stickiness over Time hypothesis (H14), which predicts that as the prevailing media framing of a conflict grows increasingly entrenched over time, larger changes in reality will be required to affect media framing.

To test these predictions, we employ two key causal variables: (1) *New York Times* coverage of U.S. military and Iraqi civilian casualties in Iraq and (2) actual trends in civilian and military casualties. While, as we have argued throughout the book, media coverage clearly does not represent a faithful measure of the true tenor of elite rhetoric, it does reflect the representation of that rhetoric selected by the media and thereby capable of influencing public opinion. Our purpose in this analysis is to determine the nature and extent of such influence, as well as that of actual events.

In the latter case, we focus on civilian and military casualties as our key indicator of reality, for two reasons. First, much of the literature on public opinion regarding war emphasizes casualties in one form or another as a key factor determining public support for war. Second, U.S. military and Iraqi civilian casualties have been *by far* the most frequently cited measures of U.S. progress in Iraq.[10] They are arguably also the most appropriate such indicator, as it is difficult to conceive of stability in Iraq

---

[9]Unfortunately, because the series ends soon after the effects of the surge on journalists' attitudes and public opinion began to emerge (December 2007), we are unable to test with these data whether, as predicted by H15b, reality eventually again began to compete with the (at the time) newly reemerging effects of rhetoric. Our model suggests that some additional time would be required before the latter pattern would likely emerge.

[10]For instance, a Lexis-Nexis search indicated that, between January 2004 and January 2009, the major U.S. newspapers included in the Lexis-Nexis database were over 3 and 14 times, respectively, more likely to reference "casualties or fatalities or killed" as they were to mention "electricity or infrastructure," on the one hand, or "refugees or displaced," on the other, in headlines or lead paragraphs also mentioning "Iraq and progress" (772 vs. 243 and 55 stories, respectively).

without considering the level or trend in casualties. Indeed, proponents of the success of the troop surge in Iraq have pointed almost exclusively to declining casualty rates to support their argument. For instance, in an article entitled "Admit It: The Surge Worked," *Washington Post* columnist Peter Beinart bases this assertion *solely* on declining casualties, observing in the lead paragraph, "the number of Iraqi war dead was 500 in November of 2008, compared with 3,475 in November of 2006. That same month, 69 Americans died in Iraq; in November 2008, 12 did" (Beinart 2008).

Data and Methods

To measure trends in the effects of elite rhetoric via the mass media on public opinion regarding Iraq, we assembled a monthly time-series data set running from May 2003 through November 2007. This yields a total of 55 monthly observations.[11] The dependent variable measures monthly changes in public support for the war in Iraq. We employ the identical smoothed aggregate public war support series as in chapter 6. As noted therein, this indicator (from Jacobson 2006) represents the overall average across 10 different survey questions asked by 15 survey organizations. In this instance, however, we test our aggregate opinion hypothesis by creating a summary indicator based on the overall average war support levels across all three partisan subgroups. The primary dependent variable is thus the monthly percent change in the percentage of Americans indicating that they support the war ($\mu = .01$, $\sigma = .02$).

Our first key causal variable measures the valence of casualty coverage (U.S. and Iraqi, civilian and military) in the *New York Times*, lagged one month.[12] We coded the valence of all articles mentioning casualties during the time frame of our analysis, measuring whether each article's coverage of casualties was positive, negative, or neutral with respect to the state of the conflict, including U.S. involvement.[13] To create our final in-

---

[11]Transforming our dependent variable into a percent change resulted in the loss of several initial observations.

[12]We counted a maximum of one positive and one negative code per article. However, an article coded as positive or negative could not also be coded as neutral. Two research assistants working separately and independently coded each article. Two other research assistants serving as arbitrators resolved disagreements between the first two coders. Inter-coder reliability on the initial coding was 76%, while that of our two arbitrators was 87%. The arbitrators' reliability measure is based on dual coding of 26 records, representing 10% of the total data set.

[13]We could not employ the Media Tenor data for the present analysis, in which we are measuring the overall tenor of the story vis-à-vis the conflict, as those data code the valence of specific statements toward some target actor—say, a Democratic MC criticizing President Bush—rather than toward the conflict itself.

dicator, we employ positive coverage as a percentage of all casualty coverage (positive, negative, or neutral). We then averaged this "net positive" casualty coverage indicator for each month. This variable runs from 0 to 1, where 0 represents the *least* positive casualty coverage and 1 represents the *most* positive coverage ($\mu = .1$, $\sigma = .18$). To capture variance in the effects of media coverage over time, we interact the lagged *New York Times* casualty coverage valence indicator with a variable counting the number of months since the beginning of our series, as well as with its quadratic.

Our second key causal variable measures actual trends in casualties in Iraq. We separately measured monthly total Iraqi civilian and U.S. military casualties (see chapter 6 for descriptions and sources of our casualty data). We normalized each total to a 0–1 interval and then added them together, normalizing the resulting summary variable to a 0–1 interval ($\mu = .46$, $\sigma = .21$). Our indicator takes into account the substantially greater weight placed by typical Americans on U.S. casualties relative to Iraqi casualties.[14] For our final indicator, we employ a one-month lag on the summary casualty variable. In order to account, as fully as possible, for the distinction between media coverage of casualties and the actual casualty trend, we interact the (lagged) summary casualty measure with our month counter and its quadratic (as we did with the *New York Times* casualty coverage valence indicator).

We also include seven control variables. To account for the intensity of media coverage of casualties in Iraq, our first two controls measure the percentage of the combined total number of stories about Iraq in television (ABC, CBS, NBC, and CNN) and print (*New York Times, Washington Post, LA Times, USA Today,* and *Wall Street Journal*) news reports that mentioned casualties. Third, to account for the president's political capital, we included presidential approval lagged one month (based on CBS News and Gallup polls). Fourth, to account for the political effect of Hurricane Katrina, we include a dummy coded 1 during the month of the hurricane (September 2005) and the subsequent four months.[15] Fifth, we include a dummy for the 2004 presidential election (coded 1 for September through November 2004, including the immediate post-election period). Sixth, to account for the state of the economy, we include the national average price of gasoline, lagged one month.[16] Finally, to account

---

[14]For evidence on the importance of proximity to the relationship between casualties and public support for war, see Gartner and Segura (2000). On the disproportionate value placed by Americans on U.S. casualties relative to foreign military casualties, see Boettcher and Cobb (2006).

[15]We tested numerous variants of the Katrina control. This indicator outperformed all other specifications.

[16]This variable outperformed consumer sentiment in our models.

for possible serial autocorrelation, our OLS models include the dependent variable, lagged one month, as a causal variable.

Our test of the Framing Stickiness over Time hypothesis (H14) differs from the other tests in this section in several ways. To begin with, because this test is not dependent on the availability of opinion data, we are able to employ weekly data, thereby increasing our N to 240 weekly observations. Additionally, for this analysis we employ as our dependent variable the weekly percent change in "net positive" *New York Times* war coverage (that is, positive coverage of casualties in Iraq as a percentage of *all* coverage of casualties in Iraq). Because we anticipate that news organizations respond to events more rapidly and directly than members of the public, and given the extremely low likelihood in this instance of reverse causality (that is, the possibility that coverage could drive casualty rates), we employ the *current* (week t), rather than the *lagged* (week $t - 1$) level of casualties as our key causal variable.

The control variables for this latter analysis also differ slightly. First, a midterm election dummy, coded 1 during September through November 2006, outperformed the presidential election dummy. The latter variable had no discernable effect on news coverage. Hence, we employ the former. Second, to account for the intensity of news coverage of Iraq casualties, we employ the same measure of casualty coverage as a proportion of all Iraq coverage as noted above, this time, owing to the nature of the dependent variable, focusing only on weekly newspaper coverage.[17] Finally, to account for the possibility that a given *percent change* in news coverage from the prior to the present week could have quite differing substantive implications at different *levels* of coverage, we add a control for the total volume of Iraq coverage in the aforementioned newspapers, lagged one week.[18]

Results

We begin with the results from our tests of the Longer-term Communication (H15) and Reality Effects (H17), Event-Shift Effects corollary (H15b), and Rhetoric versus Reality (H18) hypotheses. (Models 1 and 2, respectively, in part B of table 7.A1, appendix 7.4, present the results of basic and fully specified OLS models—with the former excluding nearly all controls—testing these hypotheses.)[19] Because the core substantive re-

---

[17]Unlike the opinion model, the percentage of television coverage of Iraq mentioning casualties had no effect on our dependent variable. Hence, we exclude it from the casualty coverage model.

[18]The lagged coverage volume indicator outperformed the current week value.

[19]The reported model excludes one influential outlier observation (March 2004). (This month saw the highest level of net positive news coverage in the entire series.) Including that observation moderately weakens the results on the *New York Times* indicator (though not for the casualty indicator), but it does not fundamentally alter them.

sults from models 1 and 2 are comparable, we focus our analysis on the latter, fully specified model.[20] We again employ Clarify (King, Tomz, and Wittenberg 2000) to estimate the expected percentage of respondents supporting the war as *New York Times* casualty coverage varies from no positive coverage to one standard deviation above the mean level of positive coverage, with all control variables, including monthly changes in casualties, held constant at their mean values. We repeat this simulation for each month in our series. The top graphic in figure 7.5 presents the effects of changes in both *New York Times* coverage of casualties and in actual casualties on public support for the Iraq War. Specifically, it shows the trends in the magnitudes of the effects of these two causal variables on public war support.

The origin of the *New York Times* coverage curve in figure 7.5 indicates that in the first month of our series (May 2003), an increase from the *no* positive casualty coverage to one standard deviation above the mean level of positive casualty coverage is associated with about a 4% increase in public war support ($p < .01$).[21] The magnitude of the positive effect of favorable coverage on public war support recedes gradually, although remaining statistically significant and substantial in magnitude through March 2004, 11 months into our series and 13 months into the war. The implication is that variations in the media coverage of casualties in Iraq continued to influence public opinion, independent of the effects of the actual trend in casualties, over a year into the conflict. This is obviously far beyond the so-called rally period at the war's outset. In addition to offering support for the Longer-term Communication Effects hypothesis (H15) with respect to media representations of elite rhetoric, these results also confirm a core assumption underlying this book, namely, that in foreign policy, communication matters over both the short *and* the longer term.

After August 2005, the mean effects continue to decline through January 2006, with the direction of the relationship briefly turning negative (though the latter upward shift is statistically insignificant). This implies that in the darkest days of the conflict, the actual state of events seems to have dominated public opinion, resulting in a greatly reduced independent influence of press coverage of casualties. Indeed, presumably owing to the effects of reality, during this period positive coverage of casualties

[20]We first present the basic model (model 1), excluding all controls except presidential approval, because of the relatively small N (52–53 observations) and consequent limited available statistical leverage in our analysis. While the results predictably differ somewhat from the fully specified model, the key relationships are largely comparable--in terms of valence and relative magnitudes of causal variables--to the fully specified model. Consequently, we proceed more confidently in interpreting the latter, fully specified OLS model (model 2).

[21]Even though we lose the first several months of our series due to transformations of the dependent variable, we employ Clarify to simulate the values for those months.

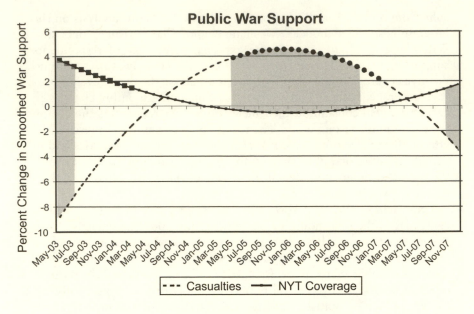

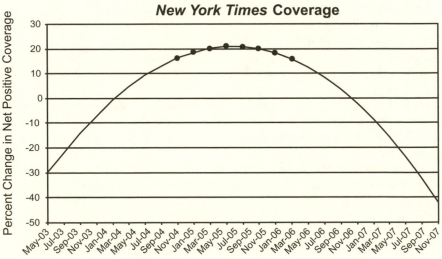

FIGURE 7.5. Estimated Percent Change in Public War Support and Net Positive *New York Times* Casualty Coverage, as Actual Casualties and *New York Times* Casualty Coverage Vary, May 2003–November 2007

Note: (1) Large circles or squares indicate statistically significant ($p < .10$ or better) effects of news coverage or casualties; shaded regions represent statistically significant differences between effects of casualties and news coverage. (2) For easier visual interpretation, the valence of the "Casualties" curve is reversed, so that we represent an increased direct relationship between *declines* in casualties and *rising* war support as a positive vertical movement along the y-axis.

might have led to further *decreases* in public support (although insignificantly so). As conditions on the ground began to improve, however, the relationship for press coverage eventually becomes direct again (that is, positive coverage is associated with more positive public attitudes about the conflict, and vice versa).

Given the apparent turnabout in events in Iraq in the second half of 2007—that is, significantly reduced Iraqi civilian and U.S. military casualties, arguably attributable to the surge in the U.S. troop presence in Iraq—the return to a direct relationship between the valence of *New York Times* coverage and public war support appears consistent with the Event-Shift Effects corollary hypothesis (H15b). However, neither the post-July 2005 declines in the effects of increased positive coverage nor the upward turn in such effects in the second half of 2007 are statistically significant. Consequently, these latter results are more suggestive than definitive. Nonetheless, the direct relationship in late 2007 approaches significance ($p < .20$), and the upward trend in the positive effects from its low point in early 2006 is itself statistically significant ($p < .10$). This suggests that these patterns most likely represent real rather than coincidental shifts.

It is, however, important to note that the most important rhetorical shift across these two periods was not a change in positive evaluations, which increased only by around 11% (from an average of 1.13 per month in the first eight months of 2007 to 1.25 during the September–November 2007 period). Rather, the late 2007 balance of rhetoric primarily reflected a massive 68% drop in negative evaluations (from 6.25 to only two per month). Thus, even as rhetoric began to regain traction and correlate more directly with public opinion, net changes in that rhetoric were mostly limited to fluctuations in *negative* evaluations. Negative evaluations continued to outpace positive ones throughout 2007, although at a reduced rate during the fall.

Turning to the Actual Casualties curve in figure 7.5, we find a quite distinct pattern. In the initial months of our series, variations in civilian and military casualties have no significant effect on public war support. The curve begins briefly in negative territory, suggesting, not entirely surprisingly, that increased casualties at the outset of the war were greeted with *increased* public support. It then gradually moves upward until, in February 2005, 25 months into our series and 27 months into the war, the effects of declines in casualties (here and subsequently from one standard deviation above the mean to zero) become statistically significantly positive. In other words, beginning in February 2005, declines in casualties are associated with significant increases in war support. This pattern persists and remains statistically significant until January 2007, peaking in December 2005, when a decline in casualties is associated with a nearly 5% increase in public war support ($p < .05$).

Beginning in February 2007, the curve moves into negative territory, indicating that falling casualties are associated with *decreases* in war support. This seemingly paradoxical reversal is not statistically significant, however, and so is of questionable substantive importance. Overall, these results clearly support the Longer-term Reality Effects hypothesis (H17), as the effects of reality—in this case, trends in civilian and military casualties—emerge gradually, and subsequently recede over time.

Also important for our theory, the two curves are themselves statistically distinct from one another during the first three months of our series, through July 2003 ($p < .10$ or better, indicated by the shaded region at the start of the curves in the top graphic of figure 7.5). During this period positive *New York Times* coverage produces a positive and significant effect on public opinion, while variations in casualties are associated with *no* statistically significant effect. Between August 2003 and April 2005 the two curves are statistically indistinguishable. From May 2005 through November 2006, declines in casualties exert a significantly more positive effect on public war support than positive news coverage, which exerts no significant effect (shown by the shaded region in the midsection of the top graphic in figure 7.5). After November 2006 the curves again become statistically indistinguishable until September 2007. Beginning in that month, positive *New York Times* casualty coverage again exerts a statistically distinguishable positive effect on public opinion ($p < .10$ or better, indicated by the shaded region toward the ends of the curves in figure 7.5) relative to declines in actual casualties, which do not significantly affect opinion.

Overall, the empirical patterns in figure 7.5 are strikingly consistent with the theory, and in particular with the model depicted in figure 2.1 of chapter 2. Initially, as predicted, rhetoric (measured by media coverage of casualties) exerts a greater influence than reality (measured by actual casualty levels). Subsequently, reality begins to exert itself, outpacing rhetoric during the medium term (represented by the middle part of our time series). Eventually, both rhetoric and reality fade to insignificance. Though the influence of both recedes over time (although at different times), consistent with the Rhetoric versus Reality hypothesis (H18), statistically significant effects persist far longer for reality than for rhetoric (19 vs. 11 months).

Our theory also predicts that even after a long period of consistent rhetoric and events on the ground, a noteworthy change in the tenor of events, such as the substantial and sustained drop in Iraqi civilian and U.S. military casualties associated with the troop surge, can eventually (after some lag period) lead the public to take a second look at a conflict and again become amenable to at least some influence by media—and by extension *elite*—framing of events, as well as, ultimately, by the actual tenor of the events themselves. In this instance, the return to a positive relationship between net positive *New York Times* coverage of casualties and public war support, as well as the reemergence of a statistically significant difference between the effects on opinion of news reports about casualties and of actual casualties, takes place in fall 2007. Presumably it is not a coincidence that this is the period where journalists began to take notice, after several months of skepticism, of declining casualty trends in Iraq. It is also worth noting that the pattern in fall 2007 essentially mirrors that from the beginning of the war, with rhetoric again exerting a greater influence on opinion than reality (although at more attenuated levels). These latter results support the Event-Shift Effects corollary hypothesis (H15b) and the Rhetoric versus Reality hypothesis (H18), and are again strikingly consistent with the theoretical model depicted in figure 2.1 in chapter 2.

Finally, we turn to our test of the Framing Stickiness over Time hypothesis (H14). (See model 3 in part B of table 7.A1 for an OLS model testing H14.) For this analysis we employ the weekly percent change in negative *New York Times* war coverage as the dependent variable and the weekly level of casualties as the key causal variable, both separately and interacted with a week counter and its quadratic. We employ the percent change in the dependent variable in order to account for the large fluctuations in *New York Times* coverage, particularly during the troop surge in the summer and fall of 2007.[22] In the bottom graphic of figure 7.5 we again use Clarify simulations to summarize the expected effects of a decline in casualties from one standard deviation above the mean to zero at each week in our time series. (While the dependent variable in this analysis is *weekly* changes in casualties, in order to make the two graphics more readily comparable we present [simulated] *monthly* probabilities in figure 7.5.)

As previously discussed, we believe that the start date of our series, in May 2003, represents the relative short term in our theoretical model. Assuming so, the implication is that our series begins in a period before reality began to exert itself, during which time elite framing is likely to exert a dominant impact on media coverage. Consequently, the elasticity of reality model anticipates a week reality effect early in the series. As we move forward in time, however, toward the medium term, reality ought

[22]By employing the percent change in coverage, while controlling for its lagged value and the overall volume of Iraq coverage in major newspapers, we take into account the magnitude of a given level change, *relative* to coverage in the recent past.

to become increasingly consequential. Hence, we anticipate that the reality curve will eventually become statistically significant. However, over time it should again recede, as new casualty information exerts relatively less influence on journalists' summary evaluations of the state of affairs in Iraq. As discussed, the troop surge is likely to revitalize the impact of rhetoric and then reality in fall 2007. However, as the prior results suggest, our series most likely ends too soon to observe a significant rebound in the influence of reality on news coverage.

The results summarized in the bottom graphic of figure 7.5 offer clear support for these expectations, and hence for the Framing Stickiness over Time hypothesis (H14). From the beginning of the series until fall 2005, casualties exert no significant effect. In fact, for most of 2003 the curve resides in negative territory, implying that rising casualty levels were associated with *more* favorable coverage. This may be an artifact of the early stages of the war, during which the U.S. and Iraqi forces fought large-scale military battles. This was a period in which elites tended to frame the conflict as a glorious U.S. victory. The initial battles that produced the apparent military success led to relatively high casualty levels on both sides. This could account for the unusual pattern of high casualty levels being greeted with favorable news coverage. Nonetheless, these patterns remain insignificant throughout and hence must be interpreted with caution.

Beginning in November 2005, declining casualties begin to exert a significantly positive effect on the tenor of casualty coverage, reaching its zenith in late May 2005, when a decrease in casualties from one standard deviation above the mean to zero is associated with a more than 21-fold increase in net positive casualty coverage. Consistent with the Framing Stickiness over Time hypothesis (H14), from this point forward the effects of the identical decline in casualties on net positive news coverage recede steadily, though they remain statistically significant through March 2006. Eventually, in 2007, the curve again turns negative, though it remains statistically insignificant for the remainder of the series.

Finally, it is useful to compare the patterns in the effects of casualties on public opinion and on news coverage. Our theory predicts that the public responds to reality primarily indirectly, based on the mediated representation of reality offered by the media. If so, we would anticipate casualties beginning to influence news coverage *before* they influence public opinion, while ceasing to significantly influence opinion *after* they cease influencing news coverage. In fact, both patterns are evident in these data. As the bottom graphic in figure 7.5 shows, casualties begin significantly influencing news coverage in November 2004. In contrast, as the top graphic in figure 7.5 reveals, casualties do not begin to influence public opinion until four months later, in March 2005. Moreover, whereas casualties continue to influence news coverage only until March 2006, their effects on public opinion last considerably longer, until January 2007.

Presidential Rhetoric and the Elasticity of Reality

Our theory also holds clear implications for over-time trends in the effects of presidential rhetoric on media coverage and public opinion. In this section we investigate several such implications, focusing in particular on the responses of journalists and citizens to presidential rhetoric regarding Iraq. In doing so, we test three hypotheses: the Longer-term Communication Effects hypothesis (H15), the Partisan Long-term Effects corollary hypothesis (H15a), the Partisan Media Convergence hypothesis (H16), and the Elasticity of Reality hypothesis (H17). The Longer-term Communication Effects hypothesis predicts that, all else equal, the effects of elite rhetoric on public opinion regarding a conflict will tend to diminish over time, while the Partisan corollary predicts that NPP partisans will decrease their war support in response to negative elite rhetoric more quickly and sharply than independents, who will be more responsive than PP partisans (with the opposite pattern arising in the case of favorable rhetoric). The Elasticity of Reality hypothesis (H17) then predicts that media coverage will grow more responsive over time to reality, and by implication less responsive to *elite framing* of reality, while the Partisan Media Convergence hypothesis (H16) predicts that this pattern will unfold in a more polarized manner in partisan media.

Data and Methods

We assembled a data set on all public presidential speeches, addresses, press conferences and press statements pertaining in significant measure to the conflict in Iraq. Our universe of data consists of a series of 347 transcripts representing all public statements by President George W. Bush that the White House defined, on its web site, as significantly focused on Iraq.[23] We include all such statements by President Bush in which, in the judgments of our coders, Iraq constituted at least one-third of the content of the statement. This yielded 74 cases, of which 67 were primarily (that is, over 50%) focused on Iraq. Our research assistants coded each transcript along a variety of dimensions, including the type of statement (e.g.,

---

[23]Throughout the George W. Bush administration, the White House transcript archive was located at the following web site: http://www.whitehouse.gov/infocus/iraq/archive.html. It is no longer publicly accessible at that URL.

address to the nation, press conference, joint appearance) and frequency of references to Iraq.[24] (See appendix 7.3 for a complete listing of variables and coding rules.)

Our media coverage dependent variables measure variations in the volume of Iraq coverage in the periods before and immediately after presidential statements. To measure television coverage, we counted the number of mentions of Iraq on the nightly newscasts of ABC, CBS, and NBC, as well as on the Fox News Channel's *Special Report with Brit Hume*, between January 2002 and September 2007. In each case, we tallied the total number of news stories mentioning Iraq during the week prior to a presidential event, and then during the week following the event.[25] For newspaper coverage, we employ the monthly tallies of mentions of Iraq in five national newspapers (*New York Times, Washington Post, Los Angeles Times, USA Today,* and *Wall Street Journal*). The newspaper data begin in March 2003 and continue through September 2007.

We separately analyze the effects of presidential rhetoric on the volume of Iraq coverage on network news, Fox, and major newspapers. For the networks and Fox we focus on the percent change in the number of Iraq stories from the week prior to a given presidential statement to the week following the statement. Owing to data limitations, for the newspaper data set we employ the percent change from the month prior to a given event to the month in which the event took place.[26]

Our public opinion dependent variables again employ the smoothed partisan war approval data introduced in chapter 6 and employed in aggregate form earlier in this chapter. (Recall that this variable combines a variety of survey questions related to support for the Iraq War.) Due to the aforementioned smoothing process, the variability in the series is quite small (indeed, significantly smaller in the partisan than in the aggre-

---

[24]Pairs of coders independently dual-coded all transcripts, subsequently resolving any disputes by discussing the disagreement until they achieved consensus. Because this coding was far more straightforward than the content analyses reported elsewhere in this book (merely entailing tallies of "hits" from Lexis-Nexis searches), we elected not to undertake arbitration of initial disputes by a third coder. Inter coder reliability testing indicated that our coders agreed on 85% of all initial (that is, first-round) coding decisions on our primary variables of interest.

[25]We count the day of the event as part of the post-event period.

[26]This latter indicator is obviously considerably less precise, as individual events took place at different times within a given month (e.g., early vs. late in the month), rendering some observations better measures of the pre-event period than others. Consequently the results for our newspaper coverage dependent variable must be interpreted with caution. Nonetheless, there is no reason to expect that this added "noise" should bias the results in our favor. In fact, all else equal, it ought to weaken rather than strengthen the results, as in some instances we are actually comparing two predominantly post-event periods (e.g., if a statement occurred near the end of the initial month).

gate series).[27] Presumably as a consequence, transforming partisan war support into percent changes results in some observations dropping from the model. Hence, as in chapter 6, we employ the simple difference between partisan (that is, Democrat, Republican, and independent) war support at poll period t (just prior to the presidential statement) and at poll period $t + 1$ (immediately following the statement).

To distinguish statements predominantly focused on Iraq from those in which most of the content focused on other issues, we include a dummy variable, coded 1 for the 67 speeches in which over half of the content focused on Iraq. We isolate the effects of the predominantly Iraq-oriented statements by interacting the Iraq focus dummy with a variable measuring the date on which a given statement occurred.[28] Because we anticipate that any trends are unlikely to be linear (or at least non-monotonic) we also include the quadratic of the date counter, and interact the quadratic with the Iraq focus dummy.

For our control variables, in order to account for potential autocorrelation we include the lagged values of our dependent variables (in level form for the news coverage models and in difference form for the opinion models).[29] We also include dummies for radio addresses in the news coverage models and statements to the press (including press conferences) in the opinion models. These two types of speeches stood apart from the others, with radio addresses less likely to influence media coverage and press statements less likely to influence public opinion relative to other types of statements.

To capture the state of events in Iraq, we include measures of the numbers of and weekly changes in U.S. and Iraqi civilian casualties. For the news coverage models, we include only the level and trend in U.S. casualties, as variations in Iraqi civilian casualties had no discernable effect on media coverage. For the opinion models, we add a measure of the weekly change in Iraqi civilian casualties, which significantly influences partisan opinion in several instances.

To account for trends in the volume of media coverage of Iraq, the opinion models also include the network news dependent variable as a

[27]In fact, the maximum change in smoothed war support between any two months (that is, from any month t to any month $t + 1$) is just .85 percentage points (for independents from November to December 2003).

[28]Statistical testing indicated that these 67 statements produced materially distinct effects from the remaining seven less Iraq-centric statements.

[29]In these models, the lagged difference substantially outperformed the lagged level among independents, performed similarly among Democrats (though slightly less strongly), and virtually identically among Republicans. We thus settled on the lagged difference form of the variable, which, on balance, slightly outperformed the lagged level. However, the key results remain similar regardless of the form of the lagged dependent variable included in the models.

control. For the network news and Fox models, in turn, we include a control for the change from week t to week $t + 1$ in the overall volume of coverage of President Bush.[30] This control is intended to account for secular trends in coverage of the president. For instance, it is possible that any trend in Iraq coverage might reflect broader trends in the media's focus on a decreasingly popular second-term president. To further account for this possibility, we also control for the president's overall approval rating in the week prior to a given statement (that is, week $t - 1$).

We also control for the number of mentions of Saddam Hussein by President Bush in each statement. Perhaps because of the familiarity to Americans, and hence the broad accessibility, of the Saddam Hussein-as-villain narrative (Baum 2003), this variable proved a reasonably strong predictor of media attention, independent of variations in the overall intensity of the president's focus on Iraq. Finally, we include three indicators of the state of the U.S. economy—the monthly change in consumer sentiment, the rate of inflation, and average gas prices—as well as a variable measuring the number of days in between presidential statements in the data set.[31]

Results

MEDIA ELASTICITY

We begin with our tests of the Partisan Media Convergence hypothesis (H16) and the Elasticity of Reality hypothesis (H17). For these tests we employ our media coverage dependent variables. (See models 1–3 in table 7.A2 in appendix 7.4 for a series of OLS analyses testing these hypotheses for network news, Fox, and national newspapers, respectively.)[32] In the top half of figure 7.6 we employ Clarify to transform the OLS results into expected changes in news coverage of Iraq, given an Iraq-focused statement, as we move from January 2002 through September 2007.[33]

[30]We again define "week $t + 1$" as beginning on the date of a presidential statement.

[31]Some models exclude up to two influential outlier observations. Including these outliers in the models modestly weakens but does not fundamentally alter the reported results.

[32]As in prior analyses, given the relatively small Ns and large numbers of controls in our fully specified models, we first tested a set of basic models. The basic models exclude all but two control variables (gas prices and network news coverage of Iraq). The results for the key causal variables, though predictably differing somewhat, were nonetheless broadly consistent in valence as well as relative magnitudes with the fully specified models. Consequently, we focus our discussion on interpreting the latter, fully specified models. (To preserve space, we do not report the base models here. Instead, these models are available from the authors upon request.)

[33]Note that for purposes of symmetry we present our results in simulated 100-day intervals. Hence, even though the final public statement on Iraq by the president in our series took place in mid-September 2007, the final simulated value extends several weeks beyond

Beginning with network news, the results indicate that from January 2002 through October 2003, a public statement on Iraq by President Bush was associated with about an 80% increase in the number of stories devoted to Iraq. At that point, the marginal effects of a presidential statement on Iraq begin to decline, reaching zero by the beginning of 2007 and then moving into negative territory, indicating that statements on Iraq by President Bush were actually greeted with declines in network news coverage of Iraq for the remainder of our series, which extends through September 2007 (and is simulated into early October 2007). The decline between 2003 and 2007 is statistically significant ($p < .05$).

The picture is similar for newspapers. This series begins with the start of the war, in March 2003. At that point, a presidential statement on Iraq was associated with about a 40% increase in national newspaper mentions of Iraq. The average effect of a statement decline steadily, reaching zero in late 2005—indicating that public statements by the president no longer influence the volume of newspaper coverage of the conflict in Iraq. At this stage the curve flattens, turning modestly negative for the duration of the series. In effect, these data suggest that by the beginning of 2006, and continuing through at least September 2007, public statements by President Bush had essentially zero effect on the intensity of newspaper coverage of Iraq. This negative trend is again statistically significant ($p < .05$).

Finally, turning to the Fox News Channel's *Special Report with Brit Hume*, here we find a starkly contrasting pattern. At the beginning of the series—in January 2002, when public and media attention were focused on the war against the Taliban and Al Qaeda in Afghanistan—a public statement on Iraq by President Bush was associated with about a 20% decline in Iraq stories on Fox. From that point forward, however, we see a steady increase, with statements by the president exerting increasing influence on coverage of Iraq, surpassing newspapers in January 2005 and network news in April 2006. The upward trend for Fox is statistically insignificant, indicating that the degree of responsiveness of Fox to presidential rhetoric is statistically invariant, over time. However, the differences between the network news and newspaper curves, on the one hand, and the Fox curve on the other are highly significant, both at the beginning and at end of the series. In other words, network newscasts and national newspapers are significantly more responsive to the president's rhetoric at the start of the series and significantly less responsive at

---

that point, to the next 100-day interval point in early October 2007. Additionally, due to missing data on several causal variables, data prior to October 2002 dropped out of the model. Consequently, the values shown in figure 7.4 for the January to September 2002 period are interpolated from the available observations. While the interpolations affect the simulated magnitudes of the effects shown in the figure and described in the text, the overall relationships remain largely unchanged.

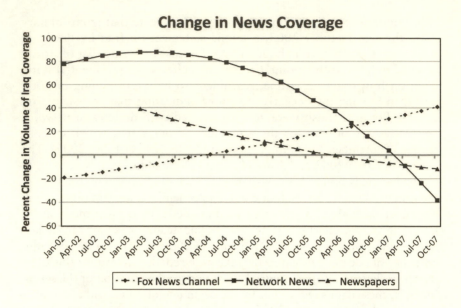

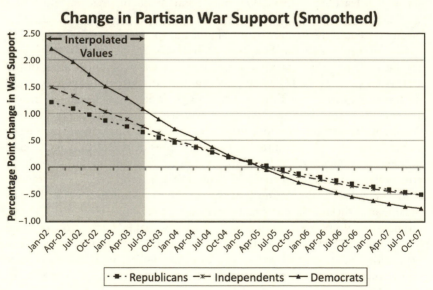

FIGURE 7.6. Estimated Effect of a Presidential Statement on Iraq on News Coverage of and Partisan Support for Iraq War, 2002–2007

the end of the series ($p < .01$ in every case). Conversely, the network news and national newspaper curves are statistically indistinguishable for most of the series, though the former curve becomes significantly more negative than the latter by fall 2007 ($p < .10$).

In essence, Fox's coverage of Iraq appears largely uninfluenced by the president's efforts to frame the debate, while network news and newspapers are heavily influenced by presidential rhetoric early on, but less so over time. Eventually, Fox becomes significantly more positively influenced by presidential rhetoric (in terms of volume) than either network news or newspapers. Taken together, these results clearly support our hypotheses. As predicted by the Elasticity of Reality hypothesis (H17), media coverage becomes less responsive to elite (in this case presidential) rhetoric over time, while, consistent with the Partisan Media Convergence hypothesis (H16), an arguably partisan news outlet (Fox) appears considerably less responsive to variations in events over the course of our series.

It is worth noting that because our series ends in September 2007 (again, simulated into early October), we are unable to account for the effects of the surge in U.S. troops on media coverage during fall 2007. Consequently, we cannot observe any changes in the responsiveness of news outlets to presidential rhetoric that may have taken place. Though the Fox curve is not significant, the fact that it is significantly more positive than the other curves in early fall 2007 raises at least the possibility that Fox was more responsive to a positive turn in events than the networks or national newspapers. If so, this too would be consistent with the Event-Shift Effects corollary hypothesis (H15b).

OPINION ELASTICITY

We turn next to our test of the Longer-term Communication Effects (H15) and Partisan Long-term Effects corollary (H15a) hypotheses. These hypotheses predict, in the former case, that the effects of elite rhetoric will tend to diminish over time (H15), and in the latter, that *negative* elite rhetoric will tend to decrease the support of NPP partisans in the electorate more quickly and sharply than that of independents, who in turn will be more responsive than PP partisans, with the inverse pattern given *positive* elite rhetoric (H15a). (Models 4–6 of table 7.A2 in appendix 7.4 test these predictions.) Once again, we transform the OLS coefficients into expected percentage point changes in war support in response to presidential statements on Iraq, over time. The bottom half of figure 7.6 graphically illustrates the results.

For all three partisan groups, a presidential statement is associated with an increase in approval of the war (either hypothetically, prior to its initiation, or retrospectively, during the conflict). Democrats display the strongest such relationship, with a presidential statement yielding about a 2.2-percentage-point increase in support for going to war against Iraq in January 2002 ($p < .01$). The corresponding increases for Republicans and independents are 1.2 and 1.5 percentage points, respectively ($p < .05$ in both cases).

Lower baseline approval rates among Democrats at the time of the survey presumably explain the relatively higher effect on Democrats. They simply had more room to rise in response to a presidential statement. Moreover, in January 2002, President Bush was in the midst the largest and most sustained rally-'round-the-flag approval spike ever recorded—a 35-percentage-point rise almost overnight (Baum 2002)—in response to the events of 9/11. Hence, at this time, Democrats were more inclined to rally in response to appeals by President Bush than was the case later in his presidency.

All three partisan groups display diminishing responsiveness over time to presidential appeals, reaching the zero point at about the same time, albeit with the Democrats, as anticipated, falling farthest and fastest (though the differences between the partisan subgroups are not statistically significant). The effects of presidential statements turn negative beginning in early 2005, with statements by the president associated with subsequent declines in war support, and remain so across all three partisan groups for the remainder of the series. Among Democrats, a presidential statement on Iraq in the final month of our series is greeted with about a .77-percentage-point decline in war support ($p < .05$). The corresponding declines among independents and Republicans are approximately a half percentage point in each case ($p < .05$).

These results offer clear support for the Longer-term Communication Effects hypothesis (H15). Across all three groups the influence of presidential rhetoric on public support for the Iraq War clearly declines over time, approaching and then surpassing zero, and ultimately turning negative. Consistent with the predictions of the Partisan Long-term Effects corollary hypothesis (H15a), in turn, we observe the largest and most rapid declines among NPP partisans (Democrats) and the shallowest decline among PP partisans (Republicans). However, because these latter differences are statistically insignificant, they must be interpreted as suggestive rather than definitive support for the hypothesis (H15a).

Comparing the Elasticity of Reality in the Partisan and Traditional Media

The Partisan Media Convergence hypothesis (H16) predicts that absent a substantial and lasting change in events, the tenor of news coverage will increasingly reflect reality over time, but that this convergence will occur more quickly for nonpartisan than for partisan media. In the context of the Iraq War (prior to the surge), this hypothesis implies that the tone of coverage related to the war should grow more negative on both the network newscasts and Fox, but more so and more rapidly on the networks. To test this prediction, we again turn to the Media Tenor data introduced in chapter 6. To properly test the Partisan Media Convergence hypothesis, which is contingent on the *absence* of a "significant and sustained change in events," we exclude the time period following the March 2007 initiation of the surge. In figure 7.7, we thus investigate whether Fox and the networks differed significantly in the negativity of their Iraq coverage between September 2004 and February 2007.

Before turning to coverage specifically focused on the Iraq War, we first investigate overall coverage, beginning with (to establish a baseline) the topics and targets in our Media Tenor data set, and then focusing on rhetoric specifically targeting the Bush administration. As shown in the upper left chart, for every year except 2004 Fox airs a significantly smaller proportion of critical evaluations (on all topics) than the networks ($p <$ .001 for 2005 and 2006; $p < .01$ for 2007), although both Fox and the networks air more criticism than praise overall. Moving to the upper right chart, we find that in every year of our series, Fox presents proportionately less criticism of the Bush administration than the networks do ($p < .001$), although again, in all cases critical evaluations outnumber positive ones.

Turning to evaluations related to the war in Iraq, the lower left chart of figure 7.7, which again includes all targets of rhetoric in the data set, shows that both Fox and the networks increased their proportions of critical evaluations related to Iraq between September 2004 and February 2007. More important, as predicted by the Partisan Media Convergence hypothesis (H16), Fox's increasing negativity lags behind that of the networks, though the differential is statistically significant in only two of the four years in our series (2005 and 2007, $p < .10$).

Focusing on Iraq-related evaluations directed specifically at the Bush administration (the lower right chart in figure 7.7), the overwhelming predominance of negativity persists for both Fox and the networks, with 2004's relatively slight negativity offset by dramatic dips in positive coverage in subsequent years. In fact, it is interesting to note that neither NBC nor CBS aired a single positive evaluation of the Bush administration related to Iraq in the first two months of 2007. Again consistent with the predictions of the Partisan Media Convergence hypothesis (H16), in every year except 2004 Fox is significantly less critical of the Bush administration than the networks ($p < .05$ for 2005 and 2006, $p <. 01$ for 2007). Taken together, regardless of whether we focus on *all* evaluations of all topics, all evaluations of the Bush administration, only Iraq-related

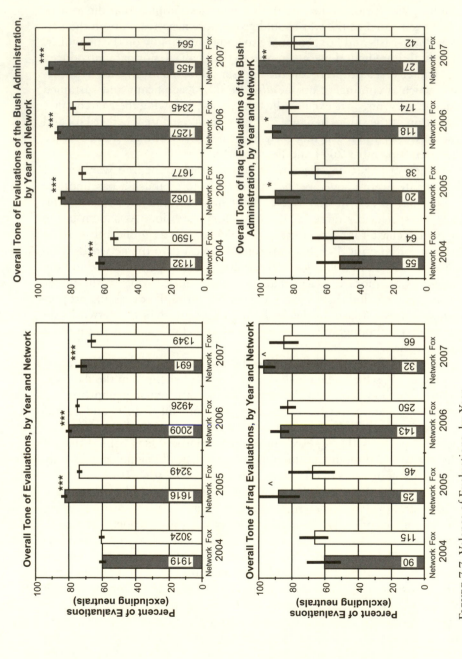

FIGURE 7.7. Valence of Evaluations, by Year

$p < .10$, $^*p < .05$, $^{**}p < .01$, $^{***}p < .001$. Ns are shown within bars. Vertical black lines denote 95% confidence intervals.

evaluations of the administration, or all evaluations of Iraq regardless of target, these results offer clear support for our Partisan Media Convergence hypothesis (H16).

Finally, in an additional test of the Elasticity of Reality hypothesis (H13), as well as our negativity assumption, we take these same evaluation data and more closely link them to specific events in Iraq. The Elasticity of Reality hypothesis (H13) predicts that over time, the tenor of media coverage of a conflict will increasingly parallel objective measures of reality. The negativity assumption simply holds that, all else equal, journalists will prefer negative over positive coverage of political events. To test these predictions, we repeat the event-based analysis introduced in figures 6.9 and 6.10 of chapter 6. In this instance, we focus on evaluations of the presidential administration and divide our sample roughly in half, defining the 2004–2005 period as relatively *early* and the 2006–2007 period as relatively *late* in the conflict. As in chapter 6, we test whether praise and criticism of the administration seem to vary directly with the severity of circumstances on the ground (see figure 6.8 in chapter 6). In this case, however, our hypothesis implies that the tenor of evaluations on the news should more closely track events on the ground in the *second* half of the sample. The negativity assumption in turn implies that to the extent the news outlets deviate from reality, they are likely to do so in a negative direction, overemphasizing critical coverage regardless of the actual tenor of events on the ground. (In table 7.A3 of appendix 7.4 we present the results from a series of logit analyses testing both predictions.) Figure 7.8 graphically illustrates the predicted probabilities derived from our logit analyses.

If one assumes, as we did in chapter 6, that a downward-sloping line is a good approximation of "resembling objective indicators of reality" in a case where the x-axis represents a shift from least to most favorable events, we find considerable support for the Elasticity of Reality hypothesis (H13) in these patterns. We also find clear support for the negativity assumption. On both Fox and the networks in the earlier time period, both positive *and* negative events on the ground in Iraq are significantly associated with increased probabilities of criticism. In contrast, in the latter half of the sample, both the Fox and network curves shift to more closely resemble a direct relationship (as exemplified in figure 6.8 of chapter 6). In other words, in the first half of the series, as the salience of an event increases so too does the volume of negative coverage, regardless of whether the event represents "bad" or "good" news for the U.S. war effort in Iraq. In contrast, in the second half of the series, the valence of coverage largely tracks that of the events. Although the downward slope for positive events on the networks is not statistically significant, its sign reverses from the earlier period. On Fox, the change to a direct rela-

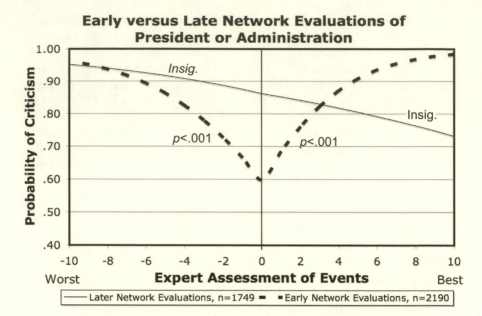

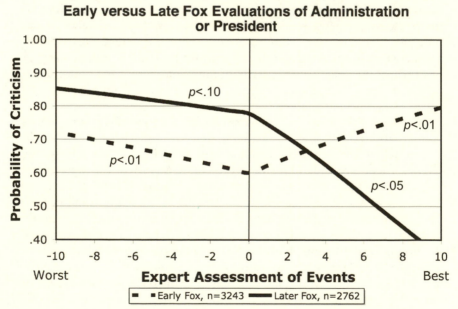

FIGURE 7.8. Estimated Effect of Events on Coverage of Elite Rhetoric, Early (2004–2005) versus Late (2006–2007)

Thickened lines denote statistically significant curves ($p < .10$ or better).

tionship is clearly significant, providing further evidence for the Elasticity of Reality hypothesis (H13).

Finally, though collapsing the temporal element in our data into two broad periods renders this analysis somewhat ill-suited for testing our partisan media predictions, it is nonetheless worth noting that the relationships are more pronounced for the networks in the early period and for Fox in the later period. In other words, the networks appear in these data more likely than Fox to feature bad news in the 2004–2005 period, regardless of the tenor of events, and to be somewhat less responsive than Fox to good news in the 2006–2007 period. These patterns are broadly consistent with our partisan media predictions.

Conclusion

We conclude by returning briefly to Thomas Paine's observation in *Common Sense*: "Time makes more converts than reason." Interestingly, and consistent with the assumptions underlying the *elasticity of reality* framework, in the first half of our data series "reason" (that is, elite rhetoric) predicted changes in war support to a greater extent than our indicators of reality for two of three partisan subgroups (Republicans and independents). Conversely, in the second half of our series the pattern reversed, with "time" (that is, our reality indicators) better predicting changes in war support for two of three partisan subgroups (again, Republicans and independents). This suggests that as the elasticity of reality shrinks over time, so too does the capacity of political elites to frame events to their own advantage, at least to the extent that such frames contradict the tenor of actual events. As VandeHei and Harris (2007) observed in fall 2007 with respect to public opinion regarding Iraq, "[I]t turns out that Washington matters less than many Democrats and even many journalists supposed in determining political momentum in the Iraq debate. Events on the ground—including regular . . . evidence that security is improving somewhat in the wake of the military's 'Surge' policy—matter more."

The implications of these findings for American foreign policy are ambiguous. On the one hand—to again reiterate a central implication of our research—in an increasingly partisan and polarized media and public opinion environment, maintaining support for any foreign policy—much less a costly, protracted one—would seem to be ever more difficult for America's leaders. On the other, one might take heart from the apparent limits we have documented on the capacity of elites to indefinitely manipulate public perceptions of reality. Sooner or later, it would seem, the public can discern the true merits of a conflict to at least some degree, regardless of elite efforts to spin events to their own partisan advantage.

Unfortunately, as we saw in our examination of the surge in late 2007, sometimes a perceived record of distortion and manipulation on the part of an administration can prevent the public from accurately perceiving the reality of a conflict, even when that reality has actually shifted. For example, Noble prize–winning *New York Times* columnist Paul Krugman responded to the proposed troop surge by writing, "The only real question about the planned 'surge' in Iraq—which is better described as a Vietnam-style escalation—is whether its proponents are cynical or delusional. . . . Iraq has become a quagmire of the vanities—a place where America is spending blood and treasure to protect the egos of men who won't admit that they were wrong" (Krugman 2007, "A Quagmire of the Vanities"). Eight months later–in September 2007, well into the turnaround precipitated by the surge–Krugman reaffirmed this stance, saying, "The smart money, then, knows that the surge has failed, that the war is lost, and that Iraq is going the way of Yugoslavia" (Krugman 2007, "A Surge").[34]

In hindsight, it seems clear that President Bush's May 2, 2003, speech aboard the aircraft carrier U.S.S. *Abraham Lincoln*, in which he declared that "In the Battle of Iraq, the United States and our allies have prevailed" (CBS News 2003) before a large banner reading "Mission Accomplished," later reduced the persuasiveness of his assertions that the U.S. military was making progress in Iraq.[35] Indeed, much like the boy

---

[34]Krugman's stance was clearly shared by the editorial board of the *Times*, which opined in January 2007 that "[T]here is nothing ahead but even greater disaster in Iraq" (*New York Times* 2007, "The Real Disaster"). They reiterated that point in late March, when they criticized Bush for not ending the surge and withdrawing troops: "Victory is no longer an option in Iraq, if it ever was. The only rational objective left is to responsibly organize America's inevitable exit. That is exactly what Mr. Bush is not doing and what the House and Senate bills try to do" (*New York Times* 2007, "Legislating Leadership"). In April, they further argued that "[T]here is no possible triumph in Iraq and very little hope left" (*New York Times* 2007, "Four Years Later"), and as late as May they claimed to have sufficient evidence of the surge's ineffectiveness to reach a firm conclusion: "Three months into Mr. Bush's troop escalation, there is no real security in Baghdad and no measurable progress toward reconciliation, while American public support for this folly has all but run out" (*New York Times* 2007, "Mr. Bush Alone").

[35]About a month later, on June 5, 2003, in a message to U.S. troops at Camp Asayliyah, President Bush reiterated his mission accomplished declaration, stating, "America sent you on a mission to remove a great threat and to liberate an oppressed people, and that mission has been accomplished" (Keen 2003). As events in Iraq deteriorated, critics of President Bush explicitly invoked his "mission accomplished" assertion to attack his credibility on the issue. Not surprisingly, these invocations varied by news outlet. On Fox News, which many observers generally perceive as sympathetic to Bush, there were 68 references to "mission accomplished" in Bush-related Iraq stories in 2004–2005, and only 40 in 2006–2007—a mild decrease. In contrast, MSNBC, which in recent years has increasingly established an anti-Bush reputation, invoked "mission accomplished" 64 times in 2004–2005, but then

who cried wolf, politicians who are too quick to claim victory or the accomplishment of a mission risk having no one believe them if or when their long-promised victory actually arrives.

Appendix 7.1. Polimetrix Survey Question Wording

1. Do you believe the prospects for a U.S. victory in Iraq (as you define it) are better, worse, or about the same as they were a year ago?
2. In your opinion, has the Bush administration's ability to influence public opinion regarding the Iraq War increased, decreased, or remained about the same since 2003?
3. Has the "surge" (that is, the U.S. counterinsurgency campaign begun in 2007 that increased the U.S. troop presence in Iraq by over 30,000) increased or decreased the likelihood of a U.S. victory in Iraq, or has it had no significant effect on the likelihood of victory?
4. Have the average monthly U.S. military and Iraqi civilian casualties in Iraq increased, decreased, or stayed at about the same level since the start of the surge?

Appendix 7.2. News Story Novelty Questions
(from Polimetrix survey)

Media Coverage Appropriate: Dummy variable derived from two questions: (1) Do you think press accounts of the war in Iraq have covered gains by coalition forces too little, about right, or too much? (2) Do you think press accounts of the war in Iraq have covered casualties too little, about right, or too much? (Coded: 1 = press accounts "about right" in both cases, 0 = otherwise)

Belief Regarding Casualty Trend: Have the average monthly U.S. military and Iraqi civilian casualties in Iraq increased, decreased, or stayed at about the same level since the start of the "surge"?[36] (Coded −1 = decreased, 0 = stayed about the same, and 1 = increased)

Democrat: Dummy variable coded 1 = Democrat, 0 = otherwise.

Republican: Dummy variable coded 1 = Republican, 0 = otherwise.

---

made more than seven times as many such references over the next two years, referencing the fateful speech 449 times in 2006–2007 (Lexis-Nexis search for [bush and Iraq and "mission accomplished"], conducted February 1, 2009 on Fox and MSNBC archived transcripts, respectively).

[36]We defined the surge in the prior question as "the U.S. counterinsurgency campaign, begun in 2007, that increased the U.S. troop presence in Iraq by over 30,000."

Ideology: Five-point scale, where 0 = very liberal, 3 = moderate, and 5 = very conservative (responses of "not sure" recoded to the mid-point).

Interest in Politics: Level of interest in politics/current events (Coded: 1 = not much interested, 2 = somewhat interested, 3 = very interested; responses of "not sure" coded as missing).

Age: Coded: 2008 minus [birth year].

Education: Scale, coded: 1 = no high school, 2 = high school graduate, 3 = some college, 4 = 2-year college degree, 5 = 4-year college degree, 5 = postgraduate degree.

Male: Dummy variable (Coded: 1 = Male, 0 = Female).

Church Attendance: Coded: 1 = almost never or never, 2 = less than once a month, 3 = a few times a month, 4 = once a week or more (responses of "not sure" recoded as missing).

Southern Resident: Dummy variable (Coded: 1 = Southern resident, 0 = otherwise).

Iraq Question Placement: Dummy variable (Coded: 1 = Iraq questions appear *after* questions about interest in generic story types; 2 = Iraq questions appear *prior* to questions about interest in generic news story types)

APPENDIX 7.3. VARIABLES AND CODING FOR PRESIDENTIAL PUBLIC RHETORIC DATA ANALYSIS

Date: Date of Statement.

Days Since Last Statement: Number of days since the last presidential statement on Iraq.

Radio Address: Dummy variable, coded 1 for radio addresses.

Press Statement/Conference: Dummy variable, coded 1 for press statements or conferences.

Bush Mentions of Saddam: Number of times Saddam Hussein was mentioned in the speech.

Iraq Focus: Coded 1 if Iraq was primary focus of presidential statement, .5 if Iraq was one of two major issues covered in statement, and 0 if Iraq was one of three or more issues covered in statement.

Network Iraq Stories: Percent change in network evening news stories mentioning Iraq between weeks t and $t + 1$.

Network Fox Bush Stories: Change in the number of evening news or Fox stories mentioning Bush between weeks t and $t + 1$.

Fox Iraq Stories: Percent change in Fox Special Report with Brit Hume news stories mentioning Iraq between weeks t and $t + 1$.

Presidential Approval$_{t-1}$: Most recent Gallup or CBS presidential approval poll rating prior to date of presidential statement on Iraq.

Gas Prices: Average weekly gas prices (from http://tonto.eia.doe.gov/dnav/pet/pet_pri_gnd_dcus_nus_w.htm).

Newspaper Mentions of Iraq: Sum of monthly number of stories mentioning Iraq in the *New York Times, Washington Post, Los Angeles Times, USA Today,* and *Wall Street Journal.*

Republican, Democratic, and Independent War Support: Smoothed Partisan War Support Series (see chapter 6 for detailed descriptions)

Weekly U.S. Casualties: Weekly tally of hostile U.S. casualties, as reported by U.S. Department of Defense.

U.S. Casualties: Weekly change in hostile U.S. casualties.

Iraqi Casualties: Weekly change in Iraqi civilian casualties, as listed on www.IraqBodyCount.org.

Consumer Sentiment: Monthly change in consumer sentiment (www.economagic.com).

CPI: Monthly net change in consumer price index (from http://inflationdata.com/inflation/ Consumer_Price_Index/CurrentCPI.asp).

Appendix 7.4. Regression Analysis Tables

Table 7.A1
Public Interest in and Effects of Information about Casualties in Iraq

A. *Multinomial Logit Analysis of Correlates of Preferring a News Story about Declining vs. Rising Casualties in Iraq*

Independent Variables	10% Decline More Interesting	10% Increase More Interesting
Media coverage appropriate	−0.203 (0.207)	0.128 (0.349)
Belief regarding casualty trend	−0.321 (0.163)*	0.510 (0.379)
Democrat	0.367 (0.273)	0.418 (0.436)
Republican	0.463 (0.280)^	−0.500 (0.674)
Ideology	0.384 (0.105)***	0.288 (0.218)
Interest in politics	−0.297 (0.134)*	0.153 (0.271)
Age	−0.005 (0.006)	−0.024 (0.011)*
Education	−0.179 (0.064)**	−0.222 (0.142)
Male	0.120 (0.177)	0.503 (0.377)
Church attendance	0.123 (0.071)^	−0.186 (0.151)
Iraq Question placement	−0.255 (0.170)	−0.664 (0.332)*
Southern resident	0.283 (0.176)	−0.416 (0.351)
Media coverage appropriate × belief regarding casualty trend	0.781 (0.258)**	−0.056 (0.470)
Constant	−1.160 (0.592)	−0.852 (1.240)
R^2 (N)	0.09 (N = 904)	

B. *OLS Analyses of Effects of Variations in Valence of New York Times Coverage of Casualties and Actual Casualties on Public Support for Iraq and Effects of Casualties on* New York Times *Coverage*

Independent Variables	(1) (War Support, Basic)	(2) (War Support, Fully Specified)	(3) (War Support, (News Coverage)
Lagged dependent variable	—	0.582 (0.159)***	−0.252 (0.043)***
NY Times net positive coverage$_{-1}$	0.071 (0.046)	0.181 (0.065)**	—
Civilian & military casualties$_{t-1}$	0.084 (0.106)	0.146 (0.105)	52.546 (36.186)
Period (month or week)	0.005 (0.002)**	0.005 (0.002)**	0.235 (0.282)
Period^2	−0.0001 (0.00003)**	−0.0001 (0.00003)**	−0.001 (0.001)
Casualties$_{t-1}$ × period	−0.009 (0.006)^	−0.013 (0.006)*	−1.598 (0.870)^
Casualties$_{t-1}$ × period^2	0.0002 (0.0001)*	0.0002 (0.0001)*	0.007 (0.0037)^
NY Times coverage$_{-1}$ × period	−0.005 (0.004)	−0.013 (0.004)**	—

TABLE 7.A1 *(continued)*

Independent Variables	(1) (War Support, Basic)	(2) (War Support, Fully Specified)	(3) (War Support, News Coverage)
NY *Times* coverage$_{-1}$ × period^2	0.0001 (0.0001)	0.0002 (0.00007)**	—
Presidential election dummy	—	−0.016 (0.007)*	—
Hurricane Katrina (5-month dummy)	—	0.018 (0.008)*	10.074 (6.411)
Presidential approval$_{t-1}$	−0.001 (0.001)	−0.002 (0.001)^	0.447 (0.486)
Proportion of TV Iraq coverage focusing on casualties	—	−0.074 (0.050)	—
Proportion of newspaper Iraq coverage focusing on casualties	—	0.209 (0.075)**	74.784 (45.429)
Gas prices$_{t-1}$	—	0.0001 (0.0001)	0.063 (0.073)
Total newspaper Iraq coverage$_{t-1}$	—	—	0.024 (0.026)
Midterm election dummy	—	—	11.331 (10.152)
Constant	0.015 (0.069)	0.035 (0.066)	−46.712 (37.878)
R^2 (N)	0.37 (N = 53)	0.59 (N = 52)	0.10 (N = 236)

^$p < .10$, *$p < .05$, **$p < .01$, ***$p < .001$

Note: In part A, base category is both stories equally interesting.

TABLE 7.A2
OLS Analyses of Effects of Bush Iraq Statements on News Coverage and Partisan War Support

Independent Variable	(1) Networks	(2) Fox	(3) Newspapers	(4) Republicans	(5) Democrats	(6) Independents
Lagged DV (t or $_{t-1}$)	-0.004 (0.002)^	-0.090 (0.022)***	-0.000 (0.000)	0.009 (0.249)	-0.508 (0.317)	-0.395 (0.240)
Iraq focus	2.442 (0.605)***	1.347 (0.965)	28.318 (16.636)^	1.754 (0.487)***	2.638 (1.041)**	1.451 (0.679)*
Statement date	0.008 (0.002)***	0.024 (0.012)*	0.031 (0.018)^	0.005 (0.002)**	0.005 (0.002)*	0.004 (0.002)*
Statement date^2 (×1,000)	-0.004 (0.001)***	-0.011 (0.006)^	-0.009 (0.005)^	-0.003 (0.001)**	-0.003 (0.001)*	-0.002 (0.001)*
Iraq focus × statement date	-0.008 (0.002)***	-0.024 (0.012)*	-0.032 (0.018)	-0.006 (0.002)***	-0.008 (0.003)**	-0.006 (0.002)**
Iraq focus × statement date^2 (×1,000)	0.003 (0.001)***	0.012 (0.006)^	0.009 (0.005)^	0.003 (0.001)***	0.003 (0.001)**	0.003 (0.001)**
Network Iraq stories	—	—	—	-0.068 (0.086)	-0.007 (0.110)	-0.066 (0.099)
Network/Fox Bush stories	0.009 (0.003)*	0.037 (0.018)*	—	—	—	—
Press statement/conference	—	—	—	-0.230 (0.108)*	-0.305 (0.175)^	-0.145 (0.171)
Radio address	-0.110 (0.105)	0.128 (0.137)	-0.036 (0.036)	—	—	—
U.S. casualties	0.008 (0.005)^	-0.001 (0.006)	0.002 (0.003)	0.009 (0.005)^	0.015 (0.008)^	0.008 (0.007)
Weekly U.S. casualties$_{t-1}$	0.000 (0.006)	-0.002 (0.006)	0.004 (0.002)^	0.011 (0.007)^	0.025 (0.008)**	0.014 (0.009)
Iraqi casualties	—	—	—	0.007 (0.002)**	0.009 (0.004)*	0.011 (0.003)**
Pre-war	0.456 (0.279)	-0.370 (0.360)	—	0.500 (0.272)^	-0.106 (0.403)	0.187 (0.347)
Bush mentions of Saddam	-0.053 (0.025)*	0.000 (0.027)	-0.017 (0.006)**	-0.036 (0.016)*	-0.009 (0.023)	-0.020 (0.021)
Presidential approval$_{t-1}$	-0.033 (0.017)*	0.025 (0.026)	-0.009 (0.005)^	-0.016 (0.012)	-0.041 (0.017)*	-0.022 (0.014)
Consumer sentiment	0.006 (0.003)*	-0.001 (0.003)	0.001 (0.001)	-0.002 (0.002)	0.004 (0.003)	0.000 (0.003)
Gas prices	-0.002 (0.002)	-0.002 (0.001)	0.001 (0.001)	0.003 (0.001)**	0.005 (0.001)***	0.004 (0.001)**
CPI	0.124 (0.102)	-0.116 (0.080)	-0.034 (0.023)	-0.014 (0.046)	0.023 (0.057)	0.023 (0.057)
Days since last statement	-0.001 (0.001)	0.001 (0.001)	-0.001 (0.000)**	0.000 (0.000)	0.001 (0.000)^	0.000 (0.000)
Constant	0.416 (1.403)	-0.920 (2.211)	-27.450 (16.704)	-0.722 (0.834)	-0.137 (1.151)	-0.217 (0.974)
R^2 (N)	0.47 (N = 71)	0.70 (N = 72)	0.43 (N = 63)	0.61 (N = 71)	0.49 (N = 71)	0.45 (N = 71)

^$p < .10$, *$p < .05$, **$p < .01$, ***$p < .001$

Note: "× 1,000" indicates that, for presentational purposes, listed coefficients have been multiplied by 1,000.

TABLE 7.A3

Logit Analyses of Valence of Network News and Fox Evaluations of President and Administration Targets, as Source and Timing Vary

News Outlet	Independent Variables			
	Negative Events	All Events	Constant	Pseudo-R^2 (N)
Early Evaluations (2004, 2005)				
Network news	−0.669 (0.095)***	0.380 (0.057)***	0.401 (0.095)***	0.02 (N = 2,190)
Fox	−0.151 (0.068)*	0.096 (0.040)*	0.404 (0.072)***	0.001 (N = 3,243)
Later Evaluations (2006, 2007)				
Network news	−0.032 (0.120)	−0.083 (0.079)	1.840 (0.158)***	0.01 (N = 1,749)
Fox	0.137 (0.076)^	−0.187 (0.055)***	1.254 (0.104)***	0.01 (N = 2,762)

^$p < .10$, *$p < .05$, ***$p < .0001$.

CHAPTER 8

Barbarians inside the Gates

PARTISAN NEW MEDIA AND THE POLARIZATION
OF AMERICAN POLITICAL DISCOURSE

IN AUGUST 2007, the FBI asked media organizations in Seattle, Washington, to assist in identifying two men who were seen behaving unusually aboard several ferries in the area. The FBI asked the news outlets to publicize descriptions of the men, including photographs taken by suspicious ferry employees. The *Seattle Post-Intelligencer* published an article noting the FBI's search, but refused to include either physical descriptions or photographs of the men. This refusal ignited a firestorm of criticism. In response, the paper's managing editor acknowledged the controversy but dismissed its significance, commenting: "I understand that people have a hard time with the concept that we get to decide what is news and what isn't, and what is fair and what isn't" (McCumber 2007).

Less than a decade earlier John Chambers, the CEO of Cisco Systems, famously stated, "What people have not grasped is that the Internet will change everything" (Friedman 1998). While the impact of digital communication on the conduct of twenty-first-century political campaigning and governance became even more evident during the 2008 presidential election, the Internet's impact as a communication medium often seems hidden in plain sight.[1] Indeed, many traditional journalists—like the man-

---

[1]Examples of the former include the literatures on online deliberative democracy (e.g., Price and Cappella 2002; Fishkin and Laslett 2003), collective action (e.g., Groeling 1999; Lupia and Sin 2003; Bimber, Flanagin, and Stahl 2005), online campaigning (e.g., Bimber and Davis 2003; Hindman 2005; Trammell et al. 2006), and "e-governance" (e.g., Allen 2000; Fountain 2001; Chadwick 2003; Anttiroiko 2004). One area where fundamental changes are clearly evident is political fundraising, which the Internet does appear to have revolutionized. In his 2000 primary race against George W. Bush, Senator John McCain (R-AZ) raised over $2 million in online contributions in the three days following his upset victory in the New Hampshire primary (Romano 2003). In 2003, Howard Dean shocked the Democratic field and seized an early lead in the nomination race by raising more than $3 million online in only three months. In 2008, Barack Obama's campaign shattered fundraising records in both the primary and the general election. In the first three months of 2007, he pulled in nearly $25 million, $8 million of which came from online donors (Salant 2008). In the second quarter of 2007, over 100,000 online donors helped Barack Obama outpace frontrunner Hillary Rodham Clinton's fundraising by almost $10 million (Wilson 2007). His total fundraising for the entire election was more than $650 million, collected

aging editor of the *Post-Intelligencer*—apparently failed to grasp that the Internet's comparatively modest production and distribution costs (Hamilton 2004) removed the decision of what is news and what isn't from the exclusive province of professionals who spoke on the nation's networks or "bought ink by the barrel." Along these lines, Rupert Murdoch, chairman and chief executive of News Corp. and himself a former newspaper editor, observed,

> It used to be that a handful of editors could decide what was news— and what was not. They acted as sort of demigods. If they ran a story, it became news. If they ignored an event, it never happened. Today editors are losing this power. The Internet, for example, provides access to thousands of new sources that cover things an editor might ignore. And if you aren't satisfied with that, you can start up your own blog and cover and comment on the news yourself. (Cooper 2008)

Traditional media undoubtedly still play a central role in American political communication. Indeed, a record audience of 71.5 million viewers tuned in to television news coverage of Election Day 2008 (Gorman 2008). However, 2008 clearly also represented a breakthrough year for Internet political news. While only 10% of survey respondents in 2004 reported getting "most" of their news about the presidential campaign via the Internet, by 2008 that number had jumped to 33%, outpacing newspapers and radio, and ranking second only to television (Pew 2008, "Internet Now Major Source of Campaign News").[2] In addition, as figure 8.1 shows, demographic trends imply the impact of Internet political news should only grow in the future.

These data show that consumption of Internet campaign news is especially prevalent among younger age groups, with just about half of 18- to 29-year-olds reporting that they relied on the Internet as their *main* source of news about the 2008 presidential election. For this age group, Internet news usage tops that of newspapers and radio *combined*, and is only 12 percentage points lower than television.[3]

---

from three million different donors (Salant 2008). One analyst thus commented after Obama's victory, "No one's going to say Obama won the election because of the Internet but he wouldn't have been able to win without it" (AFP 2008).

[2] Respondents were allowed to offer multiple responses. In the 2008 survey, a similar proportion of respondents reported relying on Fox News (21%) as on "network TV" (24%) and CNN (25%). MSNBC (10%) and local TV news (13%) were substantially less popular as primary sources of election news (Pew 2008, "Internet Now Major Source of Campaign News").

[3] This contrasts with the consumption patterns of the oldest cohort (65 + -year-olds), who are 70 percentage points more likely to rely on television than Internet news, and are also more likely to rely on newspapers and radio (Pew 2008, "Internet Now Major Source of Campaign News").

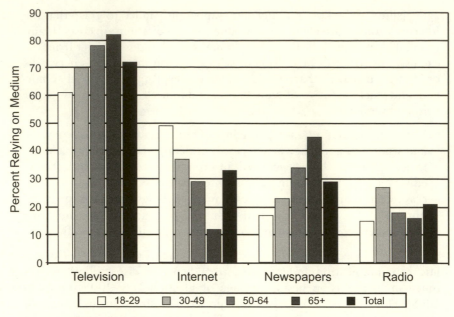

FIGURE 8.1. Percent of Public Relying on Medium for News about Campaign 2008, by Age

Note: Figures represent first or second mentions and sum to more than 100% because multiple responses were allowed. Results are based on combined Pew surveys conducted October 17–20 and October 24–27, 2008 (n = 2,011).

Many online media enthusiasts have trumpeted the rising power of the Internet, arguing that the new technology would "empower ordinary people to beat 'big media'" and "crash the gates of power" (Armstrong and Moulitsas 2006; Reynolds 2006), or at least affect the framing of elite debate among politicians and other opinion elites (Farrell and Drezner 2008). Conversely, others worry that such a trend will lead to a fragmented, "cyberbalkanized" society and deprive the nation of the "common diet" of news that, they argue, is essential for the proper functioning of modern democracy (Katz 1996; Putnam 2000; Sunstein 2001; Adamic and Glance 2005; see also Prior 2007). As Blumler and Kavanagh (1999, 221–22) argue, "[t]he presumption of mass exposure to relatively uniform political content, which has underpinned each of the three leading paradigms of political effect–agenda setting, the spiral of silence, and the cultivation hypothesis–can no longer be taken for granted."

All that said, while prior research has shown that the public has changed its consumption patterns online in a manner consistent with this sort of fragmentation (Tewksbury 2005), it remains unclear whether and to what extent the content and impact of Internet news reporting might actually differ from those of traditional media. If Internet news outlets lack their own independent newsgathering apparatus or are primarily echo chambers, repeating—albeit perhaps also magnifying—the "relatively uniform political content" of the traditional news media, then it would be difficult to justify claims of revolution, disaster, or nirvana.

In this chapter we extend our investigation of the third question guiding the book—determining the influence of new media on the relationship between public opinion and foreign policy—to assessing the role of Internet news. We begin by presenting results from parallel surveys of professional journalists and political bloggers aimed at testing several assumptions underlying our Media Partisanship hypothesis (H3), as well as several other hypotheses that we develop and test in this chapter. Next, we systematically examine the strategies for choosing news employed by Internet news providers to determine whether they differ significantly from those of the traditional news media in politically important ways, such as partisan filtering. Specifically, we consider whether and to what extent partisan new media editorial judgments systematically skew the content of news on partisan political web sites, relative to their nonpartisan peers. Finally, we explore the effects of news self-selection via the Internet on public attitudes toward the war in Iraq. These investigations test the Media Partisanship hypothesis (H3), according to which left-leaning web sites will be more likely to feature stories harmful to Republicans or helpful to Democrats, right-leaning web sites will be more likely to feature stories harmful to Democrats or helpful to Republicans, and nonpartisan web sites, like the wire services, will be equally likely to feature stories harmful to Democrats and Republicans. They also test two corollary hypotheses, explicated below, to H5 (Costly Credibility hypothesis) and H10 (Partisan Media Opinion hypothesis) concerning news selection criteria in nonpartisan media and partisan polarization patterns among Internet news consumers, respectively.

Contrasting News Standards in the Traditional and Partisan Media

To predict the content of partisan relative to nonpartisan media, we rely on an assumption concerning the preferences of news suppliers: we assume that partisan news producers will select stories based on their partisan implications rather than (or at least in addition to) traditional standards of newsworthiness. In contrast, we assume traditional journalists will largely disavow such partisan criteria or will at least be less influenced by them. If so, we should observe starkly differing attitudes about which stories in the news are "newsworthy," depending on their partisan implications. Among traditional journalists, party affiliation and ideology ought to matter less for story preferences and related attitudes than among more overtly partisan news providers. To investigate this core assumption underlying our hypothesis tests, as well as an assumption underlying our elasticity of reality framework in chapter 7, we surveyed 41 traditional journalists (we employed parts of this survey in chapter 3) and 44 politically oriented Internet bloggers. Our goal was to assess their attitudes toward different types of news stories, as well as toward news regarding the Iraq conflict.[4]

Beginning with overall news preferences, we asked the political bloggers the same battery of questions as presented in chapter 3 (vis-à-vis traditional journalists) regarding their degree of interest in eight possible types of stories (that is, Congressional Democrats or Republicans praising or criticizing their fellow partisans or the other party). We asked the bloggers to tell us which of the stories they would find most and second-most interesting, as well as the two they would find least and second-least interesting. Figure 8.2 presents the results from these questions separately for self-identified Republican and Democratic bloggers. The scales are constructed by giving each respondent two points for selecting a story as most interesting, one point for second-most interesting, -1 point for second-least interesting, and -2 points for least interesting. We then tallied the points across individuals within each partisan subgroup to produce the final news story interest score.

The first thing to note is that our Democratic bloggers mirror the traditional journalists in ranking the story in which Congressional Republicans criticize President Bush as their most preferred news story type. However, Republican bloggers do not share this preference, instead rating as their most preferred story type one in which Congressional Democrats praise President Bush. Both stories are costly, yet among bloggers, partisan interest appears to guide the choice between these two costly story types.

In general, consistent with our core theoretical assumptions, costly credibility appears to loom large, even among partisan bloggers, as each of the top four story types among Democrats and three of the top four among Republicans represent costly rhetoric (intraparty criticism or cross-party praise). However, these preferences are less ubiquitous among Republicans, who prefer congressional Republican criticism of congressional Democrats (cross-party criticism) to congressional Republican criticism of President Bush or praise of congressional Democrats (intraparty criticism and cross-party praise, respectively).

[4]We initially contacted 148 partisan bloggers who were listed in the TruthLaidBear blog "ecosystem" listing of influential partisan bloggers. See truthlaidbear.com/ecosystem.php for a full listing. Our response rate was thus 30%.

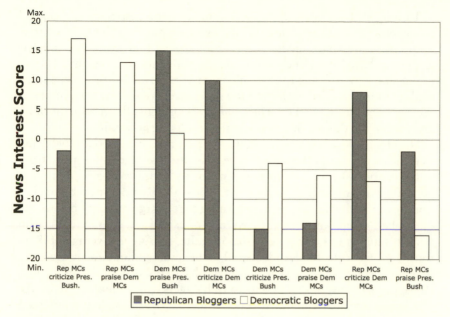

FIGURE 8.2. Estimated Effect of Events on Coverage of Elite Rhetoric, Early (2004–2005) versus Late (2006–2007)

Note: Most preferred story type = 2 points; second most preferred = 1 point; least preferred = –2 points; second least preferred = –1 point. MC, members of Congress; Rep, Republican(s); Dem, Democrat(s).

On the low end of the scale, Democratic and Republican bloggers disagree starkly on the least interesting story types. Republicans are least interested in congressional Democratic criticism of President Bush and only slightly more interested in congressional Democrats praising each other. Conversely, Democratic bloggers are least interested in congressional Republican praise of President Bush and, following that, congressional Republican criticism of congressional Democrats. In this case, congressional Democrats again mirror our traditional journalists, who were also least interested in congressional Republican praise of President Bush.

Of course, given that the figures for traditional journalists are aggregated, the closer proximity of their preferences to Democratic bloggers may reflect the pro-Democratic tilt among the traditional journalists in our sample. Nonetheless, these results clearly suggest that, consistent with our expectations, partisanship influences bloggers' preferences regarding both costly and cheap talk story types, although more starkly so in the latter case, where partisan credibility looms particularly large. This in turn leads Democratic and Republican bloggers to prefer different types of stories.

Turning to Iraq news, figure 8.3 compares the responses of political bloggers and traditional journalists by their party affiliations to four questions concerning media coverage of the war in Iraq. The top left graphic is based on a question asking respondents whether they believe the media were offering too much coverage of U.S. and Iraqi civilian casualties in Iraq (coded +1), too little such coverage (coded −1), or about the right amount (coded 0). The solid curve presents the results for bloggers, while the dashed line presents the results for journalists.

For bloggers, we see a consistent increase in the likelihood of believing that the media have offered excessive casualty coverage as we move from self-described Democratic to independent to Republican-affiliated bloggers. To be more precise, on the −1 to +1 scale, Democrats, who tend to oppose the war, average a −.7, indicating that a large majority believe the media had offered insufficient coverage of casualties. Republicans, who tend to support the war, believe the opposite, scoring an average of .8 on the −1 to +1 scale. Independents fall in the middle, though they are more likely to believe the media had overemphasized casualties than to hold the opposing view. In sharp contrast to bloggers, traditional journalists in our sample are nearly uniform in believing that the media had offered too little coverage of casualties. Moreover, partisan affiliation makes little difference among traditional journalists, as the curve remains essentially flat as we move from Democrats to independents/undeclared journalists.[5] (Unfortunately, none of our traditional journalist respondents identified themselves as Republicans, thereby truncating our partisan comparisons.)

The top right graphic presents the results from a similar analysis, this time based on a question asking respondents whether they believed press coverage of the Bush administration regarding the Iraq conflict had been too critical, not critical enough, or fair. Once again, among bloggers, as we move from self-described Democrats to independents to Republicans, we observe an increasing likelihood of believing that the media had offered excessive criticism of the Bush administration. Whereas *all* Democratic bloggers report believing that press coverage was *insufficiently* critical, Republicans average about a .9 on the −1 to +1 scale, indicating that the vast majority believe that press coverage was *too* critical. Independents again fall in between, with a plurality believing the press was too critical of the Bush administration in its Iraq coverage. As before, traditional journalists fall somewhere in between Democratic and independent bloggers, believing there was insufficient criticism of the Bush administration, on average.

[5]Our independent category includes self-identified independents and those who chose the "prefer not to answer" option. Excluding the latter individuals has no material effect on the results.

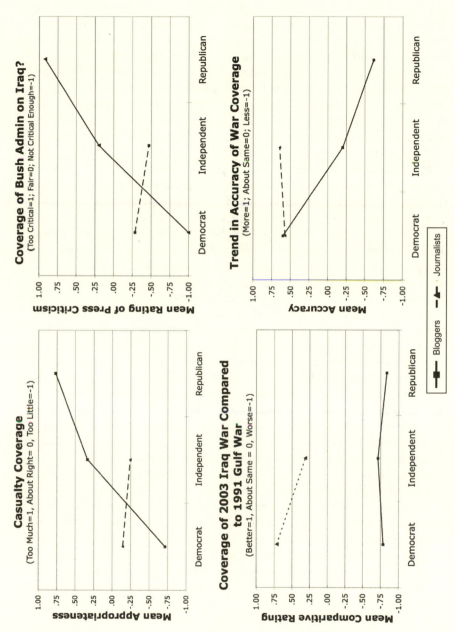

FIGURE 8.3. Journalist versus Blogger Attitudes toward Iraq Coverage

The bottom left graphic compares the attitudes of traditional journalists and bloggers on the question of whether press coverage of the Iraq War was better, worse, or about the same, relative to coverage of the first Persian Gulf War in 1991. Here, traditional journalists and bloggers offered starkly differing responses. Interestingly, in this instance, partisanship appears somewhat more salient to journalists than to bloggers, though the differences between Democratic and independent/undeclared journalists are not statistically significant. Among bloggers, this is the one instance where all three partisan subgroups are in near unanimous agreement that press coverage of the second Iraq War was inferior to that of the first (with each group averaging about a $-.8$). In stark contrast, a majority of traditional journalists, and especially self-described Democrats, believe that press coverage of the second Iraq War was superior to that of the first (with average scores of over .3 for independent/undeclared journalists and nearly .8 for self-described Democrats.

The final (bottom right) graphic in figure 8.3 is based on a question asking respondents whether they believed press coverage of the Iraq War had grown more or less accurate, or remained about the same, since the start of the war. Consistent with our elasticity of reality framework (see chapter 7), a substantial majority of journalists believe that press coverage of the war became increasingly accurate over time. Once again, partisanship matters little among traditional journalists. In contrast, bloggers fall largely along partisan lines, with Democratic bloggers mirroring their traditional journalist counterparts and independents being slightly more likely to believe that press coverage grew *less* accurate than to believe it grew *more* so. Republican bloggers take the mirror opposite position from their Democratic counterparts, believing in similarly large numbers that press coverage of the war grew less accurate over time. The gaps between independent and Republican bloggers, on the one hand, and traditional journalists on the other are striking (about .80 and 1.2 on the -1 to $+1$ scales, respectively, for independent and Republican bloggers, relative to traditional journalists).

Next, figure 8.4 reports the results of a series of questions aimed at testing an assumption underlying our elasticity of reality framework against representatives of both the traditional and partisan media. The top graphic in figure 8.4 reports the responses from traditional journalists to two questions asking whether they thought that the Bush administration was largely able to control media "spin" at the outset of the Iraq conflict, and whether they believed its capacity to influence public opinion regarding the war had increased, decreased, or remained about the same, since 2003. The results among traditional journalists could hardly be starker. Among Democrats, 100% believe that the Bush administration controlled the spin on Iraq War coverage at the outset, while 100%

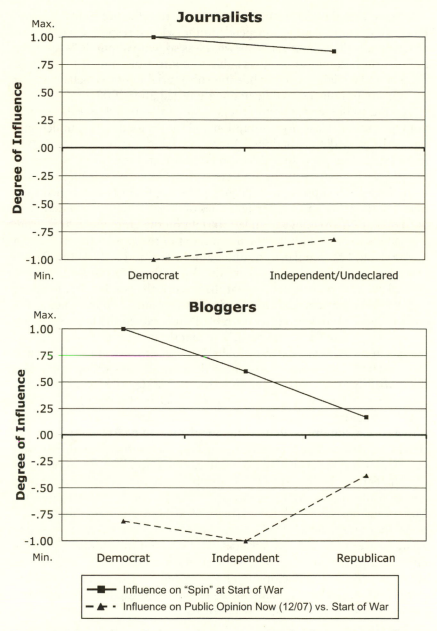

FIGURE 8.4. Journalist and Blogger Assessments of Bush Administration Influence over Framing of Iraq War at Start of War versus Over Time Trend

also agree that the administration's capacity to influence public opinion receded over time. Among independent/undisclosed respondents, the percentages are still dramatic, if somewhat less so, with about 90% agreeing that the Bush administration was able to control the spin at the start of the war and a slightly smaller but still substantial majority believing that its capacity to influence public opinion receded after 2003.

Turning to bloggers, the bottom graphic in Figure 8.4 reveals support both for the core elasticity assumption and for the assumption underlying our partisan media predictions. On the one hand, majorities of bloggers share journalists' view that the Bush administration was able to control the spin at the outset of the Iraq conflict, while also believing that the administration's capacity to influence public opinion had declined over time. On the other hand, the magnitudes of those beliefs vary widely with partisanship. As we move from left to right on the graphic—that is, from Democrats to Republicans—the magnitudes of the gaps between the two questions decline. Similar to traditional journalists, 100% of the Democratic bloggers we surveyed believe the Bush administration was able to control the spin on war coverage at the start of the conflict, while nearly 100% believe the administration's influence over public opinion had weakened since 2003. Independents resemble Democrats in the latter case, but are less likely than Democrats to believe that the administration controlled the spin at the outset of the war. Finally, Republicans are far less likely than Democrats or independents to believe that the administration controlled the spin at the war's outset, while also being considerably less likely to believe that its influence on public opinion had declined since 2003.

Taken together, these data offer clear and consistent support for several of the core assumptions underlying our theory. In nearly every instance, consistent with our assumptions regarding the motivations of partisan media, bloggers differ starkly from traditional journalists. Partisanship in turn appears to mediate the attitudes of bloggers to a greater extent than among traditional journalists, though it clearly matters for both groups. Moreover, consistent with the elasticity of reality framework, most traditional journalists believe that coverage of the Iraq War grew increasingly accurate over time that the president and his administration had strongly influenced media coverage at the outset of the Iraq conflict, and that its ability to influence public opinion had receded over time. In responding to these same questions, many bloggers shared journalists' perceptions. However, they exhibit less of a consensus, dividing more sharply along partisan lines.

While demonstrating that political bloggers differ from traditional journalists in their story preferences is suggestive, it does not demonstrate that the content of their web sites does in fact vary systematically along party lines. Journalists have long maintained that it is possible for writers to be cognizant of their own biases and to consciously avoid them in producing their final news product. Therefore, in the next section we empirically investigate whether the content on partisan web sites is as "biased" as is commonly assumed.

PARTISAN AND NONPARTISAN NEWSWORTHINESS

Establishing the presence or absence of partisan bias in news content has proven difficult. Self-described media watchdog groups such as the Media Research Center (MRC), the Center for Media and Public Affairs (CMPA), and Fairness and Accuracy In Reporting (FAIR) claim to objectively analyze media content, yet they routinely disagree on the incidence, severity, and direction of bias in the media. Scholarly attempts to assess media bias are similarly inconclusive (e.g., Efron 1971; Patterson 1993; Sutter 2001).

Among the principal difficulties in establishing the presence or absence of media bias is clearly defining what exactly constitutes bias. Several recent studies (Groseclose and Milyo 2005; Gentzkow and Shapiro 2006) have sought to empirically measure mainstream news media content against various standards, and have done so with varying results. However, few (if any) have successfully surmounted the so-called "baseline" or "unobserved population" problem (Hofstetter 1976; Groeling and Kernell 1998; Niven 2002; Groeling 2008), especially with regard to online media. In other words, finding an ideological slant in media content is one thing; attributing such a slant to politically biased editorial judgment by the media is another. After all, the observed pattern of coverage, whatever its slant, might simply reflect a balanced sampling of the actual available population of potential stories. For instance, if one observes that 90% of statements by elites on a given news outlet criticize the president, that *could* reflect biased story selection by the outlet, or it may simply reflect the fact that 90% of all statements by the elites in the pertinent time frame were, in fact, critical of the president. In the latter case, this hypothetical 90% anti-president skew in media coverage would represent an *accurate* reflection—that is, *objective* reporting—of the tenor of elite rhetoric regarding the president.

We attempt to surmount this difficulty by comparing overtly partisan web sites with other web sites that are *least* likely to incorporate partisan political preferences into their news selection decisions: the news wire services, both non-U.S. and U.S.-based. We employ the news wires as the most objective available baseline measure of the possible universe of potentially important political stories from which other news sources *could* have selected. Comparing the news choices of the wire service editors with the proprietors of more partisan web sites should allow us to assess the extent of the partisan skew of such sites. For the latter partisan sites, we selected DailyKos.com, FreeRepublic.com, and FoxNews.com. The first two outlets are commonly viewed as overtly pro-Democratic/liberal and pro-Republican/conservative, respectively, while FoxNews.com is produced by a major cable television news network with a reputation (at least among liberals and Democrats) for favoring Republican and conservative issues and candidates.

We summarize our relatively straightforward expectations here in the aforementioned Media Partisanship (H3) and Nonpartisan Media (H4) hypotheses. These hypotheses simply predict, respectively, that left-leaning web sites will disproportionately feature anti-Republican or pro-Democratic stories, right-leaning web sites will disproportionately feature anti-Democratic or pro-Republican stories, and nonpartisan web sites, such as the wire services, will be equally likely to feature stories harmful to either party.[6]

Notwithstanding assertions to the contrary by countless partisans on the right (e.g., Coulter 2003; Goldberg 2003) and left (e.g., Alterman 2003; Franken 2004), we assume that nonpartisan news media, either traditional or new *do not* select stories because they advantage a specific party or ideology. This, however, does not mean they will treat all partisan messages equally. Rather, throughout this book we have identified, and considered the implications of, many commonly held professional norms that might affect which types of partisan news stories journalists will typically prefer to select—that is, which stories they will consider newsworthy (see, e.g., Tuchman 1972; Graber 1997; Schudson 1978; Groeling 2001).

In particular, we argued in chapter 2 that for nonpartisan news, the norms of novelty, authority, conflict, and balance combine to put a premium on *costly* messages from a given party in which the party unexpectedly appears to be attacking its own members or praising the opposing party. Such messages are especially novel, as partisans have strong electoral incentives (Mayhew 1974; Groeling and Baum 2008) to reserve their attacks for the *other* party, while focusing their positive rhetoric on their fellow partisans. This suggests a corollary to our Costly Credibility hypothesis (H5):

---

[6]This assumes that other characteristics about partisans might systematically vary. Such characteristics in turn could tend to make one party relatively more newsworthy than the other. For example, in chapter 2 we argued that control of the presidency and majority status in Congress increase a party's authority and hence newsworthiness (see also Groeling 2001). In our empirical analyses, we therefore carefully control for other systematic differences in newsworthiness across the parties.

HYPOTHESIS 5A: NONPARTISAN MEDIA COROLLARY

The wire services will be more likely to cover partisan news stories featuring *costly* communication (that is, party members criticizing fellow party members or praising the other party) than those featuring *cheap* communication (that is, party members criticizing the other party or praising their own party).[7]

Newsworthiness Analysis Data and Methods

We loosely derive our research design from the classic "gatekeeper" studies. Most notably, White (1950) investigated the daily decisions of a newspaper wire service editor, "Mr. Gates." White not only examined the wire service stories appearing in the paper, he also focused specifically on the wire stories that Gates had decided should *not* appear in the paper.[8] The concept of news selection is at the heart of one of the most important modern theories of media effects and political communication, agenda-setting research (McCombs and Shaw 1972), which at its core has "focused on the relationship between the news media's ranking of issues (in amount and prominence of coverage) and the public ranking of the perceived importance of these same issues in various surveys" (Weaver, McCombs, and Shaw 1997, 257).[9]

Of course, with the new media have come new individuals and organizations that perform this same journalistic function. In this analysis, we trace the news choices of several of these organizations. This requires that we determine not only what stories an organization chooses to accept for publication but also the ones it rejects (see Groeling and Kernell 1998; Groeling 2008). Much as in the original gatekeeper studies, we have chosen to focus on wire service stories for our study population.

[7]While partisan media might be drawn to costly communication that harms the *less preferred* party, they should avoid intraparty conflict that hurts their own preferred party. Also, this hypothesis does not predict that cheap talk will be less common in the overall population of stories, as both parties prefer to praise themselves and criticize their opponents.

[8]Examining a week of wire service copy, White found that Mr. Gates included only about 10% of all wire service stories in the paper; rejecting the other 90%. A follow-up study of the choices made by the same editor in 1966 found that he chose to include nearly one in three wire service stories (Snider 1967). Subsequent gatekeeper studies have generally moved away from the idiosyncrasies of individual editors and have instead focused on organizational or societal factors (Allen 2005).

[9]Dearing and Rogers (1996) label this dominant form of agenda-setting scholarship "public agenda-setting" research. In doing so, they distinguish it from "policy agenda-setting" (which focuses on the impact of media agendas on public policy agendas) and "media agenda-setting" (which examines the "causes or consequences of changes in the media agenda"). This last strain of research is most relevant to the present study.

Specifically, our population consists of all 1,782 AP and Reuters political news story abstracts distributed between July 24 and November 14, 2006 (except for a small number that we were unable to access). This represents about 10–14 abstracts per day per wire service.[10]

Nearly all traditional U.S. news outlets typically belong to or monitor one or both of these wire services. Consequently, these stories should present a reasonable snapshot of the most important political stories available to journalists and commentators on a given day. Because the wire services in turn traditionally adhere to the "inverted pyramid" style of story construction, the headlines and abstracts should capture the most important aspects of the stories.

For each day in our sample, we also collected stories from five other Internet news sources: each of the wire services' own "top news" pages, Fox News Channel's political news feed, and the front pages of the conservative blog Free Republic and the liberal blog Daily Kos.[11] As noted above, each of these outlets provides an archetypal example of a distinct type of news organization: the wire services are the bedrock of professional, explicitly nonpartisan traditional media[12]; Fox News Channel has arguably been on the vanguard of ideologically polarized cable news content; and Free Republic and Daily Kos both represent large, partisan activist communities administered by individuals who are not professional journalists.[13] Thus, our ultimate goal is to predict and understand the

[10]We accessed wire service abstracts from their respective feeds via Breitbart.com. We collected our daily wire service stories by downloading *all* story abstracts appearing on each wire service's Top Political News listing. Note that we later try to predict which of these stories were selected for that day's top news page for that wire service. According to a telephone interview with AP, a group of editors at AP's New York headquarters decide the order of the stories, which are then sent out as "packages" to the 750 newspaper members and subscribing web sites.

[11]While we would have preferred to add other news outlets to our study, particularly CNN and the *New York Times*, the costs of adding additional outlets proved prohibitive.

[12]See, for example, Reuters Independence & Trust Principles, which state the company is "dedicated to preserving its independence, integrity, and *freedom from bias* in the gathering and dissemination of news and information" (emphasis added; see http://about.reuters.com/home/aboutus/ourcompany/independencetrust.aspx). Similarly, AP identifies its mission as one of "providing distinctive news services of the highest quality, reliability and *objectivity* with reports that are accurate, *balanced* and informed" (emphasis added; see http://www.ap.org/pages/about/about.html). Indeed, to avoid even the appearance of political conflicts of interest, AP prohibits its employees from contributing personal funds to political candidates.

[13]Of course, this capsule description glosses over many potentially important differences between these outlets. For example, the Associated Press is American in origin and emphasis, while Reuters is British and tends to be more global in its focus. The Daily Kos community is far larger than Free Republic (Baum and Groeling 2008) and also tends to have a less structured main page format.

editorial decisions—that is, the decisions regarding which stories to select and emphasize—of these several news outlets.[14]

While it is relatively straightforward to determine which wire service political stories were also chosen for that wire's top news listing for a particular day, the same task is somewhat more complex for the three other news organizations. Because other organizations might choose to use a competing organization's coverage of the same story or repackage the wire service story in such a way as to obscure its sourcing, it is not immediately obvious what should count as a wire service story "appearing" on another outlet. To address this problem, we coded appearances of given wire service stories on the other outlets along a continuum indicating whether the sourcing, subject, and actors involved matched those of the wire service. For most of the analysis that follows, we have chosen to count coverage of the same issue on the same day—in addition to coverage where the wire service story is explicitly cited—as an "appearance" of that wire service story on a given outlet.[15]

To test why a given organization featured particular stories, we content analyzed the wire services' political stories for information relating both to our predictions and to predictions derived from the broader literature on editorial decision making and news values. For example, the literature has clearly established that the president is an especially newsworthy figure in American politics (Robinson and Appel 1979; Tidmarch and Pitney 1985; Graber 1997). Thus one should expect stories related to the president to receive broader coverage than equivalent stories discussing a member of Congress (MC) or a dogcatcher. By accounting for these common determinants of news value, we can isolate the independent effects of our hypothetical relationships. In addition to coding factors such as the

[14]It should be noted that there are some important differences in the implied meaning of these choices across organizations. For the wire services, the choice of whether or not to repackage a political story into their top news pages is largely a measure of its newsworthiness; the wires have ascribed some base level of newsworthiness to the story by the decision to devote resources to reporting it in the first place, and they have already published the story in at least one section of their site (the politics page). In contrast, for other organizations the wire service story serves as a baseline measure of common political information for that day, although the organizations (particularly Fox) might be able to marshal their own resources to cover that same topic, rather than relying on the wire copy. In both cases, the wire service story helps illuminate a baseline or population of potential stories from which all of the news organizations could potentially draw.

[15]As a robustness test, we replicated our results using a more restrictive dependent variable in which we counted only stories that were explicitly identical to those appearing on the wire services in the same day. This lowered the number of positive occurrences considerably, and thereby weakened the statistical significance of our results. However, the results remained substantively similar. This increases our confidence that our operationalization is not fundamentally distorting the pattern of "positive" and "negative" outcomes.

novelty and severity of the event covered, we also attempted to account for instances of particularly dramatic action, controversial topics, issue areas, and praise, criticism or other mentions of various figures and institutions. Our models thus include a large array of controls for a variety of story topical and content elements, as well as for the state of the nation (the economy, war, and so forth) at the time of a given story. (See appendix 8.1 for definitions and coding of all control variables.) To maximize confidence in the final data, three separate human coders working independently and anonymously, via an online database we constructed, coded each record in the data set.[16] The inter-coder agreement for our model's explanatory variables across the three sets of this initial coding exceeded 94%.[17] As noted, our dependent variable examined whether the wire service political story was published, either verbatim or the same topic, in each outlet during the 24-hour period following its original appearance.

[16]Following their participation in a series of training seminars and assignments, 40 UCLA undergraduate students participated in the content analysis. Because each wire service used exactly the same headline and text for both the political and top-news page versions of the stories, we were able to mechanically match appearances for their own sites with perfect accuracy. For the other sites, three independent coders located the "best" match of the wire service story. To be counted as a match on Daily Kos or Free Republic's front page, or on the Fox News politics feed, the outlet had to feature the same topic in the 24-hour period after its original publication. An alternative method considered for this content analysis was the use of machine coding. Many scholars have used this sort of coding to study topics related to political rhetoric (see Hart 2000; Jarvis 2005). While we may have been able to conduct some aspects of the current project using computerized content analysis, the core explanatory variables (including those establishing the valence and direction of political evaluations by specific partisan figures) were too nuanced and specific for such tools. Another alternative would have been to rely on single-coded data collected by a much smaller number of highly trained coders (typically graduate students), and then randomly overlapping the coding on a small subset of the data to ensure that the coders were making similar coding judgments. When such a system achieves high enough reliability on the sampled comparison data, the researcher has greater confidence that the coders *would have* agreed on their coding throughout the entire range of their single-coded data. Our method, which uses the output of *three independent coders for every observation*, is more labor-intensive than either of the above methods, but better allows for the distribution of coding responsibilities across a larger pool of labor. Our coding process also allows far greater confidence in the resulting coding than might be conferred by typical methods, such as the dominant use of single-coded data relying on a kappa statistic derived from a small overlapping subset of the coding.

[17]Pairwise comparisons across our eight main rhetoric variables (praise/criticism of the president, administration, Republicans and Democrats) showed agreement of between 94.3% and 99.5%. In the vast majority of cases (84%), where all three coders agreed on the coding, the unanimous coding was passed on to the final data set. In the 14% of instances in which two coders agreed in their coding but disagreed with a third coder, we used the agreed-upon coding. In the 1% of cases in which all three coders disagreed or the computer could not find matches, an additional student arbitrated the differences to deliver a final code. (Missing codes count as disagreements, potentially understating actual unanimity.) In some cases, the flagged disputes appeared to have been the result of unfinished records. The additional coders also processed the values of all non-empty text fields, such as the field provided for pasting headlines or abstracts, because the database could not reliably compare these fields.

Overview of Coverage Patterns

Before turning to our hypothesis tests, we briefly review each news outlet's aggregate story choices. In figure 8.5 we summarize the distribution of several key characteristics across stories that *were* and *were not* selected as top news by each outlet. For each outlet, the shaded bar shows the proportion of stories with the noted characteristic among all stories that were not selected as top news, while the unshaded bar shows that proportion for stories that *were* selected. If a story characteristic is significantly more common among the *selected* stories on a given outlet relative to the *unselected* stories, this suggests that the outlet considered that characteristic newsworthy.

The top left graphic in figure 8.5 indicates that, all else equal, Fox, Daily Kos, and AP, but not Reuters or Free Republic, are more likely to feature stories involving scandals than stories *not* involving scandals ($p < .05$ or better). Similarly, the top right graphic suggests that all outlets except Fox consider stories involving the Iraq conflict especially newsworthy ($p < .001$ in each case).

The bottom two graphics in figure 8.5 show the relative prominence of stories involving Congress and the president. (It is important to bear in mind that our content analysis covers the period leading up to and following the 2006 congressional midterm elections.) For Congress (bottom left graphic), we see that Reuters, Daily Kos, and Fox view congressional news as significantly more newsworthy than noncongressional news ($p < .10$ or better), while every outlet except Daily Kos appears to regard presidential news as significantly more newsworthy than nonpresidential news, all else equal ($p < .001$ in each case).

In figure 8.6, we examine news choices over "good" and "bad" partisan news, beginning with (in the top left graphic) the relative prevalence of stories coded as bad news for Democrats—but not Republicans (so-called "pure bad news for Democrats"). The top right graphic presents the equivalent summary of purely bad stories for Republicans.

Most outlets appear to have regarded bad news for Democrats as relatively uninteresting. Only Daily Kos is significantly ($p < .05$) more likely to select than to ignore such stories (although, as discussed below, political blogs often select such stories for purposes of rebuttal rather than endorsement). In sharp contrast, Republicans are awash in a veritable sea of bad news—unsurprisingly, given the tenor of the 2006 election cycle. *Every* news outlet apparently regarded such purely bad news stories as significantly more newsworthy than other stories ($p < .001$ for all outlets except Fox; $p < .10$ for Fox).

For each story, we created a Raw Skew variable index, which combines the raw bad news scores for each party into a scale in which stories that are purely bad for Democrats are coded as 1, stories purely bad for

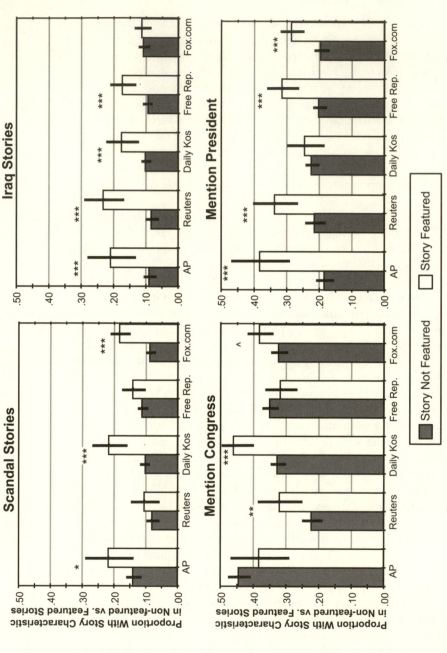

Figure 8.5. Relative Prevalence of Story Characteristics across Stories Featured and Not Featured on Web Site, by Story Characteristic and Outlet

^p < .10, *p < .05, **p < .01, ***p < .001. Vertical black lines denote 95% confidence intervals. Ns for selected (not selected) stories are as follows: AP—115 (800), Reuters—181 (684), Daily Kos—217 (1,510), Free Republic—340 (1,421), Fox.com—578 (1,202).

Note: Differences in the number of Daily Kos, Free Republic, and Fox cases are due to a small number of days in which the target web site was unavailable or did not download correctly. In cases where we were unable to retrieve these items from an archive, the observations were dropped.

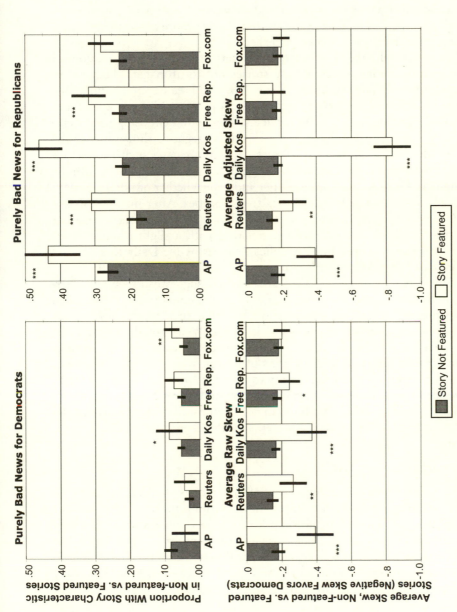

FIGURE 8.6. Story Characteristics across Stories Featured and Not Featured on Web Site, by Story Characteristic and Outlet

*p < .05, **p < .01, ***p < .001. Vertical black lines denote 95% confidence intervals. Ns for selected (not selected) stories are as follows: AP—115 (800), Reuters—181 (684), Daily Kos—217 (1,510), Free Republic—340 (1,421), Fox.com—578 (1,202).

Note: Differences in the number of Daily Kos, Free Republic, and Fox cases are due to a small number of days in which the target website was unavailable or did not download correctly. In cases where we were unable to retrieve these items from an archive, the observations were dropped.

Republicans are coded as -1, and stories that are bad for both or neither are coded as zero. The bottom left graphic in figure 8.6 shows further evidence of a pervasive wave of bad news for Republicans, with every outlet except Fox preferring stories that skewed more against the Republicans on average ($p < .05$ or better).

Unfortunately, the Raw Skew index has an important limitation: in some cases, outlets selected these stories not to propagate them but to attack them. In particular, both Daily Kos and Free Republic (unlike the wire services or the Fox RSS politics feed) produced heavily edited and skewed presentations of wire service stories, often choosing to criticize their reporting or emphasize only the most negative dimension of the story (depending on the story's target). To capture cases such as these, we asked three coders to compare the original wire service summary with the summary that appeared on the outlet and code whether or not the outlet's version was more or less damaging to the parties. After making this adjustment in a new variable (Adjusted Skew), Free Republic's apparent anti-Republican skew disappears, replaced with a slight (though insignificant) skew *against* anti-Republican stories, while Daily Kos appears even *more* skewed against Republicans ($p < .001$).

Of course, while single-factor analyses are suggestive, they are inherently limited by the assumption that all else is equal (as in a controlled experiment). Here, it is exceedingly clear that such party comparisons take place in a setting where all else is decidedly *not* equal. For example, as we argued in chapter 2, one should expect more scrutiny of Republican errors when they hold the reins of power; when Democrats were in the minority, they had less capacity to influence policy outcomes. Hence, for our hypothesis tests below, we employ multivariate regression analysis in an attempt to account for many of the most likely alternative causal explanations for the observed patterns of coverage.

Internet Blog Story Selection

The Media Partisanship hypothesis (H3) predicts that left-leaning web sites will disproportionately feature news harmful to Republicans and/or helpful to Democrats, while right-leaning sites will disproportionately feature news harmful to Democrats and/or helpful to Republicans. The Nonpartisan Media corollary hypothesis (H5a) in turn predicts that nonpartisan web sites—in our case, the wire services—will base their story selection on costliness rather than on the partisan implications of story content.

Because we consider the Adjusted Skew variable a more accurate measure than our Raw Skew indicator of the actual partisan skew in news content, we focus our discussion primarily on the former dependent variable. (Table 8.A1 in appendix 8.2 presents a series of logit analyses testing these hypotheses. Models 1–6 each test Media Partisanship [H3]. Models 1–3 employ our adjusted measure of pro-Republican skew as the dependent variable. However, as a robustness check, models 4–6 replicate models 1–3, employing the Raw Skew indicator. The results—though, as expected, slightly weaker for Daily Kos and Free Republic—largely mirror those described below.)

In table 8.1, as in prior chapters, we employ Clarify to transform the logit coefficients into expected probabilities, as the key causal variables vary from a pro-Democratic to a pro-Republican skew, as well as to determine whether the differences in the effects of (and across) the causal variables are themselves statistically significant.

The results shown in the top section of table 8.1 indicate that, overall, Daily Kos is far more likely to select a story for its top news summary if it is skewed in a pro-Democratic direction. Moving from a pro-Republican to a pro-Democratic skew is associated with a 48-percentage-point increase in the probability that a given story will be featured on Daily Kos's top news summary (from .00 to .48, $p < .01$). In other words, Daily Kos has a near zero likelihood of selecting for its top news summary a story skewed in a pro-Republican direction. Conversely, it has a nearly 50% probability of selecting a pro-Democratic skewed story. This clearly supports the liberal variant of the Media Partisanship hypothesis (H3).

To investigate the implications of the Media Partisanship hypothesis (H3) for conservative outlets, we focus on the two outlets where we anticipate a preference for pro-Republican news, FoxNews.com and Free Republic.com.[18] Beginning with Fox, table 8.1 indicates that the network is indeed significantly more likely to feature stories with pro-Republican slants on its top news summary. Moving from a pro-Democratic to a pro-Republican skew is associated with about an 8-percentage-point increase in the probability that a given story will be featured on Fox's top news summary ($p < .10$). This effect, though obviously less dramatic than that for Daily Kos, is nonetheless sizable, thereby clearly supporting the conservative variant of the Media Partisanship hypothesis (H3).

Interestingly, in this model no such pattern emerges for Free Republic. The coefficient for Free Republic is correctly signed but highly insignificant.

[18]This does not imply that conservative blogs are uniformly supportive of Republicans, or that liberal blogs are uniformly supportive of Democrats. In other words, we do not equate "conservative" with "Republican" or "liberal" with "Democrat." Indeed, conservative blogs sometimes criticize Republicans, while liberal blogs sometimes criticize Democrats (particularly if they view those Republicans and Democrats as insufficiently conservative or liberal, respectively). However, on balance, we believe it is reasonable to characterize conservative blogs as tending to sympathize with Republicans, and to be relatively more sympathetic to Republicans than Democrats, and liberal blogs as tending to sympathize with Democrats, and being relatively more sympathetic to Democrats than Republicans.

TABLE 8.1
Probability of Selecting Story for "Top News" Summary

News Outlet	Adjusted Skew		
	Anti-Dem.	Anti-Rep.	Difference
All Stories Included			
FoxNews.com	0.370	0.292	−0.078^
DailyKos.com	0.001	0.482	0.481**
FreeRepublic.com	0.186	0.180	−0.006
Reuters.com	0.186	0.266	0.080
AssociatedPress.com	0.055	0.135	0.080**
Election-Related Stories Excluded			
FoxNews.com	0.388	0.263	−0.125*
DailyKos.com	0.001	0.434	0.433**
FreeRepublic.com	0.255	0.126	−0.129
Reuters.com	0.163	0.279	0.116
AssociatedPress.com	0.067	0.150	0.083^
Post-Election and Election-Related Stories Excluded			
FoxNews.com	0.382	0.266	−0.116^
DailyKos.com	0.000	0.448	0.448**
FreeRepublic.com	0.298	0.096	−0.202*
Reuters.com	0.148	0.266	0.118
AssociatedPress.com	0.052	0.145	0.093*
	Raw Skew		
All Stories Included			
FoxNews.com	0.375	0.287	−0.088*
DailyKos.com	0.037	0.107	0.070**
FreeRepublic.com	0.177	0.183	0.006
Reuters.com	0.193	0.261	0.068
AssociatedPress.com	0.055	0.132	0.077**
Election-Related Stories Excluded			
FoxNews.com	0.398	0.259	−0.139*
DailyKos.com	0.033	0.067	0.034^
FreeRepublic.com	0.209	0.148	−0.061^^
Reuters.com	0.168	0.274	0.106
AssociatedPress.com	0.067	0.147	0.080
Post-Election and Election-Related Stories Excluded			
FoxNews.com	0.389	0.262	−0.127*
DailyKos.com	0.028	0.057	0.029^
FreeRepublic.com	0.219	0.132	−0.087^
Reuters.com	0.152	0.262	0.110
AssociatedPress.com	0.054	0.140	0.086*

^^$p < .15$, ^$p < .10$, *$p < .05$, **$p < .01$.

To determine whether our assumptions about Free Republic's story preferences were fundamentally invalid, we replicated our initial analysis, this time excluding stories that directly pertained to the 2006 midterm election (see model 2 in table A.8.1). Our reasoning is that as a pro-Republican web site, Free Republic's coverage may have reflected mounting dissatisfaction with the party's performance as the election approached and Republican prospects in the election grew increasingly bleak. The middle section of table 8.1 appears to bear this out. The predicted effects for Fox and Daily Kos are similar to those described above, if somewhat stronger for Fox (a 12.5- vs. 7.8-percentage-point change) and slightly weaker for Daily Kos (a 43- vs. 48-percentage-point change). The increased magnitude and significance for Fox appear consistent with our conjecture, as does the modest decline in magnitude for Daily Kos. For Free Republic, the magnitude of the effect increases dramatically (although the coefficient remains insignificant), indicating about a 13-percentage-point greater probability of featuring an article with a pro-Republican skew than one with a pro-Democratic skew.

To more fully control for the potential effects of election-related self-reflection, we further restricted the story content to also exclude post election coverage (shown in model 3 of table A.8.1). During the post election period, pro-Republican web sites featured an unusual amount of criticism and recrimination directed against the Republican Party for its perceived failure in the election. This could further distort the "normal" pattern of coverage. In the bottom section of table 8.2, we present the corresponding probabilities derived from this latter analysis.

Once again, this restriction has little effect on Fox and Daily Kos. However, the effect on Free Republic is dramatic. Having excluded election-related and post-election coverage, we find that for all other stories, representing more than 60% of all coded reports on Free Republic, the web site is about 20 percentage points more likely to feature a story on its top news summary if it has a pro-Republican skew than if it has a pro-Democratic skew (0.30 vs. .10, $p < .05$). This latter result is consistent with the Media Partisanship hypothesis (H3).

To further test the Media Partisanship hypothesis (H3), we next investigate whether similar patterns emerge for the news wires. Our hypothesis predicts no such relationships. In fact, this is just what we find for Reuters. Regardless of whether we include election-related reporting or post-election stories, Reuters demonstrates no statistically significant preference for stories with a pro-Republican or pro-Democratic skew. This again supports hypothesis H3.

However, contrary to our expectations, in these data, AP is between eight and nine percentage points more likely to feature among its top news summaries stories critical of the Republican Party, depending on whether election-related coverage and post-election reporting are included ($p < .01$ for all stories, $p < .10$ for non-election-related stories, and $p < .05$ for pre-election, non-election-related stories). This difference between Reuters and AP *may* be attributable to the previously noted fact that while AP is U.S.-based, Reuters is a non-American company based in the United Kingdom. Consequently, all else equal, Reuters would seem less likely to be affected by the shifting political winds surrounding American elections. Though we sought to account for any likely factors that might tend to produce secular trends in favor of one or the other party, AP's apparent slant *could* nonetheless reflect the overwhelming anti-Republican tenor of the 2006 campaign. Regardless, this latter result is robust and inconsistent with the predictions of the Media Partisanship hypothesis (H3).

We turn next to our corollary to the Nonpartisan Media corollary hypothesis (H5a), which predicts that, all else equal, news wires, but not partisan web sites, will select political stories for their top news summaries based on their perceived costliness (that is, newsworthiness). To test this hypothesis, we focus on the subset of stories that included evaluations of Democrats or Republicans by members of either party. This could include MCs, the president, cabinet officials, or other party representatives. We collapse all rhetoric into two categories, cheap or costly. Cheap rhetoric involves praising one's own party or criticizing the other party, while costly rhetoric entails the opposite: criticizing one's own party or praising the other party.

For this analysis, we are somewhat restricted in that AP did not select any of the 13 instances of costly rhetoric for their top news page. Consequently, we cannot analyze the two wire services separately. We therefore present two analyses, one focused only on Reuters and the second combining the two wire services.[19]

Preliminary testing indicated that about 10% of the observations, those focused on Iraq, differ materially from all other reporting. Specifically, virtually no costly rhetoric is available on Iraq. In other words, nearly all Iraq-related stories during this time period involve Republicans praising fellow Republicans or criticizing Democrats, or, alternatively, Democrats praising fellow Democrats or criticizing Republicans. Overall, less than two-tenths of 1% of all Iraq-related observations (three in total) featured costly rhetoric, and *all three* featured Republicans criticizing fellow Republicans. Including the Iraq observations thus significantly skews our

---

[19]Preliminary testing where data existed across both wire services revealed no significant differences in their respective preferences for different types of partisan evaluations across those categories. This finding suggests that combining the two may be less of a concern for this test than might have been the case in our tests of the Media Partisanship (H3) and Nonpartisan Media corollary (H5a) hypotheses.

results. Consequently, while for purposes of full disclosure we present our results both with and without the Iraq observations, the discussion that follows focuses on the 90% of stories that did not concern Iraq. (Models 7 and 8 in table 8.A1 present the results from our comparison of costly vs. cheap rhetoric, excluding and including AP and the Iraq-related stories, respectively.) In table 8.2, we again transform the results from our logit analyses into probabilities of selecting a story for the top news summary of a given web site.

The top half of table 8.2 (derived from model 7 of table 8.A1) focuses on Reuters and excludes Iraq-related observations. Here, the results support the Nonpartisan Media corollary hypothesis (H5a). For Fox, Free Republic, and Daily Kos, the costliness of rhetoric, or the lack thereof, has no significant effect on the propensity to feature a given story on the top news summary. Conversely, for the news wires, costly rhetoric is significantly more likely to appear as top news. Specifically, for Reuters, a story involving costly rhetoric is nearly 32 percentage points more likely than one including cheap talk to appear on the Reuters top news summary (0.06 vs. .38, $p < .05$). When we combine the two wire services, the effects are predictably, given the imbalance in the AP data, somewhat weaker. Nonetheless, for the combined wire stories, costly rhetoric remains about 10 percentage points more likely than cheap rhetoric to appear on the AP or Reuters top news summaries (0.06 vs. .16). This latter difference is nearly, though not quite, statistically significant ($p < .13$). The results shown in the bottom half of table 8.2, which include Iraq stories, are also predictably—given the aforementioned skew in available rhetoric on Iraq—somewhat weaker and less significant. Nonetheless, Reuters's apparent preference for costly rhetoric remains substantial in magnitude and nearly significant. Consequently, we interpret these results as largely if imperfectly supportive of the Nonpartisan Media corollary hypothesis (H5a).

Internet Blog Story Selection and Foreign Policy

Thus far, our hypothesis tests have been general, and not focused on foreign policy. However, our earlier findings, particularly for Free Republic, suggest there may be some significant differences in the partisan story selection criteria that Internet blogs employ for foreign policy, relative to other political issues. To investigate this possibility, we replicated our statistical analyses reported in table 8.A1 (employing the adjusted skew indicators), dividing our data by topical areas.[20] Specifically, we investi-

---

[20]For this analysis, we exclude several controls that dropped out of one or more of the three restricted models.

TABLE 8.2
Probability of Featuring Stories with Costly vs. Cheap Talk on "Top News" Summaries

News Outlet	Cheap	Costly	No. of Eval.	Difference (Cheap to Costly)	Difference (None to Costly)	Difference (None to Cheap)
			Iraq-Related Observations Excluded			
Reuters Only						
FoxNews.com	0.280	0.177	0.281	−0.103	−0.104	−0.001
DailyKos.com	0.082	0.075	0.045	−0.007	0.030	0.037
FreeRepublic.com	0.265	0.106	0.159	−0.159	−0.053	0.106
Reuters.com	0.063	0.381	0.186	0.318*	0.195	−0.123*
Reuters+AP Combined						
FoxNews.com	0.258	0.315	0.320	0.057	−0.005	−0.062
DailyKos.com	0.065	0.064	0.065	−0.001	−0.001	0.000
FreeRepublic.com	0.187	0.073	0.163	−0.114	−0.090	0.024
News wires	0.062	0.160	0.132	0.098^^	0.028	−0.070*
			All Observations Included			
Reuters Only						
FoxNews.com	0.222	0.178	0.276	−0.044	−0.098	−0.054
DailyKos.com	0.092	0.080	0.053	−0.012	0.027	0.039
FreeRepublic.com	0.256	0.102	0.166	−0.154	−0.064	0.090
Reuters	0.157	0.378	0.198	0.221^^	0.180	−0.041
Reuters+AP Combined						
FoxNews.com	0.222	0.343	0.314	0.121	0.029	−0.092^^
DailyKos.com	0.066	0.085	0.070	0.019	0.015	−0.004
FreeRepublic.com	0.176	0.088	0.174	−0.088	−0.086	0.002
News wires	0.110	0.131	0.149	0.021	−0.018	−0.039^^

^^$p<.15$, *$p<.05$.

gate three subsets of the data: (1) stories involving foreign policy (see definition below), (2) stories *not* involving foreign policy, and (3) stories mentioning the conflicts in either Iraq or Afghanistan. We define foreign policy stories as any story involving one of the following coded foreign policy criteria: Iraq, Iran, North Korea, China, war or military issues, terrorism, and weapons of mass destruction. (Table 8.A3 in appendix 8.2 presents the results of these analyses.) In table 8.3, we transform the results from our logit analysis into probabilities of featuring a story on the top news summary of a given web site, with all other causal variables held constant at their mean values.

Table 8.3
Probability of Featuring Different Types of Stories on Web Site
(Adjusted Skew)

News Outlet	Anti-Dem	Anti-Rep	Difference
Non-Foreign Policy			
FoxNews.com	0.349	0.287	−0.062
DailyKos.com	0.001	0.486	0.485**
FreeRepublic.com	0.118	0.180	0.062
Reuters.com	0.149	0.260	0.111^
AssociatedPress.com	0.047	0.095	0.048^
Stories Mentioning Iraq or Afghanistan			
FoxNews.com	0.268	0.365	0.097
DailyKos.com	0.002	0.664	0.662**
FreeRepublic.com	0.275	0.323	0.048
Reuters.com	0.412	0.409	−0.003
AssociatedPress.com	0.096	0.398	0.302*
Foreign Policy Stories Not Mentioning Iraq or Afghanistan			
FoxNews.com	0.529	0.268	−0.261^
DailyKos.com	0.005	0.308	0.303*
FreeRepublic.com	0.540	0.132	−0.408^
Reuters.com	0.297	0.200	−0.097
AssociatedPress.com	0.051	0.325	0.274*

$^{\wedge}p < .10$, $^{*}p < .05$, $^{**}p < .01$.

Several noteworthy patterns emerge in table 8.3. To begin with, in comparing AP and Reuters, we see that Reuters is about 10 percentage points more likely than AP to cover non-foreign policy stories critical of the Democrats and about 16 points more likely to cover domestic anti-Republican stories. The gaps for anti-Democrat stories are far larger, and those for anti-Republican stories are far smaller, for foreign policy stories, especially those involving Iraq or Afghanistan. In the latter case, Reuters is more than 30 percentage points more likely to cover anti-Democratic war-related stories and about equally as likely as AP to cover anti-Republican war-related stories. For other foreign policy issues, the anti-Democratic gap remains nearly as large, about 25 points, while the pattern for anti-Republican stories reverses, with Reuters nearly 13 percentage points *less* likely than AP to cover anti-Republican foreign-policy-related stories not involving war.

Finally, whereas Reuters demonstrates a significant ($p < .10$) anti-Republican skew in its domestic coverage, it shows no statistically significant partisan slant in its coverage of foreign policy. In stark contrast, in these data AP demonstrates a clear propensity to feature anti-Republican stories more frequently than anti-Democratic stories, especially on foreign policy ($p < .05$).

Once again, a possible (at least partial) explanation for these sometimes-stark differences between Reuters and AP stems from Reuters's afore-mentioned status as a non-U.S.-based wire service, in contrast to AP, which is U.S.-based. AP's greater institutional proximity to Washington, D.C. may simply render it more closely attuned to the tenor of American domestic political debates. In the summer and fall of 2006, for instance, such debate trended in an anti-Republican direction to a greater extent with respect to Iraq than virtually any other issue, and arguably more so on foreign than on domestic policy (except perhaps Hurricane Katrina and its aftermath). Reuters's non-U.S. status may also help account for its greater overall emphasis on U.S. foreign affairs coverage relative to its coverage of domestic U.S. policy.

Turning to the partisan web sites, we see that Fox is least likely to cover anti-Democrat rhetoric on Iraq or Afghanistan and most likely to do so on other foreign policy issues, with domestic issues falling in between. Conversely, Fox is most likely to cover anti-Republican stories dealing with Afghanistan or Iraq and least likely to do so on other foreign policy stories. It is worth noting here that most of this effect is driven by Iraq rather than by Afghanistan; excluding the latter only marginally alters the results. Indeed, because Iraq was consistently more salient to the American public and more prominent in the media than Afghanistan during this period, most of the war-related patterns described herein are primarily attributable to coverage of Iraq. Overall, Fox displays no statistically significant partisan favoritism on domestic issues or on the wars. However, it is significantly more likely to cover anti-Democratic than anti-Republican stories on non-war, foreign-policy-related topics (0.53 vs. .27, $p < .10$).

Turning to Free Republic, here we see no statistically significant differences in preferences for anti-Democratic or anti-Republican stories on either domestic or war-related topics, though Free Republic does appear substantially more likely to cover war-related stories than domestic ones. However, when we focus on non-war-related foreign policy stories, Free Republic demonstrates a large (41-percentage-point) and statistically significant ($p < .10$) preference for anti-Democratic over anti-Republican stories (0.54 vs .13).

On the left, Daily Kos demonstrates a strong preference for anti-Republican over anti-Democratic stories across all issue areas. However, this pro-Democratic slant is substantially stronger on war-related stories (0.00 vs. .66, $p < .01$) than on either domestic or non-war foreign policy stories. Interestingly, nearly all of the variance in Daily Kos's coverage emerges in their relative preferences for anti-Republican stories on different topics; their probability of covering an anti-Democratic story is nearly zero, regardless of the subject matter.

These last results do not directly test the hypotheses discussed thus far in this chapter. They do, however, offer some evidence in support of the Partisan Media Convergence hypothesis (H16). By the summer and fall of 2006, the wars in Iraq and Afghanistan were sufficiently past the "short-term" phase (recall figure 2.1 in chapter 2) that the elasticity of reality would have constricted substantially from the early stages of the conflicts. Given that by all accounts, the war in Iraq was going poorly, while progress in Afghanistan was reportedly slipping, the implication is that it would be difficult for pro-war partisans (mostly Republicans and their supporters) to frame either conflict, but especially Iraq, in a positive light. Conversely, it would be relatively easy for anti-war partisans (mostly Democrats) to frame the wars—again, especially Iraq—in a negative light. The reason is that, all else equal, in an environment in which reality skewed negatively and the elasticity of reality was relatively constrained, positive stories about the conflict would be less credible than critical ones. The empirical implication is that relative to other foreign policy issues, we would anticipate seeing a smaller anti-Democratic slant from pro-Republican web sites on Iraq- or Afghanistan-related stories relative to other foreign policy stories. Conversely, we would anticipate a larger anti-Republican slant on pro-Democratic web sites for war-related stories relative to other foreign policy stories.[21]

In fact, the results shown in table 8.3 offer clear support for both predictions. The two pro-Republican web sites, Fox and Free Republic, revealed stronger preferences for anti-Democratic stories on non-war-related foreign policy topics relative to war-related topics. Specifically, Fox's pro-Republican slant—that is, its preference for pro-Republican stories over pro-Democratic stories—was 16 percentage points greater for war-related stories (0.26 vs. .10), while Free Republic's pro-Republican tilt was nearly 36 percentage points greater for non-war-related foreign policy stories relative to war-related stories (0.41 vs. .05). In both cases the pro-Republican slant for war-related stories was insignificant, while that for other foreign policy stories was statistically significant ($p < .10$). The precise opposite pattern emerges for Daily Kos, whose pro-Democratic slant is 36 percentage points greater for war-related stories relative to non-war foreign policy stories (0.66 vs. .30). Each of these results is con-

---

[21]The Partisan Media Convergence hypothesis (H16) obviously does not apply to non-partisan web sites, but the Elasticity of Reality hypothesis (H13) would predict that at this point in the conflict, media coverage should have increasingly paralleled objective indicators of reality.

sistent with the aforementioned implication of the Partisan Media Convergence hypothesis (H16).

Partisan Consumer Selection and Attitudes toward Iraq

Finally, we turn to the implications of the partisan story selection patterns identified in our content analysis of Internet blogs for the attitudes of news consumers. We once again focus on public opinion regarding the Iraq War, a particularly salient foreign policy topic. We argued in chapter 2 that consumers are increasingly able to seek out news sources, including partisan web sites, that reflect their own ideological preferences. Evidence of this pattern is apparent in table 8.4, derived from a 2006 Pew Research Center survey on media consumption habits (Pew 2006). The figures in the table represent the percentages of self-reported *regular* users of various news genres and outlets who indicated that they prefer news "from sources that share YOUR political point of view" over "sources that DON'T have a particular point of view."

Out of 14 general news genres, shown in the top half of table 8.4, regular users of Internet blogs report a higher propensity to prefer self-reinforcing news (26% of self-reported regular blog users) than regular consumers of all other types of news, save political magazines like *The Weekly Standard* and *The New Republic*. This exception may be an artifact of the question wording, which specifically mentions two overtly partisan political magazines. In contrast, the Internet blog response makes no mention of a specific web site, hence avoiding a specific partisan prime in the question.

Despite its lack of specificity—and hence the absence of an overt partisan prime—the generic Internet blog response also outpaces most of the specific news outlets included in the survey (shown in the bottom half of table 8.4) in self-reported preference for news that reinforces respondents' preexisting beliefs, falling behind only regular viewers of *The O'Reilly Factor* on the Fox News Channel and listeners to Rush Limbaugh's radio program. This suggests that partisan self-selection is likely to be more acute on the Internet than in most mainstream news media, such as network TV newscasts, where all viewers are exposed to relatively comparable (if not necessarily identical) information.[22] The impli-

[22]However, this is not to say that such self-sorting does not occur at all; we simply expect the effect to be far stronger as consumers perceive the outlet as being more partisan. For example, the 2008 Pew study referenced in figure 8.1 also correlated respondents' preferred sources of broadcast news with their party identification. For the outlets with the most partisan reputations in the 2008 election (Fox and MSNBC), the results showed that only 17% of those who got most of their campaign news from Fox were Democrats (compared

TABLE 8.4
Preferences of Respondents Who Report "Regularly" Consuming Different
Types of News Genres and Outlets

News Genre, Outlet, or Show	Prefer Reinforcing News[a]	Talk about News	
		Overall[b]	"Completely Agree"[c]
New Genres			
Internet blogs	0.26	2.34	0.50
Daily newspaper	0.22	2.14	0.39
Network TV News (CBS, ABC, or NBC)	0.22	2.14	0.39
Cable news (CNN, MSNBC, or Fox News)	0.25	2.18	0.41
Local TV news	0.22	2.10	0.36
Newsmagazine shows (60 Minutes, 20/20, or Dateline)	0.23	2.23	0.44
Online news magazines (Slate.com or National Review online)	0.19	2.56	0.67
Magazines like Harpers, Atlantic, The New Yorker	0.23	2.26	0.42
Late-night TV shows (Letterman or Leno)	0.22	2.08	0.38
Political magazines (The New Republic, The Weekly Standard)	0.31	2.31	0.49
Sunday news shows (Meet the Press, This Week, Face the Nation)	0.22	2.26	0.47
News magazines (Time, Newsweek, or U.S. News)	0.22	2.24	0.44
Network news web sites (CNN.com, ABCnews.com, MSNBC.com)	0.22	2.29	0.46
National Newspaper Web sites (USAToday.com, NewYorkTimes.com, Wall Street Journal online)	0.16	2.37	0.53
Specific News Shows or Outlets			
The Daily Show with Jon Stewart	0.19	2.15	0.47
The O'Reilly Factor with Bill O'Reilly	0.32	2.24	0.44
Fox News Channel	0.28	2.23	0.43
CNN	0.19	2.24	0.46
National Public Radio	0.23	2.19	0.39
Jim Lehrer NewsHour	0.23	2.20	0.40
Rush Limbaugh's Radio Show	0.40	2.21	0.46

Source: Pew (2006).

[a]Proportion of respondents preferring self-reinforcing news.

[b]Based on 0–3 scale, where 3 represents maximum propensity to talk about news with friends and family.

[c]Proportion of respondents who "completely agree" that they often discuss politics with friends and family.

cation is that attitude polarization is likely to be particularly acute among individuals who rely on the Internet as a source of news about politics and international affairs. A third corollary to the Partisan Media Opinion hypothesis (H10) follows:

HYPOTHESIS 10c: PARTISAN MEDIA OPINION COROLLARY:
    Individuals who rely on the Internet as a source of news about international affairs will be more polarized along partisan lines than their counterparts who rely on mainstream news outlets, such as network television news.

However, as in our analysis of Iraq attitudes among Fox and CNN consumers in chapter 5 (see hypotheses H10a and H10b, the Iraq Democratic and Iraq Republican corollaries, respectively), it is important to also consider an alternate hypothesis: that differences between the characteristics of respondents who choose to watch network television news and those who rely on the Internet for their political and international news could be driving any observed relationship between outlet preferences and war attitudes rather than, or in addition to, the *content* of news to which they are exposed. As was the case when we tested for this possibility in chapter 5 with Fox and CNN, we find relatively little evidence of such a pattern. Democratic Internet news consumers in this survey are about 13% more likely to identify themselves as liberal than their network news–watching counterparts. However, Republican Internet consumers are virtually identical to Republican network news watchers in their ideological self-placements. As we will see, most of the attitude differences across media outlets emerge among Republicans rather than Democrats. This suggests that greater ideological polarization among Internet users—which could emerge if ideological extremeness predicted reliance on the Internet as a news source—cannot account for the patterns we identify. (To further assess the possibility that selection effects could account for differences in attitudes regarding the war, in table 8.A3 of appendix 8.3 we investigate the correlates of relying on the Internet or network newscasts for news about national and international politics. The results reveal no clear evidence that the observed relationships are artifacts of endogeneity.) We therefore proceed somewhat more confidently to our analysis.[23]

---

to 52% Republican), while only 11% of those relying on MSNBC were Republican (compared to 50% Democrats). CNN split 13% Republican/45% Democrat, while the network newscasts split 23% Republican/36% Democrat (Pew 2008, "Internet Now Major Source of Campaign News").

[23]As we discussed in chapter 5, an alternative means of addressing endogeneity concerns would be an instrumental variable approach. However, as before, we are unable to derive a persuasive instrument for media consumption preferences. For the same reasons as in our

Data and Methods

To test the Partisan Media Opinion corollary hypothesis (H10c), we rely on the same Pew Research Center survey as we employed in chapter 5 (with identical control variables and definitions). As before, our dependent variable is based on the following question: "How well is the U.S. military effort in Iraq going?" (coded 1 = very or fairly well, and 0 = not too well or not at all well).[24] We compare responses to this question across individuals with different partisan affiliations who claim to get most of their news about politics and international affairs from the Internet or from network TV newscasts. Specifically, given the relatively greater capacity of Internet users to self-select into news environments that tend to reinforce their preexisting beliefs and attitudes, we investigate whether Democrats and Republicans who rely on the Internet for their news about politics and international affairs are more polarized in their attitudes regarding the Iraq War than their counterparts who rely primarily on network television news (our Partisan Media Opinion corollary hypothesis [H10c]).

RESULTS

As in chapter 5, we interact respondents' partisan affiliations with their preferred sources of news about politics and international affairs. We also include the identical battery of demographic and political control variables, as well as controls for overall trust in the news media and interest in the war. (Table 8.A4 in appendix 8.2 reports the results of a logit model testing the effects of news preferences and partisan affiliation on attitudes toward the Iraq War.)[25] In figure 8.7, we transform the results from this logit analysis into probabilities of believing things are "going well" in Iraq as the primary source of news about politics and international affairs varies from the Internet to network news.

Voluminous evidence indicates that Republicans are dramatically more supportive of the war than Democrats (Jacobson 2006). Hence, to the extent partisan Internet consumers are self-selecting into environments

---

prior analyses of Fox and CNN, this not a fundamental concern for our approach, as we are primarily interested in determining the extent to which attitudes toward Iraq do or do not predict such preferences.

[24]We code 54 responses of "don't know" or refusals to answer as missing.

[25]The reported results exclude three influential outlier observations. Including these outliers modestly weakens, but does not materially alter, the reported results. In this instance, unlike the analysis in chapter 5 based on the same Pew Research Center data set, we do not employ probability weighting, as doing so does not materially affect the results.

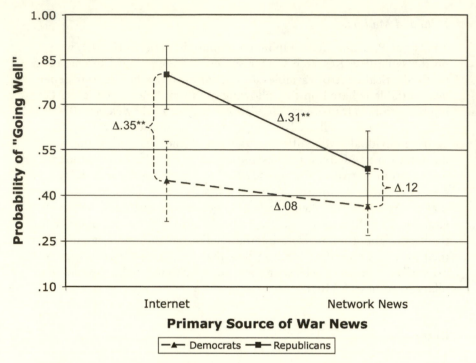

FIGURE 8.7. Estimated Probability of Believing the Iraq Conflict Is "Going Well," as Source of War News and Party Identification Vary
**p < .01. Error bars denote 95% confidence intervals.

where their attitudes are likely to be reinforced, we would anticipate greater attitude polarization across partisan Internet consumers than across their network news–consuming counterparts, who are presumably exposed to comparable war-related information. This is precisely what we find. After controlling for a variety of correlates of attitudes toward Iraq, no statistically significant difference emerges between Democrats and Republicans who prefer network news as their primary source of news about politics and international affairs. In contrast, Republicans who primarily consume their news about politics and international affairs from the Internet are 35 percentage points more likely than their Democratic counterparts to believe the Iraq War is going well (0.80 vs. .45, p < .01). Also of interest, while Democratic Internet and network news consumers do not significantly differ in their attitudes toward the war, Republican Internet news consumers are considerably more likely to believe the war is going well than Republican network news consumers. These results support the Partisan Media Opinion corollary hypothesis (H10c).

Unlike our analysis of Fox and CNN in chapter 5, there is no evidence in this instance that ideological differences between Internet and network news consumers could account for some of the differences we report. After all, as noted, although Democratic Internet users are modestly more liberal than their network news-consuming counterparts, the two groups do not differ significantly in their attitudes toward Iraq. Conversely, among Republicans, who do not differ at all ideologically across Internet and network news consumers, we find stark differences in attitudes toward the war's progress. This further suggests that differences in the information to which the two groups of Republican media consumers were exposed, rather than in their internal characteristics, are driving the patterns we report.

CONCLUSION

In June 2007, a legislative "grand bargain" on immigration supported by both the Republican administration and leaders of both parties in the House and Senate unexpectedly failed. While it is difficult to precisely determine the ultimate cause of any legislative outcome, in this case both political commentators and politicians attributed the defeat to a grass-roots conservative revolt incited by one-sided commentary in conservative niche media, especially talk radio. Republican Senate Minority Whip Trent Lott (MS) complained prior to the bill's ultimate defeat that such coverage "defined [the bill] without us explaining that there were reasons for it and the good things that were in it" (*Fox News Sunday*, June 24, 2007). Appearing on the same program, Senator Dianne Feinstein (D-CA) complained that coverage of the bill on talk radio "tends to be one-sided. It also tends to be dwelling in hyperbole. It's explosive. It pushes people to, I think, extreme views without a lot of information."

Feinstein added that she was willing to consider mandating a return to the so-called fairness doctrine to ensure greater balance. Other prominent Democrats agreed. For instance, Senate Majority Whip Dick Durbin (D-IL) commented, "It's time to reinstitute the Fairness Doctrine . . . when Americans hear both sides of the story, they're in a better position to make a decision" (Bolton 2007). Following the election of Barack Obama, House Speaker Nancy Pelosi (D-CA) refused to rule out a return to the policy, and Senator Charles Schumer (D-NY) created a stir by implying that the same FCC powers that allowed regulation of pornography should be used to promote fairness and balance in broadcasting (Eggerton 2008).

If the results of this study are any guide, Democratic attempts to rein in the "one-sided" content of conservative talk radio seem misguided, and perhaps even disingenuous. Even as Democratic leaders decry the bias and influence of conservative talk radio, Democratic activists and candidates have been quick to rally around an impressively biased and increasingly influential community online, including such web sites as DailyKos.com, MoveOn.org, and HuffingtonPost.com. Our findings suggest that if Durbin is correct in his belief that hearing both sides of the story helps Americans make better decisions, the increased reliance of many politically attentive Americans on partisan web sites like Daily Kos and Free Republic could potentially pose a significant challenge to American democracy.

Regardless of their normative implications, our findings offer a striking validation for those who complain about one-sided coverage of politics in the so-called blogosphere. Daily Kos on the left and Free Republic and Fox News on the right demonstrate clear and strong preferences for news stories that benefit the party most closely associated with their own ideological orientations. While some evidence of such partisan selection emerged for AP, overall, the news wires demonstrated far weaker tendencies to select news based on its implications for one or the other political party. This was especially the case for the British-based Reuters news wire.

Interestingly, elements of our findings offer some support for the claims of partisans on both the left and right concerning ideological bias in the media. On the one hand, our results arguably present more direct evidence concerning the right-skewed political orientation of Fox News (at least online) than other studies of media bias (e.g., Groseclose and Milyo 2005; Gentzkow and Shapiro 2006) that rely on proxies of ideological orientation, such as references to interest groups with ideological reputations or the similarity of a news outlet's rhetoric to that of different MCs. Indeed, our findings appear to validate the arguments of left-leaning partisans that Fox News (again, at least online) tends to favor Republican and conservative interests.

On the other hand, as noted, we also find some evidence that the self-consciously nonpartisan AP prefers stories critical of Republicans, which may constitute evidence supporting the often cited conservative claim of liberal bias in the mainstream news media. Of course, it could also reflect the exceptionally anti-Republican mood in the nation in the run-up to the 2006 midterm election, a period in which the news was dominated by stories about domestic political scandals enveloping the Republican Party and the perceived failure of the administration's policies in Iraq. Nonetheless, AP's anti-Republican skew persisted even when these alternative explanations were explicitly controlled in our models.

These differences may hold important implications for political discourse in America. While the audiences for partisan niche websites continue to be smaller than those for most mainstream media outlets (Baum and Groeling 2008), their typical consumers differ from the median citizen in important ways. For instance, blog users are more likely than typical individuals to discuss politics with others and, in doing so, to disseminate their views to the broader public. In the aforementioned 2006 Pew Research Center survey (see table 8.4), fully half of self-reported regular blog users report that they "often talk about the news with friends and family." This figure exceeds that for all but two of the genres or outlets included in the survey (online news magazine and national newspaper web site readers). This suggests that while relatively small (though growing) in number, blog users are disproportionately likely to be opinion leaders. In other words, blog users tend to be individuals to whom typical members of the public turn for interpretations of political issues and events. Their significance to broader patterns of public opinion, and hence American politics, thus in all likelihood exceeds their raw numbers. Indeed, news coverage in the blogosphere and the attitudes of blog consumers may increasingly influence, and as a consequence ultimately reflect, political opinion among the broader citizenry. This suggests that further systematic study is needed into the effects on mass public attitudes—direct through personal exposure, or indirect via discussion with those directly exposed—of news coverage by partisan web sites.

APPENDIX 8.1. INTERNET BLOG VARIABLE DEFINITIONS

Top News (*Dependent Variable*): Binary variable indicating whether the wire service story in question was covered by each outlet on their "top news" page (for the wire services), front page (for Daily Kos and Free Republic), or politics RSS feed (for Fox). In addition to exact matches of the wire service story itself, we counted coverage of the same issue on the same day. We coded each story along a continuum indicating whether the sourcing, subject, and actors involved matched those of the wire service.[26] That coding was then collapsed into a binary variable in which coverage of the same issue on the same day counts as an "appearance" of that wire service story on a given outlet. We collected news content from Fox from each day's

---

[26]At the top end of the continuum were stories in which the exact wire service story was explicitly cited. Note that all hits on the wire services' top news page fell into this category and were mechanically matched using computerized comparison of story text. Our final binary variable also counts cases in which the same actor and same topic was covered, and also when the same topic was covered, as coded by a team of three coders. We did not count instances where the same actor was covered in relation to a different topic.

Politics RSS feed. We collected all other news using a custom daily script that downloaded an html version of the relevant web page.

Outlet Dummy Variables (AP, DailyKos.com, FoxNews.com, Free Republic.com, and Reuters.com): For each wire service story, these dummies indicate the news organization whose news choices are being examined.

Associated Press Story: Takes a value of 1 if the record concerns choices regarding an AP wire service story, 0 if the wire service story was from Reuters.

Raw Skew: The baseline, "raw" skew indicator measures whether the original wire service story was "bad news" for one or both parties. Coders were asked, "Overall, does the story appear to be bad news for Republicans, Democrats, the President, or none of the above?" They could select multiple responses for each record. Good news for one party was coded as bad news for the other party. This coding formed the basis for the index where 1 indicated the story was bad news for Democrats, 0 indicated bad news for neither or both parties, and -1 = bad news for Republicans and/or the president.

Adjusted Skew: For Daily Kos and Free Republic, which presented highly edited or modified text on their news pages, coders compared the original wire service story to the version appearing on that news outlet.[27] If the web site version was more pro-Democratic (pro-Republican) than the matching wire service story, an intermediary variable was coded as 1 (-1), which was then subtracted from the original raw skew variable. The *Adjusted Skew* index runs from -2 (e.g., if a wire service story that was already bad for Republicans was presented in an even more negative fashion on the outlet) or 0 (e.g., if that same bad story were presented in a manner that mitigated its damage against Republicans) or 1 (-1) (e.g., if a story originally coded as having no skew or being balanced was presented in a pro-Republican [pro-Democratic] way).[28]

Cheap Rhetoric: Dummy coded 1 if member of a party (members of Congress, president, cabinet officials, or other party representatives) explicitly criticizes (praises) member(s) of other (their own) party.

Costly Rhetoric: Dummy coded 1 if member of one party criticizes (praises) her own (other) party.

[27]For example, a wire service story titled "GOP Makes Conditions on Wage Increase" became "GOP Holds Working Poor Hostage to Paris Hilton" on Daily Kos.

[28]The coders adjusted a total of 39 Free Republic and 142 Daily Kos skews. The three coders were instructed to code cases where the outlet "took the initial story and clearly attempted to spin it more favorably for one of the two parties (or against the other). So if a story previously had both positive Republican and negative Republican aspects and they only include the positive ones (or say the negative ones are wrong), that would constitute spinning the story towards the Republicans."

Iraq *New York Times* Coverage: Number of front-page stories mentioning Iraq in the *New York Times* on a given day.

August, September, October, Pre-election November: Dummy variables for month of observation (post-election November is the excluded category).

China, Iran, Iraq, North Korea: Dummies coded 1 if that nation was mentioned in wire service story.

Economy/Jobs, Election Story, Environment, Scandal, Social Issues, Terrorism, Polls, War/Military, WMD: Dummies coded 1 if pertinent issues were mentioned in wire service story.

Dramatic, Pop Stars/Celebrities, Tragedy, Political Figures: Dummies coded 1 if the story included these newsworthy elements.

Consumer Sentiment: University of Michigan Consumer Sentiment score, taken from http://www.federalreserve.gov/BOARDDOCS/HH/2007/february/figure7.htm.

Gas Prices: Average national retail gasoline prices, all grades, all formulations (cents per gallon). Data taken from U.S. Department of Energy, Energy Information Administration, Excel file pet_pri_gnd_dcus_nus_w.xls, updated 5/21/2007.

Trend: Dummy coded 1 if story appears to be part of a larger trend, and not an isolated incident.

Urgency: Four-category scale coded: -1 = proposed development; 0 = likely development, not of "life-and-death" severity; 1 = actual development, not of "life and death" severity; and 2 = actual development of "life-and-death" severity.

Appendix 8.2. Regression Analyses

Table 8.A1
Logit Analyses of Correlates of Featuring News Stories on Web Site "Top News" Summaries

Independent Variable	(1) Adjusted Skew (All)	(2) Adjusted Skew (Non-Elec.)	(3) Adjusted Skew (Pre-Elec., Non-Elec.)	(4) Raw Skew (All)
FoxNews.com	1.659 (0.137)***	1.480 (0.175)***	1.633 (0.195)***	1.670 (0.137)***
DailyKos.com	–1.042 (0.209)***	–1.571 (0.276)***	–1.740 (0.325)***	–0.318 (0.166)^
FreeRepublic.com	0.852 (0.141)***	0.670 (0.177)***	0.798 (0.196)***	0.859 (0.141)***
Reuters.com	1.117 (0.170)***	0.908 (0.207)***	0.974 (0.228)***	1.136 (0.170)***
Daily Kos × skew	–1.672 (0.171)***	–1.768 (0.243)***	–1.947 (0.282)***	—
Fox × skew	0.179 (0.103)^	0.289 (0.153)^	0.265 (0.159)^	—
Free Republic × skew	0.006 (0.123)	0.215 (0.176)	0.360 (0.188)^	—
Reuters × skew	–0.232 (0.184)	–0.344 (0.244)	–0.376 (0.261)	—
AP × skew	–0.503 (0.172)**	–0.472 (0.238)*	–0.588 (0.259)*	—
Daily Kos × raw skew	—	—	—	–0.581 (0.166)***
Fox × raw skew	—	—	—	0.197 (0.103)^
Free Rep. × raw skew	—	—	—	–0.022 (0.118)
Reuters × raw skew	—	—	—	–0.204 (0.184)
AP × raw skew	—	—	—	–0.487 (0.171)**
Wires × costly	—	—	—	—

(5) Raw Skew (Non-Elec.)	(6) Raw Skew (Pre-Elec., Non-Elec.)	(7) Costly vs. Cheap (Non-Iraq Reuters)	(8) Costly, vs. Cheap (Non-Iraq Newswires Combined)	(9) Costly vs. Cheap (All Reuters)	(10) Costly vs. Cheap (All Newswires Combined)
1.492 (0.176)***	1.647 (0.196)***	0.539 (0.140)***	1.123 (0.097)***	0.426 (0.127)***	0.960 (0.088)***
−0.807 (0.213)***	−0.826 (0.241)***	−1.580 (0.205)***	−0.791 (0.125)***	−1.482 (0.172)***	−0.852 (0.112)***
0.682 (0.177)***	0.805 (0.197)***	−0.182 (0.153)	0.242 (0.105)*	−0.215 (0.137)	0.181 (0.095)^
0.923 (0.207)***	0.992 (0.228)***	—	—	—	—
—	—	—	—	—	—
—	—	—	—	—	—
—	—	—	—	—	—
—	—	—	—	—	—
—	—	—	—	—	—
−0.396 (0.238)^	−0.415 (0.257)	—	—	—	—
0.318 (0.153)*	0.293 (0.159)^	—	—	—	—
0.221 (0.171)	0.316 (0.184)^	—	—	—	—
−0.312 (0.243)	−0.343 (0.260)	—	—	—	—
−0.448 (0.237)^	−0.564 (0.258)*	—	—	—	—
—	—	0.948 (0.718)	0.112 (0.592)	0.856 (0.723)	−0.262 (0.573)

(continued)

TABLE 8.A1 *(continued)*

Independent Variable	(1) Adjusted Skew (All)	(2) Adjusted Skew (Non-Elec.)	(3) Adjusted Skew (Pre-Elec., Non-Elec.)	(4) Raw Skew (All)
Wires × cheap	—	—	—	—
Fox × costly	—	—	—	—
Fox × cheap	—	—	—	—
Daily Kos × costly	—	—	—	—
Daily Kos × cheap	—	—	—	—
Free Republic × costly	—	—	—	—
Free Republic × cheap	—	—	—	—
Adjusted skew	—	—	—	—
July	3.103 (0.250)***	2.790 (0.305)***	2.970 (0.323)***	2.904 (0.206)***
August	3.840 (0.391)***	3.612 (0.446)***	3.817 (0.474)***	3.581 (0.302)***
September	2.212 (0.288)***	1.954 (0.333)***	2.080 (0.351)***	2.045 (0.228)***
October	−0.637 (0.194)***	−0.681 (0.259)**	−0.726 (0.265)**	−0.532 (0.184)**
Post-election	0.234 (0.167)	−0.068 (0.229)	—	0.306 (0.166)^
Election story	−0.193 (0.081)*	—	—	−0.172 (0.080)*
Political figures	0.307 (0.036)***	0.316 (0.045)***	0.342 (0.047)***	0.320 (0.035)***
War/military	0.026 (0.089)	0.088 (0.095)	0.079 (0.099)	0.031 (0.088)

(5) Raw Skew (Non-Elec.)	(6) Raw Skew (Pre-Elec., Non-Elec.)	(7) Costly vs. Cheap (Non-Iraq Reuters)	(8) Costly, vs. Cheap (Non-Iraq Newswires Combined)	(9) Costly vs. Cheap (All Reuters)	(10) Costly vs. Cheap (All Newswires Combined)
—	—	−1.451 (0.782)^	−0.961 (0.483)*	−0.345 (0.472)	−0.384 (0.334)
—	—	−0.794 (0.807)	−0.088 (0.493)	−0.765 (0.802)	0.086 (0.465)
—	—	−0.048 (0.478)	−0.331 (0.321)	−0.364 (0.446)	−0.496 (0.286)^
—	—	0.323 (0.875)	−0.279 (0.868)	0.137 (0.868)	0.004 (0.685)
—	—	0.536 (0.545)	−0.057 (0.338)	0.467 (0.535)	−0.100 (0.324)
—	—	−1.002 (1.264)	−1.175 (0.824)	−1.047 (1.247)	−0.933 (0.658)
—	—	0.594 (0.581)	0.119 (0.348)	0.487 (0.476)	−0.008 (0.307)
—	—	−0.252 (0.120)*	−0.332 (0.070)***	−0.293 (0.107)**	−0.354 (0.065)***
2.845 (0.270)***	2.959 (0.276)***	2.784 (0.349)***	2.896 (0.213)***	2.497 (0.316)***	2.795 (0.200)***
3.754 (0.381)***	3.874 (0.391)***	3.441 (0.470)***	3.490 (0.308)***	3.248 (0.442)***	3.429 (0.293)***
2.054 (0.291)***	2.131 (0.298)***	2.337 (0.361)***	2.115 (0.238)***	2.132 (0.331)***	1.968 (0.222)***
−0.668 (0.252)**	−0.710 (0.256)**	−0.050 (0.343)	−0.352 (0.208)^	−0.359 (0.279)	−0.527 (0.183)**
−0.049 (0.229)	—	0.359 (0.306)	0.339 (0.189)^	0.172 (0.248)	0.219 (0.165)
—	—	0.182 (0.146)	−0.150 (0.087)^	0.082 (0.132)	−0.189 (0.080)*
0.335 (0.044)***	0.358 (0.047)***	0.394 (0.063)***	0.333 (0.040)***	0.362 (0.055)***	0.314 (0.037)***
0.086 (0.094)	0.083 (0.098)	0.037 (0.151)	0.120 (0.110)	−0.052 (0.119)	0.030 (0.087)

(continued)

TABLE 8.A1 *(continued)*

Independent Variable	*(1)* Adjusted Skew *(All)*	*(2)* Adjusted Skew *(Non-Elec.)*	*(3)* Adjusted Skew *(Pre-Elec., Non-Elec.)*	*(4)* Raw Skew *(All)*
Terrorism	0.332 (0.162)*	0.339 (0.174)*	0.352 (0.180)*	0.370 (0.158)*
Tragedy	−0.220 (0.247)	−0.125 (0.256)	−0.084 (0.266)	−0.226 (0.245)
Economy/jobs	−0.368 (0.115)***	−0.377 (0.123)**	−0.384 (0.125)**	−0.392 (0.114)***
Scandal	0.513 (0.100)***	0.445 (0.128)***	0.436 (0.133)***	0.564 (0.099)***
Environment	−0.753 (0.325)*	−0.627 (0.322)*	−0.516 (0.328)	−0.766 (0.325)*
Pop stars/celebrities	−0.448 (0.191)*	−0.713 (0.352)*	−0.685 (0.349)*	−0.440 (0.189)*
Trend	−0.0376 (0.059)***	−0.387 (0.072)***	−0.441 (0.076)***	−0.363 (0.059)***
Urgency	0.346 (0.062)***	0.331 (0.071)***	0.305 (0.074)***	0.346 (0.062)***
U.S. fatalities— Afghan	−0.105 (0.058)^	−0.097 (0.078)	−0.090 (0.079)	−0.084 (0.056)
U.S. fatalities— Iraq	−0.024 (0.014)^	−0.049 (0.019)**	−0.035 (0.020)^	−0.024 (0.014)^
Iraq civilian deaths	0.001 (0.001)	0.001 (0.001)	0.000 (0.001)	0.001 (0.001)
Iraq *New York Times* coverage	−0.009 (0.034)	−0.004 (0.042)	−0.009 (0.043)	−0.014 (0.034)
Afghan *New York Times* coverage	−0.046 (0.067)	0.007 (0.081)	0.005 (0.083)	−0.043 (0.066)
Gas prices	−0.000 (0.004)	−0.004 (0.005)	−0.004 (0.005)	−0.001 (0.004)
Consumer sentiment	0.411 (0.060)***	0.385 (0.069)***	0.403 (0.072)***	0.382 (0.050)***
Associated Press story	0.211 (0.081)**	0.393 (0.101)***	0.371 (0.107)***	0.207 (0.080)**

(5) Raw Skew (Non-Elec.)	(6) Raw Skew (Pre-Elec., Non-Elec.)	(7) Costly vs. Cheap (Non-Iraq Reuters)	(8) Costly, vs. Cheap (Non-Iraq Newswires Combined)	(9) Costly vs. Cheap (All Reuters)	(10) Costly vs. Cheap (All Newswires Combined)
0.373 (0.172)*	0.385 (0.177)*	0.595 (0.260)*	0.576 (0.182)**	0.384 (0.218)^	0.350 (0.158)*
−0.133 (0.255)	−0.092 (0.264)	−0.148 (0.329)	−0.245 (0.254)	−0.158 (0.317)	−0.240 (0.244)
−0.403 (0.123)***	−0.407 (0.124)***	−0.532 (0.151)***	−0.340 (0.118)**	−0.553 (0.150)***	−0.362 (0.115)**
0.507 (0.128)***	0.506 (0.133)***	0.648 (0.178)***	0.564 (0.103)***	0.548 (0.167)***	0.489 (0.100)***
−0.632 (0.321)*	−0.511 (0.326)	−1.209 (0.500)*	−0.659 (0.322)*	−1.306 (0.493)**	−0.760 (0.319)*
−0.726 (0.353)*	−0.696 (0.349)*	−0.563 (0.304)^	−0.390 (0.195)*	−0.554 (0.293)^	−0.433 (0.191)*
−0.368 (0.072)***	−0.423 (0.076)***	−0.641 (0.097)***	−0.434 (0.065)***	−0.565 (0.088)***	−0.371 (0.059)***
0.319 (0.070)***	0.294 (0.073)***	0.292 (0.100)**	0.318 (0.072)***	0.307 (0.084)***	0.330 (0.062)***
−0.080 (0.076)	−0.073 (0.077)	0.008 (0.096)	−0.067 (0.061)	−0.028 (0.085)	−0.096 (0.056)^
−0.050 (0.019)**	−0.035 (0.020)^	−0.067 (0.024)**	−0.030 (0.016)^	−0.060 (0.022)**	−0.029 (0.014)*
0.000 (0.001)	0.000 (0.001)	−0.001 (0.001)	0.000 (0.001)	0.001 (0.001)	0.001 (0.001)
−0.007 (0.042)	−0.013 (0.043)	−0.021 (0.060)	−0.003 (0.037)	−0.015 (0.054)	−0.010 (0.034)
0.005 (0.081)	0.004 (0.082)	−0.037 (0.109)	−0.122 (0.073)^	0.004 (0.098)	−0.061 (0.066)
−0.003 (0.005)	−0.003 (0.005)	0.005 (0.007)	−0.002 (0.005)	0.008 (0.006)	0.000 (0.004)
0.402 (0.062)***	0.414 (0.063)***	0.377 (0.082)***	0.350 (0.054)***	0.402 (0.074)***	0.371 (0.050)***
0.389 (0.100)***	0.367 (0.106)***	—	0.057 (0.080)	—	−0.025 (0.072)

(continued)

TABLE 8.A1 *(continued)*

Independent Variable	(1) Adjusted Skew (All)	(2) Adjusted Skew (Non-Elec.)	(3) Adjusted Skew (Pre-Elec., Non-Elec.)	(4) Raw Skew (All)
Social issues	0.705 (0.273)**	0.587 (0.339)^	0.575 (0.372)	0.731 (0.283)**
WMD	0.461 (0.315)	0.543 (0.323)^	0.474 (0.336)	0.449 (0.308)
North Korea	0.448 (0.215)*	0.403 (0.234)^	0.624 (0.255)*	0.403 (0.210)*
Iran	0.159 (0.325)	0.188 (0.330)	0.107 (0.365)	0.140 (0.320)
Iraq	0.385 (0.117)***	0.403 (0.139)**	0.333 (0.151)*	0.397 (0.116)***
China	−0.353 (0.417)	−0.341 (0.420)	−0.278 (0.434)	−0.365 (0.414)
The polls	0.266 (0.167)	−0.467 (0.445)	−1.204 (0.682)^	0.265 (0.166)
Dramatic	0.301 (0.134)*	0.227 (0.152)	0.246 (0.161)	0.309 (0.131)*
Constant	−40.156 (6.244)***	−36.651 (7.212)***	−38.281 (7.458)***	−37.482 (5.340)***
Pseudo-R^2 (N)	0.16 (N = 7,022)	0.17 (N = 4,627)	0.18 (N = 4,253)	0.14 (N = 7,025)

^p < .10; *p < .05; **p < .01; *** p < .001. Robust standard errors in parentheses.
Note: All models exclude between one and three extreme outlier observations.

(5) Raw Skew (Non-Elec.)	(6) Raw Skew (Pre-Elec., Non-Elec.)	(7) Costly vs. Cheap (Non-Iraq Reuters)	(8) Costly, vs. Cheap (Non-Iraq Newswires Combined)	(9) Costly vs. Cheap (All Reuters)	(10) Costly vs. Cheap (All Newswires Combined)
0.566 (0.343)^	0.548 (0.370)	1.092 (0.370)**	0.927 (0.284)***	0.995 (0.361)**	0.728 (0.272)**
0.527 (0.316)^	0.456 (0.327)	0.455 (0.371)	0.470 (0.332)	0.556 (0.352)	0.429 (0.307)
0.373 (0.230)	0.595 (0.249)*	0.693 (0.272)*	0.579 (0.225)**	0.499 (0.253)*	0.467 (0.212)*
0.179 (0.325)	0.102 (0.359)	0.305 (0.395)	0.232 (0.354)	0.107 (0.374)	0.145 (0.320)
0.433 (0.137)**	0.369 (0.149)*	—	—	0.729 (0.161)***	0.377 (0.116)***
−0.357 (0.416)	−0.288 (0.428)	−0.280 (0.467)	−0.253 (0.419)	−0.337 (0.459)	−0.351 (0.415)
−0.484 (0.451)	−1.237 (0.699)^	0.779 (0.317)*	0.405 (0.175)*	0.594 (0.314)^	0.233 (0.169)
0.242 (0.150)	0.259 (0.159)	0.468 (0.211)*	0.393 (0.151)**	0.371 (0.182)*	0.303 (0.131)*
−38.360 (6.582)***	−39.456 (6.685)***	−37.271 (8.805)***	−33.810 (5.742)***	−40.151 (7.891)***	−35.880 (5.301)***
0.15 (N = 4,628)	0.16 (N = 4,254)	0.18 (N = 3,020)	0.15 (N = 6,254)	0.16 (N = 3,407)	0.13 (N = 7,024)

TABLE 8A.2
Logit Analyses of Correlates of Relying on the Internet or Network News as for Political and International News

Internet News	(1)	(2)	(3)	(4)
Democrat	−0.337 (0.153)*	−0.277 (0.159)^	−0.124 (0.171)	−0.126 (0.173)
Republican	−0.026 (0.165)	−0.098 (0.177)	−0.167 (0.185)	−0.219 (0.187)
Conservative	−0.168 (0.156)	−0.193 (0.160)	−0.217 (0.169)	−0.223 (0.169)
Liberal	0.427 (0.161)**	0.445 (0.161)**	0.396 (0.167)*	0.401 (0.168)*
Republicans more correct on national security	—	−0.020 (0.117)	−0.063 (0.119)	−0.088 (0.120)
Republicans more correct on taxes and spending	—	0.200 (0.114)^	0.136 (0.120)	0.122 (0.120)
Republicans more correct on social policy	—	−0.013 (0.109)	−0.069 (0.114)	−0.078 (0.114)
Network TV news favorability	—	—	−0.338 (0.101)***	−0.322 (0.102)**
Local newspaper favorability	—	—	−0.105 (0.096)	−0.101 (0.097)
National newspaper favorability	—	—	0.141 (0.098)	0.143 (0.098)
Local TV news favorability	—	—	−0.264 (0.097)**	−0.268 (0.098)**
Cable news favorability	—	—	0.008 (0.093)	0.011 (0.094)
Media too critical of president	—	—	0.191 (0.103)^	0.152 (0.107)
News quality scale	—	—	−0.031 (0.065)	−0.041 (0.064)
Know U.S. casualty level in Iraq	—	—	—	0.225 (0.136)^
Follow Iraq War	—	—	—	−0.008 (0.077)
Iraq War right	—	—	—	0.203 (0.173)
Constant	−1.052 (0.120)***	−1.038 (0.121)***	0.188 (0.452)	0.029 (0.529)
Pseudo-R^2 (N)	0.01 (N = 1,406)	0.01 (N = 1,406)	0.04 (N = 1,380)	0.04 (N = 1,376)

Network TV News	(5)	(6)	(7)	(8)
Democrat	0.503 (0.145)***	0.435 (0.151)**	0.418 (0.156)**	0.442 (0.158)**
Republican	0.066 (0.158)	0.168 (0.167)	0.224 (0.173)	0.295 (0.178)^
Conservative	−0.178 (0.142)	−0.129 (0.146)	−0.150 (0.151)	−0.149 (0.150)
Liberal	−0.353 (0.161)*	−0.390 (0.164)*	−0.298 (0.168)^	−0.326 (0.169)*
Republicans more correct on national security	—	−0.074 (0.107)	−0.045 (0.110)	−0.033 (0.112)
Republicans more correct on taxes and spending	—	−0.110 (0.101)	−0.126 (0.107)	−0.116 (0.109)
Republicans more correct on social policy	—	−0.073 (0.096)	−0.062 (0.100)	−0.064 (0.101)
Local newspaper favorability	—	—	0.070 (0.087)	0.065 (0.087)
National newspaper favorability	—	—	−0.034 (0.087)	−0.025 (0.087)
Local TV news favorability	—	—	0.576 (0.095)***	0.561 (0.095)***
Cable news favorability	—	—	−0.172 (0.087)*	−0.191 (0.089)*
Media too critical of president	—	—	−0.004 (0.097)	0.024 (0.101)
News quality scale	—	—	0.031 (0.056)	0.042 (0.057)
Know U.S. casualty level in Iraq	—	—	—	−0.308 (0.127)*
Follow Iraq War	—	—	—	−0.051 (0.071)
Iraq War right	—	—	—	−0.119 (0.163)
Constant	−0.940 (0.117)***	−0.969 (0.118)***	−2.344 (0.445)***	−1.948 (0.513)***
Pseudo-R^2 (N)	0.01 (N = 1,406)	0.01 (N = 1,406)	0.04 (N = 1,382)	0.05 (N = 1,378)

^$p < .10$; *$p < .05$; **$p < .01$. ***$p < .001$. Robust standard errors in parentheses. All models employ probability weighting ("pweight" in Stata).

TABLE 8.A3
Logit Analyses of Correlates of Selecting News Stories for Web Site "Top News" Summaries: Domestic Stories, Iraq/Afghanistan, and Non-War Foreign Policy Stories

Independent Variable	(1) Domestic	(2) Non-War Foreign Policy	(3) Iraq or Afghanistan
FoxNews.com	1.883 (0.163)***	1.494 (0.399)***	0.630 (0.365)^
DailyKos.com	−0.879 (0.255)***	−1.747 (0.644)**	−1.521 (0.504)**
FreeRepublic.com	0.861 (0.172)***	1.014 (0.396)**	0.517 (0.360)
Reuters.com	1.235 (0.213)***	0.761 (0.452)^	1.037 (0.442)*
Daily Kos × Skew	−1.740 (0.204)***	−1.393 (0.630)*	−1.826 0.386)***
Fox × Skew	0.138 (0.118)	0.590 (0.344)^	−0.238 (0.295)
Free Republic × Skew	−0.134 (0.148)	0.566 (0.372)	−0.057 (0.266)
Reuters × Skew	−0.367 (0.232)	0.249 (0.555)	−0.016 (0.420)
AP × Skew	−0.393 (0.204)*	−1.168 (0.523)*	−1.018 (0.463)*
July	3.103 (0.292)***	4.650 (0.848)***	1.890 0.539)***
August	3.573 (0.442)***	7.224 (1.250)***	1.869 (0.895)*
September	2.191 (0.328)***	4.275 (0.876)***	0.428 (0.671)
October	−0.324 (0.231)	−1.708 (0.874)*	−0.879 (0.454)*
Post-election	0.359 (0.201)^	−0.435 (0.805)	0.315 (0.402)
Election story	−0.083 (0.090)	−0.690 (0.408)^	−0.500 (0.248)*
Political figures	0.324 (0.044)***	0.344 (0.099)***	0.142 (0.089)
Tragedy	−0.185 (0.299)	−0.228 (0.721)	1.390 (1.287)
Economy/jobs	−0.404 (0.135)**	−0.329 (0.303)	−0.164 (0.804)
Scandal	0.587 (0.108)***	0.455 (0.541)	−1.561 (0.676)*
Trend	−0.485 (0.071)***	−0.337 (0.163)*	0.035 (0.177)
Urgency	0.431 (0.091)***	0.187 (0.129)	0.313 (0.124)*
U.S. fatalities— Afghan.	−0.183 (0.078)*	0.049 (0.127)	−0.104 (0.149)
U.S. fatalities—Iraq	−0.021 (0.017)	−0.013 (0.038)	−0.043 (0.043)
Iraq civilian deaths	0.001 (0.001)	0.000 (0.002)	0.003 (0.002)^
Iraq New York Times coverage	−0.057 (0.043)	0.138 (0.080)^	−0.093 (0.100)
Afghan New York Times coverage	−0.125 (0.084)	0.030 (0.169)	0.312 (0.182)^
Gas prices	−0.003 (0.005)	0.015 (0.013)	0.007 (0.012)
Consumer sentiment	0.333 (0.068)***	0.919 (0.180)***	0.323 (0.146)*
Associated Press story	0.328 (0.097)***	0.388 (0.225)^	−0.173 (0.212)
Dramatic	0.244 (0.214)	0.522 (0.247)*	−0.268 (0.234)
Constant	−32.710 (7.122)***	−89.636 (18.233)***	−32.144 (15.463)*
Pseudo-R^2 (N)	0.17 (N = 5,293)	0.20 (N = 938)	0.15 (N = 791)

^$p < .10$; * $p < .05$; ** $p < .01$; *** $p < .001$. Robust standard errors in parentheses.
Note: All models exclude three extreme outlier observations.

TABLE 8.A4

Logit Analysis of Likelihood of Believing the Conflict in Iraq Is "Going Well," as News Source and Party Identification Vary

Independent Variable	Coefficient (Std. Err.)
Democrat	−0.041 (0.243)
Republican	0.562 (0.240)*
Network news primary news source	0.300 (0.261)
Internet primary news source	0.020 (0.273)
Democrat. × Network news primary news source	−0.766 (0.379)*
Democrat × Internet primary news source	−0.131 (0.407)
Republican × Network news primary news source	−0.853 (0.388)*
Republican × Internet primary news source	0.934 (0.462)*
Know U.S. casualty level in Iraq	0.052 (0.152)
Follow Iraq War	0.068 (0.090)
Iraq right	1.993 (0.169)***
Media too critical of president	0.615 (0.111)***
News quality scale	0.149 (0.064)*
Age	−0.004 (0.004)
Education	−0.244 (0.071)***
Male	−0.118 (0.152)
Family income	0.025 (0.036)
Hispanic	−0.394 (0.282)
White	−0.592 (0.344)^
African American	−0.537 (0.412)
Asian	−1.317 (0.568)*
Ideology	−0.345 (0.086)***
Voted in 2004	0.000 (0.219)
Constant	0.031 (0.703)
Pseudo-R^2 (N)	0.34 (N = 1,340)

^$p < .10$; *$p < .05$; ***$p < .001$. Robust standard errors in parentheses.

Appendix 8.3. Testing for Selection Effects

The key question we address in this appendix is whether and to what extent knowledge about or attitudes toward the war, net of other factors, influence the decision to prefer the Internet or network newscasts. We begin with the Internet, shown in models 1– 4 in table 8.A2 in appendix 8.2.

Model 1 in table 8.A2 includes dummy variables for party (Democrat, Republican) and ideology (liberal, conservative). The results indicate that Democrats are significantly *less* likely to rely on the Internet (relative to independents, who are the excluded category), while, net of party, liberals are significantly *more* likely to do so. In model 2, we add the identical three dummy variables to our base model derived from the same questions as employed in chapter 5 asking respondents about the appropriateness of the Democratic and Republican Party positions on national security and foreign policy, economic policies, and social issues. (See appendix 5.3 in chapter 5 for question wording and coding of casual variables employed in our survey analyses.) The results indicate that only the government economic policy item significantly ($p < .10$) influences the tendency to prefer the Internet as a news source.

In model 3 of table 8.A2, we add several indicators of attitudes toward the media. While attitudes regarding the overall quality of the news media have no effect, favorability toward network and local TV news are each negative and significant ($p < .01$ and $p < .001$, respectively), indicating that, as one might anticipate, a favorable attitude toward TV news is negatively correlated with a preference for Internet news. Believing the news media are too critical of President Bush also positively influences the propensity to prefer news on the Internet ($p < .10$). However, all three relative partisan issue correctness variables are now insignificant. Finally, in model 4, we add the same set of indicators of knowledge about and attitudes toward the war in Iraq as in chapter 5. These include dummies measuring whether the respondent: (1) reports following the Iraq conflict fairly or very closely, (2) knows the approximate number of U.S. casualties, and (3) believes invading Iraq was the right thing to do. Neither following the war nor believing (retrospectively) that it was the right thing to do is significantly related to the preference for Internet news; as before, neither is preferring the Republican Party's policies regarding national security and foreign affairs. However, knowing the level of U.S. casualties is positively related to relying on the Internet for news ($p < .10$). We discuss the implications of this latter finding below.

We replicated model 4 (not shown), dropping the Iraq and foreign policy questions, except whether or not invading Iraq was the right thing to do. The Iraq attitude indicator remained insignificant. In other words, once attitudes toward the news media and general partisanship and ideology are controlled, neither a general preference for Republican policies on national security and foreign affairs nor attitudes toward the war significantly predict respondents' propensities to prefer the Internet for news about politics and international affairs. These results indicate that attitudes toward the mainstream news media and partisan/ideological predispositions mediate respondents' propensity to prefer Internet news. However, while we see some limited evidence that more knowledgeable individuals prefer Internet news, attitudes regarding Iraq do not appear in these data to influence respondents' propensity to rely on the Internet for their political and international news.

Turning to network TV newscasts, models 5–8 in table 8.A2 replicate models 1–4, with preference for network TV news as the dependent variable. The key results are similar to those for the Internet. Hence, we do not discuss them in detail. There are, however, several noteworthy differences. First, while Democrats are *less* and liberals *more* likely to prefer Internet news, the effects reverse for network news, with Democrats *more* and liberals *less* likely to rely on network news. Second, while knowing the U.S. casualty level in Iraq was *positively* associated with relying on the Internet for news, it is *negatively* associated with relying on network news ($p < .05$). However, as before, neither attention to the war nor believing that it was the right thing for the U.S. to do is significantly related to a preference for network news.

Finally, comparing pseudo-R^2 values across models 3 and 4 for the Internet and models 7 and 8 for Network news indicates that while knowing the level of casualties is significantly related to the decision to rely on the Internet or network news, the Iraq casualty knowledge and attitude items add hardly any explanatory power to the models (+.0048 for network news for and +.0034 for Internet news). In light of these results, we tentatively conclude that selection effects based on attitudes toward Iraq, the key potential selection effect for our purposes, do not appear to be fundamentally driving the decision to consume network or Internet news.

CHAPTER 9

Back to the Future

FOREIGN POLICY IN THE SECOND
ERA OF THE PARTISAN PRESS

IN FEBRUARY 1968, *CBS Evening News* anchor Walter Cronkite gave what is often regarded as the most important commentary of his long and distinguished career. In his first broadcast since concluding a fact-finding tour of Vietnam following the shocking 1968 Tet Offensive, Cronkite somberly editorialized that, while not on the "edge of defeat," the United States was "mired in stalemate," and that "the only rational way out then will be to negotiate, not as victors, but as an honorable people who lived up to their pledge to defend democracy, and did the best they could" (Cronkite 1968).

In the halls of the White House, the reaction to Cronkite's apparent turn against the war was shock and dismay. According to one famous account, President Johnson himself was deeply shaken by Cronkite's editorial because it meant he had lost the center, as "Walter both was the center and reached the center" (Halberstam 2000, 514). Indeed, after watching Cronkite's declaration, Johnson reportedly commented to an aide, "If I've lost Cronkite, I've lost America" (PBS 2006). In his analysis of the event, Halberstam asserted that the editorial did "change the balance" in the debate over the war, concluding that "it was the first time in American history a war had been declared over by an anchorman" (514).

While no contemporary media figure holds the stature or wields the influence of Walter Cronkite, the news media clearly continue to play a vital role in the conduct of American foreign policy. We began this book by highlighting an apparent gap between what elites typically say about foreign policy and what the media say those elites are saying. Most of the current scholarly literature on the relationship between political elites and the mass media, as notably exemplified by the Media Indexing hypothesis, did not anticipate this gap. Its existence raised questions about the validity, or at least the general applicability, of one of the most widely accepted arguments concerning the relationship between public opinion and foreign policy, which we termed the Opinion Indexing hypothesis. We also sought to bridge the divide between scholars studying the immediate or short-term effects of foreign policy on public attitudes and those studying the longer-term relationships between foreign policy events and public opinion. Through content analysis of media coverage of U.S. foreign policy crises over a 25-year period, we found that journalists' preferences exert a powerful effect on the representation of elite rhetoric to which the public is ultimately exposed. We also found that the nature of journalists' preferences has evolved as the mass media have fragmented over the past several decades. Traditional journalistic norms and values are no longer hegemonic in the media milieu.

Citizens, moreover, are not the passive recipients of elite frames that scholars and observers of public opinion and foreign policy since the eras of Walter Lippmann (1920) and Gabriel Almond (1950) have frequently assumed them to be. Rather, citizens are able to negotiate the minefield of partisan political debate by employing some simple information short-cuts that help them to assess the persuasiveness of different types of rhetoric. As discussed in chapter 1, the opinions of trusted elites represent an important and widely employed shortcut (Sniderman, Brody, and Tetlock 1991; Popkin 1994), especially for citizens attempting to determine whether to support or oppose a president's foreign policy, an issue area where typical Americans are particularly ill-informed (Delli-Carpini and Keeter 1996; Baum 2003; Holsti 2004). If, as our data suggest, the media present an inaccurate representation of elite rhetoric, then reliance on this shortcut may produce perverse results, leading many citizens to draw conclusions they might not otherwise have drawn had the media exposed them to a truly representative sample of elite rhetoric.[1]

IMPLICATIONS FOR PUBLIC OPINION AND FOREIGN POLICY

The media coverage and citizen response patterns we have described are likely to be troubling to some democratic theorists and political communication scholars who believe that an informed public is necessary for the proper functioning of democracy (Dahl 1961; Bennett 1997, 2003; Patterson 2000, 2003). It may also call into question the prevailing

[1]The potential for such miscalculations may be more severe under particular circumstances. For instance, our theory and evidence suggest that if the president's party receives disproportionate coverage in unified government, journalists are unlikely to select for broadcast any praise they offer, and most members of the public are unlikely to find such praise persuasive. Conversely, any criticism they offer should be exceptionally newsworthy and influential on opinion. In contrast, in divided government, the opposition party tends to dominate the news, paradoxically to the benefit of the president. Under such circumstances, any NPP praise is exceptionally newsworthy and influential on public opinion, and, while NPP criticism is newsworthy, the public is likely to discount it as cheap talk.

counterargument to media critics (e.g., Patterson 2000; Bennett 2003) offered by advocates of "low information rationality" (e.g., Popkin 1994; Lupia and McCubbins 1998), who argue that citizens can make reasoned decisions with relatively little information by using information shortcuts, or heuristic cues.

Regardless of their implications for democratic theory, our results hold clear implications for the study of public opinion and American foreign policy. Any such study that assumes relatively passive media, thereby ignoring the strategic intervening role of journalists, is likely to paint an inaccurate picture of the relationship between political debates surrounding American foreign policy and subsequent public reactions to the nation's foreign policy initiatives. Such inaccuracies in scholarly research in turn could lead future policymakers astray as they seek to build and maintain public support for presidential foreign policy initiatives. Thus, it seems clear that the combination of journalists' assessments regarding the newsworthiness of different stories and citizens' assessments concerning the persuasiveness of such stories profoundly influences the nature and extent of public support for U.S. foreign policy.

Our investigation of the Iraq conflict indicated that these effects can persist for an extended period of time, far beyond the rally-'round-the-flag period. Indeed, consistent with our theory, we found that rhetoric and objective indicators of reality, separately and in interaction, influence public opinion to varying degrees at different stages of a conflict. Coverage by traditional media outlets tends to track elite rhetoric more closely than it tracks reality in the relatively early stages of a conflict, while tracking reality more closely if a conflict persists for an extended period of time. While our data suggest that more partisan outlets, such as the Fox News Channel, also respond to the shrinking elasticity of reality over time, they do so differently than nonpartisan outlets, delaying judgment on stories perceived as unfavorable to their preferred party while rushing to broadcast stories supportive of their preferred party.

Absent a major turn of events, consumers become relatively less susceptible to the influence of elite rhetoric regarding a conflict or the unfolding of events surrounding it as they gather more information, reassess the reliability of old information, and consequently form stronger judgments about the conflict over time. Stated differently, as the elasticity of reality recedes, media consumers grow less responsive to new information, particularly when it conflicts with their prior beliefs. This is precisely the pattern of public opinion regarding the Iraq War we described in chapter 7. Prior to fall 2007, partisans had grown increasingly firm in their convictions regarding the merits and trajectory of the conflict, with Democrats increasingly impervious to news suggesting the war in general, or the surge in particular, was going well, and Republicans equally impervious to news suggesting the opposite (Jacobson 2007). However, after several months of substantial and sustained reductions in the level of violence in Iraq, the media and the public began to reassess, at least in part, this previously "settled" judgment that the war was a failure.[2] In fact, by Election Day 2008, a Rasmussen poll showed that a plurality of Americans (42%) thought that the war would be seen as a success in the long run, while a majority thought the situation there would improve over the next six months (Rasmussen Reports 2008).[3]

As of this writing, the audiences for mainstream media continue to outstrip those for emerging partisan outlets (see chapters 5 and 8). Consequently, we believe the constricting of the elasticity of reality depicted in chapter 7 continues to represent the most common relationship between reality, rhetoric, and public opinion during military conflicts. However, as new and more partisan media continue to expand, both in number and in reach, this balance may well shift.

Democratic theorists, pundits, and political activists presumably will welcome such a shift. After all, many such individuals routinely hail the new media in general, and the Internet in particular, as a revolutionary force for expanding and enhancing democratic citizenship. In at least some respects, this is most likely true. Most notably, the Internet makes it possible for typical individuals to choose the information to which they expose themselves to a greater extent than any previous technology. On its face, this appears to represent a boon for freedom and democracy.[4]

---

[2]Conversely, some political elites apparently did not participate in this reassessment. Recall from chapter 2, for instance, that as late as February 2008, Speaker of the House Nancy Pelosi (D-CA) publicly judged the war in Iraq to be a "failure," called for "the redeployment of our troops out of Iraq," and labeled the troop surge unsuccessful, claiming "there haven't been gains" (Allen 2008).

[3]Interestingly, despite perceiving greater progress in the war since the troop surge, a sizable majority of the public remained firm in viewing the war in Iraq as a mistake. Depending on question wording, only a relatively consistent minority of 30%–40% of Americans thought the war was the right choice throughout 2007 and 2008, while a similarly consistent majority of 50%–70% (again, depending on question wording) disagreed. For example, when asked whether they "favor or oppose the U.S. war in Iraq," 33% responded affirmatively in November 2006. This percentage remained within ±3% of that value in all but one of the subsequent 26 polls (as of November 2008) by the same organization asking the identical question (CNN/Opinion Research polls, archived at http://www.pollingreport.com/iraq).

[4]Though not foreign policy related, those favoring this relatively positive view of the effects of the Internet frequently point to the politics of presidential elections to justify their optimism. In some respects, recent presidential campaigns, like those of Howard Dean in 2004 and Barack Obama in 2008, appear to demonstrate the power of the Internet to "democratize" electoral politics (see chapter 8). These candidates' success in attracting hundreds of thousands (Dean) or even millions (Obama) of individual donors, primarily via the Internet, dramatically broadened the base of their support and arguably reduced their dependence on the handful of big-money donors that have dominated U.S. party politics in

Yet, as mankind has repeatedly learned throughout history, and perhaps most sensationally with the splitting of the atom, technology is frequently a double-edged sword. Proponents of the Internet-as-democracy-enhancer perspective typically assume that, when given the opportunity, citizens will choose to avail themselves of more, and implicitly also "better," civic information. However, there is reason to doubt this assumption. Indeed, more and more citizens find themselves possessing the means, motive, and opportunity to self-select into friendly media environments while avoiding information that challenges their preexisting beliefs. This could lead to what Cass Sunstein (2001) refers to as "cyberbalkanization," whereby extreme audience fragmentation enhances rather than mitigates polarization in public attitudes about politics and public policy (see also Althaus 2007).

For instance, as the proportion of the population with access to high-speed Internet connections continues to expand, a larger segment of the population will have the means to self-select into niche-targeted, or narrowcast, news and information environments. These outlets have exploded in number and diversity over the past decade, giving such individuals greater opportunity to find an outlet or set of outlets with political leanings similar to their own. Research in social and political psychology (e.g., Campbell et al. 1960; McGuire 1968; Zaller 1992) has long shown that, given the opportunity, typical individuals are highly motivated to seek out confirmatory information while avoiding dissonance. Additional research (Baum and Kernell 1998; Prior 2007) suggests that increasing numbers of Americans are taking advantage of the ever-expanding diversity of media alternatives to entirely opt out of consuming political news, at least as traditionally defined.

As we have argued throughout the book, new, more partisan media may threaten the bipartisan foreign policy consensus that emerged during the cold war era. That consensus depended in part on news media maintaining independent reservoirs of credibility that successive presidents from both parties could tap to rally the public around their policies. As larger portions of the public tune into news outlets that regularly adhere to one or the other party's preferred framing of politics, it seems likely that public opinion will become less constrained by the elasticity of reality in the aggregate. This raises the troubling possibility that elites may gain a greater capacity to manipulate public opinion regarding foreign policy over time, especially among their fellow partisans, and to sustain such manipulations for longer periods of time. In Abraham Lincoln's par-

---

recent decades. This suggests that millions of small donations by individual voters can supplement and perhaps ultimately even supplant large-scale donors as the primary fuel, or at least one of the core fuels, of presidential politics in America.

lance, it might soon be possible to fool at least some of the people (self-selecting partisans) all of the time.

LESSONS FROM HISTORY

This is, however, by no means the first time in American politics that partisan media have strongly influenced public debate. Instead, it appears to be a somewhat ironic coincidence that modern social science arrived in the postwar era just in time to study a mass media system that was almost nothing like what had preceded it. The existence of this atypical postwar information environment was arguably an artifact of an unusual regulatory context that artificially limited competition and enforced nonpartisanship in the nation's dominant media (Hamilton 2003). Viewed in a broader context, overwhelmingly nonpartisan journalism appears to have been a historical anomaly that may not repeat itself.[5]

To better understand the implications of our increasingly polarized information environment, one might actually be well served to examine the partisan press of the nineteenth century and early twentieth century. In that era, citizens who wanted an accurate picture of the political landscape could read multiple newspapers with differing partisan loyalties in order to triangulate on "the truth."[6] Such a strategy could offset to some extent the potentially harmful effects of partisan-oriented media. Yet the question remains as to whether typical citizens in the contemporary period are likely to embrace a triangulation approach to news consumption. The present differs from the past in numerous important respects, not least of which is the explosion in the twenty-first century of entertainment mass media and other competitors for scarce public attention.[7]

[5]Even some politicians' renewed interest in restoring the fairness doctrine (see chapter 8) is unlikely to address this new media partisanship, as it would be exceptionally difficult to apply outside of broadcast media.

[6]For example, in their famous "Middletown" study of what they regarded as a typical American city in the 1920s, Robert and Helen Lynd (1929, 471) found that "The local morning paper distributes 8,851 copies to the 9,200 homes of the city, and the afternoon paper 6,715, plus at least half of an additional 785 sold on the street and news-stand. In addition, the circulation of out-of-town-papers ... now totals 1200 to 1500 a day."

[7]For instance, at the height of the partisan press era in the early nineteenth century, only about 2% of U.S. adults subscribed to newspapers. By 1870, the era of the commercially oriented "penny press," that number had expanded tenfold, to about 20% of U.S. adults (Schudson 1978). Nonetheless, relative to the contemporary era of near universal media access, that percentage was quite small, with newspaper subscriptions still mostly limited to relatively well-off segments of the population. Multiple newspaper subscriptions were thus most likely available only to individuals possessing both the motive (interest in partisan politics) and opportunity (wealth) to engage in the triangulation strategy. In sharp contrast,

While it may be the case that politically attentive Americans in the twenty-first century are proportionately similar in number to their counterparts in prior news eras, a far larger portion of the contemporary population enjoys and, notwithstanding the often decried low voting rates, exercises the franchise than was the case in the nineteenth-century. Moreover, the ability of party organizations to reliably direct the voting of their members has declined with the death of party machines and the waning influence of state party bosses. Consequently, the *breadth* of consensus necessary to forge a bipartisan accord is far greater in the twenty-first century, and modern communication and polling technology allows nervous politicians to sense precisely when that consensus is eroding. Of course, gaining consent first requires capturing public attention, and even politically attentive citizens are unlikely to be able to attend to all of the competing messages in the modern media environment.

Not only is it possible to consume nearly limitless political news from virtually any ideological perspective, it is also possible to consume equally limitless soft news (Baum 2003)—from crime to sports to public health to celebrity gossip—or pure entertainment, while rarely if ever encountering politics (Prior 2007). This raises the opportunity costs for typical consumers of seeking out alternative political perspectives. Survey evidence, such as the 2006 Pew Center Survey cited in table 8.4 of chapter 8, suggests that substantial portions of the public also appear to lack the motive to do so. In that survey, more than one in five (22%) respondents, including more than one-quarter of self-described regular users of Internet blogs, reported preferring news that reinforced their preexisting beliefs over news that challenged those beliefs. Not surprisingly, as shown in figure 9.1, preferences for reinforcing news increase with strength of political ideology. Among ideologues (those defining themselves as "strong" liberals or conservatives), more than four in ten report preferring news consistent with their political points of view.

If the emerging second partisan press era is characterized more by *reinforcement seeking* than by triangulation, forging and sustaining bipartisan consensus on foreign policy will likely prove a daunting and perhaps all but insurmountable task for future leaders. Evidence of this dilemma is abundant in public reactions to the 2003 U.S. invasion and subsequent occupation of Iraq, a conflict that produced the greatest partisan divide ever recorded in scientific polling, both in terms of support for a U.S.

---

the contemporary mass media penetrate every strata of society and provide a bounty of non-news content that competes for news consumers' attention (Baum and Kernell 1999). Thus, while modern media have dramatically decreased the unit costs of becoming exposed to competing viewpoints, they have also raised the opportunity costs of such information strategies by offering potentially attractive alternative entertainment content that must be forgone in order to attend to competing news content.

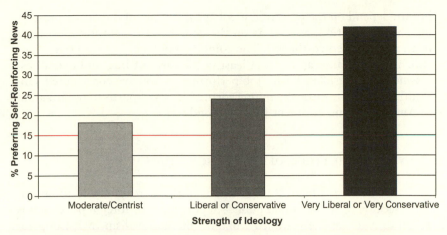

FIGURE 9.1. Preferences for Self-Reinforcing News, as Strength of Ideology Increases
Source: Pew (2006).

military conflict and in terms of overall presidential approval (Jacobson 2006). Scholars (e.g., Kull, Ramsay, and Lewis 2003–2004; Della Vigna and Kaplan 2003; Jacobson 2007) continue to debate the media's role in sharpening, if not altogether producing, the partisan gulf in evaluations of the president and the Iraq War. Jacobson (2007), for instance, speculates that a combination of differences in content and partisan self-selection into friendly news environments—such as Fox for Republicans and conservatives, PBS, MSNBC, and CNN for Democrats and liberals, and network news for independents and moderates—may contribute to partisan differences in perceptions of the war and the president leading it.

As the prior discussion attests, we certainly agree that self-selection, a concept dating back to Campbell and colleagues' (1960) theory of minimalism, may be sharpening partisan polarization, and that this phenomenon seems likely to expand in the future. However, our research suggests a second, perhaps complementary, culprit: ideologically driven credibility assessments. In other words, contemporary citizens possess, arguably to a greater extent than their predecessors, the means to engage in a multi-pronged dissonance-avoidance strategy. Selective exposure, or avoiding dissonant information altogether, presumably represents the first such prong. However, even when this first defense mechanism fails and individuals are exposed to ideologically hostile news, they increasingly possess the means—by assigning ideological reputations to individual sources and media outlets—to systematically discount it. In other words, consumers appear also to selectively accept or reject information to which they are exposed based on its perceived credibility. Credibility assessments in turn depend on the perceived ideological leaning of the outlet presenting the information, as well as on the content of the information itself (e.g., its perceived costliness). The combined influence of selective exposure and acceptance appears, at least in the cases of Iraq and overall assessments of President Bush's job performance, to have contributed substantially to the historically unprecedented levels of partisan polarization in America during President Bush's second term.

CONVERTING THE FLOCK, OR PREACHING TO THE CHOIR?

To understand the practical implications of these trends for future presidents seeking to attract broad public support for their foreign policies, it is useful to consider the so-called Militant Internationalism (MI)/Cooperative Internationalism (CI) Index developed by Wittkopf and Maggiotto (1981; see also Holsti and Rosenau 1990; Wittkopf 1990; Holsti 2004). The MI/CI Index divides the public into four categories, based on support for or opposition to *militant internationalism* (that is, support for unilateral pursuit of American national security interests, including the unilateral use of military force abroad), and support for or opposition to *cooperative internationalism* (that is, support for international engagement through multilateral institutions and limiting the use of force to multilateral contexts).

Wittkopf and Maggiato classify people who support MI and oppose CI as hard-liners, those who support CI and oppose MI as accommodationists, those who support both MI and CI as internationalists, and those who oppose both MI and CI as isolationists. Holsti and Rosenau, 1996, report that a majority of liberals are accommodationists, while conservatives are about equally divided between hard-liners and internationalists. Consistent with what one would anticipate, they further report that in their data, most Republicans identify themselves as conservative (55%), while most Democrats identify themselves as liberal (77%).[8]

These patterns suggest that with the possible exception of the earliest stages of full-scale wars, Republican presidents will find it difficult to persuade Democratic partisans (mostly relatively liberal) in the electorate to support their foreign policy initiatives, particularly uses of military force involving traditional national security missions. Ironically, Democratic presidents may not face as severe a dilemma, because Republicans (mostly relatively conservative) tend to be more likely than Democrats to

[8]Though Holsti and Rosenau have not updated the MI/CI Index since 1996, we strongly suspect that if they did so, they would find that the ideological orientations of partisans have further stratified, with even larger percentages of Republicans and Democrats identifying themselves as conservative or liberal, respectively.

support the use of military force, either unilaterally (hard-liners) or multilaterally (internationalists). Consequently, some Republicans are likely to support the use of force, either unilaterally or multilaterally, even if advocated by a Democratic president. A concrete example of such a partisan reversal occurred in the early days of the Obama administration, when a Pew Research Center survey (March 16, 2009) showed that more Republicans and independents than Democrats approved of Obama's plan to send 17,000 more troops to Afghanistan.[9]

Conversely, because Democrats are predominantly accommodationists, they are likely to primarily support multilateral uses of force aimed at nontraditional goals, such as humanitarian relief. As a result, Democrats will tend to be ideologically disinclined to support traditional uses of force by Republican presidents.

While this tension has long existed, the presence of mass media perceived as relatively nonpartisan and hence credible by a majority of the public across partisan lines muted its practical implications. This situation allowed presidents of either party to promote their foreign policy initiatives fairly effectively not only to their ex ante supporters but also to opposition party identifiers and independents. As citizens increasingly perceive the media as partisan, and hence less credible, and as they gain more capacity to limit their exposure to news inconsistent with their partisan preferences, it is likely to become ever more difficult for presidents to reach across party lines to gain bipartisan support for their foreign policy initiatives.

This trend has potentially important implications for the conduct of American foreign policy. Recent research (e.g., Fearon 1994; Smith 1998; Schultz 2001; Baum 2004; Slantchev 2006) suggests that domestic populations can influence the outcomes of international bargaining processes by enhancing or inhibiting leaders' credibility during such negotiations. According to this view, a democratic leader can enhance her bargaining position by making public threats or promises. By doing so, and thereby risking political punishment at home, a leader can effectively "tie her hands," thereby enhancing her credibility to an adversary. This is because upon publicly issuing a threat, a democratic leader who is accountable to her domestic population ups the political ante by generating domestic audience costs, defined as the domestic political punishment a leader suffers if she issues a public threat and subsequently retreats. Once generated, such costs make it more difficult to back down (Fearon 1994). Consequently,

---

[9]Nearly two-thirds of Republicans (63%) approved of the plan, while 53% of independents and only 49% of Democrats expressed similar support (Pew 2009). Of course, it is possible that some of this difference stemmed from the association of the conflict with the prior administration of George W. Bush.

audience costs can help a democratic leader signal resolve (Fearon 1994; Smith 1998; Schultz 2001).

Domestic audience cost theory, as specified above, implicitly assumes that citizens—the "audience" in domestic audience costs—will rally behind their leaders whenever they call (Baum 2004). Our evidence calls this latter assumption into question. Consequently, if, as Schultz (2001) argues, expressions of opposition to a leader's foreign policy from the opposition party can undermine the credibility of that leader's commitments abroad, then, for the same basic reasons, public opposition to the president's foreign policy goals also seems likely to be capable of undermining the president's credibility (Baum 2004; for a similar logical argument, see Slantchev 2006). To the extent that, as we have argued, the valence of media coverage of foreign policy mediates citizens' propensities to support presidential foreign policy initiatives, then the coverage patterns and resulting increases in partisan polarization we have identified seem likely to weaken presidents' hands in international bargaining situations. Such patterns may reduce their capacity to generate the domestic audience costs necessary for signaling resolve in international negotiations.

Presidents wishing to avoid this potential pitfall by persuading significant numbers of opposition identifiers to support their preferred policies will increasingly be forced to reach out to sources and media aligned with the other party. While such outreach beyond one's base is likely to be costly and frequently ineffective, it does have the silver lining of endowing considerable credibility to those pro-presidential messages in the (presumably relatively infrequent) event that "hostile" media and partisan figures choose to deliver them (see chapters 3 and 5). In an era of extreme partisan polarization, such a strategy may afford presidents their best and perhaps only opportunities to reach beyond their bases to form bipartisan coalitions in support of American foreign policy.

However, while these changes in media polarization and dispersion have made it more difficult for presidents to gain bipartisan support for their foreign policy initiatives, recent history has also shown the reverse to be true with respect to gaining support from within their own party. Support across the aisle may be scant and fleeting, yet support among the president's own partisans will be reliable in a way seldom seen in most of the postwar era, throughout which independently credible media institutions wielded sufficient power to occasionally drive away even the president's most ardent supporters.

To illustrate this point, one need only return to a variation on the theme that opened this chapter: a *CBS News* anchor speaking out against the war. In Vietnam, Cronkite's measured but ultimately pessimistic assessment not only helped convince a president that the war was unwinnable, it also reportedly solidified President Johnson's decision not to seek re-election (Halberstam 2000). In the case of the Iraq War, CBS's Katie Couric followed up her own fact-finding trip to a war zone with a speech before the National Press Club on September 26, 2007, in which she argued that it was "pretty much accepted" that the war had been a mistake, and that "people in this country had been misled in terms of the rationale for war."[10]

The response to Couric's speech, however, was much different from that to Cronkite's. Peter Feaver, a National Security Council staff member during the Bush administration, observed that network anchors "are still very influential and the White House does take pains to court them." However, he added that:

> Their influence has waned somewhat because of the rise of cable and new media. An anchor like Couric does not have the agenda-setting power that [former CBS anchor Dan] Rather had; and Rather's influence was markedly less than Cronkite's, whose skewed coverage of Vietnam set the tone for everyone else. Thus, Couric's speech on Iraq had far less traction than comparable partisan advocacy by Cronkite during the Vietnam War. (Feaver 2008; correspondence with author)

In addition, bloggers across the political spectrum (though mostly on the right) savaged Couric for her remarks. For example, a diarist on the antiwar DailyKos.com criticized Couric's "too-little, too-late" criticism of the war in a post titled "Snapshot! The Death of American News" (DailyKos.com 2007). In contrast, a conservative commentator mockingly praised her honesty in exposing her apparent biases toward the war, saying, "Maybe it's because she is a lightweight, a news neophyte promoted over her abilities, that she's willing to strip the emperor" (Crittenden 2008).

Ultimately, the impact of Couric's critique was at best a pale echo of Cronkite's. Couric was watched by fewer Americans than Cronkite, and was trusted by even fewer. Consequently, her words served mostly to provide critics of the mainstream media additional ammunition to discredit news with which they disagreed. Far from indicating a turning

---

[10]Ironically, Couric also indicated that she thought discovering the truth about Iraq was "incredibly complicated" and required the public to read "24/7 publications with every point of view" to fully understand the conflict. She also cautioned that four years into the war, "almost everyone who discusses Iraq has an agenda that is fairly entrenched ... you have to read a variety of points of view. ... So I think you really, if you seek it out, then I think you can keep getting the news and information you need. The question is, do people really want to seek it out at this point in time?"

point in the war, her remarks became merely another talking point in a seemingly never-ending war of words as the real conflict in Iraq continued unabated.

As the media landscape in which America's partisan battles are fought continues to evolve, this war of words threatens to become ever more divorced from the strategic interests of the country as a whole. Increasing numbers of news outlets—print, broadcast, cable, radio, and Internet—are responding to the changing information landscape by seeking loyal niche audiences. Some do so for economic reasons, others for ideological reasons. But regardless of the motivation, one niche-targeting strategy that growing numbers of outlets will almost certainly pursue is tailoring their content to segments of the public with particular partisan leanings.

Perceived partisan alignment among news providers challenges the media's role as neutral arbiter. As this longstanding media function erodes, future leaders are likely to find themselves facing a paradoxical political environment in which they are at once better able to rally their bases—that is, *preach to the choir*—but less able to *convert the flock*—that is, to persuade Americans beyond their base to support their policies. Bridging this gap has always been an important challenge for America's foreign policy leadership; in the future it may prove to be the central political challenge facing the nation's foreign policy—essential, yet increasingly elusive. How America's leaders respond to this challenge may determine whether the nation will be able to pursue a coherent foreign policy in the twenty-first century.

References

Adamic, Lada A., and Natalie Glance. "The Political Blogosphere and the 2004 U.S. Election: Divided They Blog." In *Proceedings of the 3rd International Workshop on Link Discovery*, 36–43. Chicago, August 21–25, 2005. Link-KDD '05. New York: ACM, 2005. http://doi.acm.org/10.1145/1134271.1134277 (accessed December 1, 2008).

AFP. "Obama Surfs the Web to the White House." *Sydney Morning Herald*, November 5, 2008. http://news.smh.com.au/technology/obama-surfs-the-web-to-the-white-house-20081105-5icx.html (accessed December 1, 2008).

Alan, Jeff, and James Martin Lane. *Anchoring America: The Changing Face of Network News*. Chicago: Bonus Books, 2003.

Allen, Barbara Ann, Luc Juillet, Gilles Paquet, and Jeffrey Roy. *E-governance and Government Online in Canada: Partnerships, People, and Prospects*. Ottawa: Faculty of Administration, University of Ottawa, 2000.

Allen, Cleo J. "Foreign News Coverage in Selected U.S. Newspapers 1927–1997: A Content Analysis." Ph.D. diss., Louisiana State University, 2005.

Allen, Mike. "Pelosi Calls Iraq a 'Failure.'" *Politico*, February 10, 2008. http://www.politico.com/news/ stories/ 0208/ 8422.html (accessed December 1, 2008).

Almond, Gabriel A. *The American People and Foreign Policy*. New York: Praeger, 1950.

Alterman, Eric. *What Liberal Media?* New York: Basic Books, 2003.

Althaus, Scott L. "Free Falls, High Dives, and the Future of Democratic Accountability." Paper presented at the Princeton Conference on Media and Accountability. Princeton, NJ, November 30–December 1, 2007.

Althaus, Scott, Jill Edy, Robert Entman, and Patricia Phalen. "Revising the Indexing Hypothesis: Officials, Media, and the Libya Crisis." *Political Communication* 13:407–21, 1996.

Altman, Douglas G. *Practical Statistics for Medical Research*. London: Chapman and Hall, 1991.

American Society of Newspaper Editors (ASNE). *ASNE Statement of Principles*. Revised August 28, 2002. http://www.asne.org/kiosk/archive/principl.htm (accessed September 7, 2005).

Anttiroiko, Ari-Veikko. *Introduction to Democratic E-Governance*. Hershey, PA: IGI Publishing, 2004.

Armstrong, Jerome, and Markos Moulitsas Zúniga. *Crashing the Gate: Netroots, Grassroots, and the Rise of People-Powered Politics*. White River Junction, VT: Chelsea Green Publishing Co., 2006.

Arnold, R. Douglas. *The Logic of Congressional Action*. New Haven, CT: Yale University Press, 1992.

Associated Press. 2007. "Associated Press Facts and Figures," April 16, 2007. http://www.ap.org/pages/about/about.html (accessed December 1, 2008).

Bacon, Perry, Jr. "Can Lieberman Survive Iraq?" *Time,* June 25, 2006. http://www.time.com/time/magazine/article/0,9171,1207783,00.html (accessed December 1, 2008).

Bai, Matt. "Preview: Working for the Working-Class Vote." *New York Times Magazine*, October 15, 2008. http://www.nytimes.com/2008/10/19/magazine/19obama-t.html (accessed December 1, 2008).

Baker, William D., and John R. Oneal. "Patriotism or Opinion Leadership? The Nature and Origins of the "Rally 'Round the Flag" Effect." *Journal of Conflict Resolution* 45 (October): 661–87, 2001.

Baum, Matthew A. "The Constituent Foundations of the Rally-Round-the-Flag Phenomenon." *International Studies Quarterly* 46:263–98, 2002.

———. *Soft News Goes to War: Public Opinion and American Foreign Policy in the New Media Age*. Princeton, NJ: Princeton University Press, 2003.

———. "Going Private: Public Opinion, Presidential Rhetoric, and the Domestic Politics of Audience Costs in U.S. Foreign Policy Crises." *Journal of Conflict Resolution* 48 (October): 603–31, 2004.

———. "How Public Opinion Constrains the Use of Force: The Case of Operation Restore Hope." *Presidential Studies Quarterly* 34 (June): 187–226, 2004.

Baum, Matthew A., and Tim Groeling. "New Media and the Polarization of American Political Discourse." *Political Communication* 25 (4): 345–65, 2008.

Baum, Matthew A., and Philip Gussin. "In the Eye of the Beholder: How Information Shortcuts Shape Individual Perceptions of Bias in the Media." *Quarterly Journal of Political Science* 3: 1–31, 2008.

Baum, Matthew A., and Samuel Kernell. "Has Cable Ended the Golden Age of Presidential Television?" *American Political Science Review* 93:99–114, 1999.

Baum, Matthew A., and Philip B. K. Potter. "The Relationship between Mass Media, Public Opinion and Foreign Policy: Toward a Theoretical Synthesis." *Annual Review of Political Science* 11:39–66, 2008.

Beaumont, Thomas. "Iowa's Top Statesmen Have Low U.S. Profile." *The Des Moines Register,* online edition, October 10, 2005. http://nl.newsbank.com (accessed December 1, 2008).

Beckel, Robert. Interview with Fox News' Catherine Herridge, June 16, 2007.

Beinart, Peter. "Admit It: The Surge Worked." *Washington Post*, January 18, 2009, B07.

Bennett, W. Lance. "Toward a Theory of Press-State Relations in the United States." *Journal of Communication* 40:2, 1990.

———. *News: The Politics of Illusion*. 3rd ed. New York: Longman, 1997.

———. "The Burglar Alarm That Just Keeps Ringing: A Response to Zaller." *Political Communication* 20 (April/June): 131–38, 2003.

Bennett, W. Lance, Regina Lawrence, and Steven Livingston. "None Dare Call It Torture: Indexing and the Limits of Press Independence in the Abu Ghraib Scandal." *Journal of Communication* 56 (3): 467–85, 2006.

———. *When the Press Fails: Political Power and the News Media from Iraq to Katrina*. Chicago: University of Chicago Press, 2007.

Berinsky, Adam. "Assuming the Costs of War: Events, Elites, and American Public Support for Military Conflict." *Journal of Politics* 69:975–97, 2007.

Berinsky, Adam, and James N. Druckman. "Public Opinion Research, Presidential Rhetoric, and Support for the Iraq War." *Public Opinion Quarterly* 71 (Spring): 126–41, 2007.

Bethell, Tom. "Strange New Respect." *The American Spectator* 25 (9), September 1992.

Bigg, Matthew. "Talk Show Hosts Voice Alarm at McCain's Rise." Reuters.com, February 6, 2008. http://www.reuters.com/article/politicsNews/idUSN062819 0220080206?feedType=RSS&feedName=politicsNews&rpc=22&sp=true.

Bimber, Bruce, and Richard Davis. *Campaigning Online: The Internet in U.S. Elections*. New York: Oxford University Press, 2003.

Bimber, Bruce, Andrew Flanagin, and Cynthia Stohl. "Reconceptualizing Collective Action in the Contemporary Media Environment." *Communication Theory* 15:365–88, 2005.

Blechman, Barry, and Stephen Kaplan. *Force Without War: U.S. Armed Forces as a Political Instrument*. Washington, DC: Brookings Institution Press, 1978.

Blumler, Jay G., and Dennis Kavanagh. "The Third Age of Political Communication: Influences and Features." *Political Communication* 16:209–30, 1999.

Boettcher, William A. III, and Michael D. Cobb. "Echoes of Vietnam? Casualty Framing and Public Perceptions of Success and Failure in Iraq." *Journal of Conflict Resolution* 50 (December): 831–54, 2006.

Bolton, Alexander. "GOP Preps for Talk Radio Confrontation." *The Hill*, June 27, 2007.

Bowers, Chris. "ACTION: Freeze Out Fox News." Posted to MyDD.com, February 21, 2007. http://www.mydd.com/story/2007/2/21/131213/634 (accessed December 1, 2008).

Brecher, Michael, and Jonathan Wilkenfeld. *International Crisis Behavior Project, 1918–2004*. Version 7, 2006. http://www.cidcm.umd.edu/icb (accessed December 1, 2008).

Bresnahan, John. "Reid Labels Military Leader 'Incompetent.'" *Politico*, June 14, 2007. http://www.politico.com/news/stories/0607/4490.html (accessed July 6, 2007).

Brody, Richard. *Assessing Presidential Character: The Media, Elite Opinion, and Public Support*. Stanford: Stanford University Press, 1991.

Brody, Richard, and Catherine R. Shapiro. "Policy Failure and Public Support: The Iran-Contra Affair and Public Assessment of President Reagan." *Political Behavior* 11 (4): 353–69, 1989.

Bumiller, Elisabeth. "In Aftermath of Article, McCain Gathers Donations." *New York Times* online edition, February 23, 2008. http://www.nytimes.com/2008/02/23/us/politics/23mccain.html?_r=2&hp&oref=slogin&oref=slogin (accessed December 1, 2008).

Campbell, Angus, Philip E. Converse, Warren E. Miller, and Donald E. Stokes. *The American Voter*. New York: Wiley, 1960.

Canes-Wrone, Brandice. *Who Leads Whom? Presidents, Policy, and the Public*. Chicago: University of Chicago Press, 2006.

Caplan, Bryan. *The Myth of the Rational Voter: Why Democracies Choose Bad Policies*. Princeton, NJ: Princeton University Press, 2007.

Cappella, Joseph N., and Kathleen H. Jamieson. *Spiral of Cynicism: The Press and the Public Good*. New York: Oxford University Press, 1997.

CBS News. "Text of Bush Speech: President Declares End to Major Combat in Iraq," May 1, 2003. http://www.cbsnews.com/stories/2003/05/01/iraq/main551946.shtml (accessed December 1, 2008).

CBS/*New York Times*. "The Connecticut Democratic Primary Exit Poll," August 9, 2006. http://www.cbsnews.com/htdocs/CBSNews_polls/ctexitpoll.pdf (accessed December 1, 2008).

Chadwick, Andrew. "Bringing E-Democracy Back In: Why It Matters for Future Research on E-Governance." *Social Science Computer Review* 21 (Winter): 443–55, 2003.

Chapman, Terrence, and Dan Reiter. "The United Nations Security Council and the Rally 'Round the Flag Effect." *Journal of Conflict Resolution* 48:886–909, 2004.

Clayman, Steven, and John Heritage. "Questioning Presidents: Journalistic Deference and Adversarialness in the Press Conferences of U.S. Presidents Eisenhower and Reagan." *Journal of Communication* 52:749–75, 2002.

Clinton, Hillary. "Senator Clinton Questions General David Petraeus and Ambassador Ryan Crocker on Iraq at Senate Armed Services Committee Hearing," September 11, 2007. http://clinton.senate.gov/news/statements/record.cfm?id=282410.

CNN. "McCain, Obama Go Head to Head in Last Debate," October 15, 2008. http://www.cnn.com/2008/POLITICS/10/15/debate.transcript/ (accessed December 1, 2008).

Cobb, Michael D. "Casualties of War: Media, Knowledge and Opinions about the War in Iraq." North Carolina State University. Unpublished manuscript, 2008.

Congressional Quarterly Almanac. Washington, DC: CQ Press, 1953–2006.

Converse, Philip E. "The Nature and Origin of Belief Systems in Mass Publics." In *Ideology and Discontent*. Edited by David Apter, 15–46. New York: Free Press, 1964.

Cook, Timothy. "Domesticating a Crisis: Washington Newsbeats and Network News after the Iraqi Invasion of Kuwait." In *Taken by Storm: The Media, Public Opinion and U.S. Foreign Policy in the Gulf War*. Edited by W. Lance Bennett and David Paletz, 105–30. Chicago: University of Chicago Press, 1994.

Cooper, Charles. "Murdoch to Media: You Dug Yourself a Huge Hole." *CNET News*, November 16, 2008. http://news.cnet.com/8301-10787_3-1009819460.html.

Cooper, Michael, and Jeff Zeleny. "Obama Strives to Retain Some Flexibility on His Iraq Policy." *New York Times,* July 3, 2008. http://www.nytimes.com/2008/07/03/us/politics/03cnd-policy.html?_r=1&hp=&pagewanted=all (accessed December 1, 2008).

Coulter, Ann. *Treason*. New York: Crown Forum, 2003.

Couric, Katie. "Speech to National Press Club." Transcript, UCLA Communication Studies Archive online, September 26, 2007.

Cox, Gary, and Eric Magar. "How Much Is Majority Status in the U.S. Congress Worth?" *American Political Science Review* 93:299–309, 1999.

Cox, Gary, and Mathew McCubbins. *Legislative Leviathan: Party Government in the House.* Berkeley and Los Angeles: University of California Press, 1993.

Crawford, Vincent, and Joel Sobel. "Strategic Information Transmission." *Econometrica* 50:1431–51, 1982.

Crittenden, Jules. "From the Mouths of Babes." *Pajamas Media Online,* October 4, 2007. http://pajamasmedia.com/2007/10/katie_get_your_gun.php (accessed December 1, 2008).

Cronkite, Walter. "We Are Mired in Stalemate." *CBS Evening News,* February 27, 1968.

Dahl, Robert A. *Who Governs?* New Haven, CT: Yale University Press, 1961.

Dailykos.com. "Nationalizing 'The Kiss,'" August, 11, 2006. http://www.daily kos.com/ storyonly/2006/8/11/1801/33929 (accessed December 1, 2008).

———. "Snapshot: The Death of American News." *Daily Kos Diary by Kangro X,* September 26, 2007. http://www.dailykos.com/storyonly/2007/9/26/111344/ 859 (accessed December 1, 2008).

Davis, Richard, and Diana Owen. *New Media and American Politics.* New York: Oxford University Press, 1998.

Dearing, James W., and Everett M. Rogers. *Agenda-Setting.* Thousand Oaks, CA: Sage, 1996.

Della Vigna, Stefano, and Ethan Kaplan, "The Fox News Effect: Media Bias and Voting." Unpublished manuscript. Berkeley, CA, March 30, 2003. http://elsa .berkeley.edu/~sdellavi/wp/foxvote06–03–30.pdf (accessed December 1, 2008).

Delli Carpini, Michael X., and Scott Keeter. *What Americans Know about Politics and Why it Matters.* New Haven, CT: Yale University Press, 1996.

Department of Defense (DoD). "Comments by Secretary of Defense Donald Rumsfeld. Department of Defense Press Briefing," February 12, 2002.

Downie, Leonard, and Robert G. Kaiser. *The News about the News: American Journalism in Peril.* New York: Knopf, 2002.

Druckman, James N. "On the Limits of Framing Effects: Who Can Frame?" *The Journal of Politics* 63 (4): 1041–66, 2001.

———. "Using Credible Advice to Overcome Framing Effects." *Journal of Law, Economics, & Organization* 17:62–82, 2001.

———. "Political Preference Formation: Competition, Deliberation, and the (Ir)relevance of Framing Effects." *American Political Science Review* 98 (4): 671–86, 2004.

Dutton, Donald. "The Maverick Effect: Increased Communicator Credibility as a Result of Abandoning a Career." *Canadian Journal of Behavioral Science* 5:145–51, 1973.

Eagly, Alice H., Wendy Wood, and Shelly Chaiken. "Causal Inferences about Communicators, and Their Effect on Opinion Change." *Journal of Personality and Social Psychology* 36:424–35, 1978.

Edwards, George C. III. *The Public Presidency.* New York: St. Martin's Press, 1983.

Efron, Edith. *The News Twisters.* Los Angeles: Nash Pub, 1971.

Eggerton, John. "Schumer Comments Prompt New Fairness Doctrine Concerns." *Broadcasting and Cable,* November 5, 2008. http://www.broadcastingcable.

com/index.asp?layout=talkbackCommentsFull&talk_back_header_id=6566 552&articleid=ca6611851 (accessed December 1, 2008).

Eichenberg, Richard. "Victory Has Many Friends: U.S. Public Opinion and the Use of Military Force, 1981–2005." *International Security* 30:140–77, 2005.

Eichenberg, Richard C., Richard J. Stoll, and Matthew Lebo. "War President: The Approval Ratings of George W. Bush." *Journal of Conflict Resolution* 50 (December): 783–808, 2006.

Entman, Robert M. *Projections of Power: Framing News, Public Opinion, and U.S. Foreign Policy.* Chicago: University of Chicago Press, 2004.

Erskine, Hazel. "The Polls: Exposure to Public Information." *Public Opinion Quarterly* 27:658–62, 1963.

Exit Poll. United States General Election Exit Poll, 2006. http://www.foxnews .com/projects/pdf/ushouse.pdf (accessed December 1, 2008).

Farrell, Henry, and Daniel Drezner. "The Power and Politics of Blogs." *Public Choice* 134:15–30, 2008.

Fearon, James D. "Domestic Political Audiences and the Escalation of International Disputes." *American Political Science Review* 88:577–92, 1994.

Feaver, Peter D., and Christopher Gelpi. *Choosing Your Battles: American Civil-Military Relations and the Use of Force.* Princeton, NJ: Princeton University Press, 2004.

Feenstra, Robert C., Robert E. Lipsey, Haiyan Deng, Alyson C. Ma, and Hengyong Mo. "World Trade Flows: 1962–2000." Working Paper 11040. Cambridge, MA: National Bureau of Economic Research, 2005. http://www.nber .org/papers/w11040 (accessed December 1, 2008).

Fishkin, James. S., and Peter Laslett, eds. *Debating Deliberative Democracy.* Boston: Blackwell, 2003.

Fordham, Benjamin, and Christopher Sarver. "Militarized Interstate Disputes and United States Uses of Force." *International Studies Quarterly* 45:455–66, 2001.

Fountain, Jane. *Building the Virtual State: Information Technology and Institutional Change.* Washington, DC: Brookings Institution Press, 2001.

Franken, Al. *Lies (and the Lying Liars Who Tell Them).* New York: Plume, 2004.

Franklin, Charles. "Ten Months of Opinion Change on War and More." Pollster. com. http://www.pollster.com/blogs/ten_months_of_opinion_change_o.php. November 6, 2007.

Friedman, Thomas. "The Internet Wars." *New York Times*, April 11, 1998, 25.

Ganassi, Michelle. "Marine Sues Murtha for Slander." *The Daily American.* September 26, 2008. http://www.dailyamerican.com/articles/2008/09/26/news/ news/news451.txt.

Gartner, Scott S. "The Multiple Effects of Casualties on Public Support for War: An Experimental Approach." *American Political Science Review* 102 (February): 95–106, 2008.

Gartner, Scott S., and Gary M. Segura. "Race, Casualties, and Opinion in the Vietnam War." *Journal of Politics* 62 (February): 115–46, 2000.

Gelpi, Christopher, Peter Feaver, and Jason Reifler. "Casualty Sensitivity and the War in Iraq." *International Security* 30 (3): 7–46, 2005–2006.

Gentzkow, Matthew, and Jesse M. Shapiro. "What Drives Media Slant? Evidence from U.S. Daily Newspapers." Unpublished manuscript. University of Chicago and NBER, 2006.

Gibler, Douglas M., and Meredith Reid Sarkees. "Measuring Alliances: The Correlates of War Formal Interstate Alliance Dataset, 1816–2000." *Journal of Peace Research* 41 (2): 211–22, 2004.

Goldberg, Bernard. *Bias*. Washington, DC: Regnery, 2003.

Gorman, Bill. "Record 71+ Million Watch Election Night TV Coverage." *TVby thenumbers.com*, November 5, 2008. http://tvbythenumbers.com/2008/11/05/record-71-million-watch-election-night-tv-coverage/7667 (accessed December 1, 2008).

Graber, Doris. *Mass Media and American Politics*. Washington, DC: CQ Press, 1997.

Groeling, Tim. "Virtual Discussion: Web-based Discussion Forums in Political Science" September 1, 1999. Department of Communication Studies, UCLA. Paper 19990901. http://repositories.cdlib.org/commstudies/19990901 (accessed December 1, 2008).

———. "When Politicians Attack: The Causes, Contours, and Consequences of Partisan Communication." Ph.D. diss., University of California, San Diego, 2001.

———. "Who's the Fairest of Them All? An Empirical Test for Partisan Bias on ABC, CBS, NBC, and Fox News." *Presidential Studies Quarterly* 38:628–54, 2008.

Groeling, Tim, and Matthew A. Baum. "Crossing the Water's Edge: Elite Rhetoric, Media Coverage and the Rally-Round-the-Flag Phenomenon." *Journal of Politics* 70 (October): 1–21, 2008.

———. "Journalist Incentives and Media Coverage of Elite Foreign Policy Evaluations." *Conflict Management and Peace Science* 26, 2009.

Groeling, Tim, and Samuel Kernell. "Is Network News Coverage of the President Biased?" *Journal of Politics* 60:1063–87, 1998.

Groseclose, Tim, and Jeffrey Milyo. "A Measure of Media Bias." *Quarterly Journal of Economics* 120:1191–237, 2005.

Halberstam, David. *The Powers that Be*. Champaign-Urbana: University of Illinois Press, 2000.

Hallin, Daniel. *The 'Uncensored War': The Media and Vietnam*. Berkeley and Los Angeles: University of California Press, 1986.

Hamilton, James T. *All the News That's Fit to Sell: How the Market Transforms Information into News*. Princeton, NJ: Princeton University Press, 2003.

Hamilton, Lee. "How to Forge Ahead." *Washington Quarterly* 24 (Spring): 123–30, 2001.

Harper, Tim. "Obama Takes His Lumps on Website: Democrat Nominee's Perceived Shift to Centre Has His Backers Fuming That He Has Sold out." *Toronto Star*, July 5, 2008. http://www.thestar.com/article/454847 (accessed December 1, 2008).

Harrington, Joseph E., Jr. "Economic Policy, Economic Performance, and Elections." *American Economic Review* 83:27–42, 1993.

Hart, Roderick P. *Campaign Talk: Why Elections Are Good for Us*. Princeton, NJ: Princeton University Press, 2000.

Hazlett, Thomas W., and David W. Sosa. "Was the Fairness Doctrine a 'Chilling Effect'? Evidence from the Post-deregulation Radio Market." *The Journal of Legal Studies* 26:279–301, 1997.

Hermann, Richard, Philip Tetlock, and Penny Visser. "Mass Public Decisions to Go to War: A Cognitive-Interactionist Framework." *American Political Science Review* 93:553–73, 1999.

Herrmann, Richard, James Voss, Tonya Schooler, and Joseph Ciarrochi. "Images in International Relations: An Experimental Test of Cognitive Schemata." *International Studies Quarterly* 41:403–33, 1997.

Hess, Stephen. *Live from Capitol Hill. Studies of Congress and the Media*. Washington, DC: Brookings Institution, 1991.

Hetherington, Marc J., and Michael Nelson. "Anatomy of a Rally Effect: George W. Bush and the War on Terrorism." *PS: Political Science and Politics* 36:37–42, 2003.

Hindman, Douglas B. "Media System Dependency and Public Support for the Press and President." *Mass Communication and Society* 7:29–42, 2004.

Hindman, Matthew. "The Real Lessons of Howard Dean: Reflections on the First Digital Campaign." *Perspectives on Politics* 3:121–28, 2005.

Hofstetter, C. Richard. *Bias in the News: Network Television Coverage of the 1972 Election Campaign*. Columbus: Ohio State University Press, 1976.

Holsti, Ole. *Public Opinion and American Foreign Policy*, rev. ed. Ann Arbor: University of Michigan Press, 2004.

Holsti, Ole R., and James N. Rosenau. "The Structure of Foreign Policy Beliefs among American Leaders." *Journal of Politics* 52:94–125, 1990.

———. "Liberals, Populists, Libertarians, and Conservatives: The Link between Domestic and International Affairs." *International Political Science Review* 17 (January): 29–35, 1996.

Howell, William, and Douglas Kriner. "Congress, the President, and the Iraq War's Domestic Political Front." In *Congress Reconsidered*. 9th ed. Edited by Lawrence C. Dodd and Bruce I. Oppenheimer. Washington, DC: CQ Press, 2008.

———. "Political Elites and Public Support for War." Unpublished manuscript, 2008.

Howell, William G., and Jon C. Pevehouse. *While Dangers Gather: Congressional Checks on Presidential War Powers*. Princeton, NJ: Princeton University Press, 2007.

Hurst, Steven. "Both Left and Right Pile on Obama: Supporters Say It's a Smart Move to the Middle; GOP Sees a Wedge." AP story on MSNBC, July 5, 2008. http://www.msnbc.msn.com/id/25536472/ (accessed December 1, 2008).

Hurwitz, Jon, and Mark Peffley. "How Are Foreign Policy Attitudes Structured? A Hierarchical Model." *American Political Science Review* 81:1099–120, 1987.

iMedia Connection. "The Score: The Popularity of Blogs." July 13, 2006. http://www.imediaconnection.com/content/10359.asp (accessed December 1, 2008).

Iyengar, Shanto, and Donald R. Kinder. *News That Matters*. Chicago: University of Chicago Press, 1987.

Iyengar, Shanto, and Adam Simon. "News Coverage of the Gulf Crisis and Public Opinion: A Study of Agenda-Setting, Priming, and Framing." *Communication Research* 20 (3): 365–83, 1993.

Jacobson, Gary C. *A Divider, Not a Uniter: George W. Bush and the American People*. New York: Pearson Longman, 2006.

———. "The War, the President, and the 2006 Midterm Congressional Elections." Paper presented at the annual meeting of the Midwest Political Science Association, Chicago, April 12–15, 2007.

Jaffe, Matthew. "Democrats Already Discrediting Upcoming Petraeus Report: Senators Suggest They Don't Expect Any New Information, Just White House Spin." ABC News. September 8, 2007. http://abcnews.go.com/print?id=3575785 (accessed December 1, 2008).

Jamieson, Kathleen Hall, and Paul Waldman. *The Press Effect: Politicians, Journalists, and the Stories That Shape the Political World*. New York: Oxford University Press, 2007.

Jarvis, Sharon. *The Talk of the Party*. Lanham, MD: Rowman and Littlefield, 2005.

Jentleson, Bruce W. "The Pretty Prudent Public: Post Post-Vietnam American Opinion on the Use of Military Force." *International Studies Quarterly* 36:49–74, 1992.

Jentleson, Bruce W., and Rebecca L. Britton. "Still Pretty Prudent: Post-Cold War American Public Opinion on the Use of Military Force." *Journal of Conflict Resolution* 42:395–417, 1998.

Katz, Elihu. "And Deliver Us from Segmentation." *Annals of the American Academy of Political and Social Science* 546:22–33, 1996.

Keen, Judy. "Bush to Troops: Mission Accomplished." *USA Today*, June 5, 2003. http://www.usatoday.com/news/world/iraq/2003–06–05-bush-qatar_x.htm (accessed December 1, 2008).

Kernell, Samuel. *Going Public*. 3rd ed. Washington, DC: CQ Press, 1997.

Kernell, Samuel, and Gary Jacobson. *The Logic of American Politics*. 3rd ed. Washington, DC: CQ Press, 2006.

King, Gary, Michael Tomz, and Jason Wittenberg. "Making the Most of Statistical Analyses: Improving Interpretation and Presentation." *American Journal of Political Science* 44 (April): 341–55, 2000.

Koeske, Gary, and William Crano. "The Effect of Congruous and Incongruous Source-Statement Combinations upon the Judged Credibility of a Communication." *Journal of Experimental Social Psychology* 4:384–99, 1968.

Koppelman, Alex. "Who Wanted to 'Cut and Run' from Somalia?" *Salon.com*, http://www.salon.com/politics/war_room/2006/09/25/clinton/index.html September 26, 2006.

Kovach, Bill, and Tom Rosenstiel. "Campaign Lite: Why Reporters Won't Tell Us What We Need to Know." Washington Monthly, January 1, 2001.

Krosnick, Jon A., and Donald R. Kinder. "Altering the Foundations of Support for the President through Priming." *American Political Science Review* 84:497–512, 1990.

Krugman, Paul. "Quagmire of the Vanities." *New York Times*, January 8, 2007.

———. "A Surge, and Then a Stab." *New York Times*, September 14, 2007.

Kuhberger, Anton. "The Influence of Framing on Risky Decisions: A Meta-analysis." *Organizational Behavior and Human Decision Processes* 75 (July): 23–55, 1998.

Kuklinski, James, and Norman Hurley. "On Hearing and Interpreting Political Messages: A Cautionary Tale of Citizen Cue-Taking." *The Journal of Politics* 56:729–51, 1994.

Kull, Steven, and I. M. Destler. *Misreading the Public: The Myth of a New Isolationism.* Washington, DC: Brookings Institution Press, 1999.

Kull, Steven, and Clay Ramsey. "The Myth of the Reactive Public: American Public Attitudes on Military Fatalities in the Post-Cold War Period." In *Public Opinion and the International Use of Force.* Edited by Phillip Everts and Pierangelo Isneria. London: Routledge, 2001.

Kull, Steven, Clay Ramsay, and Evan Lewis, "Misperceptions, the Media, and the Iraq War," *Political Science Quarterly* 118 (Winter): 575–90, 2003–2004.

Kurtz, Howard. "Republican Convention Gets Under Way; Kerry Interviewed on 'The Daily Show.'" CNN's *Reliable Sources,* August 29, 2004.

———. "Controversy over Limbaugh's Statement; Justice Thomas Assails Anita Hill." CNN's *Reliable Sources,* October 7, 2007. http://transcripts.cnn.com/TRANSCRIPTS/0710/07/rs.01.html (accessed December 1, 2008).

Larson, Eric V. *Casualties and Consensus: The Historical Role of Casualties in the Domestic Support for U.S. Military Operations.* Santa Monica, CA: RAND, 1996.

———. "Putting Theory to Work: Diagnosing Public Opinion on the US Intervention in Bosnia." In *Being Useful: Policy Relevance and International Relations Theory.* Edited by Miroslav Nincic and Joseph Lepgold. Ann Arbor: University of Michigan Press, 2000.

Lau, Richard, and David Redlawsk. "Voting Correctly." *American Political Science Review* 91:585–98, 1997

Levy, Jack S. "The Diversionary Theory of War: A Critique." In *Handbook of War Studies.* Edited by M. I. Midlarsky. New York: Unwin-Hyman, 1989.

Lippmann, Walter. *Liberty and the News.* New York: Harcourt, Brace, and Howe, 1920.

———. *Public Opinion.* New York: Macmillan, 1922.

———. *The Method of Freedom.* New York: Macmillan, 1934.

———. *Essays in the Public Philosophy.* Boston: Little, Brown, 1955.

Livingston, Steven, and Todd Eachus. "Humanitarian Crises and U.S. Foreign Policy: Somalia and the CNN Effect Reconsidered." *Political Communication* 12:413–29, 1995.

Loven, Jennifer. "Obama: Media Response to Iraq Remarks Overblown." Associated Press, July 5, 2008. http://2008caucus.blogspot.com/2008/07/obama-says-media-response-to-iraq.html (accesed July 5, 2008).

Lupia, Arthur, and Mathew D. McCubbins. *The Democratic Dilemma: Can Citizens Learn What They Need to Know?* New York: Cambridge University Press, 1998.

Lupia, Arthur, and Gisela Sin. "Which Public Goods Are Endangered? How Evolving Communication Technologies Affect the Logic of Collective Action." *Public Choice* 117:315–31, 2003.

Lynd, Robert, and Helen Merrell Lynd. *Middletown: A Study in Modern American Culture*. Orlando, FL: Harcourt Brace, 1929.

Maggiotto, Michael A., and Eugene R. Wittkopf. "American Public Attitudes toward Foreign Policy." *International Studies Quarterly* 25:601–31, 1981.

Mayhew, David. *Congress: The Electoral Connection*. New Haven, CT: Yale University Press, 1974.

McCombs, Maxwell E., and Donald L. Shaw. "The Agenda-Setting Function of the Mass Media." *Public Opinion Quarterly* 36:176–87, 1972.

McCormack, Megan, Scott Whitlock, and Rich Noyes. "The Iraq War on Cable TV." Media Research Center Report, 2006. http://www.mrc.org/SpecialReports /2006/IraqWarCableTV/ report121906_p1.asp (accessed December 1, 2008).

McCumber, David. "A Ferry Captain, the FBI, and Benjamin Franklin." *Seattle Post-Intelligencer* Big Blog. August 22, 2007. http://blog.seattlepi.nwsource.com/ thebigblog/archives/120525.asp (accessed December 1, 2008).

McGirk, Tim. "Collateral Damage or Civilian Massacre in Haditha?" *Time*, March 19, 2006. http://www.time.com/time/world/article/0,8599,1174649,00 .html (accessed December 1, 2008).

McGuire, William J. "Personality and Susceptibility to Social Influence." In *Handbook of Personality Theory and Research*. Edited by Edgar F. Borgatta and William W. Lambert, 1130–87. Chicago: Rand McNally, 1968.

McIntyre, Jamie. "Lawmaker says Marines Killed Iraqis 'in Cold Blood.'" *CNN .com*, May 19, 2006. http://www.cnn.com/2006/WORLD/meast/05/18/murtha .marines/index.html (accessed December 1, 2008).

McManus, John. "What Kind of Commodity Is News?" *Communication Research* 19:787–805, 1992.

Meernik, James, and Peter Waterman. "The Myth of the Diversionary Use of Force by American Presidents." *Political Research Quarterly* 49 (3): 573–90, 1996.

Mendelsohn, Harold, and Irving Crespi. *Polls, Television and the New Politics*. Scranton, PA: Chandler Publishing Co., 1970.

Mermin, Jonathan. "Television News and American Intervention in Somalia: The Myth of a Media-Driven Foreign Policy." *Political Science Quarterly* 112 (Fall): 385–404, 1997.

Milstein, Jeffrey. "Changes in Domestic Support and Alternative Military Actions in the Vietnam War 1965–1968." Presented at the annual meeting of the Western Political Science Association, Honolulu, April 3, 1969.

———. "The Vietnam War from the 1968 Tet Offensive to the 1970 Cambodian Invasion." In *Mathematical Approaches to Politics*. Edited by Hayward R. Alker, Karl W. Deutsch, and Antoine H. Stoetzel. New York: Elsevier Science, 1973.

———. *Dynamics of the Vietnam War: A Quantitative Analysis and Predictive Computer Simulation*. Columbus: Ohio State University Press, 1974.

Milstein, Jeffrey S., and William C. Mitchell. "Dynamics of the Vietnam Conflict: A Qualitative Analysis and Predictive Computer Simulation." Paper presented at a meeting of the Peace Research Society, Cambridge, MA, June 1968.

Mueller, John E. *War, Presidents and Public Opinion*. New York: John Wiley & Sons, 1973.

———. *Policy and Opinion in the Gulf War*. Chicago: University of Chicago Press, 1994.

National Institute of Standards and Technology (NIST). *NIST/SEMATECH e-Handbook of Statistical Methods,* 2006. http://www.itl.nist.gov/div898/hand book/ (accessed December 1, 2008).

National Security Council (NSC). "A National Security Strategy for a New Century," 1997. http://clinton2.nara.gov/WH/EOP/NSC/Strategy (accessed December 1, 2008).

———. "National Strategy for Victory in Iraq," 2005. http://www.whitehouse .gov/infocus/iraq/iraq_strategy_nov2005.html (accessed December 1, 2008).

Nelson, Thomas, and Jennifer Garst. "Values-based Political Messages and Persuasion: Relationships among Speaker, Recipient, and Evoked Values." *Political Psychology* 26:489–516, 2005.

New York Times. "The Real Disaster." *New York Times*, January 11, 2007.

New York Times. "Legislating Leadership on Iraq." *New York Times*, March 29, 2007.

New York Times. "Four Years Later in Iraq." *New York Times*, April 12, 2007.

New York Times. "Mr. Bush Alone." *New York Times*, May 11, 2007.

Nicholson, Stephen P., Gary M. Segura, and Nathan D. Woods. "Presidential Approval and the Mixed Blessing of Divided Government." *The Journal of Politics* 64 (4): 701–20, 2002.

Niven, David. *Tilt? The Search for Media Bias*. Westport, CT: Praeger, 2002.

Oneal, John R., Brad Lian, and James H. Joyner, Jr. "Are the American People Pretty Prudent? Public Responses to U.S. Uses of Force, 1950–1988." *International Studies Quarterly* 40:261–80, 1996.

Page, Benjamin, and Marshall M. Bouton. *The Foreign Policy Disconnect: What Americans Want from Our Leaders but Don't Get*. Chicago: University of Chicago Press, 2006.

Page, Benjamin, and Robert Entman. "The News before the Storm." In *Taken by Storm: The Media, Public Opinion, and U.S. Foreign Policy in the Gulf War*. Edited by W. Lance Bennett and David L. Paletz, 82–101. Chicago: University of Chicago Press, 1994.

Paine, Thomas. *Common Sense*. Online Pamphlet. Library, University of Delaware. http://www.lib.udel.edu/ud/spec/exhibits/treasures/history/paine.html. 1776.

Patrick, Brian A., and Trevor A. Thrall, "Beyond Hegemony: Classical Propaganda Theory and Presidential Communication Strategy after the Invasion of Iraq." *Mass Communication & Society* 10 (1): 95–118, 2007.

Patterson, Thomas. E. *Out of Order*. 2nd ed. New York: Knopf, 1993.

———. "Bad News, Period." *PS: Political Science and Politics* 29:17–20, 1996.

———. "Doing Well and Doing Good." Research report. Cambridge, MA: Joan Shorenstein Center on the Press, Politics and Public Policy, Harvard University, 2000.

———. "The Search for a Standard: Markets and the Media." *Political Communication* 20 (April/June): 139–43, 2003.

PBS. *Witness to History: Walter Cronkite*, 2006. http://www.pbs.org/wnet/american masters/database /cronkite_w.html (accessed December 1, 2008).

Perla, Hector, Jr. "Days of Decision: A Framing Theory of Public Opposition to the Use of Force Abroad." Presented at the annual meeting of the American Political Science Association, Washington, DC, 2005.

Peters, Charles. "The Case for Facing Facts: Why We Need to Acknowledge That the News from Iraq Has Been Getting Better." *Newsweek* 41, December 3, 2007.

Pew Research Center for the People and the Press. *News Interest/Media Update.* Washington, DC: Pew, June 2005.

———. *News Interest/Believability Survey.* Washington, DC: Pew, June 2006.

———. *Internet Now Major Source of Campaign News: Continuing Partisan Divide in Cable TV News Audiences.* Washington, DC: Pew, October 31, 2008. http://pewresearch.org/pubs/1017/internet-now-major-source-of-campaign-news (accessed December 1, 2008).

———. *Bush and Public Opinion.* Washington, DC: Pew, December 18, 2008. http://peoplepress.org/reports/pdf/478.pdf (accessed March 31, 2009).

———. *Obama's Approval Rating Slips amid Division over Economic Proposals.* Washington, DC: Pew, March 16, 2009.

Phillips, Kate. 2007. "Fox Sets 2 Debates with Congressional Black Caucus." *New York Times*, in-house blog "The Caucus," March 29, 2007. http://thecaucus.blogs.nytimes.com /2007/03/29/fox-sets-2-debates-with-congressional-black-caucus/ (accessed December 1, 2008).

Plato. *The Apology.* Rev. ed. Edited by James J. Helm. Wauconda, IL: Bolchazy-Carducci Publishers, 1997.

Popkin, Samuel. *The Reasoning Voter.* 2nd ed. Chicago: University of Chicago Press, 1994.

Powlick, Philip, and Andrew Z. Katz. "Defining the American Public Opinion/Foreign Policy Nexus." *International Studies Quarterly* 42:29–61, 1998.

Price, Vincent, and Joseph N. Cappella. "Online Deliberation and Its Influence: The Electronic Dialogue Project in Campaign 2000." *IT & Society* 1:303–29, 2002.

Prior, Markus. *Post-Broadcast Democracy: How Media Choice Increases Inequality in Political Involvement and Polarizes Elections.* New York: Cambridge University Press, 2007.

Project for Excellence in Journalism (PEJ). "Local TV News Project—2002," 2002. http://www.journalism.org/node/225 (accessed December 1, 2008).

———. "2005 Annual Report—Cable TV Content Analysis," 2005. http://www.journalism.org/node/709 (accessed December 1, 2008).

Putnam, Robert. *Bowling Alone: The Collapse and Revival of American Community.* New York: Free Press, 2000.

Pyle, Richard. "Haditha Killings Recall Vietnam's My Lai." Washington Post, June 2, 2006. http://www.washingtonpost.com/wpdyn/content/article/2006/06/02/AR2006060200936.html (accessed December 1, 2008).

Rahn, Wendy. "The Role of Partisan Stereotypes in Information Processing about Political Candidates." *American Journal of Political Science* 37:472–96. 1993.

Rasmussen Reports. "War on Terror Update: Confidence in War Hits New High, But Voters Less Sure When Troops Coming Home," November 13, 2008. http://www.rasmussenreports.com/public_content/politics/mood_of_america/war_on_terror/war_on_terror_update (accessed December 1, 2008).

Reeder, Glenn D. "The Attribution of Morality." *Journal of Personality and Social Psychology* 44:736, 1983.

Reuters. "Reuters Independence and Trust Principles," 2007. http://about.reuters .com/home/aboutus/ourcompany/independencetrust.aspx (accessed December 1, 2008).

Reuters. "FACTBOX—Quotes from Republican Presidential Debate." *Reuters Alertnet*, January 31, 2008. http://www.alertnet.org/thenews/newsdesk/N302l 57299.htm (accessed December 1, 2008).

Reynolds, Glenn H. *An Army of Davids: How Markets and Technology Empower Ordinary People to Beat Big Media, Big Government, and Other Goliaths*. Nashville, TN: Nelson Current, 2006.

Robinson, Michael J., and Kevin R. Appeal. "Network News Coverage of Congress." *Political Science Quarterly* 94:407–18, 1979.

Romano, Lois. "Internet Becoming Candidates' Domain: Dean Leads Democrats in Using Web." *Washington Post*, A04, June 29, 2003.

Rosenau, James N. *Public Opinion and Foreign Policy*. New York: Random House, 1961.

Rosenstiel, Tom. "What Are the Master Narratives about the Candidates in 2004 and How Is the Public Reacting to Them?" Internet release. Washington, DC: Project for Excellence in Journalism, July 2004. www.journalism.org/ resources/research/campaign2004 /character/default.asp (accessed December 1, 2008).

Rosenthal, Andrew. "Talk to The Times: Editorial Page Editor Andrew Rosenthal." *New York Times Online*. http://www.nytimes.com/2007/09/17/business/ media/24askthetimes.html. 2007.

Russett, Bruce. *Controlling the Sword: The Democratic Governance of National Security*. Cambridge, MA: Harvard University Press, 1990.

Sabato, Larry. *Feeding Frenzy: How Attack Journalism Has Transformed American Politics*. New York: Free Press, 1991.

Salant, Jonathan. "Obama Leveraged Record Fundraising, Spending to Defeat Rivals." Bloomberg.com, November 5, 2008. http://www.bloomberg.com/apps/ news?pid=20601087&refer=home&sid=axZ6QT0Qr3YQ (accessed December 1, 2008).

Sanchez, Ricardo S. "Military Reporters and Editors Luncheon Address," Washington, DC, October 12, 2007.

Sandlow, Marc. "America's referendum on war. Pelosi's countdown: She ticks off a list of changes, including a new Iraq strategy." *San Francisco Chronicle*, November 5, 2006. http://www.sfgate.com/cgi-bin/article.cgi?file=/c/a/2006/11/05/ PELOSI.TMP (accessed December 1, 2008).

Sargent, Greg. "Politico Story Saying Reid Called Generals 'Incompetent' Is Denied." *TPM Café Election Central*, June 14, 2007. http://electioncentral.tpm-cafe.com/blog/electioncentral/2007/jun/14/reid (accessed December 1, 2008).

Schudson, Michael. *Discovering the News: A Social History of American Newspapers*. New York: Basic Books, 1978.

Schultz, Kenneth A. *Democracy and Coercive Diplomacy*. Cambridge: Cambridge University Press, 2001.

————. "The Politics of Risking Peace: Do Hawks or Doves Deliver the Olive Branch?" *International Organization* 59 (Winter): 1–38, 2005.

Schwartz, Benjamin C. *Casualties, Public Opinion, and U.S. Military Intervention: Implications for U.S. Regional Deterrence Strategies.* Santa Monica, CA: RAND, 1994.

Sears, David O. "College Sophomores in the Laboratory: Influences of a Narrow Data Base on Social Psychology's View of Human Nature." *Journal of Personality and Social Psychology* 31 (3): 515–30, 1986.

Sigal, Leon V. "Sources Make the News," In *Reading the News: A Pantheon Guide to Popular Culture.* Edited by R. K. Manoff and M. Shudson. New York: Pantheon Books, 1986.

Singer, J. David, and Melvin Small. National Material Capabilities Data, 1816–1985. Computer file. Ann Arbor: J. David Singer, University of Michigan; Detroit, MI: Melvin Small, Wayne State University (producers), 1990.

Skowronski, John, and Donald Carlson. "Social Judgment and Social Memory: The Role of Cue Diagnosticity in Negativity, Positivity, and Extremity Biases." *Journal of Personality and Social Psychology* 52:689–99, 1987.

————. "Negativity and Extremity Biases in Impression Formation: A Review of Explanations." *Psychological Bulletin* 106:131–42, 1989.

Slantchev, Branislav. "How Initiators End Their Wars: The Duration of Warfare and the Terms of Peace." *American Journal of Political Science* 48 (4): 813–29, 2004.

————. "Politicians, the Media, and Domestic Audience Costs." *International Studies Quarterly* 50 (2): 445–77, 2006.

Smith, Alastair. "Diversionary Foreign Policy in Democratic Systems." *International Studies Quarterly* 40:133–54, 1996.

————. "International Crises and Domestic Politics." *American Political Science Review* 92:623–38, 1998.

Snider, Paul. "'Mr. Gates' Revisited: A 1966 Version of the 1949 Case Study." *Journalism Quarterly* 3:419–27, 1967.

Sniderman, Paul, Richard Brody, and Phillip Tetlock. *Reasoning and Choice: Explorations in Political Psychology.* New York: Cambridge University Press, 1991.

Sobel, Richard. "What Have We Learned About Public Opinion in U.S. Foreign Policy?" In *Public Opinion in U.S. Foreign Policy: The Controversy over Contra Aid.* Edited by Richard Sobel, 269–78. Lanham, MD: Rowman and Littlefield, 1993.

Spence, A. Michael. *Market Signaling.* Cambridge, MA: Harvard University Press, 1973.

Sunstein, Cass R. *Republic.com.* Princeton, NJ: Princeton University Press, 2001.

Suskind, Ron. "Faith, Certainty and the Presidency of George W. Bush." *New York Times Magazine,* November 17, 2004. http://www.nytimes.com/2004/10/17/magazine/17BUSH.html?_r=1&oref=slogin (accessed December 1, 2008).

Sutter, Daniel. "Can the Media Be So Liberal? The Economics of Media Bias." *Cato Journal* 20 (3): 431–51, 2001.

Tewksbury, David. "The Seeds of Audience Fragmentation: Specialization in the Use of Online News Sites." *Journal of Broadcasting & Electronic Media* 49:332–49, 2005.

Tidmarch, Charles M., and John J. Pitney, Jr. "Covering Congress." *Polity* 17: 463–83, 1985.

Tomz, Michael, Gary King, and Langche Zeng. "ReLogit: Rare Events Logistic Regression." *Journal of Statistical Software* 8 (2), 2003. http://www.jstatsoft .org/v08/ i02/paper (accessed December 1, 2008).

Trammell, Kaye D., Andrew Paul Williams, Monica Postelnicu, and Kristen D. Landreville. "Evolution of Online Campaigning: Increasing Interactivity in Candidate Web Sites and Blogs Through Text and Technical Features." *Mass Communication and Society* 9:21–44, 2006.

Tuchman, Gaye. *Making News: A Study in the Construction of Reality*. New York: Macmillan, 1972.

Tumulty, Karen. "John McCain, Maverick No More." *Time*, July 12, 2007. http: //www.time.com/time/magazine/article/0,9171,1642900,00.html (accessed December 1, 2008).

UCLA Film and Television Archive, Research and Study Center. News and Public Affairs (NAPA) collection. 1980–2003.

VandeHei, Jim, and John F. Harris. "Democrats Remain Stalled on Iraq Debate." *The Politico*, November 30, 2007. http://dyn.politico.com/printstory.cfm?uuid= 3602EDC4–3048–5C12-005578659CDA41C0 (accessed December 1, 2008).

Vandenberg, Arthur H., Jr. *The Private Papers of Senator Vandenberg*. Boston: Houghton-Mifflin, 1952.

Walster, Elaine, Elliot Aronson, and Darcy Abrahams. "On Increasing the Persuasiveness of a Low Prestige Communicator." *Journal of Experimental Social Psychology* 2:325–42, 1966.

Weaver, David, Maxwell McCombs, and Donald Shaw. "Agenda-Setting Research: Issues, Attributes, and Influences." In *Handbook of Political Communication Research*. Edited by Lynda Lee Kaid. Mahwah, NJ: Lawrence Erlbaum, 1997.

Weisberg, Jacob. "Ballot Box: Why the Press Loves John McCain." *Slate.com*, October 4, 1999. http://www.slate.com/?id=1003748 (accessed December 1, 2008).

Wheaton, Sarah. "Political Sites Drawing More Eyeballs." *New York Times*, Politics Blog, June 18, 2007.

Whitcomb, Dan. "Democrats Cancel Fox News Debate." *Reuters.com*, March 9, 2007. http://www.reuters.com/article/topNews/idUSN0918742820070310 (accessed December 1, 2008).

White, David M. "The 'Gatekeeper': A Case Study in the Selection of News." *Journalism Quarterly* 27: 383–90, 1950.

Wilson, Chris. "Cashing in on a Net Gain." *US News and World Report,* July 8, 2007. Downloaded from http://www.usnews.com/usnews/news/articles/070708/ 16wild.fund.htm

Wittkopf, Eugene R. *Faces of Internationalism: Public Opinion and American Foreign Policy*. Durham, NC: Duke University Press, 1990.

Yon, Michael. "Resistance is Futile: You Will Be (Mis)Informed." *MichaelYon. com*, October 22, 2007. http://www.michaelyon-online.com/wp/resistance-is-futile.htm (accessed December 1, 2008).

Zaller, John. *The Nature and Origins of Mass Opinion.* Cambridge, UK: Cambridge University Press, 1992.

Zaller, John. "Elite Leadership of Mass Opinion: New Evidence from the Gulf War." In *Taken by Storm: The Media, Public Opinion, and U.S. Foreign Policy in the Gulf War.* Edited by W. Lance Bennett and David L. Paletz, 82–101. Chicago: University of Chicago Press, 1994.

———. "A Theory of Media Politics: How the Interests of Politicians, Journalists and Citizens Shape the News." Unpublished manuscript, 1999.

Zaller, John, and Dennis Chiu. "Government's Little Helper: U.S. Press Coverage of Foreign Policy Crises, 1941–1995." In *Decisionmaking in a Glass House.* Edited by Brigitte L. Nacos, Robert Y. Shapiro, and Pierangelo Isernia, 61–84. New York: Rowman and Littlefield, 2000.

Zaller, John, and Stanley Feldman. "A Simple Theory of the Survey Response: Answering Questions versus Revealing Preferences." *American Journal of Political Science* 36:579–616, 1992.

Zalta, Edward N., principal ed. "Bayes' Theorem." In *Stanford Encyclopedia of Philosophy* (online), 2008. http://plato.stanford.edu/entries/bayes-theorem/.

Index